The Creative Curriculum® for Infants, Toddlers & Twos

Volume 3

Objectives for Development & Learning: Birth Through Kindergarten

Cate Heroman; Diane C. Burts, EdD; Kai-leé Berke; Toni S. Bickart

English Language Acquisition Objectives by Patton Tabors, EdD
Foreword by Diane Trister Dodge

Contributing Authors: Hilary Parrish Nelson, Laurie Taub, Kelly Boyle

TeachingStrategies® · Washington, D.C.

Design and layout: Jeff Cross, Abner Nieves
Cover design: Julie Sebastianelli

Teaching Strategies, Inc.
P.O. Box 42243
Washington, DC 20015

www.TeachingStrategies.com

978-1-60617-417-3

Teaching Strategies, The Creative Curriculum, and Teaching Strategies GOLD names and logos are registered trademarks of Teaching Strategies, Inc., Washington, D.C. Brand-name products of other companies are suggested for illustrative purposes only and are not specifically required for implementing the curriculum.

Library of Congress Cataloging-in-Publication Data

Dodge, Diane Trister.
  The creative curriculum for infants, toddlers & twos / Diane Trister Dodge, Sherrie Rudick, Kai-leé Berke ; Donna Bloomer ... [et al.], contributing authors. -- 2nd ed., rev.
    p. cm.
  ISBN 978-1-60617-415-9 (v. 1) -- ISBN 978-1-60617-416-6 (v. 2) -- ISBN 978-1-60617-417-3 (v. 3)
  1. Education, Preschool--Curricula--United States. 2. Child care--United States. 3. Curriculum planning--United States. 4. Child development--United States. I. Rudick, Sherrie. II. Berke, Kai-leé. III. Title.

LB1140.4.D632 2011
372.19--dc22

2010038683

Printed and bound in the United States of America.
2016   2015   2014   2013   2012
11 10 9 8 7 6 5 4 3

Acknowledgments

We would like to give special thanks to the users of this volume. The successes and frustrations that you shared helped us understand your challenges. We have tried to respond to your needs.

We would like to acknowledge many people for their essential role in developing this tool. Foremost, we would like to recognize the leadership and inspiration of Diane Trister Dodge, our president and founder. Thank you to Hilary Parrish Nelson and Laurie Taub for their tireless dedication to this product. We appreciate the thorough research work of Kelly Boyle, Jeffrey Capizzano, and Jennifer Mosley, who oversaw extensive field testing. Dr. Richard Lambert of the University of North Carolina deserves recognition for his evaluation and research work, as does Dr. Renee Casbergue for drafting language and literacy items.

We would like to thank our content reviewers of the first draft. They provided insightful and valuable advice: Dr. Laura Berk, Illinois State University; Jenna Bilmes, MEd, author and early childhood consultant; Dr. Renee Casbergue, Louisiana State University; Dr. Juanita Copley, University of Houston; Dr. Rosalind Charlesworth, Weber State University; Dr. Cynthia F. DiCarlo, Louisiana State University; Dr. Linda Espinosa, University of Missouri–Columbia; Dr. Beth Graue, University of Wisconsin–Madison; Dr. Craig Hart, Brigham Young University; Candy Jones, MEd, author and early childhood consultant; Dr. Faith Lamb-Parker, Columbia University; Dr. Lea McGee, Ohio State University; Dr. Jennifer Park, early childhood consultant; Dr. Susan Sandall, University of Washington; Dr. Steve Sanders, University of South Florida; Dr. Anne Stonehouse, Monash University (Melbourne); and Monica Vacca, early childhood consultant.

Teachers at our field-test sites played an essential role by providing feedback about *Objectives for Development & Learning: Birth Through Kindergarten*. They helped us make it as applicable and reliable as possible. We thank the leaders and users at the following field-test sites: Chicago Public Schools, Karen Carradine, EdD, Director of Assessment and Accountability; Easter Seals Child Development Center of Silver Spring, MD, Marion A. Entwisle, Director; Easter Seals Child Development Center of Washington, DC, Kate Jordan-Downs, Director; Innovation Station Child Development Center/Bright Horizons Family Solutions, Greta M. Duncan, Training and Curriculum Specialist; Howard Area Community Center, Family Center and its staff, Cindy Coudek, Yan Ferguson, and Becky Rube.

The University Child Development Center of North Carolina had three participating sites: North Cross, Gina Jones, Director; University Park, Stella L. Fogle, Director; Highland Creek, Phillippe Locke, Director. Community Action Head Start of Washington County, Oregon's Part Day, Pre-K Program had nine participating sites: Beaverton, Hiteon/Mill, Tigerton, Tigard–Tualatin, Hillsboro, Newhill, Hillsboro Child Development Center, Beaverton Child Development Center, Part Day/Full Year Early Head Start. Thanks to Lori Balch, Education Coordinator, for her cooperation. Acelero Learning, Monmouth County, NJ had five participating sites: Head Start Freehold Center, Head Start Neptune Center, Head Start Redbank Center, Head Start Keyport Center, and Head Start Howell Center. Thanks to Rachel Bragin, Vice President, Education & Training, and Linda Fourch, Director of Curriculum and Instruction Development, Community Action Project.

The Louisiana State University Child Development Laboratory Preschool, which is affiliated with the School of Human Ecology in the College of Agriculture, participated in the Phase 1 Instrument Review Pilot. We would like to thank the following people who were very helpful in this pilot: Carol Aghayan, Rachel Crockett, Dr. Cyndi DiCarlo, Michele D. Fillastre, Undrea Kwain Guillory-Smith, Susanna Melikyan, and Lindsay Sanches.

We also extend a special thanks to the teachers and staff of the Women's League Child Development Center in Hartford, CT. On the basis of their feedback, we further refined our materials for the next instrument review. We especially appreciate the participation of the following teachers and staff at the Fairfax County Employees' Child Care Center: Shadawna Brown, Tonya Nolen, Shirley Palmer, Asria Rafiqzad, Ruth Stover, and Keo Zelaya. Their insightful feedback was invaluable to us during the Phase 2 Instrument Review.

We thank Dr. Dina Castro, Dr. Linda Espinosa, Antonia Lopez, Dr. Lisa Lopez, and Dr. Patton Tabors of our Latino Advisory Council and Dawn Terrill for their assistance in developing our dual-language learning component. We deeply appreciate the contributions of Dr. Espinosa and Dr. Lopez to the Spanish literacy and language objectives. We are also grateful to the Oregon Child Development Coalition, Donalda Dodson, Executive Director, for piloting the Spanish materials of *Teaching Strategies GOLD®*. Diane Meisenheimer, Lead Education Specialist, and Clarissa Martinez, Education Specialist, oversaw the pilot test at two sites. For providing direct support to teachers during the pilot, deep thanks are extended to Berni Kirkpatrick, Education Manager for the Polk County site, and Patricia Alvarado, Education Coordinator for the Washington County site.

The creation of volume 3 of *The Creative Curriculum® for Infants, Toddlers & Twos* was an ambitious undertaking that would not have been possible without a unified effort. We recognize the entire staff of Teaching Strategies, who used their relentless energy to make this product the best for our users. A special thank you to Margot Ziperman, Production Manager, and our Creative Services team, who were so focused on designing a beautiful and engaging product. We also thank Rachel Friedlander Tickner for her detailed work on the references.

Contents

Volume 1: The Foundation 1–186

Volume 2: Routines and Experiences 187–385

Volume 3: Objectives for Development & Learning

Foreword vii

Introduction ix

   Objectives for Development & Learning x

   Scaffolding Children's Learning xv

   Planning for Children's Learning xvi

   Working With Children With Disabilities xvii

   Working With English-Language or Dual-Language Learners xviii

   Home Language Survey xix

   Widely Held Expectations xx

   Key Parts of the System xxiii

Areas of Development and Learning 1

   Social–Emotional Development 3

   Physical Development 25

   Language Development 43

   Cognitive Development 59

   Literacy 81

   Mathematics 105

   Science and Technology 125

   Social Studies 139

   The Arts 151

   English Language Acquisition 163

Glossary 173

References 177

Foreword

Clearly defined objectives for children's development and learning play a central role in a meaningful curriculum. Having a curriculum that does not include them is like having a road map but not knowing where you want to go. Objectives give you a clear destination, defining what you want children to know and learn during their time with you.

When these objectives include progressions of development and learning—clear sequences—you see all of the steps along the route. In this way, the curriculum can inform and guide your decisions about where you want to go.

I am very excited to introduce this new addition to our curriculum: *The Creative Curriculum® for Infants, Toddlers & Twos, Volume 3: Objectives for Development & Learning: Birth Through Kindergarten*. It explains 38 objectives for children from birth through kindergarten. Of course, not all objectives apply to children under age 3. A color-coded system shows you when children generally begin to demonstrate the behaviors and skills related to each objective.

You will become familiar with these objectives because they are referenced throughout the first two volumes of the curriculum. However, simply knowing how the objectives for children's development and learning are stated is not sufficient. Teachers who use *The Creative Curriculum®* should know not only *what* the objectives of the curriculum are, but *why* these particular objectives were selected. They need to understand what the research tells us about why each objective is important for children's school achievement. Research findings confirm that what you do every day in your work with infants, toddlers, and twos is vital. It builds a strong foundation for children's success in school and in life.

Volume 3: Objectives for Development & Learning is an integral part of *The Creative Curriculum® for Infants, Toddlers & Twos*. It has many advantages for educators involved in programs serving infants, toddlers, and twos.

It offers a comprehensive overview of child development. Good practice is grounded in an understanding of child development—what children are like at each stage of development and learning. The first chapter of *Volume 1: The Foundation* gives an overview of children's development from birth to age 3. *Volume 3* presents detailed progressions of development and learning in the areas of social–emotional, physical, language, and cognitive development. It shows widely expected skills, behaviors, and knowledge at each stage of early childhood.

It helps teachers focus on what matters most. You choose to work with very young children because you want to make a difference. By focusing on the skills and knowledge that are most important to children's later success in school and in life, you are helping to build a strong foundation for each child's future development and learning. Extensive research clearly identifies the first 23 objectives as predictors of school success.

It offers a way to follow each child's progress. The best way to help children make progress is to understand what they currently know and can do and what steps they are ready to take next. The color-coded progressions enable you easily to determine where to begin thinking about each child's development and to follow his or her progress.

Strategies support responsive caring and teaching. When you identify a child's current level of development for each objective, you can refer to the strategies page to find suggestions for appropriate support. They are a quick reference for individualizing care and teaching.

It includes valuable information to share with families. When you meet with families, you can show them the objectives and explain their importance. You will have a way of reassuring them that their child is developing and learning and that wide differences in development are perfectly typical. (These might be differences across developmental areas for an individual child, and they might be differences between one child's development and that of chronological peers.) You also will find specific information related to children with disabilities and how differences in family beliefs and expectations may affect the ways children learn.

Every day in your work with very young children—especially in your interactions—you have opportunities to address the objectives of *The Creative Curriculum*® and help children become enthusiastic, engaged learners. This volume will help you decide how to respond to each child and assist you in making hundreds of decisions about materials and experiences that will interest and appropriately challenge children.

I am sincerely indebted to the authors of *Volume 3: Objectives for Development & Learning: Birth Through Kindergarten*. They collaborated over many years to extensively research, identify, describe, and refine this critical resource for implementing *The Creative Curriculum*® *for Infants, Toddlers & Twos*. I hope you will think of it as a map that points you in the right direction as you plan each day for very young children. You will expand your knowledge of child development and learning, recognize how you are building a strong foundation for children's success in school, and be able to communicate effectively about the important work you do.

Diane T. Dodge

Diane Trister Dodge
Founder and President
Teaching Strategies, Inc.

Introduction

Teachers make decisions every day that help lay a solid foundation for children's present and future development and learning. In order to make good decisions, they need a deep understanding of three aspects of early childhood education:

1. child development
2. content knowledge
3. strategies for caring and teaching

Effective teachers understand **child development**—who children are and how they develop and learn. They use this information to guide planning and decision making. They get to know children as individuals—their interests, strengths, experiences, needs, language, and family background. With that information, they individualize caring and teaching in order to build meaningful relationships with children and help each child succeed. They know and understand general areas of development: social–emotional, physical, language, and cognitive.

Effective teachers also know **content**—the subject matter appropriate for the early childhood years. They are familiar with the knowledge, skills, and understanding of concepts that are important for children to acquire. They know the learning progressions that children typically follow as they develop the foundation for competence in literacy and mathematics and begin to explore science and technology, social studies, and the arts.

Effective teachers also have a broad range of **caring and teaching strategies** that interweave their knowledge of child development and their content knowledge in ways that support children's development and make learning meaningful and engaging for each child. *Volume 3: Objectives for Development & Learning: Birth Through Kindergarten* is like a compass that will point you in the right direction as you plan each day. It will help you make decisions about how to care for and interact with each child, which materials to select, the experiences you provide, and how you will scaffold children's development and learning. Refer to this volume for information about child development, content knowledge, and appropriate strategies.

Objectives for Development & Learning:
Birth Through Kindergarten

Social–Emotional

1. Regulates own emotions and behaviors
   a. Manages feelings
   b. Follows limits and expectations
   c. Takes care of own needs appropriately

2. Establishes and sustains positive relationships
   a. Forms relationships with adults
   b. Responds to emotional cues
   c. Interacts with peers
   d. Makes friends

3. Participates cooperatively and constructively in group situations
   a. Balances needs and rights of self and others
   b. Solves social problems

Physical

4. Demonstrates traveling skills
5. Demonstrates balancing skills
6. Demonstrates gross-motor manipulative skills
7. Demonstrates fine-motor strength and coordination
   a. Uses fingers and hands
   b. Uses writing and drawing tools

Language

8. Listens to and understands increasingly complex language
   a. Comprehends language
   b. Follows directions

9. Uses language to express thoughts and needs
   a. Uses an expanding expressive vocabulary
   b. Speaks clearly
   c. Uses conventional grammar
   d. Tells about another time or place

10. Uses appropriate conversational and other communication skills
    a. Engages in conversations
    b. Uses social rules of language

The Creative Curriculum® for Infants, Toddlers & Twos

11. Demonstrates positive approaches to learning
   a. Attends and engages
   b. Persists
   c. Solves problems
   d. Shows curiosity and motivation
   e. Shows flexibility and inventiveness in thinking

12. Remembers and connects experiences
   a. Recognizes and recalls
   b. Makes connections

13. Uses classification skills

14. Uses symbols and images to represent something not present
   a. Thinks symbolically
   b. Engages in sociodramatic play

Literacy

15. Demonstrates phonological awareness
   a. Notices and discriminates rhyme
   b. Notices and discriminates alliteration
   c. Notices and discriminates smaller and smaller units of sound

16. Demonstrates knowledge of the alphabet
   a. Identifies and names letters
   b. Uses letter–sound knowledge

17. Demonstrates knowledge of print and its uses
   a. Uses and appreciates books
   b. Uses print concepts

18. Comprehends and responds to books and other texts
   a. Interacts during read-alouds and book conversations
   b. Uses emergent reading skills
   c. Retells stories

19. Demonstrates emergent writing skills
   a. Writes name
   b. Writes to convey meaning

Mathematics

20. Uses number concepts and operations
    a. Counts
    b. Quantifies
    c. Connects numerals with their quantities
21. Explores and describes spatial relationships and shapes
    a. Understands spatial relationships
    b. Understands shapes
22. Compares and measures
23. Demonstrates knowledge of patterns

Science and Technology

24. Uses scientific inquiry skills
25. Demonstrates knowledge of the characteristics of living things
26. Demonstrates knowledge of the physical properties of objects and materials
27. Demonstrates knowledge of Earth's environment
28. Uses tools and other technology to perform tasks

Social Studies

29. Demonstrates knowledge about self
30. Shows basic understanding of people and how they live
31. Explores change related to familiar people or places
32. Demonstrates simple geographic knowledge

The Arts

33. Explores the visual arts
34. Explores musical concepts and expression
35. Explores dance and movement concepts
36. Explores drama through actions and language

English Language Acquisition

37. Demonstrates progress in listening to and understanding English
38. Demonstrates progress in speaking English

Objectives for Development and Learning

Child development and learning is complex. It would be overwhelming to try to identify every skill and behavior children demonstrate in these early years. *Volume 3: Objectives for Development & Learning* includes the knowledge, skills, and behaviors that are most predictive of school success. It also includes objectives that help you focus on competencies valued in state early learning standards and standards of professional organizations. The objectives will guide your program planning and decision making.

Thirty-six of the **objectives** are organized into nine **areas of development and learning.** The first four areas describe major areas of child growth and development:

- Social–Emotional
- Physical
- Language
- Cognitive

The following five areas focus on content learning that is often called *outcomes* in early learning standards:

- Literacy
- Mathematics
- Science and Technology
- Social Studies
- The Arts

A tenth area, English Language Acquisition, helps you to follow a child's progress in acquiring both receptive and expressive language in English.

Many of the objectives include **dimensions** that are more specific descriptions of aspects of the objective. For example, the dimensions of Objective 1, *Regulates own emotions and behaviors*, include the child's managing feelings, following limits and expectations, and taking care of his or her own needs appropriately.

A complete list of the objectives can be found on pages x–xii.

Volume 3: Objectives for Development & Learning is based on an extensive review of the most current research and professional literature in the field of early childhood education. Each part of this resource is described briefly on the next few pages.

The overview of each **area of development and learning** explains the research about why the area is important. The objectives included in the area are listed in a shaded box.

The **research foundation page** summarizes the important research findings related to the objective. It provides a broad picture of development and learning from birth through kindergarten, and it explains what is being measured and why. Cultural and linguistic considerations, as well as considerations for children with disabilities, are included in this foundation.

Progressions of development and learning include indicators and examples based on standard developmental and learning expectations for various age-groups and for classes or grades.

Objective 1 Regulates own emotions and behaviors

a. Manages feelings

Levels	Not Yet	1	2	3	4	5	6	7	8	9
Indicators (in bold)			**Uses adult support to calm self**		**Comforts self by seeking out special object or person**		**Is able to look at a situation differently or delay gratification**		**Controls strong emotions in an appropriate manner most of the time**	
Examples (bulleted)			• Calms self when touched gently, patted, massaged, rocked, or hears a soothing voice • Turns away from source of overstimulation and cries, but is soothed by being picked up		• Gets teddy bear from cubby when upset • Sits next to favorite adult when sad		• When the block area is full, looks to see what other areas are available • Scowls, "I didn't get to paint this morning." Pauses and adds, "I have an idea. I can paint after snack."		• Asserts, "I'm mad. You're not sharing the blocks! I'm going to play with the ramps." • Says, "I'm so excited! We're going to the zoo today!" while jumping up and down	
Age range expectations										

The **levels** (numbers above each box) are used to label each point along the progression of development and learning. The "in-between" boxes allow for more steps in the progression, so the teacher can indicate that a child's skills are emerging in this area but not yet solid. These in-between levels also enable the teacher to indicate whether a child needs adult support (verbal, physical, or visual) to accomplish the indicator.

Colors are used to indicate the age or the class/grade ranges for these expectations. Red, orange, and yellow code each year of life for the first 3 years. Green, blue, and purple code classes/grades for the next 3 years.

Notice that some colored bands of a progression are longer or shorter than others. Some bands begin in the "Not Yet" category. While there is a typical progression for each objective, it is not rigid; development and learning is uneven, overlapping, and interrelated. Sometimes a skill does not begin to develop until a child is 2 years old, and another skill may not emerge until age 3 or 4. The colored bands might show you at a glance that it is typical, for example, for children to enter the pre-K year with a particular skill emerging at level 5 and then for the children to progress to level 8 by the end of the year if they are given appropriate support and experiences.

Finally, the **strategies page** offers ways to promote development and learning in relation to the objective.

Birth to 1 year

1 to 2 years

2 to 3 years

Preschool 3 class

Pre-K 4 class

Kindergarten

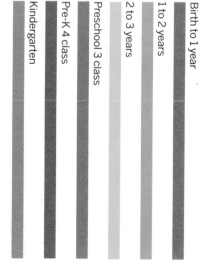

Scaffolding Children's Learning

Teacher–child interactions play an essential role in guiding children's learning. You *scaffold* children's development and learning through these interactions. Just as a carpenter uses a scaffold as he works on an area that is difficult to reach, you provide children with support as they work to develop skills that are just beyond their current levels. As children acquire the necessary skills, you offer less and less support as children learn to accomplish particular tasks independently.

For example, consider Objective 12, Dimension b, *Makes connections*. You notice that a child is at level 2, *Looks for familiar persons when they are named; relates objects to events*. You look ahead to level 4, *Remembers the sequence of personal routines and experiences with teacher support*. To scaffold learning, consider the strategies you will use to support the child on his or her path to the next level. You might use one of the strategies provided in the "Strategies" section for Objective 12. One suggestion is *Demonstrate and explain how different routine experiences relate, e.g., "Your sweater goes over your head, just as your T-shirt goes over your head."*

Refer to *Objectives for Development & Learning* as you consider how to support children's learning. The information in this volume will help you choose a wide range of caring and teaching strategies.

Planning for Children's Learning

You make many decisions every day as you observe children and respond in appropriate ways. As you think about each child and consider how best to provide support, your observations often lead you to ask more questions. *Objectives for Development & Learning: Birth Through Kindergarten* is an important resource for finding answers about a child's development with regard to each objective. The objectives address all areas, so they help you gain a comprehensive picture of the child's development and learning.

Planning for children is an art. There are no formulas or quick solutions. It would be wonderful to be able to say that, if you were to conduct a particular activity, the child would automatically progress to the next level. It takes time, practice, and reflection to determine what support a child or group of children needs.

However, you can plan for the specific needs of individual children. Think about what you know about your group of children and consider the expected outcomes identified in this volume and in your state early learning standards. Use this information to shape what you do each day. Think about the progressions of development and learning as you determine how and when to adapt activities to make them more simple or complex.

Involve others in planning for the children in your group. Consider what you know about children as you plan changes to your physical environment. Are the materials challenging but not frustrating for the children? Do you want to nurture a child's particular interest? Would adapting materials make them more useful for children? Might a dual-language learner demonstrate competencies in all areas if the materials were more linguistically appropriate?

Working With Children With Disabilities

To ensure that all children, including those with disabilities, are making progress, teachers recognize the many possible emergent skills that precede the development of these widely expected skills of children in the early years. A wide range of progressive skills and behaviors for objectives are included in this volume. They serve as a guide to seeing how all children are progressing in the nine areas of development and learning, while acknowledging that children show what they know in different ways. The progressions of development and learning emphasize to teachers that all children have skills and behaviors upon which to build.

The Creative Curriculum® objectives for development and learning help you plan for children who may be struggling in some areas by understanding the individual skills and specific needs of each child. You can then identify support strategies such as simplifying instructions or a change in materials used, to make it easier for children to participate and make progress through daily experiences.

Because *Volume 3: Objectives for Development & Learning* provides a picture of development through kindergarten, children with disabilities or those who struggle to learn are able to demonstrate progress. Keep the child with disabilities in mind as you read this volume and consider the intent of the objectives for individual children. Observe how each child progresses toward meeting the objective while using individualized modifications, assistive devices, or adult supports as necessary. For example, a child with a physical impairment might use a walker or a wheelchair to move around the classroom. The intent of Objective 4, "Demonstrates traveling skills" is that the child is able to move or propel herself to get where she wants to go. Any means that a child uses, such as adaptive equipment, scooting on her bottom, or crawling, meets the intent of the objective.

Objectives for Development & Learning can be used to support tiered models of supportive instruction and individualize intervention by identifying a child's strengths in relation to those of classmates. You can design learning experiences for skill building and practice for natural groupings of children that create opportunities to learn new skills. For some children, *Objectives for Development & Learning* can help identify areas of need so that collaborative teams of educators, other professionals, and family members can design more explicit interventions to assist with skill attainment and expansion.

You can use *Objectives for Development & Learning* to guide the development of an Individualized Family Service Plan (IFSP) for each child. IFSPs look closely at the child's present levels of development, major outcomes to be achieved for the child and family, and the specific early intervention services that will be provided in a given period of time. The progressions for development and learning presented in *Volume 3* will help you identify the more advanced skills and behaviors that a child is likely to develop next. Additionally, the "in-between" levels of the progressions can help you determine what support a child will require as he or she makes progress. Statements of expected outcomes are often worded similarly to the objectives. They identify the interrelated and progressive skills that help a child participate and progress in an appropriate natural environment.

Working With English-Language or Dual-Language Learners

In areas other than language and literacy, the objectives presented in this book will help you gather information, no matter which language children prefer to use as they demonstrate what they know and can do. However, the indicators, dimensions, and examples for the language and literacy objectives (8–10 and 15–19) show the progression of English-language development (e.g., Is the child able to understand directions given in English? Does the child associate English sounds with the letters of the alphabet?).

Dual-language learners are children who are learning two or more languages at the same time, and they are continuing to develop their home language(s). If you are in a program that uses a dual-language approach and Spanish is one of the languages, also refer to *Teaching Strategies GOLD®: Objetivos para el desarrollo y el aprendizaje.*

The "Home Language Survey" may provide information that will assist you in planning and individualizing learning experiences for infants, toddlers, and 2-year-olds. However, Objectives 37 and 38 are only used for English- and dual-language learners in preschool 3, pre-K 4, and kindergarten classrooms. This is because those children are in the process of learning English after already establishing a beginning foundation in their family languages.

Answer the survey questions about the child and the family members who care for the child. Respond, using a scale ranging from "only English" to "only home language." Try to gather as much information as possible to help you answer the questions. If you are unable to answer a question because you do not know the answer or because the child is not yet speaking, circle "N/A" for "not applicable."

Home Language Survey*

☐ Check here if the child's parents or legal guardians decline to provide information for this survey.

A. What language do family members use when speaking to the child in the home?

	1	2	3	4	5
	only English	mostly English but sometimes home language	both equally	mostly home language but some English	only home language (not English)

(write in home language: _____)

B. What language does the child use when speaking to family members in the home?

N/A	1	2	3	4	5
Not applicable	only English	mostly English but sometimes home language	both equally	mostly home language but some English	only home language (not English)

C. What language does the child use when speaking to other children in the classroom?

N/A	1	2	3	4	5
Not applicable	only English	mostly English but sometimes home language	both equally	mostly home language but some English	only home language (not English)

D. What language does the child use when speaking to the teachers?

N/A	1	2	3	4	5
Not applicable	only English	mostly English but sometimes home language	both equally	mostly home language but some English	only home language (not English)

Sum of circled numbers   Number of questions answered

_____ / _____ = _____

If this value is 2 or greater and the child is in a preschool 3, pre-K4, or kindergarten class, use Objectives 37 and 38.

*These research reports helped guide our thinking in the development of the "Home Language Survey":

Aikens, N. L., Caspe, M. S., Sprachman, S., López, M. L., & Atkins-Burnett, S. M. (June 2008). *Paper Symposium: Development of a language routing protocol for determining bilingual Spanish–English speaking children's language of assessment.* Biennial Head Start Research Conference. Washington, DC.

Puma, M., Bell, S., Cook, R., Heid, C., López, M. L., et al. (2005). *Head Start impact study: First year findings.* Washington, DC: U.S. Department of Health and Human Services, Administration for Children and Families.

Gutiérrez-Clellen, V. F., & Kreiter, J. (2003). Understanding child bilingual acquisition using parent and teacher reports. *Applied Psycholinguistics, 24*(2), 267–88.

Widely Held Expectations

Objectives and Dimensions	Ranges (color-coded)
SOCIAL–EMOTIONAL	
1. Regulates own emotions and behaviors	
a. Manages feelings	
b. Follows limits and expectations	
c. Takes care of own needs appropriately	
2. Establishes and sustains positive relationships	
a. Forms relationships with adults	
b. Responds to emotional cues	
c. Interacts with peers	
d. Makes friends	
3. Participates cooperatively and constructively in group situations	
a. Balances needs and rights of self and others	
b. Solves social problems	
PHYSICAL	
4. Demonstrates traveling skills	
5. Demonstrates balancing skills	
6. Demonstrates gross-motor manipulative skills	
7. Demonstrates fine-motor strength and coordination	
a. Uses fingers and hands	
b. Uses writing and drawing tools	
LANGUAGE	
8. Listens to and understands increasingly complex language	
a. Comprehends language	
b. Follows directions	
9. Uses language to express thoughts and needs	
a. Uses an expanding expressive vocabulary	
b. Speaks clearly	
c. Uses conventional grammar	
d. Tells about another time or place	
10. Uses appropriate conversational and other communication skills	
a. Engages in conversations	
b. Uses social rules of language	

Legend:
- ■ Birth to 1 year
- ■ 1 to 2 years
- ■ 2 to 3 years
- ■ Preschool 3 class
- ■ Pre-K 4 class
- ■ Kindergarten

Objectives and Dimensions

Ranges (color-coded)

COGNITIVE

11. Demonstrates positive approaches to learning
    a. Attends and engages
    b. Persists
    c. Solves problems
    d. Shows curiosity and motivation
    e. Shows flexibility and inventiveness in thinking
12. Remembers and connects experiences
    a. Recognizes and recalls
    b. Makes connections
13. Uses classification skills
14. Uses symbols and images to represent something not present
    a. Thinks symbolically
    b. Engages in sociodramatic play

LITERACY

15. Demonstrates phonological awareness
    a. Notices and discriminates rhyme
    b. Notices and discriminates alliteration
    c. Notices and discriminates smaller and smaller units of sound
16. Demonstrates knowledge of the alphabet
    a. Identifies and names letters
    b. Uses letter–sound knowledge
17. Demonstrates knowledge of print and its uses
    a. Uses and appreciates books
    b. Uses print concepts
18. Comprehends and responds to books and other texts
    a. Interacts during read-alouds and book conversations
    b. Uses emergent reading skills
    c. Retells stories
19. Demonstrates emergent writing skills
    a. Writes name
    b. Writes to convey meaning

Objectives and Dimensions — Ranges (color-coded)

MATHEMATICS

20. Uses number concepts and operations
    - a. Counts
    - b. Quantifies
    - c. Connects numerals with their quantities
21. Explores and describes spatial relationships and shapes
    - a. Understands spatial relationships
    - b. Understands shapes
22. Compares and measures
23. Demonstrates knowledge of patterns

SCIENCE AND TECHNOLOGY

No progressions for Science and Technology

24. Uses scientific inquiry skills
25. Demonstrates knowledge of the characteristics of living things
26. Demonstrates knowledge of the physical properties of objects and materials
27. Demonstrates knowledge of Earth's environment
28. Uses tools and other technology to perform tasks

SOCIAL STUDIES

No progressions for Social Studies

29. Demonstrates knowledge about self
30. Shows basic understanding of people and how they live
31. Explores change related to familiar people or places
32. Demonstrates simple geographic knowledge

THE ARTS

No progressions for The Arts

33. Explores the visual arts
34. Explores musical concepts and expression
35. Explores dance and movement concepts
36. Explores drama through actions and language

ENGLISH LANGUAGE ACQUISITION

Progressions included, but not age-level designations

37. Demonstrates progress in listening to and understanding English
38. Demonstrates progress in speaking English

Key Parts of the System

Here are definitions of important terms used in *Volume 3: Objectives for Development & Learning*:

area of development and learning

the broadest domains of development and learning, e.g., "Social–Emotional"

objective

a statement of expectations of knowledge, skills, and behaviors, e.g., "Regulates own emotions and behaviors"

dimensions

a specific aspect or subskill of an objective, e.g., "Manages feelings," "Follows limits and expectations"

indicators

descriptions of knowledge, skills, or behaviors that children demonstrate at four levels of each developmental progression. These statements are in **bold** underneath levels 2, 4, 6, and 8, e.g., "Accepts redirection from an adult"

examples

different ways that children show what they know and can do, e.g., *"Moves to the sand table at the suggestion of an adult when there are too many at the art table"*

colored bands

colored bands or lines (red, orange, yellow, green, blue, and purple) that show the age or the class/grade ranges for widely held developmental and learning expectations

progressions of development and learning

paths, or trajectories, that children typically follow when acquiring a skill or behavior

levels

"Not Yet"; levels 1, 2, 3, 4, 5, 6, 7, 8, 9

teaching strategies

what teachers can do to support and scaffold children's learning as it relates to a particular objective

Areas of Development and Learning

Social–Emotional Development

Young children's social–emotional development involves learning how to understand their own and others' feelings, regulate and express their emotions appropriately, build relationships with others, and interact in groups (Rubin, Bukowski, & Parker, 1998). Social–emotional development flourishes when children have close, supportive, and trusting relationships with adults (Howes & James, 2002). When adults are responsive, when they express pleasure about children's accomplishments and discoveries, and when they create an environment in which children can participate actively in daily routines and experiences, children know that adults consider them to be important, interesting, and competent.

Children's interactions with others are crucial to their learning. Problematic childhood relationships with adults and peers have been linked to negative outcomes such as emotional and mental health problems, lower school achievement, higher dropout rates, peer rejection, and delinquency. When their interactions are positive, young children are more likely to have positive short- and long-term outcomes (Rubin et al., 1998; Smith & Hart, 2002). The strong connection between early relationships and later behavior and learning makes it especially important for teachers to assess children's social–emotional development accurately and to support their growth and competence in this area.

SOCIAL–EMOTIONAL DEVELOPMENT OBJECTIVES

1   Regulates own emotions and behaviors

2   Establishes and sustains positive relationships

3   Participates cooperatively and constructively in group situations

Regulates own emotions and behaviors

1

In order to manage emotions and regulate his or her behavior, a child must learn to control impulses, tolerate frustration, cope with strong emotions, follow limits and expectations, and delay gratification. A crying infant calms when rocked by a loving adult. A 2-year-old sits in a quiet place hugging a stuffed bear after his mother leaves for work. A preschooler acts out a birthday party, thanking her guests for coming. A 5-year-old tells you when others are not following the rules.

To be able to regulate their emotions and behaviors, children must: 1) develop a basic understanding that actions have positive and negative consequences, 2) know what behaviors are acceptable, 3) be aware that they are capable of controlling their behavior, and 4) know that they have the power to manage their emotions (Bilmes, 2004). Children learn how to manage their emotions and regulate behavior in an environment that is warm and nurturing, and where the adults are trustworthy and responsive to each child's needs. Discussing the reasons for limits and the consequences of behavior helps children know why limits and rules are necessary. Teachers usually provide reasons for moral rules that apply in every setting, such as not hitting or taking another child's toy. They usually do not explain the social reasons for rules such as putting blocks back on the shelf neatly (Charlesworth, 2008; Smetana, 1984).

Children who regulate their emotions positively do better in school (Blair & Razza, 2007; Bronson, 2000) and have an easier time getting along with peers (Copple & Bredekamp, 2009; Ponitz, McClelland, Jewkes, Conner, Farris, & Morrison, 2008). Noncompliant, problematic behavior in preschool tends to continue in later school years (Charlesworth, 2008; Campbell, 1995; Campbell, Pierce, March, Ewing, & Szumowski, 1994). Self-regulation is ranked as the most important characteristic necessary for school readiness by kindergarten teachers, who also indicate that over half of their children lack effective self-regulatory skills (Rimm-Kaufman, Pianta, & Cox, 2000). Children who have warm, supportive, secure relationships with their teachers exhibit fewer behavioral problems than children who do not have positive relationships (Bronson, 2006; Howes & Ritchie, 1998), so teachers' role in helping children follow limits and expectations is important to children's future school success.

Objective 1 Regulates own emotions and behaviors

Various factors, such as a disability, life experiences, and family practices, influence the way children express their feelings and emotions. Some children are taught to avoid expressions of emotion, while others are encouraged to express their feelings openly (Trawick-Smith, 2006). Difficulty in learning to manage emotions may be an early warning sign of a disability or future psychological problems (Diamond, 2002; National Scientific Council on the Developing Child, 2004). Infants who have trouble remaining calm may need special help to develop self-regulatory skills (Cook, Klein, & Tessier, 2004). Children who cannot control their emotions at age 4 are likely not to be able to follow the teacher's directions at age 6 (Bodrova & Leong, 2005).

Differences in family beliefs and expectations affect the way children respond to classroom limits. The ways people express opinions, discuss ideas and feelings, and take turns in conversations differ from one culture to another and often from one family to another. Children from some cultural backgrounds look others straight in the eye during conversations while other children are taught to avoid eye contact (McAfee & Leong, 1994). There are also differences in the strategies families use when children do not follow the established limits (Trawick-Smith, 2006). Frequent communication between teachers and families is therefore necessary to guide children's behavior and to work toward shared goals.

Children's ability to meet their own needs appropriately is valued and typically expected by some cultures (Pierce & Schreibman, 1994). When children take care of themselves in these cultures, they build their confidence, and this influences their emotions and behaviors. Children who feel competent, or who have belief in their abilities, are better able to face life's challenges (Curry & Johnson, 1990). Children develop confidence by participating successfully in everyday activities. When children can communicate their needs, move from place to place, use tools, and participate in classroom routines, they have more opportunities to build self-confidence. Children with physical disabilities may be viewed by their nondisabled peers as being less able to perform certain tasks or to participate fully in everyday classroom activities (Diamond & Hestenes, 1996). It is therefore important for teachers to support children with disabilities appropriately in their efforts to do things for themselves and to give them, whenever possible, the same opportunities to participate in classroom activities as their typically developing peers. Teachers may need to provide children with disabilities as well as English-language learners with pictorial examples depicting various sequences of a routine or activity. The pictures support children's abilities to complete tasks by themselves (Macrina, Hoover, & Becker, 2009; Pierce & Schreibman, 1994).

Objective 1 Regulates own emotions and behaviors

a. Manages feelings

Not Yet	1	2	3	4	5	6	7	8	9
		Uses adult support to calm self • Calms when touched gently, patted, massaged, rocked, or hears a soothing voice • Turns away from source of overstimulation and cries, but is soothed by being picked up		**Comforts self by seeking out special object or person** • Gets teddy bear from cubby when upset • Sits next to favorite adult when sad		**Is able to look at a situation differently or delay gratification** • When the block area is full, looks to see what other areas are available • Scowls and says, "I didn't get to paint this morning." Pauses and adds, "I have an idea. I can paint after snack."		**Controls strong emotions in an appropriate manner most of the time** • Asserts, "I'm mad. You're not sharing the blocks! I'm going to play with the ramps." • Says, "I'm so excited! We're going to the zoo today!" while jumping up and down	

b. Follows limits and expectations

Not Yet	1	2	3	4	5	6	7	8	9
		Responds to changes in an adult's tone of voice and expression • Looks when adult speaks in a soothing voice • Appears anxious if voices are loud or unfamiliar • Touches the puddle of water when adult smiles encouragingly		**Accepts redirection from adults** • Moves to the sand table at suggestion of adult when there are too many at the art table • Initially refuses to go inside but complies when the teacher restates the request		**Manages classroom rules, routines, and transitions with occasional reminders** • Indicates that only four persons may play at the water table • Cleans up when music is played • Goes to rest area when lights are dimmed		**Applies rules in new but similar situations** • Walks and uses a quiet voice in the library • Runs and shouts when on a field trip to the park • Listens attentively to a guest speaker	

Objective 1 Regulates own emotions and behaviors

c. Takes care of own needs appropriately

Not Yet	1	2	3	4	5	6	7	8	9

Indicates needs and wants; participates as adult attends to needs
- Cries to show discomfort, hunger, or tiredness
- Opens mouth when food is offered
- Raises knees to chest when on back for diaper changing
- Pulls off own socks
- Raises arms while being lifted out of buggy

Seeks to do things for self
- Asserts own needs by pointing, gesturing, or talking
- Holds hands under faucet and waits for adult to turn on water
- Tries to zip jacket, but throws to ground in frustration
- Attempts to clean up toys

Demonstrates confidence in meeting own needs
- Washes hands and uses towel to dry
- Stays involved in activity of choice
- Uses materials, utensils, and brushes appropriately
- Takes off coat and hangs it up
- Puts away toys
- Volunteers to feed the fish

Takes responsibility for own well-being
- Completes chosen task
- Waits for turn to go down slide
- Creates a "Do not touch" sign for construction
- Tells why some foods are good for you
- Takes care of personal belongings

Objective 1 Regulates own emotions and behaviors

Strategies

- Stay nearby when babies are lying or sitting close to each other. Gently separate them if they touch each other too roughly, showing them how to be gentle.

- Use clear, simple language to communicate which behaviors are acceptable, e.g., say, "Pat Tamika's arm gently."

- Establish and practice consistent routines.

- Only put acceptable play materials within reach. This will limit the number of times you have to say *no*.

- Acknowledge when children show self-discipline, e.g., say, "You wanted to grab Tommy's car, but you waited until he was finished playing with it."

- Use simple, clear language and facial expressions to communicate acceptable behaviors.

- Create clear boundaries to help children learn to control themselves. Use visual aids, such as carpet squares or floor tape, to mark boundaries with preschool children.

- State rules positively rather than negatively. Tell children what behavior is expected, e.g., say, "Walk when you are inside," instead of saying, "Don't run."

- Give children alternative ways to express their anger, e.g., tell the child, "If you feel angry, tell us. Say, 'I'm angry!' That way we can help you."

- Set clear, reasonable, age-appropriate expectations that children can understand. When children do not behave in acceptable ways, assess whether the adult expectation is appropriate in the given situation. Respond by consistently structuring consequences that are related to the behavior, e.g., have the child help clean up dumped paint instead of using time-out.

- Model taking deep breaths, counting to five, or doing relaxation exercises when situations are stressful. Talk to toddlers about how you are taking deep breaths to help you relax. Engage older children in doing relaxation exercises with you.

- Explain the reasons for rules, and help children understand why particular behaviors are not acceptable, e.g., "Be kind to others. Hitting hurts people's bodies," or "Only three children may play at the sand table. When there are too many children, some can't reach the toys."

- Use gestures and other visual cues while telling children the rule or limit.

- Respond positively and firmly when a child's behavior is challenging. To help a child change his or her behavior, observe systematically, talk with others who know the child, develop a plan of action, and implement and evaluate the plan.

- Provide opportunities for children age 2 and older to help create the rules for their classroom.

- Ask families about the self-care activities in which the child participates at home.

- Describe what you are doing during caregiving routines, so children can learn the sequence of actions to care for themselves.

- Serve food that children can feed to themselves. Be prepared for messes.

- Use picture cues so nonverbal children or children with certain disabilities can communicate through photos, such as to express, "Hello," "I'm thirsty," or "I'm sleepy." Children point to the pictures until they learn the words in English or until they can do the activities for themselves.

- Talk with children about their feelings during routine activities. For example, you might say, "I know you're unhappy having your diaper changed now, but soon I'll be done and you can play. Here's a ball to hold."

- Provide opportunities for preschool and older children to engage in extended make-believe play in which they can act out strong emotions.

- Provide picture and word cues to assist toddlers and older children as they participate in self-care tasks, e.g., use a recipe for making a snack or post cue cards with the steps of feeding the class pet.

Objective 1 Regulates own emotions and behaviors

Strategies, *continued*

- Model using self-talk with older children to help them verbalize their thoughts and guide their own behavior. For example, tell them "Say to yourself, 'Stop. Calm down. I'm getting mad, but I don't need to hit anyone'."

- Discuss photos of people showing various emotions. Encourage older preschool and kindergarten children to create stories about the source of the person's feelings. Guide them to come up with appropriate ways the person might respond to the situation.

- Provide child-sized cleaning materials such as sponges, mops, brooms, and dust pans so children can assist with meaningful classroom cleaning.

- Include clothing of various sizes so children can practice dressing themselves. Slightly larger-sized clothes and those with large fasteners are easier for young children and children with certain disabilities to manipulate.

- Display posters made by kindergarten children that depict things they do to take responsibility for their own well-being. Posters might focus on healthy eating habits, exercise, or personal hygiene. Create individual calendars and have each child record their healthy behaviors during the week. Review at the end of the week and determine which habits need more attention.

- Allow plenty of time to let children take responsibility for self-care routines.

- Provide a variety of self-care materials for children to explore, e.g., dolls to dress and undress, shoes to lace and tie, dress-up clothes with fasteners of varying difficulty.

- Provide only as much help as necessary for children to accomplish tasks, e.g., put socks on the child's toes and then encourage him or her to pull them up the rest of the way.

- When appropriate, encourage families to involve their children in simple household tasks, as appropriate, e.g., hanging clothes, pouring beverages, and setting the table.

Objective 2

Establishes and sustains positive relationships

Being able to establish caring relationships and to enter successfully into ongoing social interactions are essential skills for school and for success in life. There are four dimensions to this objective: establishing and sustaining positive relationships with adults; making and keeping friends; relating to other children in groups; and interpreting the emotional cues of others and responding appropriately.

Relationships With Adults

The ability to establish caring relationships between a child and the important people in his or her life is called *attachment.* An infant squeals with laughter as a trusted adult plays with him. A toddler struggles to say good-bye to her mother at drop-off time. A 2-year-old runs into the room and hugs her teacher hello every morning. A preschool child works and plays with friends but knows when to ask an adult for help. A kindergartner engages a teacher in a conversation about their shared interest in horses.

Children's ability to form positive relationships with adults is important to their social development and academic success (Berk, 2006; Bronson, 2006; Howes, 2000; Howes et al., 2008; Palermo, Hanish, Martin, Fabes, & Reiser, 2007; Pianta, 1999). The model for all future relationships begins with the infant's early interactions with parents and other primary caregivers (Lamb, Bornstein, & Teti, 2002; Rubin, Bukowski, & Parker, 1998). Responding to infants' signals is critical to the development of a trusting, secure relationship with their primary caregivers (Peterson & Wittmer, 2008).

Various factors can interfere with a child's ability to form secure attachments with adults. Risk factors such as poverty, disabilities, or stress may influence the formation of secure attachments (Diamond, 2002; Ray, Bowman, & Brownell, 2006; Sigman & Ruskin, 1999; Trawick-Smith, 2006). Family socialization practices, such as encouraging dependence, may also affect how the child separates from the primary caregiver, how the child responds to other adults, and how other adults respond to the child (Chen, 1996; Harwood, Miller, & Irizarry, 1995; Trawick-Smith, 2006).

Objective 2 Establishes and sustains positive relationships

The classroom is an important setting for the development of positive relationships with adults outside the family (Pianta, 1999). Just as in the parent–child relationship, the quality of the teacher–child relationship can support or limit children's development and learning (Howes et al., 2008; Palermo et al., 2007; Schmidt, Burts, Durham, Charlesworth, & Hart, 2007). Teacher–child relationships may be close and affectionate, distant and formal, filled with conflict, or overly dependent (Coplan & Prakash, 2003; Howes & Matheson, 1992; Pianta, 1999). Overly dependent relationships and teacher–child relationships marked by lots of conflict can interfere with children's learning and academic achievement (Coplan & Prakash, 2003; Palermo et al., 2007; Ray et al., 2006). Teachers must build respectful and trusting relationships with children and their families. This is particularly true when the family's home culture and socioeconomic background differs from the teacher's (Ray et al., 2006). Supportive relationships with teachers can help children overcome the challenges associated with living in high-risk circumstances and help children whose early relationships have not been positive (Pianta, 1999). Children who have secure attachment relationships with primary caregivers and teachers have an easier time interacting with peers, forming positive relationships, and being a part of the group.

Interpreting the Emotional Cues of Others and Responding Appropriately

Learning to recognize and respond to the emotional cues of other people involves learning a set of skills that adults model. When an infant smiles back at a smiling face and a toddler moves near a crying child, they are beginning to recognize and respond to the emotions of others. Two-year-olds respond to others with empathy and understanding when they offer a crying child a special toy and tell the teacher, "He's sad." Preschoolers and kindergartners understand the reasons for people's emotions and begin to learn that feelings are complex, for example, that someone can be happy and disappointed at the same time.

Emotional understanding is critical to positive social relationships and peer acceptance (Denham, von Salisch, Olthof, Kochanoff, & Caverly, 2002; Eisenberg et al., 1997; Hubbard & Coie, 1994; Hyson, 2004). Social acceptance depends on a child's ability to understand, predict, and interpret the emotions of others (Mostow, Izard, Fine, & Trentacosta, 2002). Children who can accurately interpret emotional signals are more likely to respond appropriately to others and less likely to become angry or aggressive. Children who exhibit challenging behaviors may not recognize what others are feeling (Webster-Stratton & Herbert, 1994). But some children who bully others may "read" emotions correctly, but respond inappropriately. Adults must combat bullying behavior by being proactive and taking preventive actions.

Families introduce young children to cultural rules about ways of feeling and displaying emotions (Denham et al., 2002). Some children are taught to openly express their emotions, while others are encouraged to avoid outward expressions (Day, 2006; Trawick-Smith, 2006). Children who have suffered abuse or witnessed abuse often have difficulty managing their own emotions (Beland, 1996; Ontai & Thompson, 2002).

Some disabilities may affect children's sensitivity to emotions. For example, some children with autism spectrum disorders have difficulty reading the emotions of others (Baron-Cohen, 1995). They may not recognize the meaning of basic emotional signals such as facial expressions, tone of voice, or words (Ayoub & Fischer, 2006). The more adults acknowledge children's emotional reactions and describe emotional signals, the better children become at interpreting them (Berk, 2006; Denham & Kochanoff, 2002).

Objective 2 Establishes and sustains positive relationships

Interacting With Peers and Making Friends

The ability to enter successfully into ongoing social interactions is an important social skill. This ability begins with an infant's early interactions with a primary caregiver and quickly grows into an interest in watching other children at play. A toddler who laughs with another child as they both finger paint with their own materials becomes a 2-year-old who takes turns dipping his fingers in a shared pot of paint. The preschooler who talks about friendships becomes a kindergartner who establishes and maintains relationships over time with special friends.

Children's ability to build positive relationships with peers affects their social competence, school adjustment, academic success, and mental health in adulthood (Berk, 2006; Katz, Kramer, & Gottman, 1992; Ladd, Birch, & Buhs, 1999; Ladd, Buhs, & Seid, 2000; Peisner-Feinberg et al., 1999; Raver & Zigler, 1997; Shonkoff & Phillips, 2000; Wentzel & Asher, 1995). Some children's interactions put them at risk for developing negative relationships with peers. Once children develop negative reputations, they are likely to be rejected by their peers unless adults intervene (Black & Hazen, 1990; Kaiser & Rasminsky, 2003). Children who are not well liked often exhibit expressions of anger, hostility, or aggression (Cillessen & Bellmore, 2002; Denham, McKinley, Couchoud, & Holt, 1990; Hartup & Abecassis, 2002). Aggressive behaviors are not only physical. Aggression also may be verbal, e.g., name calling; nonverbal, e.g., mean faces; or relational, e.g., excluding children from an activity (Ostrov, Woods, Jansen, Casas, & Crick, 2004). Both the aggressor and the victim need adult intervention and support to develop positive peer relationships.

Children who are successful in their peer relationships use strategies such as making comments that are appropriate to the ongoing interaction. Children who are not well liked use behaviors such as calling attention to themselves or trying to control the interaction (Cillessen & Bellmore, 2002; Dodge, Schlundt, Schocken, & Delugach, 1983; Putallaz & Gottman, 1981). Many children need adult assistance to learn how to enter group play successfully. Children with disabilities may need help to enter the group or to initiate social contacts with potential social partners (Buysse, Goldman, & Skinner, 2003; Hart, McGee, & Hernandez, 1993; Kantor, Elgas, & Fernie, 1993; Pettit & Harrist, 1993; Robinson, Anderson, Porter, Hart, & Wouden-Miller, 2003).

Through interactions with peers over time, children begin to form friendships. These friendships can help children acquire positive social skills and develop more complex social competence (Katz, Kramer, & Gottman, 1992; Shonkoff & Phillips, 2000). Friend relationships are different from other relationships that children have with peers. Friends are more likely to be the same sex, ethnicity, and have similar behaviors, both positive and negative. They spend more time with one another (Hartup & Abecassis, 2002). Most children with disabilities who are in programs with typically developing peers have at least one friend (Buysse, 1993).

Play is an important context for developing close relationships. Creative learning activities such as fantasy play, block play, and open-ended art activities provide opportunities for children to build positive relationships with peers (Wishard, Shivers, Howes, & Ritchie, 2003).

Objective 2 Establishes and sustains positive relationships

a. Forms relationships with adults

Not Yet	1	2	3	4	5	6	7	8	9

Demonstrates a secure attachment to one or more adults

- Appears uneasy when held by a stranger but smiles broadly when mom enters room
- Calms when a familiar adult offers appropriate comfort
- Responds to teacher during caregiving routines

Uses trusted adult as a secure base from which to explore the world

- Moves away from a trusted adult to play with a new toy but returns before venturing into a new area
- Looks to a trusted adult for encouragement when exploring a new material or physical space

Manages separations without distress and engages with trusted adults

- Waves good-bye to mom and joins speech therapist in a board game
- Accepts teacher's explanation of why she is leaving the room and continues playing

Engages with trusted adults as resources and to share mutual interests

- Talks with teacher every day about their pets
- Brings in photos of home garden to share with teacher who also has a garden

b. Responds to emotional cues

Not Yet	1	2	3	4	5	6	7	8	9

Reacts to others' emotional expressions

- Cries when hears an adult use an angry tone of voice
- Smiles and turns head to look at person laughing
- Moves to adult while watching another child have a tantrum

Demonstrates concern about the feelings of others

- Brings a crying child's blanket to him
- Hugs a child who fell down
- Gets an adult to assist a child who needs help

Identifies basic emotional reactions of others and their causes accurately

- Says, "She's happy because her brother is here." "He's sad because his toy broke."
- Matches a picture of a happy face with a child getting a present or a sad face with a picture of a child dropping the banana she was eating

Recognizes that others' feelings about a situation might be different from his or her own

- Says, "I like riding fast on the trike, but Tim doesn't."
- Shows Meir a picture of a dinosaur but doesn't show it to Lucy because he remembers that she's afraid of dinosaurs

Objective 2 Establishes and sustains positive relationships

c. Interacts with peers

Not Yet	1	2	3	4	5	6	7	8	9

	Plays near other children; uses similar materials or actions	**Uses successful strategies for entering groups**	**Initiates, joins in, and sustains positive interactions with a small group of two to three children**	**Interacts cooperatively in groups of four or five children**
	• Sits next to child playing an instrument	• Watches what other children are doing for a few minutes and then contributes an idea	• Sees group pretending to ride a bus and says, "Let's go to the zoo on the bus."	• Works on tasks with others toward a common goal
	• Imitates other children building with blocks	• Asks, "Can I run with you?"	• Enters easily into ongoing group play and plays cooperatively	• Plays and works together for extended periods of time
	• Looks at other child's painting and chooses the same color			

d. Makes friends

Not Yet	1	2	3	4	5	6	7	8	9

	Seeks a preferred playmate; shows pleasure when seeing a friend	**Plays with one or two preferred playmates**	**Establishes a special friendship with one other child, but the friendship might only last a short while**	**Maintains friendships for several months or more**
	• Leaves library area to greet another child upon his arrival	• Builds block tower with another child during choice time and then looks at books with same child later in the day	• Talks about having friends and what friends do together	• Finds her friend's favorite purple marker and gives it to her
	• Seeks preferred child to sit next to at group time	• Joins same two friends for several days to play a running game outside	• Seeks out particular friend for selected activities on a regular basis	• Works through a conflict and remains friends after a disagreement

Objective 2 Establishes and sustains positive relationships

Strategies

- Learn to distinguish an infant's cries so you can respond appropriately, e.g., know if he or she is hungry, tired, lonely, or needs a diaper changed.

- Exaggerate your response to an infant's behavior, e.g., widening your eyes and changing the pitch of your voice to show excitement over a new accomplishment.

- Engage in experiences that help infants and toddlers understand how to interact with others, e.g., play peek-a-boo.

- Acknowledge children's positive interactions, e.g., comment as two children interact, "You touched Omar's face very gently."

- Label and talk about emotions and their causes, e.g., "Christina is angry because you took her truck," and "Willard is sad because he dropped his sandwich."

- Read simple books showing different emotions. Discuss why the people look and feel the way they do, e.g., say, "She's smiling because she is happy. She's happy because her mommy is home."

- Discuss and read books about friendships, e.g., how friends treat one another, the things they do for each other.

- Build positive relationships with each child by making purposeful observations every day, talking to each child respectfully, being sensitive to the child's feelings, and validating accomplishments and progress.

- Assist parents or caregivers as they leave. Help them understand that separation may be more difficult for toddlers than it is for infants and preschoolers.

- Interact one-on-one with children daily, playing and talking with them.

- Display family pictures in the classroom to validate children's most important relationships.

- Respond promptly and consistently to children's needs.

- Show respect in handling children, e.g., say, "I'm washing your face to get the food off."

- Smile frequently at children as you interact with them. This helps to establish positive relationships.

- Show appropriate affection, e.g., rub backs at nap time, hold children's hands as you walk around the playground, give hugs as children arrive in the morning.

- Talk to children at their eye level.

- Make each child feel special. Make time for him or her to share special interests with you, e.g., show you a favorite book or tell you about a recent experience. Tell children about your interests, e.g., things you like to do, what you liked to do as a child.

- Model respectful relationships with other adults in the program, e.g., tell children how other adults help. Say, "Mr. Jonas keeps our play yard clean and safe," or, "Thank you, Ms. Kelly, for getting the trikes out for us."

- Provide duplicates of favorite toys.

- Model cooperative behavior.

- Make accommodations for children with disabilities. You may need to pair a child with a disability with a peer partner, hold a prop for the child to use during group play, or give guidance and language for entering a peer group.

- Pay close attention to a child who is likely to act aggressively. Help the child control his or her emotions and behavior before another child gets hurt.

- Help children detect and interpret cues about how someone feels, e.g., say, "He looks angry. His forehead is wrinkled, his mouth turns down, and his fists are tight."

Objective 2 Establishes and sustains positive relationships

Strategies, *continued*

- Read stories to preschool and older children about various emotions. Discuss why the characters in the story look, feel, and act the way they do.

- Observe children as they try to enter group activities both indoors and outdoors. Help children who need assistance find play partners. Teach them positive strategies for entering and participating in group activities.

- Address all types of aggressive behavior. With twos and older children, assist the victim and the aggressor to develop prosocial behaviors such as helping, sharing, and including others in group activities and play. Call attention to positive changes in the child's behavior. Guide the other children toward responding to the child in new, more positive ways.

- Create spaces in the room for two preschool children to work together.

- Help preschool children learn how to enter a group by

    1) waiting, watching, and listening without speaking;

    2) imitating the actions of the children in the group; and

    3) saying something positive that relates to what the group is doing such as suggesting roles they could play.

- Explain that people have a variety of emotional responses to particular events (loss, injury, pain, birthday, going home, etc.) and they do not always react the same way.

- Explain that people express the same emotion in different ways, e.g., sometimes when people are sad they cry; sometimes they turn the corners of their mouths down like this and furrow their brows like this, but they do not cry.

- Engage children in informal conversations about your life and theirs. Listen attentively while they speak.

- Label your own feelings as you share experiences from your life and how you felt. Talk about things that made you happy, sad, or excited. Explain and model some of the ways you expressed your emotions.

- Provide opportunities for kindergarten children to work together on group projects over time. Model how children can help each other and work through conflict situations.

Objective 3

Participates cooperatively and constructively in group situations

Functioning as a member of a group requires an understanding of the feelings and rights of others and the ability to balance personal needs and desires with those of other people. When an infant babbles to the children at the lunch table, he is showing his interest in belonging to the group. When a 2-year-old waits for a turn on a bike, she is learning that other people's needs are important, too. When a preschool child works with others to paint a class mural, he is cooperating and sharing materials and ideas. And, an experienced kindergartner knows how to negotiate a trade of toys so that he gets what he wants. The foundational skills for being a productive member of social and learning groups are established during the early childhood years, and they are important for early school success (Ladd, Birch, & Buhs, 1999).

Being a productive member of a group involves complex interactions. Children must gradually learn to cooperate, negotiate, lead and follow, and express their feelings and ideas in socially acceptable ways. Positive group participation includes work-related skills like listening, following directions, behaving appropriately, staying on task, and organizing work materials. Poor work-related skills in kindergarten are related to behavioral difficulties and lower academic achievement in the primary grades (McClelland, Morrison, & Holmes, 2000).

Children who are socially competent interpret social situations and match their behavior accordingly. They comply with group expectations, and they work and play collaboratively. Social, cultural, and ethnic differences may create a mismatch between the kinds of behaviors expected at school, e.g., working independently to complete a task, and those expected at home, e.g., working together to complete a task (Ray, Bowman, & Brownell, 2006; Trawick-Smith, 2006). Adult guidance helps children learn how to act and adapt to the different expectations they encounter in diverse group settings.

Objective 3 Participates cooperatively and constructively in group situations

Younger children and children with poor peer relationships may use negative strategies, such as grabbing or hitting, to meet their needs (Berk, 2009; Downey & Walker, 1989; Yeates, Schultz, & Selman, 1991). Children with peer difficulties often assert their needs in ways that drive friends away (Erdly & Asher, 1999; Youngstrom et al., 2000). Some children come from homes where violence is the most frequently used problem-solving strategy. Children who experience difficulty processing social information often give up easily and resort to aggression (Kaiser & Rasminsky, 2003). Aggressive children are especially at risk for developing more serious problems throughout childhood and adolescence (Campbell, 1995; Parker & Asher, 1987), but intervention can help (Burton & Denham, 1998; Denham & Burton, 1996, 2003; Shure, 1997). Limited language skills can also be a barrier to social problem solving.

Conflicts are important opportunities for children to learn the give-and-take necessary for mature, successful social interactions that require negotiation and compromise (Kimple, 1991). It is tempting for an adult to fix children's social problems, but children need opportunities to think about and implement their own solutions. Good social problem-solving skills enable children to speak up for themselves, build self-esteem, and develop competence in other areas (Dinwiddle, 1994; Gonzalez-Mena, 2002),

and such skills deter aggressiveness (Richard & Dodge, 1982; Kaiser & Rasminsky, 2003). Children who think of multiple ways to solve a problem are better able to solve problems without resorting to aggression.

Children are more likely to use prosocial behaviors, such as cooperating or consoling and helping others, when their teachers use positive guidance strategies and a curriculum that emphasizes the values of a community (DeVries, Haney, & Zan, 1991; Schmidt, Burts, Durham, Charlesworth, & Hart, 2007).

In addition, adult guidance helps children develop a repertoire of effective problem-solving strategies. Children benefit from learning a process for solving social problems (see strategies at the end of this section) (Committee for Children, 2002; Gonzalez-Mena, 2002; Kaiser & Rasminsky, 2003; Levin, 2003; Slaby, Roedell, Arezzo, & Hendrix, 1995).

Objective 3 Participates cooperatively and constructively in group situations

a. Balances needs and rights of self and others

Not Yet	1	2	3	4	5	6	7	8	9

Responds appropriately to others' expressions of wants
- Gives another child a ball when asked
- Makes room on the sofa for a child who wants to look at the book with him

Takes turns
- Waits behind another child at the water fountain
- Says, "It's your turn now; the timer is up."

Initiates the sharing of materials in the classroom and outdoors
- Gives another child the gold marker to use but asks to use it again when the other is done
- Invites another child to pull the wagon with her

Cooperates and shares ideas and materials in socially acceptable ways
- Leaves enough space for someone else to work at the table
- Pays attention to group discussions, values the ideas of others, and contributes own ideas in a respectful manner

b. Solves social problems

Not Yet	1	2	3	4	5	6	7	8	9

Expresses feelings during a conflict
- Screams when another child touches his crackers
- Gets quiet and looks down when another child pushes her

Seeks adult help to resolve social problems
- Goes to adult, crying, when someone takes the princess dress she wanted to wear
- Calls for the teacher when another child grabs the play dough at the same time he does

Suggests solutions to social problems
- Says, "You ride around the track one time; then I'll take a turn."
- Says, "Let's make a sign to keep people from kicking our sand castle like we did in the block area."
- Asks teacher to make a waiting list to use the new toy

Resolves social problems through negotiation and compromise
- Says, "If I let you use the ruler, will you let me use the hole punch?"
- Responds, "Hey, I know! You two can be the drivers to deliver the pizza."

Objective 3 Participates cooperatively and constructively in group situations

Strategies

- Provide opportunities for infants and toddlers to play and interact with other children, staying nearby to offer redirection and to prevent harm to children.

- Coach toddlers to use the words, *stop* and *no*, when they are in conflict. Respond to the situation and expand a child's language, e.g., "I heard you say *no*. It sounds like you don't want Mica to touch the truck."

- Explain conflicts to children when they take place, describing people's feelings and the reasons for those feelings.

- Carefully watch a situation that is becoming a conflict. Allow children the chance to work out difficulties for themselves if no one will be hurt, but be prepared to offer support if needed.

- Coach children to use assertive (not aggressive) language, e.g., say, "Zory, you tell him, 'It's my turn now'."

- Establish respectful and meaningful interactions between families and teachers. Share the objectives and expectations of your program.

- Communicate what you and other adults at school do to support children in group situations. Explain how family members can help their children develop work- and play-related skills, to assume responsibility, and to cooperate.

- Provide opportunities for infants to spend time watching and interacting with other children, e.g., hold the infant on your lap while you watch the toddlers painting, put the child's blanket in a place where he can observe others at play.

- Sing songs, do fingerplays, and read books with small groups of toddlers. Keep these activities short and interactive to hold their interest.

- Give older children, and toddlers as soon as they are able, opportunities to help in the classroom, e.g., setting out the mats at nap time, looking for another child's missing shoe.

- Help twos and older children learn about cooperation by providing ample time, materials, and opportunities for children to engage in play and other cooperative activities with multiple children.

- Use positive strategies to guide children's behavior and to help them learn how to cooperate with others. Encourage cooperative interactions by suggesting turn taking and sharing and by modeling cooperation.

- Use role-play, games, and books to help preschool children to practice conflict resolution when there is not an immediate problem. When a conflict does arise, help children think about the sequence of events that led to it. Guide children through the problem-solving process and help them experiment with possible solutions.

- Teach preschool and older children the steps involved in resolving conflicts: 1) Identify and model how to state the problem, e.g., say, "Juan wants the truck, but you're playing with it." 2) Brainstorm solutions. Discuss possible solutions with the children involved. Accept all ideas as possibilities. 3) Evaluate solutions. Use open-ended prompts to help children predict outcomes, e.g., say, "I wonder what would happen if...." 4) Help children choose and try a solution. 5) Help children evaluate the outcome. Discuss what worked and what did not. Encourage the children to try other solutions if necessary.

- Encourage preschool and older children to watch for and record, through drawings or writing, the cooperative acts of others. Keep them in a special place, e.g., a "kindness jar." Before the day is over, read the children's notes aloud (Whitin, 2001).

- Begin to coach toddlers and twos and older children as needed about taking turns and sharing.

Physical Development

Physical development includes children's gross-motor (large muscle) and fine-motor (small muscle) skills. Balance; coordination; and locomotion, or traveling, are part of gross-motor development. Motor development progresses predictably, from simple to complex, in a head-to-toe direction. An infant lifts his head, lifts his trunk, rolls, crawls, sits, stands, walks, and then becomes a toddler who runs. Children gain control of their bodies in a predictable sequence as well, from the center of their bodies and outward to their fingers and toes. A child first catches a ball by trapping it against her whole body, then by holding out her arms to catch it, and finally by catching it with her hands. Similarly, fine-motor skills progress from the child's grabbing an object with a whole hand, picking up a small item with thumb and index finger, and eventually controlling the fine hand muscles needed for writing. Children need many opportunities to practice their gross-motor skills, e.g., pulling, climbing, running, kicking, throwing, jumping. and their fine-motor skills, e.g., cutting, drawing, writing.

As they develop physically, children master increasingly sophisticated tasks and are able to meet more of their own physical needs, such as feeding and dressing themselves. Motor and other aspects of physical development are influenced by gender, heredity, nutrition, health, environment, economic level, experience, culture, and disabilities (McKenzie, et al., 1997; Spaulding, Gottlib, & Jensen, 2008; Trawick-Smith, 2006).

PHYSICAL DEVELOPMENT OBJECTIVES

4 Demonstrates traveling skills

5 Demonstrates balancing skills

6 Demonstrates gross-motor manipulative skills

7 Demonstrates fine-motor strength and coordination

Physical development affects other areas of development. Brain research points to the importance of early, positive movement experiences to brain development (Gabbard, 1998; Robert, 1999). Physical development is linked to children's emotional development and their school performance (Pica, 2006; Rule & Stewart, 2002; Sanders, 2002; Son & Meisels, 2006). The ability to be physically active influences social well-being and mental health. Regular physical activity helps children build and maintain healthy bones, muscles, and joints. It helps them to control weight and prevents or delays health conditions such as high blood pressure (McKenzie, et al., 1997; Pica, 2006; Sanders, 2002). The more children can do physically, the more willing they are to interact with other children and to try new and challenging physical tasks (Kim, 2005). This establishes a positive cycle that affects overall learning and health.

Motor development is not automatic. If children are to develop physical competence, they need a variety of equipment and materials; planned, appropriate movement experiences; and opportunities to practice and apply previously learned skills (Barbour, 1999; Epstein, 2007; Gallahue, 1995; Manross, 2000; Sanders, 2006).

Demonstrates traveling skills

4

Traveling involves moving the body through space. When an infant rolls over, a toddler takes a few steps, a preschooler rides a tricycle, and a kindergartner skips across the playground, they are traveling. The early years are critical for the development of the large muscles needed for traveling. Basic traveling movements, like running, galloping, and marching, can be combined in even more complex movements for dance and sports.

Environmental conditions, e.g., lack of space and weather, the demands of the task, family background, and disabilities influence a child's ability to perform a motor task. Some children with motor impairments achieve traveling movements by using a wheelchair or other adaptive technology. Children without independent mobility may become socially isolated if adults do not support their efforts to participate in ongoing activities (Harper & McCluskey, 2002). The strong desire to play with their peers may motivate children with motor impairments to work toward more independent mobility (Kim, 2005). When children with disabilities achieve greater independent mobility, they show improved social and language development (Charlesworth, 2008; Kim, 2005).

Children learn some motor skills primarily through exploration and discovery. In order to develop more proficient movement skills, children need a combination of unstructured play and appropriate, planned movement experiences (Deli, Bakle, Zachopoulou, 2006; Manross, 2000; Pica, 1997). Adult guidance is especially important for learning skills such as marching, galloping, and skipping. Verbal cues and modeling can help children learn to perform the skills more successfully (Breslin, Morton, & Rudisill, 2008; Sanders, 2006).

Objective 4 Demonstrates traveling skills

Not Yet	1	2	3	4	5	6	7	8	9

Moves to explore immediate environment
- Rolls over several times to get toy
- Crawls
- Cruises
- Takes a few steps
- Takes steps, pushing a push-toy or chair
- Moves from crawling to sitting and back again

Experiments with different ways of moving
- Walks across room
- Uses a hurried walk
- Walks backwards
- Pushes riding toy with feet while steering
- Uses a walker to get to the table
- Marches around room

Moves purposefully from place to place with control
- Runs
- Avoids obstacles and people while moving
- Starts and stops using wheelchair
- Walks up and down stairs alternating feet
- Climbs up and down on playground equipment
- Rides tricycle using pedals
- Gallops, but not smoothly

Coordinates complex movements in play and games
- Runs smoothly and quickly, changes directions, stops and starts quickly
- Steers wheelchair into small playground spaces
- Jumps and spins
- Moves through obstacle course
- Gallops and skips with ease
- Plays "Follow the Leader," using a variety of traveling movements

Objective 4 Demonstrates traveling skills

Strategies

- Create a protected space for young infants to explore movement safely while lying on their stomachs and backs.

- Provide push toys, e.g., toy shopping carts and doll strollers, in the classroom and outside to help children who are learning to walk maintain balance.

- Provide time every day for outdoor play. Make sure there is sufficient space for running, jumping, skipping, and galloping.

- Play music during movement activities. Incorporate dances that may be familiar to families in your program. Model, describe, and suggest ways for children to respond to music by using a variety of movements.

- Use traveling movements to transition children from one activity to another. Invite children to walk slowly, quickly, sideways, or backwards.

- Provide riding toys for children to push with their feet and eventually pedal.

- Provide movement activities that involve all children actively. Avoid activities where children spend much time waiting or watching others participate.

- Include activities that have a range of appropriate ways to participate so that every child is successful most of the time.

- Use movement activities to enhance stories, e.g., encourage a wild rumpus as in *Where the Wild Things Are* or together act out *Going on a Bear Hunt*.

- Set up an obstacle course so preschool and older children can practice particular skills, e.g., hopping, skipping, running. Help children who need assistance with a skill or to be safe. Adjust the difficulty of tasks to match and slightly challenge children's current ability levels.

- Involve older children in traveling games where they start, stop, and change directions quickly, e.g., hopscotch or "Travel, Stop, Change." For "Travel, Stop, Change," call out a traveling movement (e.g., spin, jump, gallop, run). When the whistle blows, children immediately stop that movement and change quickly to the next movement called.

- Use traveling cards with kindergarten children to direct their movements. For example, the card might indicate, "Gallop 6 steps with right foot," "Walk backwards 10 steps," or "Skip to the end of the sidewalk."

Demonstrates balancing skills

5

Balancing involves movements to help stabilize the body's position when the person is not at rest (Payne & Rink, 1997). Balance is required for an infant to sit unsupported, for a toddler to stoop to pick up a toy and stand up again without tipping over, for a 3-year-old to jump off the bottom step on the climber and land on two feet, and for a kindergartner to walk across a narrow balance beam.

Turning, stretching, stopping, rolling, jumping and landing, swinging, swaying, and dodging require balance (Sanders, 2002). Balancing is difficult for very young children because of their uneven body proportions. As children become less top heavy, their ability to balance improves.

Balance can be static or dynamic. Static balance involves holding a particular position while the body is stationary, such as standing on one foot or sitting. Dynamic balance requires holding a stable position while the body is moving, such as while jumping and landing (Sanders, 2002).

Children's ability to balance affects their performance of gross-motor tasks (Ulrich & Ulrich, 1985). Appropriate instruction, practice, and safe materials and equipment are needed to help children improve their balancing skills (Bosma, Domka, & Peterson, 2000; Wang & Ju, 2002). Children often use materials in unique and sometimes dangerous ways to help them balance (Berger, Adolph, & Lobo, 2005). It is important to be sure that equipment is stable and in good repair.

Various factors influence children's ability to ba[...] For example, performance on the balance beam [...] affected by changes in beam width, length, and [...] and whether the child is moving (Robert, 1999)[...] Certain disabilities also influence children's bala[...] Children with Down syndrome, visual impairments, or motor disabilities such as cerebral palsy may need adaptations to assist them with balancing tasks, or they may need to participate in activities for shorter periods of time (Gould & Sullivan, 1999).

Objective 5 Demonstrates balancing skills

Not Yet	1	2	3	4	5	6	7	8	9

Balances while exploring immediate environment

- Sits propped up
- Rocks back and forth on hands and knees
- Sits a while and plays with toys
- Sits and reaches for toys without falling

Experiments with different ways of balancing

- Squats to pick up toys
- Stands on tiptoes to reach something
- Gets in and out of a chair
- Kneels while playing
- Straddles a taped line on the floor
- Sidesteps across beam or sandbox edge

Sustains balance during simple movement experiences

- Walks forward along sandbox edge, watching feet
- Jumps off low step, landing on two feet
- Jumps over small objects
- Holds body upright while moving wheelchair forward

Sustains balance during complex movement experiences

- Hops across the playground
- Hops on one foot and then the other
- Walks across beam or sandbox edge, forward and backwards
- Attempts to jump rope

Objective 5 Demonstrates balancing skills

Strategies

- Provide supervised opportunities for young infants to play on their stomachs to build strength.

- Play games with toddlers to promote balance. Place a few objects, such as beanbags, several feet away from a large bucket. Encourage the child to walk from the bucket to the beanbags, pick one up, walk back to the bucket, and drop it in.

- Modify the environment and learning experiences to accommodate a range of abilities.

- Stay close to catch or support a child if he or she loses balance. Use soft surfaces, such as rugs or mats, to help cushion falls indoors.

- Encourage children to stop, change directions, or walk up and down low ramps to promote their balance as they walk.

- Place masking tape or brightly colored yarn on the floor and encourage children to practice balancing by walking on it. Coach children about how to hold their arms out to steady themselves. Hold their hands as needed to provide support.

- Encourage twos and older children to practice walking with bean bags on different body parts, e.g., on head, shoulder, elbow, or under the chin.

- Introduce balance beam activities to twos and older children by offering a wide, low (not more than 4–5 inches off floor) beam. Have children walk with arms out to the side. Increase the challenge by having children walk forward, backward, or sideways, or walk forward while carrying a light object in their hands. Tilt the beam slightly so children can walk up or down the beam. Provide support as needed, such as holding a hand for the first few times a child walks along the beam.

- Provide opportunities for preschool and older children to practice static balance. Have children stand on one foot. Give the cue *freeze* when you want the children to hold their positions (for at least 3 seconds). When they can do that, ask them to balance on the other foot or with their eyes closed.

- Create balancing cards that show animals, objects, or people in various positions. For example, you might have a stork standing on one foot, a frog squatting, a toy soldier, an airplane, a person in yoga position, etc. Children select a card and then carry out the act. The other children try to guess what they represent.

Demonstrates gross-motor manipulative skills

6

Gross-motor manipulative skills involve giving force to or receiving force from balls or similar objects. A toddler picks up a large ball, lifts it over her head, brings it forward again as fast as she can, and then drops the ball in front of her. A preschooler holds a whiffle ball in one hand, moves the ball back along the side his head, takes a step while moving his arm forward, and propels the ball. Both of these children are demonstrating their gross-motor manipulative skills by attempting to throw a ball. In addition to throwing, these skills include collecting or catching, bouncing, kicking, and striking. Children can throw at advanced levels before they can catch objects.

The early years are important for the development of fundamental gross-motor manipulative skills. Children should explore and experiment with balls and similar objects of various sizes and weights. Equipment that is proportionate to the sizes and weights of the children is critical to developing mature gross-motor manipulative skills (Payne & Rink, 1997).

Developing competence with basic ball skills increases children's potential for learning more advanced skills such as those used in organized sports. These skills may also have a positive effect on self-concept and social skill development. Previous learning experiences; size, shape, and weight of the ball or object; and the presence of a disability can affect how children perform gross-motor manipulative tasks. Some children with motor impairments may need adaptations to participate in gross-motor activities (Gould & Sullivan, 1999).

When children's movements become more consistent and less haphazard, they are ready for more specific instruction in how to perform a particular gross-motor manipulative task. One way to do this is through the use of cue words or phases. For example, when helping children learn to catch, you might say, "Watch the ball. Reach with your hands. Pull it into your body." When you tell children discreet actions to take, you help them focus on the skill so they can perform it more efficiently (Breslin, Morton, & Rudisill, 2008; Sanders, 2002). As children play with balls and similar objects, they also need to learn how to maintain their position in relation to people and objects. This is an important safety component (Breslin, et al., 2008). Adults are crucial in helping children build a foundation for later skill development and in the safe use of equipment.

Objective 6 Demonstrates gross-motor manipulative skills

Not Yet	1	2	3	4	5	6	7	8	9

Reaches, grasps, and releases objects

- Reaches for object
- Pushes ball
- Drops objects
- Grasps a rolled ball or other object with two hands
- Bats or swipes at a toy

Manipulates balls or similar objects with stiff body movements

- Carries a large ball while moving
- Flings a beanbag
- Throws a ball or other object by pushing it with both hands
- Catches a large, bounced ball against body with straight arms
- Kicks a stationary ball

Manipulates balls or similar objects with flexible body movements

- Throws a ball or other object
- Traps thrown ball against body
- Tosses beanbag into basket
- Strikes a balloon with large paddle
- Kicks ball forward by stepping or running up to it

Manipulates balls or similar objects with a full range of motion

- Steps forward to throw ball and follows through
- Catches large ball with both hands
- Strikes stationary ball
- Bounces and catches ball
- Kicks moving ball while running

Objective 6 Demonstrates gross-motor manipulative skills

Strategies

- Avoid activities that encourage competition or that eliminate children from participating.

- Provide sufficient equipment for each child to participate. Include a variety of shapes, sizes, textures, and weights to encourage experimentation and active participation.

- Ensure children's safety by helping them adjust their position in space in relation to other children and objects. Some children need particular guidance about how to notice and move around other people and objects. Teach the safe use of each piece of equipment.

- Provide balls of various sizes, textures, and grips to explore. Include balls with chimes, bells, and visible items rolling inside.

- Provide opportunities for toddlers to practice releasing balls into targets such as large baskets, buckets, or a small basketball hoop.

- Use scarves or Mylar® balloons to practice catching. These items are easier to catch than balls because they move slowly and give children time to position themselves for a catch.

- Provide lightweight clubs or mallets and balls of various sizes for toddlers and older children to practice hitting along the ground.

- Provide equipment that is appropriate in scale. Young preschool children like to throw and catch large rubber or beach balls. Smaller, softer balls are good for kicking. Also provide yarn balls or beanbags for catching or for throwing against a wall with varying force. Use short-handled, oversized plastic or foam paddles or bats for striking.

- Make modifications for children with disabilities or who have less developed manipulative skills. Use lower targets; provide easy-to-see, bright objects to strike; or reduce the distance between the child and target. Offer balls or similar materials that are lightweight. Hang paper balls for children to hit without having to retrieve them.

- Use specific cues with individual children to help them increase proficiency, e.g., "Look at the target before you throw." Use consistent terminology to avoid confusion.

- Provide kindergarten children with plastic cups and tennis or foam balls to practice throwing and catching skills. Increase difficulty by having children throw and catch while sitting, standing, crouching, or walking.

Objective 7

Demonstrates fine-motor strength and coordination

7

Fine-motor skills involve grasping and releasing objects using fingers and hands, as well as using both hands together and often coordinating these movements with the eyes. They require hand and finger strength and dexterity. An infant who slowly picks up Cheerios® one at a time with his thumb and index finger will become a 2-year-old who scribbles with a crayon. A 3-year-old who squeezes and pounds play dough will become a 5-year-old who cuts a picture out of a magazine accurately. Dramatic changes occur in what children can accomplish as they gradually gain control of the small muscles in their hands and fingers. Fine-motor skills improve with regular practice and can be supported through routines and play activities.

Fine-motor skills are important in the performance of daily routines and many school-related tasks. The pincer grasp (using the thumb and index finger, or forefinger, in opposition to one another) develops at the end of the first year, enabling the child to manipulate small objects. Fine-motor development progresses slowly during the preschool years. By kindergarten, children who have often experimented with various materials engage in fine-motor activities for longer periods of time and with less frustration than children who have not had opportunities to handle materials.

Hand and finger strength and control enable children to perform a variety of self-care tasks, such as eating, toileting, dressing, toothbrushing, and nose blowing. These skills give children the experience of doing things on their own and build confidence. Self-care skills are learned gradually and mastered with repetition. Complex skills, such as tying shoes, require children to have an adequate attention span, memory for a series of complex hand movements, and the dexterity to carry them out. Children who have difficulty coordinating the small muscles in their hands have trouble dressing and feeding themselves (Rule & Stewart, 2002).

Gender and family background also affect the development of children's fine-motor skills. Girls tend to be more advanced than boys in fine-motor skills (Sanders, 2006). Some children from at-risk families may have less-developed fine-motor skills. The risk factors were low maternal education, welfare dependency (poverty), only one parent in the home, and having parents whose primary home-language was not English (National Center for Education Statistics, 2000).

Objective 7 Demonstrates fine-motor strength and coordination

Children with disabilities and others who have difficulty coordinating the small muscles in their hands may struggle with using pencils, crayons, and scissors (Rule & Stewart, 2002). They may avoid fine-motor activities because the activities are difficult for them, they tire, or they become anxious and give up in frustration. Modification of activities and materials to fit their developmental levels, as well as more structure and guidance, can help children increase fine-motor skills (Stewart, Rule, & Giordano, 2007).

Young children in some cultures perform self-care tasks and family chores that most children in the United States do not perform until they are older, e.g., preparing food (Trawick-Smith, 2006; Whiting & Edwards, 1988; Whiting & Whiting, 1975). Some children are not expected to perform self-care tasks such as dressing themselves until after their preschool years because their families value interdependence (doing things for each other) over personal independence.

Objective 7 Demonstrates fine-motor strength and coordination

a. Uses fingers and hands

Not Yet	1	2	3	4	5	6	7	8	9

Reaches for, touches, and holds objects purposefully
- Bats or swipes at a toy
- Transfers objects from one hand to another
- Releases objects voluntarily
- Rakes or scoops objects to pick them up
- Picks up food with fingers and puts in mouth
- Bangs two blocks together
- Crumbles paper

Uses fingers and whole-arm movements to manipulate and explore objects
- Places shape in shape sorter
- Points at objects and pokes bubbles
- Releases objects into containers
- Uses spoon and sometimes fork to feed self
- Dumps sand into containers
- Unbuttons large buttons
- Rotates knobs
- Tears paper

Uses refined wrist and finger movements
- Squeezes and releases tongs, turkey baster, squirt toy
- Snips with scissors, then later cuts along straight line
- Strings large beads
- Pours water into containers
- Pounds, pokes, squeezes, rolls clay
- Buttons, zips, buckles, laces
- Uses hand motions for "Itsy Bitsy Spider"
- Turns knobs to open doors
- Uses eating utensils
- Sews lacing cards

Uses small, precise finger and hand movements
- Uses correct scissors grip
- Attempts to tie shoes
- Pushes specific keys on a keyboard
- Arranges small pegs in pegboard
- Strings small beads
- Cuts out simple pictures and shapes, using other hand to move paper
- Cuts food
- Builds a structure using small LEGO® pieces

b. Uses writing and drawing tools

Not Yet	1	2	3	4	5	6	7	8	9

Grasps drawing and writing tools, jabbing at paper

Grips drawing and writing tools with whole hand but may use whole-arm movements to make marks

Holds drawing and writing tools by using a three-point finger grip but may hold the instrument too close to one end

Uses three-point finger grip and efficient hand placement when writing and drawing

Objective 7 Demonstrates fine-motor strength and coordination

Strategies

- Provide a wide variety of fine-motor activities that interest and appeal to all children in the program. Include items that are easy to manipulate by hand and add more challenging activities as quickly as possible without causing frustration.

- Offer activities that strengthen infants' and toddlers' hand grasp, e.g., transferring an object from one hand to another, pulling scarves from a hole cut in a box.

- Engage children in activities that encourage them to move their fingers individually, e.g., finger plays, pointing at pictures.

- Provide activities to strengthen the hand grasp and release of toddlers and older children, e.g., using squirt bottles, medicine droppers, punching holes, using clothespins, and handling play dough.

- Include activities for toddlers and older children that support eye-hand coordination, e.g., stringing beads on pipe cleaners or laces, picking up objects with tongs or tweezers, placing various sized pegs in holes, and folding paper. Encourage kindergarten children to fold paper into halves, fourths, very small, etc. and/o to create shapes or animals.

- Include activities for twos and older children that require using two hands together, e.g., tearing paper, opening and closing containers, using wind-up toys.

- Have children watch as you demonstrate a task and describe the steps. Vary your language to accommodate different developmental levels.

- Allow plenty of time for children to explore materials and complete tasks.

- Take advantage of self-care activities (e.g., handwashing and scraping plates) throughout the day to support the development of children's fine-motor skills.

- Give simple, clear, verbal instructions and physically guide, model, or use picture cues to help children perform tasks successfully.

Language Development

Language is the principal tool for establishing and maintaining relationships with adults and other children. Children's desire to communicate their thoughts, ideas, needs, and feelings with others motivates them to develop language (Epstein, 2007). Learning to understand and use words is complex. Language also involves learning about the structure and sequence of speech sounds, vocabulary, grammar, and the rules for engaging in appropriate and effective conversation (Berk, 2009).

Language development begins at birth, but many children do not receive the ongoing experiences that support this learning. By age 3, differences in children's understanding and use of language are enormous (Copple & Bredekamp, 2009; Strickland & Shanahan, 2004). Strong language skills are essential for children's success in school and life (Hart & Risley, 2003; Heath & Hogben, 2004; Jalongo, 2008; Kalmar, 2008). Oral language, including grammar, the ability to define words, and listening comprehension, helps provide the foundation and is an ongoing support for literacy (National Early Literacy Panel, 2008; Strickland & Shanahan, 2004).

LANGUAGE DEVELOPMENT OBJECTIVES

8 Listens to and understands increasingly complex language

9 Uses language to express thoughts and needs

10 Uses appropriate conversational and other communication skills

Children use language to think and to solve problems. Because words represent objects and ideas, language development is closely related to cognitive development. Children with certain types of disabilities face particular challenges in learning to understand and use language effectively.

Family background and culture also affect how children learn language. There are differences in how much mothers talk with their children and what they talk about. Some parents focus on social norms such as turn-taking; others discuss what people are thinking and feeling. There are major differences in the kinds of questions they ask (Peña & Mendez-Perez, 2006).

Teachers are very important in helping children develop a strong foundation in language. Teachers influence language development through the language they use, the way they set up the environment, and the types of experiences they provide. The opportunities children have for sociodramatic play and the level of that play affect children's language development. Higher levels of play allow for increased language and more complex language structures (Heisner, 2005).

Listens to and understands increasingly complex language

8

Children must be able to comprehend what they hear. *Receptive language* includes listening to, recognizing, and understanding the communication of others. An infant turns to the sound of her mother's voice, a 2-year-old answers simple questions, and a kindergartner follows detailed, multistep directions. To comprehend language, children must focus their attention and listen with a purpose. They must accurately and quickly recognize and understand what they hear (Roskos, Tabors, & Lenhart, 2004). Receptive language starts to develop before expressive language, but they are closely connected (Hirsch-Pasek, Golinkoff, & Naigles, 1996; Strickland, 2006). Expressive language is dependent upon receptive language.

Young children connect what they hear with their background knowledge and experiences (Strickland, 2006). The more children understand about the world around them, the better able they are to make sense of what they hear. Through conversations with adults, listening to stories read aloud, and engaging in meaningful experiences, children develop new concepts and acquire new vocabulary that helps them to understand increasingly complex language.

Some children with hearing impairments may be learning other forms of communication such as sign language or cued speech. Children with receptive language difficulties may have difficulty understanding the meaning of what they hear. They may understand only a word or two and then guess the meaning of the rest of the words.

English-language learners who are not proficient in their home language may find it harder to learn English (Jalongo, 2008; Tabors & Snow, 2001). Environments that are noisy make it even more difficult for them to recognize English words (Jalongo, 2008). Positive language interactions with skillful English speakers are critical to helping them become proficient in English (Piker & Rex, 2008).

Nonverbal communication is an important part of the listening experience and may have different meanings in different cultures. Some people value direct eye contact while listening, and others perceive eye contact as a sign of disrespect (Trawick-Smith, 2006).

Objective 8 Listens to and understands increasingly complex language

a. Comprehends language

Not Yet	1	2	3	4	5	6	7	8	9

Shows an interest in the speech of others
- Turns head toward people who are talking
- Recognizes familiar voice before the adult enters the room
- Looks at favorite toy when adult labels and points to it
- Responds to own name

Identifies familiar people, animals, and objects when prompted
- Picks up cup when asked, "Where's your cup?"
- Goes to sink when told to wash hands
- Touches body parts while singing "Head, Shoulders, Knees, and Toes."

Responds appropriately to specific vocabulary and simple statements, questions, and stories
- Finds his favorite illustration in a storybook when asked
- Listens to friend tell about cut finger and then goes to the dramatic play area to get a Band-Aid®
- Responds using gestures to compare the sizes of the three leaves

Responds appropriately to complex statements, questions, vocabulary, and stories
- Answers appropriately when asked, "How do you think the car would move if it had square wheels?"
- Builds on ideas about how to fix the broken wagon
- Acts out the life cycle of a butterfly after the teacher reads a story about it

b. Follows directions

Not Yet	1	2	3	4	5	6	7	8	9

Responds to simple verbal requests accompanied by gestures or tone of voice
- Waves when mother says, "Wave bye-bye," as she waves her hand
- Covers eyes when adult prompts, "Wheeeere's Lucy?"
- Drops toy when teacher extends hand and says, "Please give it to me."

Follows simple requests not accompanied by gestures
- Throws trash in can when asked, "Will you please throw this away?"
- Puts the balls in the basket when told, "Put all the balls in the basket, please."
- Goes to cubby when teacher says, "It's time to put coats on to go outside."

Follows directions of two or more steps that relate to familiar objects and experiences
- Washes and dries hands after being reminded about the hand-washing sequence
- Completes a sequence of tasks, "Get the book bin and put it on the table. Then bring the paper and crayons."

Follows detailed, instructional, multistep directions
- Follows instructions for navigating a new computer program
- Follows teacher's guidance: "To feed the fish, first get the fish flakes. Open the jar and sprinkle a pinch of food on the water. Finally, put the lid on the jar and put it back on the shelf."

Objective 8 Listens to and understands increasingly complex language

Strategies

- Use *parentese* with young infants. Singsong speech and exaggerated facial expressions encourage babies to listen and focus on what is said.

- Talk often with children, using rich language to describe objects, events, and people in the environment.

- Walk over to the child instead of speaking from across the room. The child can attend more easily to what you are saying if you are nearby.

- Have the child's attention when you speak. Place yourself face-to-face at the child's level.

- Be clear and specific when making requests and giving directions.

- Use language that is easy for the child to understand, explaining new vocabulary as you use it.

- Use gestures and concrete objects to clarify what you are saying to a child.

- Use the same words and phrases for common classroom activities. This can help English-language learners associate language with meaning, e.g., say, "Hang your painting on the drying rack."

- Give adequate waiting time, so children can process what they hear and take part in discussions.

- Use precise language because young children are very literal thinkers.

- Learn about and respond appropriately to the conversational styles of the children's families.

- Use same-language and different-language peers as social peer resources. Peers can assist dual language learners in participating in classroom activities and responding appropriately to the teacher's inquires.

- Alert children when giving complex explanations. Tell them what to listen for. For example say, "This is hard to understand. Listen carefully to each step."

- Positively acknowledge when the child follows directions.

- Use multistep and unrelated directions with kindergarten children. For example, you might say, "First, take the plastic tablecloth and put it on the table. Next, get the paint, droppers, and six containers off the shelf. Put 10 drops of paint into each container. Put a container and piece of paper at each child's place." Also use multiple directions related to different tasks. For example, "Hang your coat up. Take the books back to the library. When you come back, get out your journal."

Uses language to express thoughts and needs

9

Children all over the world follow the same developmental sequence as they learn to speak. They proceed from cooing and babbling in infancy to forming words and sentences as toddlers and 2-year-olds and using more adult-like speech as preschoolers. Children talk to express feelings, make requests, discuss plans, gain information, understand concepts, solve problems, and share ideas and stories. With lots of practice over time, children develop the ability to speak clearly and to use *decontextualized language* to tell personal stories as they describe objects, people, and events that are familiar, but that occurred in another time and place (Nicolopoulou & Richner, 2007; Snow, 1991). This *narrative talk* or storytelling requires more complex language than is needed for daily conversations (Stadler & Ward, 2005).

The use of language is important to children's literacy development. Children's first writing experiences are usually based on what they learned through narrative talk (Beals, 2001; Dickinson & Tabors, 2001; Hart & Risley, 1995). Later literacy development is influenced by *explanatory talk* such as discussion of cause-and-effect relationships and connections between ideas, events, and actions (Beals, 2001; Dickinson & Tabors, 2001; Hart & Risley, 1995). Children's later literacy development also is influenced by their ability to define words and their knowledge of grammar (National Early Literacy Panel, 2008).

Children's language skills vary greatly. There are major differences due to family background and income. Family language patterns affect how much speech children use to express their feelings, needs, and ideas (Rogoff, Mistry, Goncu, & Mosier, 1993). Some children speak in complex sentences. Others make brief statements and must be supported to say more about their ideas. Children's narrative topics may be limited to a single focus with a clear beginning, middle, and end. Narratives of other children may flow from one topic into another (Stadler & Ward, 2005). By kindergarten, some children living in poverty have only one fourth of the vocabulary of their middle-class peers (Berk, 2006).

Some children use other forms of communication besides spoken language. They may use sign language or augmentative communication including pictures, switch activated devices, or other mechanisms that can speak for them (Cook, Klein, & Tessier, 2004). It is important to include children's use of these devices when assessing a child's development.

Objective 9 Uses language to express thoughts and needs

For some children, English is not their first language. They may speak only a little English or none at all. Every language has its own vocabulary and rules for how sounds, words, and larger units of meaning fit together. Many children use the structure of their home language and apply it as they learn English (August & Hakuta, 1998). English-language learners and children with language delays may find it difficult to use language that goes beyond what is familiar (Weitzman & Greenberg, 2002).

Children with language delays or hearing or cognitive impairments often speak in short, ungrammatical sentences. Children with language delays may have difficulty retrieving words from memory and may confuse word meanings (Ratner, 2001). Impairments in social interactions may make it challenging for some children with autism spectrum disorders to learn new words (Parish-Morris, Hennon, Hirsh-Pasek, Golinkoff, & Tager-Flusberg, 2007).

Teachers can influence children's language development (Copple & Bredekamp, 2009). It is important for teachers to engage in conversations with all children, even if they don't yet speak English (Piker & Rex, 2008). Reciprocal, extended conversations with more skilled speakers help children increase their vocabularies, expand their expressive skills, and move toward more conventional grammar. Through participating in extended conversations with adults or mature language users, most children gradually learn adult-like language constructions.

Objective 9 Uses language to express thoughts and needs

a. Uses an expanding expressive vocabulary

Not Yet	1	2	3	4	5	6	7	8	9

2 — **Vocalizes and gestures to communicate**
- Coos and squeals when happy
- Cries after trying several times to get toy just out of reach
- Waves hands in front of face to push away spoon during a feeding
- Uses hand gestures to sign or indicate "more"

4 — **Names familiar people, animals, and objects**
- Says, "Nana," when grandmother comes into the room
- Names the cow, horse, chicken, pig, sheep, and goat as she sees them on the trip to the farm

6 — **Describes and tells the use of many familiar items**
- When making pancakes, says, "Here is the beater. Let me beat the egg with it."
- Responds, "We used the big, red umbrella so we both could get under it."

8 — **Incorporates new, less familiar or technical words in everyday conversations**
- Uses a communication device to say, "My bird went to the vet. He has a disease. He's losing his feathers."
- Says, "I'm not sure I can put it together. It's complicated."

b. Speaks clearly

Not Yet	1	2	3	4	5	6	7	8	9

2 — **Babbles strings of single consonant sounds and combines sounds**
- Says, "M-m-m;" "D-d-d"
- Says, "Ba-ba-ba"
- Babbles with sentence-like intonation

4 — **Uses some words and word-like sounds and is understood by most familiar people**
- Refers to grandma as "Gum-gum"
- Asks, "Where bankit?" and a friend brings his blanket to him
- Says, "No go!" to indicate she doesn't want to go inside

6 — **Is understood by most people; may mispronounce new, long, or unusual words**
- Says, "I saw ants and a hoppergrass" (grasshopper)
- Speaks so is understood by the school visitor

8 — **Pronounces multisyllabic or unusual words correctly**
- Says, "Oh, that one has layers, it's a *sedimentary* rock."
- Says, "What does *ostracize* mean?" after hearing the word read in *Abiyoyo*

Objective 9 Uses language to express thoughts and needs

c. Uses conventional grammar

Not Yet	1	2	3	4	5	6	7	8	9

Uses one- or two-word sentences or phrases
- Asks, "More?"
- Says, "Daddy go."
- Uses one word, "Juice," to mean, "I want some juice."

Uses three- to four-word sentences; may omit some words or use some words incorrectly
- Says, "Bed no go."
- Says, "Daddy goed to work."
- Responds, "I want banana," when asked what she wants for snack

Uses complete, four- to six-word sentences
- Says, "I chose two books."
- Says, "We are going to the zoo."
- Says, "Momma came and we went home."

Uses long, complex sentences and follows most grammatical rules
- Says, "We are going to the zoo to see the animals. We'll learn where they live and what they eat."
- Notices when sentences do not make sense; tries to correct them

d. Tells about another time or place

Not Yet	1	2	3	4	5	6	7	8	9

Makes simple statements about recent events and familiar people and objects that are not present
- Says, "Got shoes."
- Hears helicopter, stops and says, "'copter."
- Tells, "Gran lives far away."

Tells simple stories about objects, events, and people not present; lacks many details and a conventional beginning, middle, and end
- Dictates a simple story with few connections between characters and events
- Says, "I've got new shoes. I went to the shoe store."

Tells stories about other times and places that have a logical order and that include major details
- Tells about past experiences, reporting the major events in a logical sequence
- Says, "I went to the shoe store with Gran. I got two pairs of new shoes."

Tells elaborate stories that refer to other times and places
- Dictates an elaborate story of her recent visit to the bakery, including details of who, what, when, why, and how
- Tells many details as he acts out his recent trip to the shoe store

Objective 9 Uses language to express thoughts and needs

Strategies

- Serve as a good speech model for children. Speak slowly, and model correct grammar.

- Respect children's communication styles while encouraging them to achieve higher levels of communication. Instead of correcting the child's incorrect pronunciation and grammar, respond by modeling the correct language. Repeat their words with more complete, grammatically accurate, or expanded talk. For example, when the child says, "He goed," say, "Yes, Marcus went to the museum with his aunt and uncle."

- Encourage children to use explanatory talk (explaining and describing) by modeling it. For example explain, "This jar of paint is hard to open. If I put it under hot water, the cover will expand, and it will be much easier to open."

- Ask open-ended questions that encourage multiple responses. For example say, "What would happen if...?", "What do you think?", "What else could you do?". Even if children are preverbal, open-ended questions encourage children's thinking, and they benefit from hearing the rich language.

- Have one-on-one conversations with children who are reluctant to speak in a group. Support them in contributing to small group discussions.

- Provide props that encourage talking, e.g., telephones and puppets.

- Join children's dramatic play to scaffold their storytelling. For example, you might prompt a child by saying, "What did your grandma say after that?"

- Help children connect their everyday experiences and relate the familiar to the unfamiliar. For example, when introducing a new material say, "You can use these new sponge brushes to paint just like you use the big paint brushes. Let me show you."

- Tell children stories without using books. Tell about things that happened in another time and place. For example, you might tell a story about what they did at school earlier in the year. Encourage kindergarten children to tell their own stories about what they did at school earlier in the year.

- Include materials to encourage verbal children to tell stories, e.g. wordless picture books, miniature items from a story, and picture story starters.

- Help children increase the richness and diversity of their vocabulary. Introduce children to less common words through books, songs, conversations, discussions, pretend play, first-hand experiences, and in-depth studies.

- Repeat and reinforce new words. Talk about the meanings of new words by providing familiar words with similar meanings. Use new words in different contexts throughout the day.

- Use simple language and speak slowly. Use gestures, pictures, and objects to help children understand meaning.

- Play language games with kindergarten children. Have them make up sentences (some that make sense and some that don't), and have the other children indicate "sense" or "nonsense." If it's a nonsense sentence, the other children have to try and tell why it's nonsense.

- Make sure each child can respond to questions, participate in story time, make choices, initiate social conversations, and get your attention when needed. Consider a variety of communication techniques, e.g., gestures, picture boards, and recordable communication devices.

- Ask families about the child's successful communication strategies at home.

Uses appropriate conversational and other communication skills

10

Conversations involve back-and-forth exchanges. When an infant coos back at his mother while she talks to him, a 2-year-old adds her thoughts when there is a pause in the conversation, a preschooler initiates a conversation with his teacher about a recent vacation, and a kindergartner takes turns as he engages in a lengthy conversation with several friends, they are all using appropriate communication and conversational skills.

Children acquire vocabulary, other language skills, and background knowledge about many topics by participating in frequent, meaningful conversations with responsive adults. They benefit from conversations that include varied vocabulary and that challenge their thinking (Dickinson & Tabors, 2001). Such conversations contribute to early reading success. In addition, conversations are important to children's cognitive and social–emotional learning (Hart & Risley, 1995). One-to-one, extended, cognitively challenging conversations can be used to engage even reluctant talkers (Snow, Burns, & Griffin, 1998).

Children also must learn the social rules of communicating. This involves being polite, speaking so the listener understands, and turn-taking. The social rules of conversations often vary from culture to culture and from one community to another (Peña & Mendez-Perez, 2006; Trawick-Smith, 2006). Social conventions determine how much silent time is expected for thinking and for carefully selecting the right words before making a response (Rowe, 1987). In some families, children may be expected to listen to adult conversations and to speak only when asked to contribute. The following list describes differences in several social conventions (Trawick-Smith, 2006):

- Turn-taking: Some people engage in conversations where equal turn-taking is not valued; others value it highly.

- Personal space: Some people tend to stand very close together during conversations, while others stand farther apart.

- Eye contact: In some communities, eye contact with an adult is a sign of disrespect or rudeness; in others, eye contact is a sign of respect.

- Touch: A touch, e.g., on the arm or shoulder, may be offensive to some people but considered a friendly gesture by others.

- Gestures: Hand gestures, e.g., making a circle with the thumb and forefinger, may carry different meanings in different cultures.

- Politeness and formality: Some people vary formality and other ways of being polite according to the social status of the person being addressed.

Objective 10 Uses appropriate conversational and other communication skills

a. Engages in conversations

Not Yet	1	2	3	4	5	6	7	8	9
		Engages in simple back-and-forth exchanges with others		**Initiates and attends to brief conversations**		**Engages in conversations of at least three exchanges**		**Engages in complex, lengthy conversations (five or more exchanges)**	

Engages in simple back-and-forth exchanges with others
- Coos at adult who says, "Sweet Jeremy is talking." He coos again, and adult imitates the sounds
- Shakes head for *no*; waves bye-bye
- Joins in games such as pat-a-cake and peekaboo

Initiates and attends to brief conversations
- Says, "Doggy." Teacher responds, "You see a doggy." Child says, "Doggy woof."
- Asks teacher, "Home now?" Teacher responds, "Yes, I'm leaving to go home."
- Looks at teacher and points to picture of car. Teacher responds, "No, I'm going to walk home."

Engages in conversations of at least three exchanges
- Stays on topic during conversations
- Maintains the conversation by repeating what the other person says or by asking questions

Engages in complex, lengthy conversations (five or more exchanges)
- Offers interesting comments with communication device
- Extends conversation by moving gradually from one topic to a related topic

b. Uses social rules of language

Not Yet	1	2	3	4	5	6	7	8	9

Responds to speech by looking toward the speaker; watches for signs of being understood when communicating
- Hears siren and goes to adult pointing, "Fire tuck."
- Looks at adult and says, "Ball," repeatedly until adult says, "Ball. You want the ball?"

Uses appropriate eye contact, pauses, and simple verbal prompts when communicating
- Pays attention to speaker during conversation
- Pauses after asking a question to wait for a response
- Says "please" and "thank you" with occasional prompting

Uses acceptable language and social rules while communicating with others; may need reminders
- Takes turns in conversations but may interrupt or direct talk back to self
- Regulates volume of voice when reminded

Uses acceptable language and social rules during communication with others
- Uses a softer voice when talking with peers in the library and a louder voice on the playground
- Says, "Hello," back to the museum curator on a trip

Objective 10 Uses appropriate conversational and other communication skills

Strategies

- Build on the child's language. Rephrase what the child says and then add more.

- Learn as much as you can about the communication styles of the families in the program.

- Plan specific experiences where children will be encouraged to talk and to use their communication skills.

- Model appropriate conversational skills, e.g., taking turns, eye contact, speech volume, and using polite words.

- Provide many opportunities for children to hear and use language. Engage in frequent conversations with each child. Listen carefully to what is being said. Children will talk more when they know teachers listen.

- Provide interesting experiences for children to discuss.

- Try to maintain conversations with children for extended exchanges. Listen carefully to what the child is saying. Respond with related comments and open-ended questions that keep the conversation going. Try to get the child to tell you more about the topic. For preverbal children, model this conversational style using their cues to guide you. For example, when the infant reaches for a rattle and grunts, say, "Do you want your rattle? What are you going to do with your rattle?" Hand the baby the rattle and when he shakes it say, "Oh you are shaking it." When the baby squeals with delight say, "You like shaking your rattle."

- Encourage the use of social words in context, e.g., "please" and "thank you." Provide them as options on a child's communication device.

- Use the same communication system as the child, e.g. point to pictures on her picture board to ask if she wants to go outside.

- Organize kindergarten children into discussion groups of four or more. Begin with topics they want to talk about. Support them as needed to listen to others (including communicating with children using communication devices), take turns, add relevant information, stay on topic, etc. Include less skillful as well as more skilled children in the group. As children become more skillful, increase the number of children in the group.

Cognitive Development

Cognitive development, also called intellectual development, is influenced by the child's approaches to learning as well as his or her biological makeup and the environment. A child's background knowledge, or knowledge base, also affects the way a child thinks. This background knowledge influences the child's information processing, memory, classification, problem solving, language acquisition, and reading and mathematics learning (Bjorklund, 2005; McAfee & Leong, 1994). What and how children learn often varies considerably from culture to culture, and minor variations exist in the ways children within a cultural group perform specific cognitive tasks (Trawick-Smith, 2006). Some children have disabilities that interfere with the development of their conceptual and reasoning skills (Cook, Klein, & Tessier, 2004).

Children who have positive approaches to learning are more likely to succeed academically and to have more positive interactions with peers (Fantuzzo, Perry, & McDermott, 2004; Hyson, 2005, 2008). These dispositions and behaviors must be nurtured by effective curriculum and intentional teaching methods (Hyson, 2005, 2008; Hyson, Buch, Fantuzzo, & Scott-Little, 2006).

COGNITIVE DEVELOPMENT OBJECTIVES

11 Demonstrates positive approaches to learning

12 Remembers and connects experiences

13 Uses classification skills

14 Uses symbols and images to represent something not present

The physical environment of the classroom and the kinds of interactions children have with adults and other children influence the way children approach learning and influence other aspects of their cognitive development.

Play is important for learning. Researchers have found many connections between cognitive competence and play, particularly high-quality dramatic play. The benefits of play include self-regulation; memory development; divergent thinking; problem solving; language development; and academic skill development in literacy, math, social studies, and science (Bergen, 2002; Bodrova & Leong, 2004; Charlesworth, 2008; Fantuzzo & McWayne, 2002; Howes & Matheson, 1992; Klein, Wirth, & Linas, 2004; Krafft & Berk, 1998; Newman, 1990; Nourot & Van Hoorn, 1991; O'Reilly & Bornstein, 1993; Smilansky & Shefatya, 1990; Steglin, 2005).

Demonstrates positive approaches to learning

11

When children have a positive approach to learning, they are likely to want to learn more. There are five dimensions to this objective: attention and engagement, persistence, problem solving, curiosity and motivation, and flexibility and inventiveness.

Attention, Engagement, and Persistence

As children mature, they demonstrate an increasing capacity to concentrate, to persist, and therefore, to become deeply involved in what they are doing, despite distractions and interruptions. The ability to resist distractions, remain positively engaged, and persist at learning tasks are related positively to children's academic achievement, cognitive development, and peer interactions (Blair, 2003; Deater-Deckard, Petrill, Thompson, & DeThrone, 2005; Duncan et al., 2007; Fantuzzo, Perry, & McDermott, 2004; Howse, Lange, Farran, & Boyles, 2003; Hyson, 2008; Jablon & Wilkinson, 2006; Ladd, Birch, & Buhs, 1999; Normandeau & Guay, 1998).

There are variations among children's levels of attention, engagement, and persistence. Bilingual children may sometimes be more likely to attend to relevant details during attention-demanding tasks than their monolingual peers because they have had experience attending to one language while ignoring the other language (Bialystok & Martin, 2004). In general, children show greater persistence on tasks that are challenging for them (tasks that are not too easy or too difficult). They are likely to be more attentive, interested, and engaged when they make choices about their learning (Brophy, 2004; Kohn, 1993).

Some children with particular disabilities may be less likely to become engaged in activities or may show engagement in ways that are different from those of typically developing children. Children with attention deficit disorders (ADD, ADHD) may find it difficult to persist with classroom performance tasks. Children with autism spectrum disorders may repeat behaviors, continuing to do the same things again and again. They may do this even if their strategies are not successful. Children living in poverty may find it hard to regulate their attention and persist with challenging tasks if they are hungry, sick, or sleepy (Howse, Lange, Farran, & Boyles, 2003; Hyson, 2008).

Objective 11 Demonstrates positive approaches to learning

Positive evaluative feedback from adults helps children persist with difficult tasks (Berk, 2009; Burhans & Dweck, 1995; Kelly, Brownell, & Campbell, 2000). Children who are distracted easily may need to work with only a few materials and choices at one time. Sometimes a task must be presented in smaller steps so that the child can understand what to do (Gargiulo & Kilgo, 2007; Lewis, 2003).

Problem Solving

Children solve problems by using available information, resources, and materials to overcome obstacles and achieve a goal. An infant cries when hungry. A toddler backs down steps consistently once he has been taught to go down backwards. A preschool child tries several strategies, modifying them as he goes along. A kindergartner works with peers trying various suggestions for attaching new pieces to a sculpture. In order to use relevant information to solve problems, children need to have organized what they know and be able to retrieve it. Very young children independently discover many ways to solve problems as they explore their bodies and interact with materials and people.

Children become increasingly selective in and adept at using problem-solving strategies. With experience, they become better at selecting and monitoring strategies and applying them in new situations (Berk, 2002, 2009; Bjorklund, 2005). Even after using a more efficient strategy, children often return to using a less effective strategy. This switching among strategies aids cognitive development. It allows children to reason about their choices, comparing more and less effective strategies.

Play gives children many opportunities to solve problems. In particular, sociodramatic play fosters children's problem-solving skills (Bergen, 2002; Fisher, 1992). Research shows that there are cultural and individual differences in the ways children approach problem-solving tasks. Some children interact with others to solve problems. Some children watch how others work with materials before beginning to use them. Other children solve problems independently, handling materials to figure out how they work. (Bergen, 2002; Berk, 2002, 2009; Trawick-Smith, 2006). One way is not necessarily better than another.

Curiosity and Motivation

Young children want to know more about themselves and the world around them. An infant explores a block by putting it in his mouth and banging it on the ground. A toddler turns the water handle repeatedly to make the water start and stop. A 2-year-old repeatedly asks, "Why?" A preschooler who is interested in airplanes asks an adult to read a nonfiction book about how jets are made. These children are all demonstrating their curiosity and motivation to learn.

Curiosity promotes cognitive, social–emotional, and physical development throughout life by stimulating exploratory behaviors (Reio, Petrosko, Wiswell, & Thongsukmag, 2006). By responding to children's questions and providing safe environments that encourage active exploration, adults foster children's curiosity and motivation to learn. When children are motivated, they have a desire to continue with challenging tasks. Most children find new learning self-motivating (Hyson, 2008). Giving them rewards, e.g., food items, smiley faces, stickers, may lessen their curiosity and motivation to pursue the activities in the future (Arnone, 2003; Deci, Koestner, & Ryan, 2001; Elliot & Dweck, 2005; Katz & Chard, 1995; Stipek, 2002).

Objective 11 Demonstrates positive approaches to learning

All children do not show their curiosity or motivation to learn in the same ways, and teachers may interpret some children's behaviors as a lack of interest and motivation. Some children are taught not to ask questions of adults, and some watch how others use materials rather than explore them actively. Some children with particular cognitive disabilities demonstrate little apparent curiosity or motivation, and they need a great deal of adult support.

Flexibility and Inventiveness

Cognitive flexibility is important for children's academic achievement (George & Greenfield, 2005; Hyson, 2008). Children who are flexible in their thinking consider alternative possibilities, find their own ways to resolve conflicts, and solve problems with tools and materials. When a 2-year-old tries a block and then uses a broom handle to reach a toy under a bookshelf and when a preschooler makes up new lyrics to a familiar song, they are approaching tasks with flexibility and inventiveness.

Flexible thinking is critical to children's development of sorting and categorization skills, understanding of concepts, problem-solving skills, reasoning skills, divergent thinking, and inventiveness. Children need unhurried time to explore topics in depth and to complete activities; space that inspires them to create; a varied collection of found, recycled, and purchased materials and props; an encouraging classroom atmosphere that supports risk-taking, acceptance of mistakes, and innovation; and opportunities to express their innovative thinking through creative products (Pope & Springate, 1995).

Flexibility requires children to shift focus from one topic to another, recognize relevant information, and change their strategies to match changing task demands. There are age differences in children's cognitive flexibility. Infants become increasingly able to shift attention from one object or person to another (Berk, 2002). A developmental spurt in children's cognitive flexibility occurs between 3–5 years of age (Deak, 2003; Smidts, Jacobs, & Anderson, 2004). Children who are bilingual may show enhanced cognitive flexibility as they switch between languages (Bialystok, McBride-Chang, & Luk, 2005). Some children with particular disabilities, such as autism spectrum disorders, may have difficulty with flexible thinking and may need specific activities to encourage flexibility of thought (Carruthers, 1996; Gould & Sullivan, 1999; Lewis, 2003).

Objective 11 Demonstrates positive approaches to learning

a. Attends and engages

Not Yet	1	2	3	4	5	6	7	8	9

Pays attention to sights and sounds
- Watches the teacher walk across the room
- Turns head toward sound of mother's voice

Sustains interest in working on a task, especially when adults offer suggestions, questions, and comments
- Takes small blocks from adult and continues to drop them into a container
- Continues ring stacking when the teacher says, "You're putting the biggest ones on first."
- Continues the play about going to a restaurant after the teacher offers a menu

Sustains work on age-appropriate, interesting tasks; can ignore most distractions and interruptions
- Makes relevant contributions to group discussion about class pet
- Focuses on making a sign for a building while others are rolling cars down a ramp nearby

Sustains attention to tasks or projects over time (days to weeks); can return to activities after interruptions
- Returns to LEGO® construction over several days, adding new features each time
- Pauses to join in problem-solving discussion at adult's request, then returns to art project

b. Persists

Not Yet	1	2	3	4	5	6	7	8	9

Repeats actions to obtain similar results
- Repeatedly shakes a rattle to produce noise
- Hits a toy on a play gym accidentally; then waves arms to hit it again
- Puts objects in a wagon and then dumps them out over and over again

Practices an activity many times until successful
- Stacks blocks again and again until tower no longer falls
- Uses shovel in many ways to fill small bucket with sand
- Chooses the same puzzle every day until he can insert each piece quickly and easily

Plans and pursues a variety of appropriately challenging tasks
- Keeps looking through all of the magnetic letters for those that are in her name
- Works with others to learn how to use a new software program

Plans and pursues own goal until it is reached
- Keeps building a sand structure, trying multiple ways to get the bridge to hold
- Returns from lunch with a different idea about what to add to his story

Objective 11 Demonstrates positive approaches to learning

c. Solves problems

Not Yet	1	2	3	4	5	6	7	8	9

Reacts to a problem; seeks to achieve a specific goal

- Grunts when cube gets stuck in shape sorter
- Reaches for a toy that is just out of reach
- Blows on warm cereal after seeing someone blow on cereal

Observes and imitates how other people solve problems; asks for a solution and uses it

- Seeks help opening a stuck cap; pulls one end as teacher pulls the other
- Asks another child to hold his cup while he pours milk

Solves problems without having to try every possibility

- Looks at an assortment of pegs and selects the size that will fit in the hole
- Tells another child, "Put the big block down first, or the tower will fall down."

Thinks problems through, considering several possibilities and analyzing results

- Considers new information before trying a strategy: "If I put this box on top, I can see if they are the same size."
- Thinks about a book character's problem and suggests solutions

d. Shows curiosity and motivation

Not Yet	1	2	3	4	5	6	7	8	9

Uses senses to explore the immediate environment

- Turns in direction of a sound
- Moves closer to touch an object
- Shakes or bangs a toy to make it work

Explores and investigates ways to make something happen

- Enjoys taking things apart
- Turns faucet on and off
- Tilts a ramp to find out if a car will go down faster

Shows eagerness to learn about a variety of topics and ideas

- Seeks answers to questions about the storm
- Shows interest in learning how the firefighter's clothes protect him

Uses a variety of resources to find answers to questions

- Locates informational book on insects to identify the butterfly seen outside
- Asks visiting musician questions about her instrument

Objective 11 Demonstrates positive approaches to learning

e. Shows flexibility and inventiveness in thinking

Not Yet	1	2	3	4	5	6	7	8	9

Imitates others in using objects in new and/or unanticipated ways

- Notices another child reach a toy with the broom handle; then tries
- Imitates a friend, putting a basket on head to use as a hat

Uses creativity and imagination during play and routine tasks

- Strings wooden beads into a necklace as part of dramatic play
- Uses a table, sheets, and towels to build a tent

Changes plans if a better idea is thought of or proposed

- Accepts idea to use tape instead of glue to fix the tear
- Suggests building on a hard surface when structure keeps falling down

Thinks through possible long-term solutions and takes on more abstract challenges

- Offers ideas on how to make the block area larger for building
- Creates board game; thinks of how to play it from start to finish

Objective 11 Demonstrates positive approaches to learning

Strategies

- Provide one or two toys or materials at a time for young infants, exchanging them when the child's attention diminishes.

- Provide appropriate amounts of visual stimuli, e.g., pictures, mobiles, and signs, so children are neither over- nor understimulated.

- Use the child's name to get his or her attention, e.g., say, "Look, Juan!" as you begin to speak.

- Help the child stay focused by singing about an activity if it is helpful to the child, e.g., sing, "This is the way we stack the blocks, stack the blocks, stack the blocks...."

- Provide children with time, space, and a variety of interesting materials for play.

- Provide recyclable as well as new materials that can be used in a variety of innovative ways, e.g., boxes, tubes, spools, containers.

- Provide many opportunities for children to make choices from among interesting materials that are familiar and challenging, and encourage children to use them in many ways.

- Rotate materials regularly to maintain children's interest. Provide materials that build on those already familiar to the children.

- Interpret and expand on what children do and say. Model deliberate, strategic engagement in activities and self-talk to help children stay engaged and persist with challenging tasks.

- Provide opportunities for children to observe others solving problems and to work with other children and adults to solve problems together.

- Support children's efforts during challenging tasks by providing specific, positive verbal feedback or physical support while encouraging them to come up with solutions, e.g., "Keep turning the puzzle piece to figure out how it fits."

- Describe children's problem-solving strategies, e.g., "You tried reaching into the jar to get the balls out, and then you turned the jar over and dumped them."

- Limit directions to one step at a time for toddlers and two or three steps at a time for preschoolers and kindergartners. Reinforce the directions visually by demonstrating the activity, by using pictures, or by using picture and word cues.

- Encourage children to learn from their mistakes. Encourage them to make and test predictions and to examine their thinking.

- Respond to children's explorations and discoveries with enthusiasm and encouragement rather than by providing rewards like stickers or prizes.

- Support children's spontaneous interests, e.g., their examinations of the locust shells found in the play yard, in addition to offering teacher-directed activities based on the children's interests.

- Encourage children to solve problems for themselves when appropriate. Be available to offer support, encouragement, and new ideas when needed.

- Demonstrate, explain, and engage children in trying different ways of doing things. Discuss whether the strategies worked well.

- Take time to answer *why* questions, offering explanations that the child can understand.

- Encourage children's inclination to ask questions and wonder. Help them refine their questions and support them in finding answers.

- Play games that support children's curiosity and internal motivation, such as "Mystery Bag." Hide an object inside a bag. Give verbal clues about its identity. Let children feel, describe, and guess what it is before looking at it.

Objective 11   Demonstrates positive approaches to learning

Strategies, *continued*

- Encourage children's imaginations by finding images in clouds or puddles. Discuss pictures in which part of an object is hidden.

- Nurture children's curiosity by providing thought-provoking, hands-on, investigatory experiences that motivate them to apply their developing skills and prior knowledge and that challenge them to think.

- Ask children open-ended questions such as, "What do you think would happen if you...? What else could you do with...? Can you think of another way to...?"

- Point out strategies children used successfully in similar situations, e.g., prompt, "Yesterday you used the broom to get the dishes from behind the sink. I wonder if it would work to get the puzzle piece that dropped behind the shelf?"

- Organize the play environment to encourage sociodramatic play, including props, utensils, and tools to support different roles. Create new settings for dramatic play with preschool and older children, e.g., a post office, clinic, grocery store, bakery, or campsite. Serve as a sensitive play tutor, engaging in play while following the children's leads.

- Plan so that children can spend days or weeks investigating interesting objects in their environment, seeking answers to their questions, and finding solutions to problems.

- Provide well-defined boundaries for preschool and kindergarten children who need support in order to focus, e.g., use freestanding cardboard dividers for table activities and colored tape to define workspaces on the floor. Limit the number of choices they are given.

- Model flexibility by changing an activity to incorporate children's interesting ideas. To help children consider different perspectives or solutions, explain why the activity is being changed.

- Emphasize the process children use to come up with possible approaches to tasks instead of focusing on finished products and answers.

- Guide preschool and older children in doing in-depth, long-term, and open-ended studies and explorations.

- Encourage children to think of multiple ways to create something using the same materials. For example, they might see how many different ways they can make a boat using milk cartons, paper, foil, craft sticks, etc.

Remembers and connects experiences

12

Memory involves complex cognitive processes. To remember, children must attend to the important aspects of information so that it can be stored and later retrieved and used. Children store information in long-term memory if the information is meaningful to them, if they are able to connect it to something they already know, and if they sense its importance. When toddlers name common objects, preschoolers talk about something they did yesterday, and kindergartners retell a story in detail, they are remembering and connecting information and experiences.

When children determine whether something is the same as, similar to, or different from what they have encountered before, they are using *recognition memory*, e.g., the child recognizes a book he or she has heard before. *Recall memory* is harder; children must imagine something that is not present, e.g., recalls foods eaten by the hungry caterpillar without looking at the pictures. Cues improve children's free recall memory (Berk, 2002; Bjorklund, 2005).

As children develop their abilities to attend and to use memory strategies, their learning is enhanced. They use their existing knowledge and understanding as the basis for making new experiences, ideas, and concepts meaningful.

Making links between new and known information may be challenging for some children. Children with learning disabilities may find it hard to attend to relevant information or to organize information so it can be retrieved (Trawick-Smith, 2006). English-language learners must remember words and their meanings in more than one language.

Adults play an essential role in helping children improve their memory skills. Adults help children connect new experiences to prior knowledge and revise their previous thinking to fit with new experiences. Adult scaffolding, or support, helps children attend and use memory strategies such as categorizing (Barry, 2006; Larkina, Guler, Kleinknect, & Bauer, 2008; McAfee & Leong, 1994; Mussen, Conger, Kagan, & Huston, 1990).

Children from different families and communities may depend on different senses to help them obtain and retain information. Some children retain information that they hear for a longer time, while other children more easily remember information they obtained from drawings, photographs, or other graphics (Bjorklund, 2005; McAfee & Leong, 1994; Trawick-Smith, 2006).

Objective 12 Remembers and connects experiences

a. Recognizes and recalls

Not Yet	1	2	3	4	5	6	7	8	9

2 — Recognizes familiar people, places, and objects; looks for hidden object where it was last seen
- Looks for food dropped from high chair
- Uncovers bear after adult covers it with a blanket
- Says or signs names of common objects when sees them

4 — Recalls familiar people, places, objects, and actions from the past (a few months before); recalls 1 or 2 items removed from view
- Looks for horse used a few months ago in bin of toy animals
- Identifies one or two objects taken away while playing "What's Missing?"
- Shows fear of a bee after having been stung

6 — Tells about experiences in order, provides details, and evaluates the experience; recalls 3 or 4 items removed from view
- Identifies four objects taken away while playing "What's Missing?"
- Says, "We went to the baseball game. We sat way up high. We ate peanuts and drank lemonade. I really liked it a lot but my sister didn't."

8 — Uses a few deliberate strategies to remember information
- Creates an observational drawing of a fire truck and then refers to it later while building with blocks
- Tells the teacher, "I'm putting my book in my backpack so I'll remember to take it home."

b. Makes connections

Not Yet	1	2	3	4	5	6	7	8	9

2 — Looks for familiar persons when they are named; relates objects to events
- Turns head toward door when her teacher says, "Bethany, Mommy is here."
- Throws paper away when teacher says, "Please put this in the trash."

4 — Remembers the sequence of personal routines and experiences with teacher support
- Goes to attendance chart with parent upon arrival
- Gets a paper towel after teacher says, "What do we do next, after we wash our hands?"

6 — Draws on everyday experiences and applies this knowledge to a similar situation
- After hearing *A Chair for My Mother* read aloud says, "My Nana has a chair like the one Rosa and her family bought."
- Uses traffic-directing signals on the bike track after seeing a police officer demonstrate them
- Divides crayons into "fair share" groups after watching a teacher do it the day before

8 — Generates a rule, strategy, or idea from one learning experience and applies it in a new context
- Proposes a one-way sign for entering and exiting the cubby area after a neighborhood walk where children discussed one-way street signs
- Tallies friends' favorite ice cream flavors after learning how to make tally marks to count how many people wear shoes with buckles

Objective 12 Remembers and connects experiences

Strategies

- Talk about the child's home experiences and use the child's home language (if possible) to help him or her relate old and new experiences.

- Demonstrate and explain how different experiences relate, e.g., "Your sweater goes over your head, just as your T-shirt goes over your head."

- Use gestures and language to draw attention to particular features of objects and people.

- Give cues involving many senses, not just verbal cues, to help children remember and learn particular information.

- Use photos and objects to talk about the child's past experiences.

- Involve children in "Remember when..." games and discussions, e.g., Ask, "Do you remember the elephant we saw at the zoo yesterday?" Talk with toddlers about events in the immediate past, and talk with preschoolers and kindergartners about events that took place in the more distant past.

- Expand on children's fragmented recollections by asking varied questions, adding information to children's statements, and commenting about events.

- Encourage children to represent events in multiple ways. For example, after a trip to the fire station, follow up discussions by making a class book with photos and drawings of the trip. Place photos of the trip in the Block area so children can re-create the fire station or fire truck. Develop a list with children of new props to include for dramatic play. Read books or look on the internet for information about firefighters, and compare the information with what the children experienced on their trip.

- Give children enough time to think and make connections before expecting an answer.

- Play memory games like "What's Missing?" Display a few items, remove one, and invite children to tell which one is missing. Display and remove more items with older children.

- Guide older preschool and kindergarten children to make analogies. Help them to see ways in which things they learned about earlier are similar to other things. For example, after studying turtles, they may notice that crabs, crawfish, and lobsters also have shells that help protect them.

- Play games like "What Do They Have in Common?" Show children pictures of various animals, people and/or objects and have them communicate ways in which they are alike.

Uses classification skills

13

Classification refers to the grouping and organizing of objects, pictures, words, or ideas on the basis of particular criteria. When a toddler tries to put a key in a doorknob, a 2-year-old puts all of the beads in a container with a bead label, and a preschooler explains why he put the snake and lizard picture cards in one pile and the birds in another, they are using classification skills.

Children initially identify broad categories, e.g. food. Next they develop subcategories, e.g., fruit. They then differentiate further and identify additional subcategories, e.g., apples (Pauen, 2002). Exploration of objects, expanding knowledge of the world, and increased language skills contribute to children's ability to classify (Berk, 2002; Gelman & Coley, 1990). When children classify they organize their experiences and manage enormous amounts of information that can be retrieved later. The ability to classify is important for learning and remembering (Larkina, Guler, Kleinknect, & Bauer, 2008). It supports the development of logical thinking.

Children's earliest classifications are based on their sensory perceptions (Berk, 2009). By the end of the first year their classifications become more conceptual, based on common functions or behaviors. When children are particularly knowledgeable about a topic, they are likely to categorize at a more mature level (Bjorklund, 2005; Gelman, 1998). Adults help children classify more accurately and think more deeply about categories

by naming categories and by talking with children about pictures and objects (Gelman, 1998; Gelman, Chesnick, & Waxman, 2005; Gelman, Coley, Rosengren, Hartman, & Pappas, 1998). When an adult reads a picture book and explains that chickens and ducks are both birds, children begin to understand that particular similarities group them together despite their differences. Teachers can assess children's classification skills during conversations with them and as they observe children sorting and re-sorting spontaneously, e.g., grouping all shades of blue crayons together while drawing or sorting by properties suggested by someone else, e.g., "Give me all of the blue teddy bears."

Cultural unfamiliarity makes it harder for children to classify accurately and at higher levels (Lin, Schwanenflugel, & Wisenbaker, 1990). Without the support of language, some English-language learners may find sorting and classifying tasks more challenging than their English-speaking or bilingual peers. Some children with learning disabilities develop classification skills more slowly than their typically developing peers, and some may not be able to develop high-level classification skills (Trawick-Smith, 2006).

Objective 13 Uses classification skills

Not Yet	1	2	3	4	5	6	7	8	9

Matches similar objects

- Puts one sock with another sock
- Gathers all the vehicles from a shelf
- Picks out and eats only the animal crackers
- Puts only blue pegs in pegboard; leaves red and yellow pegs to the side

Places objects in two or more groups based on differences in a single characteristic, e.g., color, size, or shape

- Puts all the red beads together and all the blue beads together
- Pulls out all the trucks from the vehicle bin
- Identifies fabric pieces as being scratchy or soft
- Puts pictures into piles of babies, older children, and grown-ups

Groups objects by one characteristic; then regroups them using a different characteristic and indicates the reason

- Says, "These buttons are blue, and these are red"; then resorts buttons into big and little
- Points to groups of animals and says, "These are zoo animals and these are farm animals"; then sorts the zoo animals into those with stripes and those without stripes

Groups objects by more than one characteristic at the same time; switches sorting rules when asked, and explains the reasons

- Organizes a sticker collection into groups and subgroups and explains why and how; then creates a new grouping when the teacher makes a suggestion
- Creates four piles of shapes: big red triangles, small red triangles, big blue triangles, small blue triangles. Switches when asked to form two groups of all the big and small triangles

Objective 13 Uses classification skills

Strategies

- Provide materials that are safe for infants and toddlers to explore by using all of their senses. As they explore objects, describe the characteristics, "That fabric is soft and bumpy" and "Your block is hard and smooth."

- Model sorting and classifying, and provide opportunities for children to practice, e.g., prompt and model, "Let's pick up all the toys that are trucks."

- Play simple classification games with toddlers by gathering items that people use together, e.g., sock/shoe, flower/vase, plate/fork, and coat/hat.

- Sing, recite fingerplays, and read books that focus on colors, shapes, machines, animals, or other categories.

- Play sorting and matching games, using materials that are familiar to the child. Think about the child's family background, neighborhood, and community as you choose familiar materials, e.g., toys, clothing, utensils, food labels.

- As preschool and kindergarten children sort objects, name the categories and use gestures and statements to point out the similarities of the items in each group. Ask children about the groups, e.g., ask, "Why do these things belong together?"

- Provide preschool and kindergarten children with opportunities to arrange collections into groups by using various rules that you and the children make together.

- Use "mystery boxes" to help preschool children develop classification skills. Put one item into the box. Have each child ask one "yes" or "no" question about what is in the box, e.g., "Is it an animal? Is it brown? Does it have four legs?" Support children's efforts by periodically summarizing what is known about the object, e.g., "We know it is a brown animal with four legs. What else do we need to know?"

- Record older preschool and kindergarten children's ideas about each of two groups, e.g., cats and dogs. Ask them to find similarities between the two groups. Present their ideas in a Venn diagram.

Objective 14

Uses symbols and images to represent something not present

Children engage in symbolic thinking when they use representations of objects, events, or persons that are not present. A toddler points to a picture of a cow when an adult asks, "Where's the cow?" A preschooler builds an elaborate structure with blocks and announces, "The dragon lives in this castle!" Both of these children are engaging in abstract thinking. As children mature, they use substitutes that are increasingly different in form and/or function from what they symbolize. Thinking symbolically is necessary for language development, problem solving, reading, writing, mathematical thinking, and participating fully in society (Deloache, 2004; Younger & Johnson, 2004).

Children younger than age 3 have trouble understanding and maintaining the distinction between a symbol and what it represents (Berk, 2002; DeLoache, 1987; Fletcher & Sabo, 2006). Before children can effectively use symbols such as letters, numbers, or maps, they must understand implicitly that symbols represent other things (DeLoache, 1991). By about 18 months of age, children begin treating pictures symbolically rather than as objects to explore manually by hitting, rubbing, patting, scratching, etc. (Preissler & Carey, 2004). This marks an important point in their development of symbolic thinking (DeLoache, 2004; Fletcher & Sabo, 2006). Tools such as webs, graphs, and concept maps are symbolic representations that help preschool and kindergarten children organize and visually represent what they know and think (Birbili, 2006).

Objective 14 Uses symbols and images to represent something not present

Dramatic play, sometimes called symbolic, pretend, make-believe, fantasy, or imaginative play is an important vehicle for development and learning (Bergen, 2002; Klein, Wirth, & Linas, 2004; Nourot & Van Hoorn, 1991; Smilansky & Shefatya, 1990; Steglin, 2005). Dramatic play contributes to children's development of abstract thinking and imagination and supports their school adjustment, memory, language, and self-regulation abilities (Bodrova & Leong, 2004; Fantuzzo & McWayne, 2002; Krafft & Berk, 1998; Newman, 1990).

Sociodramatic play is a complex, abstract type of dramatic play that involves more than one child playing together. Advances in cognition and language allow children to use more involved play themes and story lines. Sociodramatic play has several important elements (Smilansky & Shefatya, 1990): *role play* (pretending to be someone else); *props* (use of real or imaginary objects); *make-believe* (enacting events); *interaction* (agreeing on roles for two or more children and relating to one another from the perspectives of their roles); *verbal communication* (interacting verbally about the play situation and roles); and *time* (remaining at play for a sustained period). As children act out their roles, they arrive at a shared understanding of the rules for behavior (Bodrova & Leong, 2004). The type of props influences children's pretend play. Children act out more familiar, everyday roles when realistic props are provided. They engage in more fantasy roles when nonrealistic props are offered (Berk & Winsler, 1995).

There are cultural differences in the ways children play. Children from some family backgrounds do not engage in dramatic play unless the classroom environment resembles their home environment (Heisner, 2005; Levy, Wolfgang, & Koorland, 1992; Trawick-Smith, 1998). English-language learners or children with language delays may find it difficult to engage in elaborate, verbal negotiations and to make their ideas about pretend themes and roles clear (Bergen, 2002; Casby, 1997). Disabilities may also affect children's dramatic play. Children with visual or hearing impairments may seek adults, rather than peers, as play partners. Some children with autism spectrum disorders do not engage readily in sociodramatic play (Trawick-Smith 2006).

Objective 14 Uses symbols and images to represent something not present

a. Thinks symbolically

Not Yet	1	2	3	4	5	6	7	8	9

Recognizes people, objects, and animals in pictures or photographs
- Touches the cow in the illustration when an adult reads, "And the cow jumped…."
- Points to photograph and says, "Mommy"
- Identifies a duck in a variety of different photos and illustrations

Draws or constructs, and then identifies what it is
- Draws various shapes and says, "This is my house."
- Glues red yarn on paper and says, "I made spaghetti."

Plans and then uses drawings, constructions, movements, and dramatizations to represent ideas
- Sees a dump truck outside and plans how to draw it
- Says, "Let's pretend to be seeds growing like in the book."

Represents objects, places, and ideas with increasingly abstract symbols
- Makes tally marks
- Makes and interprets graphs with teacher's help
- Attempts to write words to label a picture

b. Engages in sociodramatic play

Not Yet	1	2	3	4	5	6	7	8	9

Imitates actions of others during play; uses real objects as props
- Holds a toy phone to ear
- Wraps a blanket around a doll and then rocks it

Acts out familiar or imaginary scenarios; may use props to stand for something else
- Puts beads in a muffin tin, places tin in oven, and asks, "Who wants some cupcakes?"
- Uses a short rope as a fire hose
- Pretends to be the birthday boy at the party and blows out the candles on the pegboard 'cake' after others sing "Happy Birthday"

Interacts with two or more children during pretend play, assigning and/or assuming roles and discussing actions; sustains play scenario for up to 10 minutes
- Pretends to be the bus driver. Tells the other children, "You can be the passengers. Give me your tickets, and I will give you change."

Plans and negotiates complex role play; joins in detailed conversation about roles and actions; play may extend over several days
- Joins in elaborate play about taking a dog to the veterinarian, assigning roles, switching roles, creating props, and returning to the play day after day

Objective 14 Uses symbols and images to represent something not present

Strategies

- Provide many opportunities for children to learn about diverse symbols and their functions, such as language, gestures, letters, numerals, photographs, drawings, models, maps, graphs, webs, and video images.

- Provide books appropriate for the age and abilities of the child, e.g., chubby, cardboard, and cloth books for infants and toddlers.

- Point to pictures during story reading, calling attention to what the pictures mean.

- Show children common objects and encourage them to think of how to use them to represent something different.

- Collect data about the classroom routines of preschool and kindergarten children, e.g., attendance, transportation to school, or snack choices. Graph or otherwise present the information by first using concrete objects, then pictures, and then abstract symbols.

- Schedule adequate time for pretend play to take place indoors and outdoors.

- Match play props to the family backgrounds and developmental characteristics of the children.

- Model pretending, e.g., pretend to take a bite of a plastic apple or rock a baby doll to sleep.

- Provide familiar household items for children to use during pretend play, e.g., a toy broom for sweeping and empty food boxes representative of the foods children eat at home.

- Arrange the environment and introduce props that will encourage play. Observe children while they are playing to gather information about what props to include and what suggestions to make. Decide whether to sustain play by participating or by not intervening.

- Offer both highly realistic and less realistic props for pretend play to accommodate the range of developmental levels.

- Provide multipurpose, open-ended props that can represent many things, e.g., blocks and boxes. Encourage children to use gestures and descriptive language as they dramatize.

- Encourage children 18-months and older to pretend without props as another way of engaging in dramatic play.

- Describe what children are doing, offer suggestions, and make modifications for children with disabilities.

- Ask open-ended questions to extend children's imaginative play and expressive language.

- Extend children's pretend play by interacting with them. Imitate what they are doing; comment and ask questions; or take a role, using a play voice and gestures.

- Plan specific activities to enhance preschool and kindergarten children's knowledge of the world and the roles of people in various settings, e.g., field trips, book reading, visitors. Talk about people's roles.

- Encourage older preschool and kindergarten children to make their own props to use in play or to support their learning, e.g., number lines, word walls, alphabet books, etc.

Literacy

The early years are critical for literacy development. Children who do not learn to read and write by the end of the primary grades are at risk for school failure. Children who are especially likely to have difficulty learning to read in the primary grades are those who begin school with less prior knowledge, verbal abilities, phonological sensitivity, familiarity with the basic purposes and mechanisms of reading, and letter knowledge (National Early Literacy Panel, 2008; Snow, Burns, & Griffin, 1998). The level to which a child progresses in reading and writing is one of the best predictors of whether the child will function competently in school and in life (Neuman, Copple, & Bredekamp, 2000).

Literacy learning begins at birth. During the early childhood years, children engage in emergent reading and writing behaviors that form the foundation for conventional literacy, but many children do not receive the ongoing experiences that support this learning. By age 3, differences in children's understanding and use of literacy skills are enormous. Reading aloud to children appears to be one of the most important activities for building the understandings and skills needed for reading success (Neuman et al., 2000). Children from middle-class families have been read to for about 1,000 hours before beginning kindergarten. Children from families living in poverty have been read to for about 25 hours (Berk, 2006; Neuman, 2003). When children enjoy having

LITERACY OBJECTIVES

15 Demonstrates phonological awareness

16 Demonstrates knowledge of the alphabet

17 Demonstrates knowledge of print and its uses

18 Comprehends and responds to books and other texts

19 Demonstrates emergent writing skills

books read to them, and when they are excited about what they are hearing and learning, they are motivated to learn to read, and, later, to read to learn (Heroman & Jones, 2004).

Listening, speaking, reading, and writing develop interdependently in children, and each one contributes to the development of the others. Children's literacy development may be negatively affected by factors including poverty; limited English proficiency; visual, hearing, and language impairments; cognitive deficiencies; and parents who have had difficulty reading (National Early Literacy Panel, 2008; Snow et al., 1998).

Effective instruction in the early years can have a large impact on children's literacy development. Children who would otherwise be most at risk for school failure stand to benefit the most from high-quality experiences (Campbell, Ramey, Pungello, Sparling, & Miller-Johnson, 2002). Teachers are critical and can inspire children to read, write, and learn through thoughtful planning and developmentally appropriate literacy instruction (Neuman et al., 2000).

Objective 15

Demonstrates phonological awareness

Phonological awareness, or phonological sensitivity, is the ability to discern the sounds and patterns of spoken language. As this awareness develops, children learn to hear the separate sounds of oral language that are blended in ordinary speech. For some children, distinguishing the parts of spoken language is difficult because it requires them to attend to the sounds of speech separately from meaning.

Phonological awareness is an important skill in learning to read. Children typically begin to demonstrate this awareness by about age 3, and their skills improve gradually over many years (Snow, Burns, & Griffin, 1998). Phonological sensitivity is a strong predictor of later reading, writing, and spelling ability (National Early Literacy Panel, 2004, 2008). Instruction that strengthens children's phonological awareness has been shown to contribute to later reading success (Ehri et al., 2001; National Early Literacy Panel, 2008). Children become phonologically aware through experiences such as reciting poems, singing, and clapping the syllables of chanted words (Adams, 1990, 2001; Carroll, Snowling, Hulme, & Stevenson, 2003; Strickland & Schickedanz, 2004).

Phonological awareness skills are typically learned in a particular order (Anthony, Lonigan, Driscoll, Phillips, & Burgess, 2003). However, children acquire these skills in an overlapping sequence rather than by mastering one level before the next (Dickinson & Neuman, 2006).

Children who are learning two or more languages must learn very different sound systems (Gonzalez, 1998). They must distinguish English phonemes that may not be part of their native languages. A child may therefore have difficulty hearing and/or producing the sounds of English.

Objective 15 Demonstrates phonological awareness

a. Notices and discriminates rhyme

Not Yet	1	2	3	4	5	6	7	8	9

Joins in rhyming songs and games

- Hums along and joins in random words in rhyme
- Sings with a group, "One, two, buckle my shoe…"

Fills in the missing rhyming word; generates rhyming words spontaneously

- Completes the rhyme in the phrase, "The fat cat sat on the ____ (mat)."
- Chants spontaneously, "Me, fee, kee, tee, lee, bee."

Decides whether two words rhyme

- "Do *bear* and *chair* rhyme? What about *bear* and *goat*?"
- Matches rhyming picture cards

Generates a group of rhyming words when given a word

- Says, "Bat, sat, lat," when asked, "What words rhyme with *cat*?"

b. Notices and discriminates alliteration

Not Yet	1	2	3	4	5	6	7	8	9

Sings songs and recites rhymes and refrains with repeating initial sounds

- Sings, "I'm bringing home a baby bumble bee…?"

Shows awareness that some words begin the same way

- Says, "*Max* and *Maya*…our names start the same!"

Matches beginning sounds of some words

- Groups objects or pictures that begin with the same sound
- Picks up a toy bear when asked, "What begins the same way as *box*, *baby*, and *bike*?"

Isolates and identifies the beginning sound of a word

- Says, "/m-m-m/," when asked "What is the first sound of the word *milk*?"
- Responds, "/t/," after being asked, "What's the beginning sound of *toy*, *toe*, *teeth*?"

Objective 15 Demonstrates phonological awareness

c. Notices and discriminates smaller and smaller units of sound

Not Yet	1	2	3	4	5	6	7	8	9
		Hears and shows awareness of separate words in sentences • Joins in clapping each word while chanting, "I like ice cream." • Jumps upon hearing a specified word in a story		**Hears and shows awareness of separate syllables in words** • Claps each syllable of name, *Tri-na* • Puts together *pen* and *cil* to say *pencil* • Puts together *foot* and *ball* to say *football*		**Verbally separates and blends onset and rime** • Says, "Hat," after hearing /h/…/at/ • Points to Jonathan when teacher plays game and asks, "Where's _onathan?"		**Verbally separates and blends individual phonemes in words** • Claps each phoneme of the word hat: /h/ /a/ /t/ • Says, "Hat," after hearing /h/ /a/ /t/	

Objective 15 Demonstrates phonological awareness

Strategies

- Know each child's level of phonological awareness and provide appropriate experiences. Plan specific activities to help children attend to rhyme, alliteration, and smaller and smaller units of sound.

- Encourage children to listen to sounds in the environment. Record different sounds for children to identify.

- Use songs, stories, and rhymes that play with language. Informally, but intentionally, draw children's attention to the sounds of language.

- Encourage children to play with words and to make up their own rhymes.

- Have children fill in rhyming words in a verse. For example, "The cat wore a____ (hat). He slept on a ____ (mat). He played with a ____(bat)."

- Play games that focus on alliteration (initial sounds). For example, have children think of words that begin with the same sound as another child's name (Bonito, Betty, baby, bath, buttons, etc.).

- Clap or tap rhythm sticks to mark the syllables of preschool and kindergarten children's names as you say them.

- Draw children's attention to the phonemes in spoken words during daily routines. For example, dismiss children to go to lunch by saying, "If your name begins with the /m/ sound like Matthew, you may go to lunch."

- Plan activities with older preschool and kindergarten children that focus on onset and rime. For example, have children group words by their beginning sounds (*rake, rat, rose*) or create word families that emphasize the ending sounds (*ring, sing, king*).

- Encourage kindergarten children to draw pictures and write their own rhyming words to share with other children.

- Provide opportunities for older kindergarten children to make up their own alliteration sentences, e.g., a "T sentence" might be, "Tommy tells Tyron to tickle Terry."

Demonstrates knowledge of the alphabet

16

Knowledge of letters and words is an important component of literacy. It involves more than reciting the alphabet song or recognizing individual letters. Children must understand that speech can be recorded in print and that words in print can be spoken. Readers must understand that a letter is a symbol that represents one or more sounds. A more complex level of understanding requires knowing that these symbols can be grouped together to form words and that words have meanings. The idea that written words are composed of letters that represent sounds is called the *alphabetic principle*. Children's understanding of the alphabetic principle is a predictor of future reading success.

Young children's alphabet knowledge, especially their ability to rapidly name letters and numerals in random order, is a strong predictor of later reading, writing, and spelling ability (Adams, 1990; National Early Literacy Panel, 2004, 2008; Stevenson & Newman, 1986). In addition, preschool children's letter knowledge is a unique predictor of growth in phonological sensitivity across the year (Burgess & Lonigan, 1998). There is a high correlation between knowing the names of the letters and knowing the letter sounds. These appear to be overlapping skills (Lomax & McGee, 1987; Richgels, 1986; Worden & Boettcher, 1990). Children's knowledge of the alphabet is also closely related to their comprehension skills by the end of second grade (Cats, Fey, Zhang, & Tomblin, 2001).

Objective 16   Demonstrates knowledge of the alphabet

a. Identifies and names letters

Not Yet	1	2	3	4	5	6	7	8	9
		Recognizes and names a few letters in own name		Recognizes as many as 10 letters, especially those in own name		Identifies and names 11–20 upper- and 11–20 lowercase letters when presented in random order		Identifies and names all upper- and lowercase letters when presented in random order	

b. Uses letter–sound knowledge

Not Yet	1	2	3	4	5	6	7	8	9
		Identifies the sounds of a few letters		Produces the correct sounds for 10–20 letters		Shows understanding that a sequence of letters represents a sequence of spoken sounds		Applies letter–sound correspondence when attempting to read and write	

6. Shows understanding that a sequence of letters represents a sequence of spoken sounds
- Asks when writing, "How do you spell *cough*?"

8. Applies letter–sound correspondence when attempting to read and write
- Sees the word *cat*; begins to sound out the word: /k/ /a/ /t/
- Makes an *open* sign for the doctor's office by writing "opn"

Objective 16 Demonstrates knowledge of the alphabet

Strategies

- Focus on letters as part of meaningful activities. Point out particular letters as you take dictation, compose messages, and read stories. Call attention to the letter-sound relationship. For example you might say, "That word begins just like Tamika. It begins with the letter T."

- Display the alphabet at the child's eye level. Make smaller versions for children to use as references. For example, provide alphabet strips or alphabet cards in the Library area. Children can refer to these as they read or write.

- Use the children's names to help them learn the alphabet letters and their sounds. For example, have children place cards with their photos and names printed on them underneath alphabet letters posted around the room. Talk about whose names are under each letter and the sound the letter makes.

- Sing the alphabet song. Sing each letter slowly so children can hear each letter. Point to each letter on a large alphabet chart as you sing.

- Read alphabet books. For example, *Chicka, Chicka Boom Boom* (Bill Martin, Jr.) and *The Alphabet Tree* (Leo Lionni) are good for group reading. Talk about the letters, their shapes, and the names of the pictured objects that begin with the letter.

- Place alphabet books in the Library area and in other interest areas. Select books that include words with a single letter sound (snake), rather than a blend (*ship*) to avoid confusion. Younger children and English-language learners benefit from books that focus on a single letter, word, and picture per page.

- Encourage sensory exploration of the alphabet. Offer children a variety of ways to explore the alphabet: by using sandpaper or felt letters, salt trays, clay, magnetic letters, and by forming letters with their bodies.

- Support kindergarten children as they make their own letter dictionaries. They might illustrate using photographs, drawings, and/or words. Children can add additional words to their books as the year progresses.

- Have kindergarten children assist with creating lists of new vocabulary words they learned at school. They can take the list home and talk with family members about their words and what they mean.

Demonstrates knowledge of print and its uses

17

Long before they learn to read, young children try to make sense of the print around them. Children see print in their homes, in their schools, on street signs, and elsewhere throughout their communities. They see it in books, on grocery lists, and on food containers. Knowledge of print and its uses includes understanding that print carries a message and that print is organized and read in particular ways. Through print-rich environments and scaffolding by adults, children learn about the many functions of print; how books are handled; and features of print, such as punctuation. Children need these skills to be successful readers and writers.

Young children's concepts about print are a good predictor of later reading, writing, and spelling ability (National Early Literacy Panel, 2004, 2008; Clay, 1979a, 1979b; McCormick & Mason, 1986; Wells, 1985). Understanding that print is meaningful is one of the first steps children take in learning to read and write (Mason, 1980). Children learn much about print from what is included in the environment, e.g., signs and labels, and from including print in their play (McGee, Lomax, & Head, 1988; Neuman & Roskos, 1993). They learn the uses of written language before they learn its forms (Gundlach, McLane, Stott, & McNamee, 1985; Taylor, 1983). Although the first stages of reading and writing are predominately about function, children develop an interest in print conventions. However, children do not systematically progress from one stage to the next (Morrow, 2005).

Objective 17   Demonstrates knowledge of print and its uses

a. Uses and appreciates books

Not Yet	1	2	3	4	5	6	7	8	9
		Shows interest in books • Gazes at the pages of a book • Brings book to adult to read		**Orients book correctly; turns pages from the front of the book to the back; recognizes familiar books by their covers** • Hands teacher book and says, "Let's read *Corduroy!*"		**Knows some features of a book (title, author, illustrator); connects specific books to authors** • Says, "I want to read this Dr. Suess book today." • Says, "Eric Carle wrote this book. He is the author."		**Uses various types of books for their intended purposes** • Selects the book about insects to identify the butterfly seen on the playground	

b. Uses print concepts

Not Yet	1	2	3	4	5	6	7	8	9
		Shows understanding that text is meaningful and can be read • Points to the words on the sign by the fish bowl and says, "Just one pinch!"		**Indicates where to start reading and the direction to follow** • Points to beginning of text on the page when pretending to read and moves finger left to right as she continues down the page		**Shows awareness of various features of print: letters, words, spaces, upper- and lowercase letters, some punctuation** • Points to the word *hippopotamus* and says, "That's a long word." • Says, "That means stop reading," as he points to a period at the end of a sentence.		**Matches a written word with a spoken word but it may not be the actual written word; tracks print from the end of a line of text to the beginning of the next line** • Touches each word on the page while reciting the words from *Brown Bear, Brown Bear, What Do You See?* • Picks up finger and returns it to the beginning of the next line when pretend reading	

Objective 17 Demonstrates knowledge of print and its uses

Strategies

- Create a print-rich environment. Include print that is meaningful, functional, and interesting. Avoid displaying so much print that it clutters the room.

- Display print at the child's eye level. If you place print too high, children will not be able to see it or attend to its features.

- Support children's play with print as they imitate real-life situations. For example, offer books, newspapers, or magazines to add to the doctor's office. Supply paper and markers for making signs, writing checks, or creating appointment books.

- Write signs, charts, recipes, labels, and other classroom materials in the children's presence. Describe the process as children watch you write. Call attention to the features of print such as individual letters, words, spaces, upper- and lowercase letters, and punctuation.

- Distinguish between children's drawing and writing. Use the words *drawing* and *writing* when making comments about their products. For example, you might say, "You *drew* a rainbow. I see you *wrote* your name and Toben's name next to your picture."

- Point out the title, author, and illustrator as you read books with older children.

- Draw children's attention to the conventions of print. For example, when you record a child's dictation, talk about where you are starting to write, why you are beginning the sentence with an uppercase letter, and what the punctuation mark means at the end of the sentence. As you read, move your finger under the words to help children learn directionality.

- Use story and informational books and planned writing experiences to teach about print. Intentionally read books aloud to individuals, small groups, and large groups of children. Place both fiction and non-fiction books in various interest areas so children can find the information they need and discover purposes for print. For example, you might include books about plants in the Discovery area if you have plants there.

- Talk with children about the many ways print is used around them. For example, look on the Internet to check the day's weather. Read the lunch menu. Read aloud a card to be sent to a sick child.

- Talk about concepts about books when you read to children. Talk about where the writing starts on the page and which way to proceed when reading.

Comprehends and responds to books and other texts

18

Comprehension, the process of finding meaning, is the goal of reading instruction. Comprehending text involves connecting what is heard and read with background knowledge and experiences. The more the language and meaning of the text relates to a person's prior knowledge, the easier it is to make sense of what is read. Comprehension of oral language and simple texts is essential to future reading success; children learn to process what they hear and read (Teale & Yokota, 2000). Children who engage in frequent activities with books have larger, more literate vocabularies. These children learn to read better than children who have few book experiences (Dickinson & Tabors, 1991; Wells, 1986). Although most children are not reading before they enter kindergarten, the development of listening comprehension skills is important. Through meaningful language activities, children develop and integrate comprehension skills.

Children follow a typical progression in learning to read storybooks. Initially they point to and label pictures in a book, treating each page as a separate entity. As they pretend to read, the story they tell does not flow from page to page. Next they begin to talk about the pictures and follow the story across the pages. Their language transitions from sounding like "talk" to a more reading-like intonation. Finally, they begin using different strategies (known words, knowledge of letters and sounds, patterns in text, picture and context clues) to make meaning of the text (Sulzby, 1985).

Dramatic play relates to comprehension in powerful, complex ways (Christie, 1983; Pellegrini & Galda, 1982; Saltz, Dixon, & Johnson, 1997; Silvern, Williamson, & Waters, 1983). *Metaplay*, in which children assume a role and negotiate what will happen next, has been shown to increase story comprehension (Trawick-Smith, 1998). Retelling stories also helps children develop a sense of story structure and other understandings about language that contribute to their comprehension of text (Morrow, 1985). Children who speak a dialect or who are English-language learners may retell a story using the grammar of their dialect or home language. Their use of standard English grammar increases over time as they gain more experience with listening and responding to stories (Schickedanz, 1999).

Objective 18 Comprehends and responds to books and other texts

a. Interacts during read-alouds and book conversations

Not Yet	1	2	3	4	5	6	7	8	9
		Contributes particular language from the book at the appropriate time • Says, "You're not big enough," when teacher pauses in *The Grouchy Ladybug*		**Asks and answers questions about the text; refers to pictures** • Responds, "He was mad. He threw his hat down."		**Identifies story-related problems, events, and resolutions during conversations with an adult** • When prompted says, "George got put in jail. He ran out the open door and got out."		**Reconstructs story, using pictures, text, and props; begins to make inferences and draw conclusions** • Joins in story discussion then says, "I think Max was upset that he was sent to bed without his supper."	

b. Uses emergent reading skills

Not Yet	1	2	3	4	5	6	7	8	9
		Pretends to read a familiar book, treating each page as a separate unit; names and describes what is on each page, using pictures as cues		**Pretends to read, using some of the language from the text; describes the action across pages, using pictures to order the events; may need prompts from adult**		**Pretends to read, reciting language that closely matches the text on each page and using reading-like intonation**		**Tries to match oral language to words on page; points to words as reads; uses different strategies (e.g., sounding out words, known words, and patterns in text) to make meaning from print**	

Objective 18 Comprehends and responds to books and other texts

c. Retells stories

Not Yet	1	2	3	4	5	6	7	8	9
		Retells some events from a familiar story with close adult prompting • Says, "The pig builds a house from it" when the teacher asks, "What does the first little pig do with the straw?" Then says, "The wolf blows it down," when the teacher asks, "What does the wolf do to the house?"		**Retells familiar stories, using pictures or props as prompts** • Retells the basic events of *The Three Little Pigs*, using felt pieces on a felt board		**Retells a familiar story in proper sequence, including major events and characters** • Retells *The Three Little Pigs*, starting with the pigs saying goodbye to their mother, remembering the correct order in which the pigs build their houses, and ending with the wolf climbing down the chimney and falling into the pot of hot water		**Retells stories with many details about characters, events, and storylines** • Retells *The Three Little Pigs*, and includes details about how the mother felt about her children's leaving home, the pigs' personalities, and why building a house from bricks is better than building a house from straw or sticks	

Objective 18 Comprehends and responds to books and other texts

Strategies

- Provide high-quality children's literature from a variety of genres. Include picture books, poetry, and informational books. Call attention to how ideas are presented in different ways in different types of books.

- Prepare children for reading by taking a *picture walk*. Introduce the story by previewing the pictures. Ask children to predict what the story is about by looking at the cover. Turn the pages slowly as you *walk* through the book so children can make predictions about the story.

- Provide opportunities for children to talk about stories before and after they are read. Encourage them to ask questions and to make predictions.

- Support children's use of language from books. Introduce and discuss new words in meaningful contexts.

- Engage children in helping you read repeated phrases in books. For example, from *The Very Busy Spider* (Eric Carle) they might "read" with you as you point to the words, "The spider didn't answer. She was very busy spinning her web."

- Help children connect new information and ideas to what they already know. For example, you might say, "What does this remind you of _____?" "How is _____ like _____?" "Have you ever_____?"

- Facilitate story retellings. Use simple pictures, puppets, costumes, or props to help children recall the story. For example, for the story *Jump Frog, Jump!* (Robert Kalan), you might use a toy fly, frog, fish, snake, turtle, net, and basket as props.

- Support story retellings by taking turns telling parts of the story. Have children tell more of the story as they are able.

- Provide repeated readings of the same book so children can focus on different aspects of the book each time, e.g., story line, details, specific vocabulary words.

- Read chapter books with older preschool and kindergarten children.

- Model using different strategies for making meaning from print. Show children how to use picture cues, context, sounding out words, and known (high frequency) words.

Objective 19

Demonstrates emergent writing skills

19

Writing is an important aspect of emergent literacy. Writing letters or name writing is a predictor of later literacy (National Early Literacy Panel, 2008). Writing begins with making a mark. Then, when children are given the time, opportunities, and materials to practice, their writing skills continue to advance. Children begin to understand that writing is recorded speech. As their phonological awareness advances, children write a few letters that represent sounds in words. Their writing gradually becomes more conventional, typically as they enter the elementary grades.

Writing originates from drawing and is supported by make-believe play. Children learn to associate symbols with meaning (Vygotsky, 1997). To write, children need to understand that letters are symbols. By exploring writing, children learn about letters, sounds, and the meaning of text (Schickedanz & Casbergue, 2009). Understanding the mechanics of the writing system (letter naming and letter–sound correspondences) has a moderate correlation with reading in the primary grades (Stuart, 1995).

Writing letters requires children to know how each letter looks and how to put line segments together to form them. They must also know the orientation of letters and learn the particular order of the letters in each word (Schickedanz, 1999). Reversed letters are very common in preschool and kindergarten children's writing (Schickedanz & Casbergue, 2009) and are not a cause for concern. Because fine-motor skills are necessary to control writing tools, it is helpful to know that markers are easiest for children to use; followed by chalk; then crayons; and, last, pencils (Charlesworth, 2008). Hand dominance, which usually develops between 1 and 2 years of age, may not develop fully until around age 7.

Objective 19 Demonstrates emergent writing skills

a. Writes name

Not Yet	1	2	3	4	5	6	7
	Scribbles or marks	**Controlled linear scribbles**	**Mock letters or letter-like forms**	**Letter strings**	**Partially accurate name**	**Accurate name**	
	• Scribble writes deliberately • Makes marks that appear to adults to be in random order	• Scribbles lines, circles, or zigzags in rows • Often repeats action and forms	• Writes segments of letter forms, e.g., lines, curves • May use too many segments to create a letter, e.g., five horizontal lines on the letter E • May not orient letter segments correctly	• Writes some letters correctly • Writes letters in unconventional order	• Writes all the letters of own name, although some may not be sequenced correctly • Writes all the letters of own name, but some of the letters are not formed or oriented correctly	• Writes all the letters of own name in the correct sequence, form, and orientation • Uses uppercase or lowercase letters (or a combination of both) when writing name	
	Carolyn	Lilly	Paula	Emma	Vicky	Brooke	

Objective 19 Demonstrates emergent writing skills

b. Writes to convey meaning

Not Yet	1	2	3	4	5	6	7
	Scribbles or marks • Scribble writes deliberately • Makes marks that appear to adults to be in random order	**Controlled linear scribbles** • Scribbles lines, circles, or zigzags in rows • Often repeats action and forms	**Mock letters or letter-like forms** • Writes segments of letter forms, e.g., lines, curves • May use too many segments to create a letter, e.g., five horizontal lines on the letter E • May not orient letter segments correctly	**Letter strings** • Writes strings of letters • Writes some letters correctly • Writes letters in unconventional order • Begins to separate groups of letters with spaces • May copy environmental print	**Early invented spelling** • Uses first letter of word to represent whole word • Writes initial and/or final sounds of a word to represent the whole word *Note: In Spanish, early invented spelling may consist primarily of vowels.*	**Late invented spelling** • Begins to include beginning, middle, and ending sounds in words • Represents most of the sounds heard in words in the correct order	

Maya said, "Here Mommy. Read this."

Carolyn said, "That's my phone number. You can call me."

Erica said, "I'm writing my ABCs just like my sister."

Jordan said, "Here's a ticket! You're under arrest!"

Meir wrote, "Uncle Clay, I love you."

Jenna said, "I need to buy some blackberries and grapes at the store."

Objective 19 Demonstrates emergent writing skills

Strategies

- Provide ample time, materials, and space for children to write throughout the day. Offer unlined and lined paper of different sizes and shapes, pencils of various sizes, crayons, markers, and white boards, magic slate, and other writing supplies.

- Provide specific opportunities to write outdoors. For example, write letters in the dirt or sand with fingers or small sticks or write on the sidewalk with chalk or water. Encourage older preschool and kindergarten children to make meaningful signs to use during outdoor activities, e.g., "STOP" or "detour" for a puddle of water.

- Include activities that give children reasons to write their names. For example, they may write their names on drawings, letters, greeting cards, sign-up sheets for a popular activity, or attendance sheets upon arrival each day.

- Provide accurate models of children's names. Print clearly using upper- and lowercase letters. Make names available for children to use as resources as they write.

- Plan specific activities that focus on writing. For example, with older children you might write the story of the day on chart paper.

- Model writing with children. Talk about what you are doing as you write. For example, you might say, "I'm making a sign to let people know the toilet is out of order." As you write "Out of order," say each word slowly and spell it. Call attention to each phoneme by saying the sound aloud as you write the letter(s).

- Encourage children to write words that are important to them as they create drawings, messages, greeting cards, lists, signs, menus, or books.

- Support the writing efforts of children. Say words slowly, emphasizing each sound so children can write the sounds they hear. Talk about directionality and letter shapes as you form the letters.

- Encourage kindergarten children to revise their original writings. Use simple word processing software as well as writing utensils and paper. Model the process writers go through to revise their writing. Children might revise their writings by first looking back at a previous writing sample, e.g., done a month before, and revising it based on their new knowledge and skills. They also might write about a topic they wrote about previously and then go back and look at their writing and compare it to their current writing.

Mathematics

Children slowly construct informal mathematical knowledge, beginning in the first few months of life. Firsthand exploration is important for learning mathematics. As infants, children begin to use their everyday experiences to construct a variety of fundamental mathematical concepts and strategies. The knowledge children acquire informally provides the foundation for the concepts and skills that they later learn formally in school. Through the essential process skills of problem solving, reasoning, communicating, making connections, and representing, children learn mathematics content (Copley, 2000; Geist, 2009).

Research has made a clear link between early math skills and later school reading and math achievement. An analysis of six longitudinal studies showed that early math skills have the greatest predictive power, followed by reading and then attention skills (Duncan et. al., 2007). Children's knowledge at kindergarten entry is considered predictive of future mathematics success throughout their years in school. Evidence shows that high-quality early childhood education programs can make a difference in children's mathematical learning (Clements & Sarama, 2009).

MATHEMATICS OBJECTIVES

20 Uses number concepts and operations

21 Explores and describes spatial relationships and shapes

22 Compares and measures

23 Demonstrates knowledge of patterns

Regardless of social class, culture, or disability, most children develop mathematical skills. However, there are gaps in some children's informal knowledge that make it difficult for them to understand school mathematics (Benigno & Ellis, 2004; Klein & Starkey, 2004). Language plays a central role in teaching and learning mathematics. For a child with a disability, the environment or materials may need to be adapted, routines adjusted, or an activity modified. The teacher's role is to determine what special supports a child needs to participate fully (Copley, Jones, & Dighe, 2007).

Adults play a significant role in helping children learn mathematical vocabulary, concepts, and process skills. If children are to develop the knowledge needed for later formal learning, they need frequent practice with materials in play settings and adult-guided activities that include meaningful discussions and applications (Varol & Farran, 2006).

Objective 20

Uses number concepts and operations

20

Children's understanding of counting, number symbols, and number operations are fundamental to their success with more complex mathematics (Ginsburg & Baroody, 2003; Zur & Gelman, 2004). When an infant signs *more* to request another bite of applesauce, a young child proudly announces, "I 2 years old," and a preschooler counts out 18 napkins at snack time, they are using number concepts and operations. Teachers play a critical role in helping children develop an understanding of number concepts and operations through intentional teaching during planned activities and daily routines.

To count well, children must learn: 1) the verbal number sequence; 2) one-to-one correspondence, i.e., that one number name is matched to a single object in a set being counted; and 3) cardinality, i.e., that the last number named when counting objects tells how many. Children can look at a small group of objects and identify the quantity without counting, e.g., counters or domino patterns. This is *subitizing*. From this children explore concepts of more and less, how many, and parts and wholes (Clements & Sarama, 2009). As they learn to discuss mathematical ideas, they learn ordinal counting: how to indicate the position of something in a sequence, e.g., first, second, third, and so forth. Over time children develop strategies such as counting on from a quantity (rather than beginning at one), counting back, or counting by groups (skip counting), e.g., by twos, fives, or tens.

Through everyday experiences and planned learning activities, young children begin to construct understandings about the number operations of separating (subtracting) and combining (adding). Taking away is a common separating operation that makes a collection smaller and answers the question "How many are left?" Children can often solve subtraction problems before they can solve addition problems (Copley & Hawkins, 2005). Addition problems involve combining sets of objects to find out "How many in all?" Young children typically use fingers or other objects to solve problems involving combining or separating, (Baroody, 2004). Physical objects that are directly related to the problems being solved are best (Clements & Sarama, 2009).

Young children also must learn to connect quantities with their written number symbols, or numerals. Displaying numerals with representations of their quantities helps children associate the amount with the numeral (Copley, 2000; Payne & Huinker, 1993). Before children can connect quantities with numerals they must develop a mental image of each numeral and its spoken name. Children sometimes confuse numerals that are similar in appearance, e.g., 2 and 5, and 6 and 9. Numerals that are easily confused should be taught side by side so the teacher can point out how they differ (Baroody, 1987). Some children benefit from handling three-dimensional numerals with textured surfaces (Charlesworth, 2005a).

Objective 20 Uses number concepts and operations

a. Counts

Not Yet	1	2	3	4	5	6	7	8	9
		Verbally counts (not always in the correct order) • Says, "One, two, ten" as she pretends to count		**Verbally counts to 10; counts up to five objects accurately, using one number name for each object** • Counts to ten when playing "Hide and Seek" • Counts out four scissors and puts them at the table		**Verbally counts to 20; counts 10–20 objects accurately; knows the last number states how many in all; tells what number (1–10) comes next in order by counting** • Counts to twenty while walking across room • Counts ten plastic worms and says, "I have ten worms." • When asked, "What comes after six?" says, "One, two, three, four, five, six, seven…seven."		**Uses number names while counting to 100; counts 30 objects accurately; tells what number comes before and after a specified number up to 20** • Counts twenty-eight steps to the cafeteria • When asked what comes after fifteen, says "Sixteen."	

b. Quantifies

Not Yet	1	2	3	4	5	6	7	8	9
		Demonstrates understanding of the concepts of *one*, *two*, and *more* • Says, "More apple," to indicate he wants more pieces than given • Takes two crackers when prompted, "Take two crackers."		**Recognizes and names the number of items in a small set (up to five) instantly; combines and separates up to five objects and describes the parts** • Looks at the sand table and says instantly, without counting, "There are three children at the table." • Says, "I have four cubes. Two are red, and two are blue." • Puts three bunnies in the box with the two bears. Counts and says, "Now I have five."		**Makes sets of 6–10 objects and then describes the parts; identifies which part has more, less, or the same (equal); counts all or counts on to find out how many** • Says, "I have eight big buttons, and you have eight little buttons. We have the same." • Tosses ten puff balls at the hoop. When three land outside she says, "More went inside." • Puts two dominoes together, says, "Five dots," and counts on "Six, seven, eight. Eight dots all together."		**Uses a variety of strategies (counting objects or fingers, counting on, or counting back) to solve problems with more than 10 objects** • Uses ladybug counters to solve the problem, "You had eight ladybugs. Two flew away. How many ladybugs are left?" • Says, "I have ten cars. I left two at Grandma's, so now I have ten, nine, *eight* left." • Uses two-sided counters to determine different number combinations for fourteen	

Objective 20   Uses number concepts and operations

c. Connects numerals with their quantities

Not Yet	1	2	3	4	5	6	7	8	9

Recognizes and names a few numerals
- Points to the *1* when the teacher says, "Where is the numeral *1*?"
- Notices numerals around the room and calls some of them by name

Identifies numerals to *5* by name and connects each to counted objects
- Says, "Five" as she attaches five clothespins to the *5* card
- Tells her friend, "That's a *3*, and there are three puppies on this page."

Identifies numerals to *10* by name and connects each to counted objects
- Shouts, "Seven," and jumps seven times when the teacher holds up the number *7* card
- Says, "I put nine buttons in the *9* box."

Identifies numerals to *20* by name and connects each to counted objects
- Says, "Kaufee put the *12* card and twelve beads on his necklace."
- Says, "I drew fifteen flowers to go on page 15 of our number book."

Objective 20 Uses number concepts and operations

Strategies

- Provide a variety of materials to help children develop an understanding of quantity. Offer buttons, bottle caps, keys, sticks, beans, cubes, counting bears, and other materials for children to count and compare. Model comparison vocabulary. Use words like *more*, *most*, *less*, *fewer*, *least*, *same as*, or *equal*.

- Recite fingerplays or rhymes and sing songs about numbers. Read stories that include numerals and items to count.

- Observe children to determine their counting skills. For those just beginning to count, display a few identical items in a straight line. As children gain skills, change the arrangement of objects. Gradually add more and varied objects to count.

- Use everyday activities as opportunities to count. Talk aloud as you count to solve problems. For example, you might say, "I wonder how many glue sticks we need to put out so everyone at the table has one? Let's count the children to find out."

- Model counting strategies. Touch or point to each object as you count slowly, saying the number name. Show how to keep track of the objects counted. For example, you might physically move the objects toward you as you count each one. Count on from an amount, e.g., "How much is four and three more? Four...five, six, seven. Seven."

- Practice counting in ways that involve multiple learning styles and representations. Involve the senses as children touch, hear the spoken number, see the numeral, or physically move their bodies.

- Include materials and activities that associate numerals with sets.

- Use everyday situations to illustrate combining and separating. For example, when a child leaves the dramatic play area you might say, "We had three children in the dramatic play area. Tommy went to play in the blocks area. How many children are left?"

- Encourage older preschool and kindergarten children to tell *how many* stories. For example, they might tell how many children are on the climber or how many markers they have after their friend gave them more or put some away.

- Provide various materials for kindergarten children to make number combinations. For example, use two sided colored beans, e.g., white on one side and blue on the other, to make combinations for the number four. When children shake and spill the beans they will discover different number combinations for four (i.e., 1 blue and 3 white beans; 2 blue and 2 white; 3 blue and 1 white; 4 blue and 0 white beans; or 4 white and 0 blue). Children can record their findings on their Number 4 Combination chart.

Explores and describes spatial relationships and shapes

21

Understanding spatial relationships and shapes helps children build the foundation for understanding geometry. Spatial awareness, how objects are oriented in relation to one another, develops as children begin to explore the relationship between their bodies and the things around them. As they learn to navigate their environment, they learn about direction, perspective, distance, symbolization, and location. The awareness of spatial relationships develops as infants see faces from different positions and perspectives. Toddlers try to fit their bodies into boxes of different sizes. Preschoolers walk around block structures to see which sides they want to draw, and kindergartners attempt to give directions to particular locations. Children who have a strong spatial sense do better in mathematics (Clements, 2004).

Positional words describe spatial relationships and help children deepen their understanding of those relationships. Directional words describe *which way*, e.g., up, down, forward, and backward. Distance words tell *how far*, e.g., near, far, and close. Location words specify *where*, e.g., on, off, under, and over. Children from a variety of cultures generally understand the spatial terms of *in, on*, and *under* before they understand *next to* or *by* (Plumert & Hawkins, 2001).

Young children explore two- and three-dimensional shapes long before they can name and describe them. In addition to square, rectangle, triangle, and circle, preschool children can learn the three-dimensional shapes of cube ("like a box"), rectangular prism ("like a box"), cylinder ("like a can"), and sphere ("like a

ball") (Copley, Jones, & Dighe, 2007). Typically, young children form a visual prototype that they use to classify shapes by their overall appearance (Clements, 2004). For example, they say that a triangle is a triangle because it "looks like one" (Van Hiele, 1986). It is important to provide a wide variety of models of each shape so that children do not perceive that a particular shape looks only one way, e.g. think all triangles must have a point on top in the middle (Clements, Battista, & Sarama, 2001). Many types of squares and rectangles should be presented to help children understand that a square is a special type of rectangle. Double-naming, as in *square-rectangle* may be helpful (Clements & Sarama, 2009). Shapes should be rotated into different positions (e.g., on their sides or upside down), and examples should be provided for comparison (Charlesworth, 2005b).

Children do not develop their ideas about shapes by simply looking at them. They need to manipulate, draw, compare, describe, sort, and represent the shapes in a variety of ways (Charlesworth, 2005a, 2005b; Clements, 1999). Infants, toddlers, and twos explore shapes as they fit a circle into the matching hole on a shape sorter; work shape puzzles; and blow bubbles outdoors, saying "Lots of balls!" Older preschool and kindergarten children can combine shapes to produce composite shapes, e.g., using two triangles to produce a square (Clements, Wilson, & Sarama, 2004). This is an important process that helps children understand and analyze shape (Clements, 2004).

Objective 21 Explores and describes spatial relationships and shapes

a. Understands spatial relationships

Not Yet	1	2	3	4	5	6	7	8	9
		Follows simple directions related to position (in, on, under, up, down) • Follows teacher's directions to put the trash in the can • Raises hands up and down as the song directs		**Follows simple directions related to proximity (beside, between, next to)** • Follows teacher's direction to put the cup next to the plate • Sits beside her friend when he says, "Sit between me and Laura."		**Uses and responds appropriately to positional words indicating location, direction, and distance** • Says, "Look for the surprise behind the tree." • Moves game piece backward when playmate gives directions		**Uses and makes simple sketches, models, or pictorial maps to locate objects** • Constructs a map of the play yard using landscape toys • Uses a map of the classroom to find the hidden treasure	

b. Understands shapes

Not Yet	1	2	3	4	5	6	7	8	9
		Matches two identical shapes • Puts a circular puzzle piece in the circular space • Places shapes in a shape-sorting box		**Identifies a few basic shapes (circle, square, triangle)** • Looks at a wheel and says, "A circle." • Names shape pieces as he puts them on a shape lotto card		**Describes basic two- and three-dimensional shapes by using own words; recognizes basic shapes when they are presented in a new orientation** • Says, "It's a ball 'cause it rolls." • Puts hand in feely box and says, "It has three sides and three points. It's a triangle."		**Shows that shapes remain the same when they are turned, flipped, or slid; breaks apart or combines shapes to create different shapes and sizes** • Says, "It's still a triangle no matter how you turn it." • Cuts apart a rectangle to make two squares	

Objective 21 Explores and describes spatial relationships and shapes

Strategies

- Label shapes with correct names as the children use them. For example, when a child says, "I got a round one," when describing a sphere, you might say, "Yes, it is round. It looks like a ball. It's called a sphere."

- Guide children's explorations of shapes. Discuss the features as children explore. Use the word *not* as you talk about a shape. For example, you might say, "This is *not* a circle because it does not have curved lines."

- Present shapes that differ in size and orientation. For example, so that children will not think that all triangles have equal-length sides, present narrow triangles, wide triangles, and triangles rotated in various positions.

- Encourage children to create new shapes from other shapes. Use computer software that allows children to manipulate shapes and see the results as they move and combine pieces.

- Model and encourage the use of positional words as children climb in, out, on, or through objects. For example, you might say, "Lars crawled *over* the box and *under* the rope. Now he is *in* the tunnel."

- Use maps or other representations with older preschool and kindergarten children to help them think spatially. For example, provide a simple map with easily found landmarks and specific clues about the location of the hidden object or photograph classroom materials and activities from different positions. Discuss where in the classroom the materials or activities are located and where you stood to take the photo.

- Encourage older preschool and kindergarten children to represent shapes in various ways. For example, they might draw shapes and then recreate them on the geo board or with tangram pieces.

Compares and measures

22

Young children frequently compare measurement as they interact. They say, "I want so much grapes, not little bit grapes!" "I'm bigger!" or, "Joe has the longest one!" They understand that there are different ways of measuring. They begin to recognize the attributes of *length, height,* and *width* (how long, tall, and wide something is), *capacity* (how much something holds), *weight* (how heavy something is), *area* (how much space is covered), and *time* (sequence and duration). Time is a difficult measurement concept for children to learn because it is not a physical attribute of objects. In fact, telling time does not develop well until after kindergarten, but preschoolers develop an understanding of the passage of time as they go through predictable daily routines (Geist, 2009).

Children's initial ideas about size, quantity, and seriation involve comparisons related to their play materials and books. They know about the differently sized beds and bowls in *The Three Bears*. Young children experiment first by lining up objects, then they can begin to connect number to length as they use nonstandard measurement tools, e.g., links, blocks, rods (Clements & Sarama, 2009).

Experimenting with tools that give different results, e.g., sometimes measuring an object with links and later measuring the same object with rods, is an essential step to understanding why standard tools, e.g., rulers, measuring tape, are important for comparing measurements.

In addition to nonstandard measurement tools, children can benefit from exploring and using tools with uniform units, e.g., rulers and centimeter cubes, as their measurement ideas and skills are developing (Clements, 2003; Sarama & Clements, 2006). Actual measurement involves associating a numeral with an attribute of an object, e.g., "This box is 9 inches long." Understanding how to measure accurately is a skill that takes many years to learn (Mix, Huttenlocher, & Levine, 2002).

Objective 22 Compares and measures

Not Yet	1	2	3	4	5	6	7	8	9

Makes simple comparisons between two objects

- Pours sand or water from one container to another
- Indicates which ball is bigger when shown a tennis ball and a beach ball

Compares and orders a small set of objects as appropriate according to size, length, weight, area, or volume; knows usual sequence of basic daily events and a few ordinal numbers

- Puts blocks side by side in order of length
- Says, "We go outside after lunch."
- Lays two short blocks on top of a long block to see if it's the same length
- Responds, "You're second to use the computer."

Uses multiples of the same unit to measure; uses numbers to compare; knows the purpose of standard measuring tools

- Measures by using paper clips, cubes, string, hands, feet or other objects
- Measures block tower with linking cubes and says, "I made mine fifteen cubes high!!"
- Stands on scale while pretending to be in a doctor's office

Uses measurement words and some standard measurement tools accurately; uses ordinal numbers from *first* to *tenth*

- Says, "We need two cups of flour and one cup of salt to make dough."
- Says, "If I add three more tiles to this side of the scale, they'll be the same."
- Looks at the clock and says, "It's 12 o'clock. It's time for lunch."

Objective 22 Compares and measures

Strategies

- Take advantage of daily opportunities to talk about comparing and measuring. Extend children's visual comparisons of length, height, weight, and area. For example, when children debate about who found the longest rope or who has the biggest leaf, encourage them to compare by laying them side by side or placing one on top of the other.

- Provide many opportunities for children to measure using non-standard measures. For example, offer plastic snap cubes, plastic chains, paper clips, blocks, paper strips, straws, plastic cups, or large spoons. Encourage children to think of other materials they can use to measure.

- Plan activities that allow children to compare measuring with non-standard and with standard measures. For example, make a small batch of play dough using cups and spoons from dramatic play. Make another batch using standard measuring cups and spoons. As children compare the products, guide them to discover the advantages of standard measuring tools.

- Encourage children to use measuring tools in their own ways during measurement activities and during dramatic play. Model the conventional use of measuring tools during class activities. Explain tools and methods as you engage in real measurement activities. Use measurement vocabulary to describe the process.

- Offer a variety of standard measuring tools for children to investigate and use. Include rulers, yardsticks, measuring tapes, thermometers, balance scales, measuring cups, and centimeter grid paper.

- Use estimation vocabulary. Use words such as *about*, *approximate*, *nearly*, *almost*, and *close to* in the context of real-life situations. Encourage children to check their estimations by measuring.

- Involve older preschool and kindergarten children in using recipes and measuring tools to make their own snacks independently.

- Provide opportunities for kindergarten children to compare and record how much something will hold (capacity). For example, use a snack-size zip bag and see how many snap cubes, bottle tops, or counting bears it will hold when full. Have children record and compare their results.

Demonstrates knowledge of patterns

23

A pattern is a regular arrangement of something, e.g., numbers, objects, shapes, colors, sounds, or movements. Guiding children to understand patterns is a foundational skill in mathematics. As they learn to label patterns by having one name stand for something else, they are creating an algebraic representation. Children begin to identify patterns in their environment at an early age. An infant waves her arms in anticipation as you arrive with her bottle. A toddler repeats a repetitive phrase from a storybook while you read aloud. A preschooler describes a simple pattern on a shirt, "Green stripe, red stripe, green stripe, red stripe." A kindergartner describes how he counts by using even numbers, "Two, four, six, eight. I skip a number every time."

In *repeating patterns*, the core unit repeats a minimum of five times, e.g., red, blue; red, blue; red, blue; red, blue; red, blue. Children often mistakenly believe that something is a pattern because it is repeated once. Young children can recognize the relationship between repeating patterns that share the same core unit but that are perceptually different, e.g., color and movement, as in a color pattern of red, blue; red, blue; red, blue… and a movement pattern of stomp, clap; stomp, clap; stomp, clap… (Sarama & Clements, 2006).

Growing patterns are more complex than repeating patterns. In growing patterns, the pattern increases by at least plus one and continues to increase. A block staircase is an example of a growing pattern (Copley, 2000). The familiar song, "My Aunt Came Back," also is an example of a growing pattern. Children add one phrase and action to each verse, repeating the previous phrases and actions, until they reach the tenth verse with ten actions and phrases (Copley, Jones, & Dighe, 2007).

The study of patterns is exciting for young children. They first learn to copy simple patterns made with objects. They later learn to extend and create their own patterns (Clements, 2004; Klein & Starkey, 2004). Patterns help children know what comes next and to make predictions about things they cannot yet observe. Exploring patterns helps children understand some basic algebraic ideas. Learning experiences that focus on patterns facilitate children's generalizations about number combinations, counting strategies, and problem solving (Copley, 2000).

Objective 23 Demonstrates knowledge of patterns

Not Yet	1	2	3	4	5	6	7	8	9

Shows interest in simple patterns in everyday life

- Notices that a special song is played whenever it is time to clean up
- Points to the tiles in the bathroom and says, "They go this way, that way, this way, that way."

Copies simple repeating patterns

- Beats a drum as the teacher does, e.g., loud, soft; loud, soft; loud, soft; etc.
- Strings beads as her friend does, e.g., red, blue, blue; red, blue, blue; red, blue, blue; etc.

Extends and creates simple repeating patterns

- Makes a repeating movement pattern, e.g., stomp, stomp, clap, clap; stomp, stomp, clap, clap; stomp, stomp, clap, clap; etc.
- When shown pattern of cubes, e.g., red, blue, blue, red; red, blue, blue, red; etc., adds to it correctly

Recognizes, creates, and explains more complex repeating and simple growing patterns

- Describes even numbers, e.g., 2, 4, 6, 8, etc., as "skipping" every other number on a 100's chart
- Says, "If I add one to three, it's the next number: four. If I add one to four, it's the next number: five."
- Extends a growing pattern by adding one cube like a staircase, e.g., 1 cube, 2 cubes, 3 cubes, 4 cubes, etc.

Objective 23 Demonstrates knowledge of patterns

Strategies

- Identify patterns in daily routines. For example, you might say, "Every day we follow the same pattern. After choice time, we have cleanup, then snack, then story."

- Call attention to patterns in the environment. For example, you might say, "Magnus, you have a pattern in your shirt: blue stripe, red stripe; blue stripe, red stripe; blue strip, red stripe..." or "Sai, you made a pattern with your blocks: up, down; up, down; up, down..."

- Support children as they copy and extend patterns. Begin with simple repeating color patterns. Use objects that are identical except for their color. Progress to shape patterns where objects are the same color, same size, but vary in shape. Continue by using same-colored, same-shaped, but differently sized objects. Encourage children to repeat their patterns at least five times.

- Describe patterns with words, sounds, movements, and objects rather than with letters. Using letters, e.g., ab, abb, abc patterns, can be confusing to children who are learning letters and their sounds.

- Encourage children to talk about and identify patterns. For example, children can become "pattern detectives" as they describe and represent patterns they identify in the environment. Include their discoveries in a class book titled, *Patterns Discovered by Our Class*.

- Read patterning stories and verses. For example, *Mrs. McTats and Her Houseful of Cats* (Alyssa S. Capucilli), *The Napping House* (Audrey Wood), and *The Relatives Came* (Cynthia Rylant) are books that include patterns that can be acted out by children.

- Encourage kindergarten children to compare patterns and to find similarities and differences among them. For example, two patterns may use the same colors, but one is a yellow, green; yellow, green; yellow, green pattern and the other is a yellow, green, green; yellow, green, green; yellow, green, green pattern.

- Have kindergarten children create growing patterns using materials such as small cube blocks, stacking cubes, or linking chains. They can represent their patterns through drawings.

Science and Technology

Science content during early childhood typically focuses on living things (life science), the physical properties of materials and objects (physical science), and Earth's environment and how we care for it (earth science). The best way to learn science is to *do* science through integrated, hands-on, child-centered inquiry (Lind, 1997; 2001). Learning to engage in the process of scientific thinking, gaining understanding, and making connections are more important than learning scientific facts at an early age.

Young children are natural investigators. They are curious about how things work and what will happen next (Mantzicopoulos, Patrick, & Samarapungavan, 2008). Hands-on science learning begins in infancy with sensory stimulation that sharpens the infant's observation and discrimination skills. With adults' help and encouragement, this leads to more detailed exploration and discovery (Desouza & Czerniak, 2002). During the preschool and kindergarten years, scientific exploration should focus on naturalistic and informal learning that promotes exploration and discovery through everyday experiences. As children become more systematic in their explorations, their understanding deepens and their ideas come closer to current scientific understanding (Chalufour & Worth, 2004).

Young children have many scientific understandings, although they may be incomplete or inaccurate (Eshach & Fried, 2005; Hannust & Kikas, 2007; Nobes et al., 2003; Tenenbaum, Rappolt-Schlichtmann, & Zanger 2004). They can think and talk in

SCIENCE AND TECHNOLOGY OBJECTIVES

24 Uses scientific inquiry skills

25 Demonstrates knowledge of the characteristics of living things

26 Demonstrates knowledge of the physical properties of objects and materials

27 Demonstrates knowledge of Earth's environment

28 Uses tools and other technology to perform tasks

complex ways about science topics when they have related knowledge and experience (Gelman & Brenneman, 2004; Peterson & French, 2008). Adult-child conversations can support children's evolving theories of science (Tenenbaum & Callanan, 2008). When children have frequent opportunities to hear and use scientific vocabulary in meaningful contexts, they begin to use scientific words accurately (Gelman & Brenneman, 2004).

Science topics should be appropriate for children's developmental levels so that they do not develop scientific misconceptions or become disinterested. Appropriate, integrated scientific-inquiry activities can help children enjoy and feel competent about learning science (Mantzicopoulos, Patrick, & Samarapungavan, 2008). Some language can hinder children's scientific understanding. For example, saying *dead battery* or *lively music* may cloud children's understanding of living and nonliving things. Exploring which items sink or float is more appropriate than discussing the abstract concepts of buoyancy and density, that is, why things sink and float (Eshach & Fried, 2005; Tenenbaum, Rappolt-Schlichtmann, & Zanger, 2004). Some topics, such as astronomy, are difficult for young children to understand because they involve concepts that cannot be explored firsthand and objects that cannot be touched (Hannust & Kikas, 2007).

Young children need many opportunities to explore science concepts firsthand over time so they can connect new understandings to related experiences. Hurried exposure to disconnected science topics does not provide opportunities for rich conceptual growth (Gelman & Brenneman, 2004). In-depth investigations are an appropriate way for children to learn science content, the basic skills needed to use tools and other technology, and such process skills as observing, comparing, classifying, measuring, and communicating. Collaboration with peers and the guidance of a supportive teacher help children acquire basic science concepts and fundamental inquiry skills.

Objective 24

Uses scientific inquiry skills

24

Scientific inquiry is the *doing* of science (Epstein, 2007). Children use a variety of inquiry skills as they connect what they know to new experiences. Inquiry skills include making focused observations, posing meaningful questions, determining what is already known by examining books and other resources, making predictions, selecting appropriate techniques and tools, conducting investigations, reflecting on experiences, and communicating their findings (Chalufour & Worth, 2004; National Committee on Science Education Standards and Assessment, National Research Council, 1996). Adults can help children develop scientific inquiry skills through everyday experiences, such as observing worms, and helping them represent their observations in various ways, such as recording in science journals (Brenneman & Louro, 2008).

As you create exploratory opportunities and plan experiences for children, think about how each child uses the skills of scientific inquiry. Focus your observations on

HOW AND WHEN THE CHILD

- observes and explores things in the environment
- reacts to changes
- manipulates objects to understand their properties
- connects new observations to what he or she already knows
- identifies problems, makes predictions, thinks of ways to solve problems, and tries possible solutions
- organizes information
- makes comparisons and classifies
- talks with others about discoveries
- represents his or her thinking through drawing, dramatizing, graphing, or making models

Objective 24 Uses scientific inquiry skills

Strategies

- Model focused observation by showing curiosity about things in the environment, observing intently, using multiple senses, and calling attention to details. For example, when children wonder in what part of the tank a fish usually stays, encourage them to observe to find out. Involve the children in making a chart to record their observations.

- Support children as they practice scientific inquiry. Use scientific terms like *observe*, *hypothesize*, *predict*, and *estimate*. Guide children as they revisit and extend their investigations. For example, you might document their inquiry with photographs taken with a digital camera. Help children to think about their experiences, talk about the strategies they used, and analyze and synthesize the information they collected.

- Help children connect new discoveries to what they already know. For example, compare children's drawings before and after a field trip. Ask open-ended questions such as, "How is this magnet like/different from the magnet we used last week?"

- Conduct in-depth investigations with preschool and kindergarten children, using living things, objects, and materials from the local environment. Encourage children to communicate their discoveries in multiple ways. For example, they might draw, dictate, write, take photos, dramatize, make models, or graph their findings. Support children's use of explanatory language as they talk about their discoveries.

- Support kindergarten children as they record their scientific predictions and observations in their science notebooks or journals. For example, they might predict what will happen over time to the pumpkin they picked from their garden, how tall the tomato plant will grow, or what will dissolve in water. Children can record their observations using a digital camera, drawings, and/or writing and then report and discuss their findings.

Objective 25

Demonstrates knowledge of the characteristics of living things

25

Young children are interested in living things. They are especially interested in the plants and animals in their immediate environment. They want to learn about their habitats and how they grow and change. For example, children in Louisiana may want to learn more about the crawfish they see in the bayous, while children in New Mexico may want to explore the different cactus plants they see growing around them (Dodge, Colker, & Heroman, 2002). No matter what topic of the life sciences children study, they can learn the major concepts as they interact with living things. Through regular contact with nature, children expand their curiosity and observation skills, practice nurturing behaviors as they care for living things, and gain knowledge in other academic areas (Rosenow, 2008; Russo, 2008).

As you create exploratory opportunities and plan experiences for children related to living things, think about how each child is beginning to understand concepts about living things. Focus your observations on

HOW AND WHEN THE CHILD

- shows a growing ability to classify living and nonliving things
- communicates about the characteristics of living things
- demonstrates an understanding that living things grow, change, and reproduce
- shows awareness of life in different environments or habitats
- groups or categorizes living things, e.g., appearance, behavior, plant, or animal
- demonstrates awareness that living things go through a growth cycle

Objective 25 Demonstrates knowledge of the characteristics of living things

Strategies

- Include opportunities for children to care for living things. For example, they might care for a pet fish or grow a small garden in the play yard. Discuss what living things need to grow and stay healthy.

- Provide opportunities for children to observe the life cycle of living things. For example, they might observe the life cycle of a frog and record changes that occur by drawing pictures or taking photographs.

- Sing, recite fingerplays, and read stories about how living things grow and change.

- Go on nature walks to look for worms, ladybugs, roly-polies (pill bugs), grasshoppers, or other living things to observe. Use magnifying glasses to get a better look.

- Use correct terminology when discussing living things. Use words like *germinate*, *sprout*, *bud*, or *stalk* when talking about plants. Use words like *habitat*, *camouflage*, *herbivore*, *antennae*, or *predator* when talking about animals.

- Help children understand animal behavior. After observing and talking about specific behaviors, encourage children to act like their favorite animals. For example, they might dramatize how cats stalk, preen themselves, or play.

- Encourage children to categorize living things. They might group according to appearance, behavior, or whether things are plants or animals. Have children explain their classifications.

- Guide kindergarten children to look up information on the Internet about the habitats or environments of different animals and to record findings in their science journals.

Demonstrates knowledge of the physical properties of objects and materials

26

By preschool, children have already begun building scientific knowledge about the physical properties of objects and materials (Gelman & Brenneman, 2004). They learn about physical properties by observing and manipulating common objects and materials. As they use their senses to explore things, they learn about shape, color, texture, weight, temperature, and how things move and change. As teachers talk with children about the properties of objects and materials, children develop vocabulary and important background knowledge. This background knowledge helps children observe their environment more closely. For example, the child who has been exposed to ramps at school may notice the ramps they see elsewhere in the community and talk about them at home and school. Without this exposure, the ramps may have gone unnoticed by the child (Eshach & Fried, 2005).

As you create exploratory opportunities and plan experiences for children, think about how each child explores and learns about objects and materials. Focus your observations on

HOW AND WHEN THE CHILD

- examines, describes, and measures the observable features of objects

- demonstrates understanding that objects are made from one or more materials, e.g., metal, wood, plastic, or paper

- communicates that the physical properties of objects and materials can change, e.g., when solid ice becomes a liquid

- displays awareness of natural forces that affect objects and materials, e.g., wind and gravity

- explores and describes ways that objects can be moved in space, e.g., pushing, pulling, rising, or sinking

Objective 26 Demonstrates knowledge of the physical properties of objects and materials

Strategies

- Use everyday activities as opportunities for children to learn about the physical properties of objects and materials and the natural forces that affect them. Talk about what children observe throughout the day. For example, when children paint with water they learn about evaporation. When they cook, they learn about changes that occur in matter. When they push trucks up a ramp or move boats in water, they learn about how objects can be moved in space.

- Use appropriate vocabulary to describe phenomena. Use words like *sink*, *float*, *dissolve*, *melt*, *absorb*, *adhere*, *attract*, *repel*.

- Offer a variety of substances for children to explore and learn their characteristics. Include objects made from metal, wood, plastic, and paper.

- Plan experiences where children can observe changes in the physical properties of objects and materials. For example, leave an ice cube outside in the sun and observe as it becomes a liquid. Mix different materials in water to see if they dissolve.

- Repeat experiences often so children can extend their understandings. For example, use different bubble solution recipes. Offer different materials for children to use as bubble wands. Encourage them to compare their new experiences with what they learned from previous experiences.

- Make charts and/or graphs about the physical properties of objects and materials. For example, children might explore concepts such as absorb/repel, sink/float, hot/cold, or rough/smooth.

Objective 27

Demonstrates knowledge of Earth's environment

27

When children learn about Earth's environment, they learn about the composition of the Earth: rocks, sand, dirt, mud, and water. They learn about the weather, day and night, shadows, and recycling. Children learn about Earth's environment best by exploring their own natural surroundings. As children explore the properties of the world around them, they notice changes and make predictions. They begin to understand their environment, learn important ideas, and develop respect for their natural surroundings (Dodge, Colker, & Heroman, 2002).

As you create exploratory opportunities and plan experiences for children, think about how each child is learning concepts about the Earth and the environment. Focus your observations on

HOW AND WHEN THE CHILD

- demonstrates understanding that there are different kinds of weather and that weather changes

- describes and measures weather

- communicates awareness that the environment changes, e.g., season to season, sometimes slowly and sometimes suddenly

- communicates that the Earth's surface is made of different materials, e.g., rocks, sand, dirt, and water, and each material has properties that can be described

- shows awareness that different objects can be seen in the sky

- demonstrates understanding that people can affect the environment in positive and negative ways

Objective 27 Demonstrates knowledge of Earth's environment

Strategies

- Investigate properties of rocks, soil, and water. For example, children may dig in the dirt, explore puddles, or examine rocks of different hardnesses and talk about their discoveries.

- Point out changes you notice in the environment. For example, you might look out the window during diaper changing and say, "It's snowing outside. Soon the ground will be covered with white snow."

- Use collections of natural objects to help children learn more about the environment. For example, children might collect rocks, shells, leaves, or pinecones and group them by characteristics such as size, color, shape, or texture.

- Observe the Earth's environment during different times of the day and different times of the year. For example, observe the sky at different hours. Talk about what the children see. Go on nature walks at different times of the year. Document and discuss how things are the same and different during each visit.

- Use words such as *evaporation*, *condensation*, *atmosphere*, *windy*, *overcast*, *partly cloudy*, *environment*, *recycling*, *pollution*, and *litter* when talking about the Earth's environment.

- Recite fingerplays, sing, and read seasonal or weather-related books. Compare and contrast the information in books with the current season and weather.

- Go on a litter hunt. Talk about the appropriate place for various kinds of litter (recycling bin or trash can) and how children can help to keep the Earth's environment clean.

- Observe shadows during different times of the day. Measure and compare how they are alike and different.

- Involve older children in making their own recycled paper. Tear scraps of construction paper and put them in a blender with water. Blend and then pour the solution through a rectangular mesh screen. Spread so that the liquid drains and the pulp is left on the screen. During the process, talk about changes that occur. Let the pulp dry for several days, and then use the recycled paper for writing or drawing.

Objective 28

Uses tools and other technology to perform tasks

28

Tools and technology make work easier and help people solve problems (Dodge, Colker, & Heroman, 2002). Technology enables children to respond and represent their learning in individual ways (Northwest Educational Technology Consortium, Northwest Regional Educational Laboratory, 2002). Technology can increase participation for English-language learners and children with disabilities (Murphy, DePasquale, & McNamara, 2003). As children use a variety of tools, such as thermometers, funnels, magnifying lenses, balances, hammers, tape measures, measuring cups, cameras, and computers, they learn to select the most appropriate tools for the job.

As you create exploratory opportunities and plan experiences for children, think about how each child develops important concepts related to tools and technology. Focus your observations on

HOW AND WHEN THE CHILD

- shows understanding that different tools and technology are used in different places for different purposes, e.g., finding information, communicating, and designing

- demonstrates the appropriate use of various tools and other technology

Objective 28 Uses tools and other technology to perform tasks

Strategies

- Offer a variety of tools and other technology for children to use during explorations. For example, you might offer ramps, pulleys, water wheels, egg beaters, and magnets for children to explore their physical world. Include magnifying glasses, tape recorders, and a digital camera as children study living things. Offer sifters, balance scales, plastic thermometers, or rain gauges as they explore the Earth's environment.

- Encourage children to try different tools to accomplish a task. Have them evaluate and compare the results.

- Talk with children about how tools and other technology are used in daily living. For example, you might say, "The hearing aid helps Benny hear what others are saying," or "The mixer helps Mrs. Horton stir the ingredients together to make bread."

- Model technology applications in daily activities. For example, check the weather forecast for the day or look up information about ants on the Internet.

- Demonstrate the appropriate use of tools and other technology, emphasizing safety and proper care. For example, show children how to navigate a software program or operate a digital camera.

- Provide discarded items for children to take apart and find out what is inside or how they work. For example, offer record players, radios, clocks, or telephones. Remove the electrical cord and other unsafe parts before children explore. Offer different sizes and kinds of screwdrivers, pliers, and other tools. As they take these and other things apart, they discover pulleys, magnets, levers, springs, and circuit boards. Remind children not to take things at home apart unless they are given permission.

- Support older children as they write and illustrate stories using simple word processing programs, computer art programs, and digital cameras.

- When children find an interesting object outdoors, e.g., rock, fur, pine needles, dandelion helicopters, get them to observe it carefully with their naked eye and then draw what they see. Provide magnifying tools, e.g., magnifying glass, scope on a rope, microscope, jeweler's loupe, for closer study, and discuss how the magnifying devices made their observation better. Have children draw the object again and compare and discuss their drawings.

Social Studies

Social studies is the study of people and the ways they relate to others. As a discipline, social studies incorporates concepts and ideas from the fields of history, geography, anthropology, sociology, civics, and economics (Seefeldt, 1995). When young children explore social studies, they learn how to be researchers, critical thinkers, and active members of a classroom community.

Everyday experiences provide the foundation for learning social studies. Teachers can build upon children's interests and use them to introduce children to other places, traditions, and cultures. Many children today are immigrants or come from immigrant-headed households. These children face particular challenges, such as being different or learning a new language (Baghban, 2007). Issues of human diversity can be addressed through social studies as children learn how people live, work, get along with others, solve problems, and are shaped by their surroundings.

The focus of social studies during infancy and toddlerhood is on self-development within social settings (Mindes, 2005b). Young children begin with an egocentric perspective, showing interest first in themselves and then in their families. Adults enhance this self-development by providing safe, secure environments and materials that foster curiosity and exploration (Epstein, 2007). During the preschool years, children become interested in other people and their community. As they become more aware of the larger world through their

SOCIAL STUDIES OBJECTIVES

29 Demonstrates knowledge about self

30 Shows basic understanding of people and how they live

31 Explores change related to familiar people or places

32 Demonstrates simple geographic knowledge

understanding of themselves and their individual experiences, preschool and kindergarten children can engage in long-term studies of meaningful topics. Their interests lead children to ask questions, actively investigate issues, and make connections between what they are learning in their daily lives. In the process of their investigations, children learn how to be researchers, and they become experts on topics related to everyday life.

Objective 29

Demonstrates knowledge about self

29

Young children describe themselves in terms of age, gender, physical traits, material possessions, behavior, preferences, skills, experiences, role in the family, family routines, and environment. During the preschool years children begin to develop their racial identities and notice differences in social class (Feeney & Moravcik, 2005; Ramsey, 2003). The child's culture, family, and social settings (child care, school, and neighborhood) play an important role in determining what features of the self are incorporated into the child's concept of self. Personal storytelling involving family members serves as a rich source of self-knowledge and helps to instill a child's cultural values (Burger & Miller, 1999; Miller, Fung, & Mintz, 1996).

As you create exploratory opportunities and plan experiences for children, think about how each child demonstrates knowledge of him- or herself. Focus your observations on

HOW AND WHEN THE CHILD

- demonstrates understanding that each person has unique characteristics, ways of communicating, and ways of solving problems
- communicates that each person is part of a family that has unique characteristics
- shows awareness that each person has basic needs that must be met to stay healthy, e.g., food, clothing, shelter

Objective 29 Demonstrates knowledge about self

Strategies

- Offer multiple ways for children to express their individuality and preferences. For example, they might communicate their ideas and feelings through painting, drawing, storytelling, song, or dance.

- Encourage children to recognize their unique characteristics as well as characteristics they share with others. For example, use transition times to call attention to similarities and differences by saying, "If you have curly hair, you may go to the rug."

- Use photographs of children involved in classroom activities. Display photos in accessible places so children can refer to them throughout the day. For example, place individual photos in a basket or on rings for children to use during art or writing activities. Create charts or graphs showing children's likenesses and differences (eye color, hair, favorite class activity). Make puzzles using different class pictures.

- Create short stories about children in the class. Take photographs of each child involved in daily activities. Write a short sentence or two about what the child is doing. Make the books accessible during the day. Send them home so children can share them with family members. Encourage kindergarten children to create their own short stories about their daily school activities.

- Encourage families to share traditions, songs, games, or special stories they read at home with their children.

- Include materials that help children explore differences among children in the program. For example, include various shades of skin tone paint, crayons, markers, and construction paper. Offer dolls that represent different ethnicities, props, musical instruments, puzzles, books, and other materials that recognize diversity.

- Support the home languages of children in your program. For example, learn a few words in the home languages of the children. Write children's names, *hello* and *goodbye*, or names of familiar objects in English and in the home languages. Involve children and families in the process.

- Help older preschool and kindergarten children to learn their full names, addresses, and phone numbers.

- Guide older children to illustrate and write books about themselves. Topics might include "My Family," "Things I Like to Do," "Foods I Like to Eat," or "Places in My Neighborhood." Teachers can take dictation for younger children or children who cannot write.

Objective 30

Shows basic understanding of people and how they live

30

Young children are eager to learn about other people and how they live. They are interested in the physical characteristics of people; similarities and differences in habits, homes, and work; family structures and roles; and the exchange of goods and services. It is important for them to learn to respect others and to understand how people rely on each other. Reading appropriate books to children can be an effective way to help them develop positive attitudes about others and to better understand how people live throughout the world (Feeney & Moravcik, 2005).

As you create exploratory opportunities and plan experiences for children, think about how each child demonstrates understandings related to people and how they live. Focus your observations on

HOW AND WHEN THE CHILD

- shows awareness that there are similarities and differences among people and families

- demonstrates understanding of the various jobs of people in the community

- shows understanding that people buy, sell, and trade to get goods and services that they do not raise, make, or find themselves

- communicates about the various means of transportation that people use to move goods and go from place to place

- shows increasing awareness that respect for others, cooperation, and fairness help us get along in communities

- demonstrates increasing understanding that there are rules in our homes, schools, and community and that each rule has a purpose

- communicates understanding that people have various rights and responsibilities

Objective 30 Shows basic understanding of people and how they live

Strategies

- Include puzzles, block people, props, and other materials representing a range of jobs and cultures. As children play, comment on the tools people use in their jobs.

- Take frequent walks in the neighborhood. Help children notice the patterns of life and work as they see people going about their daily activities. For example, they might see street vendors selling their wares, roofers repairing a roof, a delivery person delivering a package, sanitation workers collecting trash, or a bus driver picking up passengers.

- Take trips to visit workplaces in the community. Before the trip read books, introduce new vocabulary, and discuss what children might see. During the trip ask workers to demonstrate and talk about what they do. Point out how people work together. Follow up trips by talking about the experience, adding new materials to support play, or documenting through art, writing, or making maps.

- Support older preschool and kindergarten children in interviewing people in the school, program, and community to learn more about their jobs. Guide children as they generate questions. For example, they might ask, "Why do you wear a uniform?" or "What tools do you use to do your job?"

- Help children expand their understanding of how children and families in other places are alike and different from themselves. For example, create e-mail partners with children in another part of the country or world. Guide children as they share information about themselves and generate questions to ask.

- Develop a "pen-pal" relationship with a kindergarten class in another part of the country. Share information through photographs, drawings, and writings about the activities in which the children in the class are involved or community activities that are particularly meaningful to them.

- Include books that show people from other cultures or people in unfamiliar jobs dealing with issues or doing things that are similar to the issues and activities of people with whom the children are familiar.

- Guide older children to illustrate and write books about things they can do to help others, e.g., set the table for a family meal, help a classmate clean up, teach a classmate how to perform a task or use a new material or game.

Objective 31

Explores change related to familiar people or places

31

To gain a sense of history, children must first understand that people and places change over time. Change is difficult for young children to understand because they focus on the here and now (Seefeldt, 1997). Children can learn about time and change in relation to themselves, including their daily schedule, what they did yesterday, and what they will do tomorrow. The calendar, when used appropriately, can help preschool and kindergarten children understand the passage of time. When children use the calendar to count the days until a special event, they are learning about the future. When they count the number of days since they lost their first tooth, they are learning to think about the past. Preschool children love to think about what they can do now that they could not do when they were babies. They can appreciate stories about other times and places that are relevant to their own experiences (Dodge, Colker, & Heroman, 2002).

As you create exploratory opportunities and plan experiences for children, think about how each child explores the concept of change. Focus your observations on

HOW AND WHEN THE CHILD

- demonstrates understanding that people and things change over time

- shows that time can be measured

- communicates about time, e.g., uses words such as *yesterday, today, tomorrow, day, week, month, minute, hour*

Objective 31 Explores change related to familiar people or places

Strategies

- Use children in the class to demonstrate change over time. For example, have children place photos of themselves and their friends at different ages in a series from youngest to oldest. Create scrapbooks of each child's life. Include photographs, art, dictations, notes, or other artifacts about important events and accomplishments. Talk about changes over time.

- Take photos of children engaged in the same activity or in the same location during different times of the year. Discuss changes the children notice.

- Provide opportunities for children to recall family memories or events in the community. For example, children might tell a story about something that happened when they were babies or make collages that illustrate a recent visit to grandparents.

- Involve grandparents or other senior citizens in the program. For example, ask them to tell simple stories of what life was like when they were young. Support children to generate interview questions as they talk with elders. They might ask, "What did you like to play when you were little?" or "What was your favorite fruit when you were little?" or "What is your favorite fruit now?"

- Display photographs of buildings in the community. As the year progresses, look for changes that occur. For example, children might notice that a building was painted or another had a "Going out of business" sign in the window. Talk about the changes and about what may have contributed to the changes.

- Invite the children to compare the sizes of clothes and shoes they wore at the beginning and end of the year.

- Avoid spending long periods on "calendar time" activities. Use calendars with preschool and kindergarten children in ways that are meaningful and functional. For example, you might mark special upcoming events at the beginning of the week or month. Indicate special recurring events such as, every other Thursday an elder volunteer reads a story. Indicate daily jobs such as who feeds the pet. Show what group project was completed. Involve children in determining what should be marked on the calendar and ways to do it.

Objective 32

Demonstrates simple geographic knowledge

32

Geography is the study of the earth's physical environment and the relationship of this environment to the people who live in it. The study of geography for young children needs to be relevant to their experiences. They can learn about the characteristics of the places where they live and the relationship between that place and other places (Dodge, Colker, & Heroman, 2002).

Preschool and kindergarten children often make simple maps to show their understanding of familiar places, e.g., classroom, play yard, neighborhood. Their first attempts at mapmaking may be with three-dimensional constructions in the block, sand, or art areas. Children's experiences with mapmaking help them to develop the concepts of representation, symbolization, perspective, and scale (Lenhoff & Huber, 2000).

As you create exploratory opportunities and plan experiences for children, think about how they demonstrate simple geographic knowledge. Focus your observations on

HOW AND WHEN THE CHILD

- demonstrates understanding that we are surrounded by geographical features, e.g., mountain, hill, desert, lake, river, creek, bayou, and there is specific information that identifies a location, e.g., address

- communicates that we depend on people who live far away for many necessities and information

- shows increasing understanding that maps are tools with symbols that help us locate objects, find where we are, and where we are going

Objective 32 Demonstrates simple geographic knowledge

Strategies

- Invite children to build, construct, or create various geographic landscapes. Provide materials to support their ideas. For example, you might offer sea shells, large rocks, or grasses for children to use in the sand and water table as they create mountains, the sea shore, or rivers and levees.

- Take walks in the neighborhood. Take photos of landmarks that children can use to create representations of their immediate environment. For example, you might take a picture of a nearby bridge or a hill or large mountain seen from the play yard. Attach photos with laminating paper onto blocks for children to use in block play.

- Support children as they create maps of familiar places. For example, provide chalk and encourage children to make a map of the play yard on the concrete. Offer blocks and landscape toys for children to make a map of the classroom.

- Read books and plan activities that focus on a variety of geographical regions. For example, after reading *Make Way for Ducklings* (Robert McCloskey), support children to work together to create a mural or diorama of the pond and island where the ducklings went to live.

- Use children's personal travels as a springboard for discussion of other places. With younger children, talk about possible landmarks such as a lake or tall mountain. With older preschool and kindergarten children, refer to the city and state, and locate children's travels on a map or globe.

- Assist older children in creating a "Where does it come from?" web or diagram. For example, kindergarten children might study how the milk they have at school gets to the cafeteria. They might use observation, books, the Internet, and interviews to help them get the needed information.

The Arts

Children express themselves creatively through the visual arts, music, dance and movement, and drama. In addition to using the arts to create, children can also develop an awareness and appreciation of the art of others. The arts are intrinsically rewarding as an avenue for expressing feelings and ideas that may be difficult to share verbally. Other areas of learning and development are supported when children are involved in the arts (Epstein, 2007). As children draw, paint, construct, mold, weave, dramatize, sing, dance, and move, they make new discoveries and integrate what they are learning.

The early childhood years are very important to children's realizing their creative potential (Kemple & Nissenberg, 2000). Their creative expressions and continued interest in the arts vary greatly according to the quantity and quality of their early experiences (Denac, 2008; Kemple & Nissenberg, 2000; Szechter & Liben, 2007; Zimmerman & Zimmerman, 2000). Children need time, space, supportive adults, opportunities to explore various media, and a variety of world experiences to enhance their creativity. When adults demonstrate techniques, children develop greater skill in expressing their creative ideas, but too much or too little structure can hinder the development of creative expression (Bae, 2004; Epstein, 2007; Jalongo & Isenberg, 2006). Activities such as coloring within the lines, imitating a model, competitions, and highly scripted performances do not further young children's creative expression (Jalongo & Isenberg, 2006).

THE ARTS OBJECTIVES

33 Explores the visual arts

34 Explores musical concepts and expression

35 Explores dance and movement concepts

36 Explores drama through actions and language

For children, the arts involve active exploration and inquiry. Infants respond to musical sounds by babbling and moving (Kenney, 1997). These experimentations satisfy the infants. They gain more control over vocalizations and movements during toddlerhood. During the preschool and kindergarten years, children perform, create, listen to, and describe music (Andress, 1995). Building on their early play behaviors, preschool and kindergarten children tell stories and dramatize a variety of increasingly complex, familiar, and imaginary scenarios.

Children's drawings, paintings, and other visual art creations change dramatically during early childhood (Thompson, 1995). Artwork begins almost by accident as the toddler experiments with materials. Children's creations evolve from what appear to adults to be random, unplanned expressions to more elaborate representations, during preschool and kindergarten, of people, objects, and events. During this time, the arts provide opportunities for collaboration with peers. Children engage in studies and demonstrate what they know through music, drama, dance and movement, and visual arts.

Objective 33

Explores the visual arts

33

Visual art experiences include painting, drawing, making collages, modeling and sculpting, building, making puppets, weaving and stitching, and printmaking. Children benefit from working with many different kinds of materials and having conversations about their artwork and the work of others (Bae, 2004; Colbert, 1997; Johnson, 2008). The more they are able to experiment with various media and to discuss different ways to use materials, the more children are able to express their ideas through the visual arts (Dodge, Colker, & Heroman, 2002).

As you create exploratory opportunities and plan experiences for children, think about how each child creates and responds to the visual arts. Focus your observations on

HOW AND WHEN THE CHILD

- shows appreciation for various forms of visual art
- shows appreciation for the artwork of peers
- communicates what he or she sees and how it makes him or her feel
- uses and cares for art materials
- explores different materials, tools, and processes
- shows increasing awareness of color, line, form, texture, space, and design in his or her artwork or the work of others
- communicates about his or her artwork, e.g., what it is made of, what he or she was thinking, and from where the idea comes

Objective 33 Explores the visual arts

Strategies

- Offer diverse, open-ended materials for children to explore. Include materials with different patterns, textures, and colors.

- Encourage children to explore various art media, tools, and processes. Provide opportunities to draw, paint, print, stitch, sculpt, photograph, and make collages.

- Encourage children to use various media to express their ideas. For example, they may represent the ideas expressed in a drawing by using blocks or collage materials.

- Incorporate technology. For example, offer drawing and painting software. Provide a camera. Invite children to paint while listening to different types of music.

- Encourage close observation as part of creative work. Model the examination of objects from different angles before drawing. Show children how to look from time to time to compare their drawings with the object, and to check when finished to see if anything else needs to be added.

- Demonstrate manipulative skills and how to use and care for art materials. For example, model how to cut and how to wipe a paintbrush on the edge of the cup.

- Display children's art creations attractively and prominently in the room, as much as possible at children's eye level. Show collaborative as well as individual work. Remove displays before the room becomes cluttered or when children lose interest.

- Talk about art techniques used by illustrators. For example, after reading books by Leo Lionni, discuss how he uses torn paper collage in his illustrations. Offer materials for children to experiment with and encourage them to try new techniques.

- Invite family members or local artists to share their work with the children. Get them to talk about the materials, tools, and techniques they use to create their work; how their work has changed over time; and if and where they display or sell their art.

- Ask open-ended questions that invite children to think about their creations and why they made particular choices. Take photos of their work, and record or audiotape their explanations.

- After exploring various art media, provide kindergarten children with opportunities to classify photographs of art by its medium. For example, they might sort photographs of clay sculptures, wood sculptures, fabric collages, mixed media collages, line drawings, and paintings into piles.

Objective 34

Explores musical concepts and expression

34

Music is combining voice, instrumental or mechanical sounds to create melody, rhythm, or harmony (Dodge, Colker, & Heroman, 2002). Children learn to appreciate different kinds of music and become comfortable with different forms of musical expression when they listen to recordings, create melodies, learn songs as a group, talk about sounds, and explore musical instruments. The teacher's expression of interest and choice of musical activities influence children's interest and musical development (Denac, 2008; Kenney, 1997). Music can affect children's literacy development and academic performance (Shore & Strasser, 2006; Wiggins, 2007). Musical activities that relate to story reading can focus children's attention and enhance their social interactions (deVries, 2008).

As you create exploratory opportunities and plan experiences for children, think about how each child relates to musical concepts and expression. Focus your observations on

HOW AND WHEN THE CHILD

- shows awareness and appreciation of different kinds of music

- expresses thoughts, feelings, and energy through music

- shows increasing awareness of various components of music: melody (tune), pitch (high and low sounds), rhythm (the beat), tempo (speed), dynamics (changes in volume), and timbre (sound quality distinguishing one instrument or voice from another)

Objective 34 Explores musical concepts and expression

Strategies

- Include music and movement experiences and activities throughout the day. Use musical activities as you transition children from one activity to another. Include songs or movement activities as part of most large-group activities. Sing or use musical instruments during outdoor activities.

- Encourage children to make up new lyrics and actions to familiar tunes or to create their own songs. Include software that enables children to create tunes.

- Personalize songs. For example, sing the child's name or the name of a favorite food.

- Create songbooks or song charts with pictures to illustrate songs children frequently sing.

- Play a variety of music. Offer different genres, such as jazz, country, classical, or rock and roll. Include music that inspires children to move quickly (polka) or slowly (lullaby). Discuss differences and how each type of music makes them feel.

- Include songs and lullabies from many cultures. Teach children songs that are familiar to their families so they can sing them together.

- Encourage children to focus on particular musical elements through your comments and questions. Use words such as *pitch* (*high, low, up, down*); *rhythm* or *beat* (*steady, fast, slow*); *volume* (*loud, soft*); and *duration* (*long, short*).

- Provide a variety of musical instruments from various cultures for children to explore.

- Involve children in making their own musical instruments. Encourage them to explore sounds by modifying their instruments. For example, compare the sounds of empty coffee can drums to those of drums with water in them.

- Invite musicians to bring instruments. Have them play and talk about their instruments.

- Transform the Dramatic Play area into a musical stage or recording studio. Include musical instruments, a toy microphone, an audio recorder, and other appropriate props.

- Make printed music available to children. Support older preschool and kindergarten children's experimentation with musical symbols and notations. For example, provide staff paper for beginners and encourage children to "write" music. Encourage children to "read" their music and to perform by singing or playing an instrument. Audiotape their creations.

Objective 35

Explores dance and movement concepts

35

One of the first ways that children express themselves is through movement. Each new movement gives children more information about the capabilities of their bodies (Lutz & Kuhlman, 2000). Dance involves using one's body to express ideas and feelings and to response to music. Preschool children demonstrate knowledge of dance and movement in many ways when they imitate animals or use scarves and streamers as they respond to music. Movement, taught with pretend imagery, is beneficial to children's learning and enjoyment of dance (Sacha & Russ, 2006). Teachers can help children learn *how* their bodies can move, *where* their bodies can move, and the *relationships* among parts of their own bodies, relationships with other persons, and relationships among persons in space (Sanders, 2002).

As you create exploratory opportunities and plan experiences for children, think about how each child relates to dance and movement. Focus your observations on

HOW AND WHEN THE CHILD

- communicates feelings and ideas through dance and movement

- demonstrates spatial awareness (*where* the body moves): location (separate or shared space); directions (up or down, forward or backward); levels (low, middle, high); and pathways (straight, curved, zigzag)

- demonstrates effort awareness (*how* the body moves): speed (fast or slow); force (strong or light); and control (bound or free)

- demonstrates relational awareness (*relationships* the body creates): with the physical self (body parts); with body shapes and size (big, small, straight); roles with other people (leading or following, mirroring, alternating); and in space (near or far, over or under, around or through)

Objective 35 Explores dance and movement concepts

Strategies

- Encourage children to participate in various creative movement activities. For example, they might move like an elephant, a swan, falling leaves, a kite, a windstorm, or growing plants.

- Model movements and invite children to join you. Suggest new movements and techniques or ways to combine different actions.

- Use pretend imagery. Have children first imagine the movement and then carry it out. For example, they might close their eyes and imagine reaching for a small bird in a tree, and then they carry out the movements they envisioned.

- Use objects and props to help children focus. For example, use a blue mat as a pond and have children leap over the pond as if they were deer, rabbits, or frogs.

- Provide space and materials for dance and movement activities indoors and outdoors. Use large open spaces to support their exploration of movement and direction. Use small spaces for isolated movement and specific patterns. Offer streamers, ribbons, scarves, balloons, blankets, or parachutes.

- Use vocabulary that supports children's understanding of movement concepts. Describe *how* their bodies move in space (*fast, slow, heavy, light*). Tell *where* their bodies can move (*forward, backward, low, middle, high, straight, curved, zigzag*). Describe the *relationship* of their bodies to other people or objects (*near, far, leading, following, mirroring, together, apart*).

- Ask movement experts to visit. For example, invite a member of a dance troupe to demonstrate dance techniques and how to control body movements.

- Watch videos that show examples of a wide variety of dances in other cultures. Take children to see a children's ballet or other dance performance.

- Involve children in designing and making scenery or stage sets for performances.

Objective 36

Explores drama through actions and language

36

Drama is portraying characters and telling stories though action, dialogue, or both (Dodge, Colker, & Heroman, 2002). Drama is an important part of development and learning for young children. It positively affects children's language development and literacy, self-awareness, social–emotional reasoning, and problem solving (Brown, 1990; Pinciotti, 1993; Wright, et al., 2008). As children participate with others in drama-related play, they develop basic skills and knowledge in the use of props, movement, pantomime, sound, speech, character, and story making (Pinciotti, 1993). Children learn to tell stories through repeated exchanges with people who are important to them. Experiences and cultural traditions influence what stories children tell and how they tell stories (Curenton & Ryan, 2006; Wright et al., 2008). Adult guidance is important in helping children develop the skills they need act out scenarios and stories. When teachers read stories for later dramatization or provide children with puppets to act out a story, clothing they can use for dress up, and props that can transform blocks into an imaginary city, they are teaching children drama. As children play with materials such as these, they express their feelings and process their experiences.

As you create exploratory opportunities and plan experiences for children, think about how each child explores drama. Focus your observations on

HOW AND WHEN THE CHILD

- shows that real-life roles can be enacted
- communicates a message or story through action and dialogue
- represents ideas through drama, e.g., pretends to be the big bad wolf
- shows appreciation of the dramatizations of others

Note: See Objective 14 for related information about sociodramatic play.

Objective 36 Explores drama through actions and language

Strategies

- Extend the play of children by encouraging additional scenarios. Provide a variety of props for the exploration of different roles.

- Extend children's play by helping them to see a range of actions, solutions, and possibilities. Provide opportunities to act out different characters and feelings. For example, have children make angry, fierce, sad, joyful, kind, and brooding faces. Provide an imaginary bag with imaginary costumes and have children use them in their play.

- Provide verbal prompts to support children's dramatizations. For example, to help children get started you might say, "Act as though...," "Imagine you are...," or "Once there was a..." To help them continue, say, "Then what happened?" or "What happened next?" To help them close, you might prompt, "How did it end?" or "What happened last?"

- Invite children to dramatize stories you read. Read the story, calling attention to the setting, mood, characters, and plot. Provide puppets or other props for children to use to enact the story. Read the story a second time, pausing so children can act out the various parts.

- Invite children to act out familiar stories such as *Caps for Sale*.

- Encourage children to build scenery and props for dramatization. For example, they might create houses to act out *The Three Little Pigs* or make masks to dramatize *The Three Billy Goats Gruff*.

- Encourage children to dictate stories to act out later. Send copies of stories home for children to enact with their families.

- Attend a children's theater performance or arrange for a mime, actor, or storyteller to visit.

- Provide opportunities for children to try different theater roles. For example, they might be the writer, actor, director, designer, or audience member. Support them as they develop knowledge and skills in the use of props, movement, pantomime, sound, speech, character, and storytelling.

English Language Acquisition

Language learning is a basic feature of the early development of all children. If a child is raised in a family in which English is spoken, she will learn to speak English. If a child is raised in a family in which Spanish is spoken, he will learn to speak Spanish. If a child is raised in a family in which both English and Spanish are spoken, she will become bilingual as she learns both languages. If a child is raised in a family in which Spanish is spoken and the child attends an early childhood classroom in which English is spoken, he will be a second-language learner, adding English to his home language of Spanish. Bilingual children, who are also called *simultaneous* language learners, and second-language-learning children, who are also called *sequential* language learners, are both presented with a challenging cognitive task: They must learn and maintain two languages, rather than just one. Therefore children in both of these groups are dual-language learners.

The language-learning process for simultaneous language learners closely resembles the process for monolingual children. However, because of simultaneous language learners' need to know twice as many words, their vocabulary development may be less extensive in each language in comparison to monolingual children (Oller & Eilers, 2002).

Young sequential language learners follow a slightly different developmental sequence. At first these children may continue to use their home language in a second-language setting. Later, when they realize that their home language is not being understood, they enter a nonverbal period during which they gain receptive abilities in the new language and may experiment with language sounds. Next, they begin to use memorized words and

---

ENGLISH LANGUAGE ACQUISITION

37 Demonstrates progress in listening to and understanding English

38 Demonstrates progress in speaking English

phrases in their new language, and some of the phrases might be quite long. Finally they develop productive use of the new language, constructing original sentences with the words and phrases they already know (Tabors, 2008). This sequence is not specific to a particular language, so Objectives 37 and 38 may be adapted to assess progress in acquiring any second language. The language in the examples must be modified to reflect the new language the child is learning.

Learning a second language is cumulative and often uneven. Children may sound very sophisticated in situations where they know the vocabulary and the grammar that they need in order to be understood. In other situations, however, they might be unable to communicate because of emotional or linguistic constraints (Tabors, 2008).

One of the major concerns about young children who are learning a second language in a society where that is the dominant language is that the first language may no longer be developed. The loss of the first language can be detrimental for personal, familial, religious, and cultural reasons (Wong Fillmore, 1991b). Furthermore, research shows that the second-language learners who do best in school are those who have a strong grounding in their home language (Collier, 1987).

There are considerable individual differences in how young children take on the task of learning a second language. Highly motivated children, children with more exposure to the new language, children who are older when they begin the process, and children who have more outgoing personalities may make more rapid progress. Some children may spend an entire year in the nonverbal period, while others may start to use social words right away. Second-language learners may be socially isolated because of their inability to communicate. Effective teachers use strategies to integrate these children into classroom activities, and they develop techniques for helping children begin to understand and use their new language.

Demonstrates progress in listening to and understanding English

37

The first task for second-language learners is to gain receptive understanding of the new language. Once they have learned that they are in an environment where a new language is being used and that they will need to use that language if they want to be understood, they must begin to hear the sounds of the new language and begin the process of connecting those sounds to the objects and activities around them. Children take on this task at different rates (Saville-Troike, 1988; Wong Fillmore, 1979; Itoh & Hatch, 1978). If it is possible to communicate in their home language with adults and children in the classroom, they may choose to do so without making the effort to learn the new language (Meyer, 1989). If they find that nonverbal communication is effective, they may use that for a considerable period of time.

However, once motivated to begin to understand the new language—because they want to play with peers or want to understand the teachers who are using the new language—they begin to observe and listen closely. At this time children use *spectating* behaviors, focusing their attention on how words are formed, and *rehearsing* behaviors, mouthing words or practicing by saying words to themselves (Tabors, 2008). As they acquire the phonology of the new language, children may also play with the sounds of the language by inventing new words (Saville-Troike, 1988).

Classroom routines and the language used in those contexts help children begin to understand the new language. However, assessing children's receptive abilities can be complicated by the fact that young learners are extremely good at guessing meaning from context. In order to check receptive comprehension, teachers must be careful that they are assessing understanding without providing contextual cues like gestures or eye gaze.

Objective 37 Demonstrates progress in listening to and understanding English

1	2 Beginning	3	4 Progressing	5	6 Increasing	7	8 Advancing	9
	Observes others as they converse in English during play or other small-group experiences; may engage in similar activities by imitating behavior; attends to oral use of English • Moves closer to the dramatic play area to watch a small group of children • Sits across from two children who are stringing beads and talking, and begins stringing beads, too • Watches another child hold up a cup to request milk and does the same • Participates by doing hand movements while other children and the teacher sing in the new language		**Responds to common English words and phrases when they are accompanied by gestures or other visual aids** • Joins a group in the block area when one child motions with a hand to come, and says, "Come play." • Goes to the sink when the teacher says it is time to brush teeth and pantomimes toothbrushing • Nods when classmate says, "Hello." • Sits by the teacher when she holds up a book and asks, "Would you like to read a book?"		**Responds to words and phrases in English when they are not accompanied by gestures or other visual aids** • Goes to table when teacher says, "It's lunchtime. Take your seats at the tables." • Puts the caps on the markers and then puts the markers on the shelf when reminded • Points to ear when asked, "Where's your ear?" • Picks up a car from a group of toys when asked, "Where's the car?" • Picks up the puzzle with the puppy on it when another child says, "Let's do the puppy puzzle together."		**Understands increasingly complex English phrases used by adults and children** • Responds by putting the correct block where directed when another child says, "Hey, put that square block over there by the horse to make the fence." • Points to the correct piece when the teacher asks, "Which circle is the biggest?" • Touches the car at the top of the tallest ramp when the teacher asks, "Which car do you think will roll the fastest?"	

Objective 37 Demonstrates progress in listening to and understanding English

Strategies

- Gather personal information from each family, including what language or languages are spoken at home and which family members speak them. In-depth information includes an estimate of how much time each person in the home spends using a particular language with the child, and what language or languages the child uses when speaking with each family member.

- If the child is using a language other than English at home, ask whether or not a parent feels the child is making appropriate progress in that language.

- If you do not share the home language with an English-language learner, ask the parents for a few words in the home language that can be used to welcome the child to the classroom. If parents agree, make a tape recording of these words to use in the classroom to comfort their child or to help other children hear the sounds of the child's home language.

- Set up classroom routines and use consistent language when referring to activities (clean-up time) and objects (cubby, block area) throughout the day in the classroom.

- Make sure English-language learners are included in situations in the classroom where they can hear English. Assign seating so that English-language learners are near English-speaking children during activities, or snack, group time, and rest time.

- Pair an English-language learner with an outgoing English-speaking child for certain periods during the day, so that the English-speaking child may help to integrate the English-language learner into classroom activities.

- When speaking English with an English-language learner, use these guidelines:

  - Speak slowly. This helps children hear and learn the individual words.

  - Use repetition. When children hear the same word used multiple times for an object, they are more likely to make the connection between the spoken word and the name of the object.

  - Simplify your message.

  - Place important words at the end of a sentence and emphasize those words. For example, "This is your *hand*. Do you want to trace your hand?"

  - Double the message with gestures, actions, visual aids, or directed gaze while you are talking. For example, when asking children to put on their coats, model putting on your own coat. These visual aids help children understand what is being said.

  - Use *running commentary* by telling English-language learners what you are doing as you are doing it. For example say, "Now I will put the milk in the batter."

  - Use parallel talk, describing the actions of the child, "You are stacking the blue block on top of the red block."

- Be alert to an English-language learner's use of non-verbal communication, such as pointing silently to a paint brush. Supply the words in English for what the child is trying to communicate. For example, "You want the paint brush? Here is the paint brush."

- Talk about what is right in front of the English-language-learning child, so the context will be obvious.

- Provide pictures to accompany the daily schedule, classroom rules, and other print in the classroom. This helps children know the expectations even though they may not yet understand the language.

- Use repetitive songs and games during group times. Children who are English-language learners often say their first words in English when singing familiar songs and fingerplays.

- Read books in children's home languages if possible prior to reading the book in English to them. This helps them become familiar with the words and the story line before hearing it in English. Reading it in the home language should not happen immediately prior to reading it in English, but rather earlier in the day or the week.

- Choose books with repetitive refrains when reading aloud with English-language learners. Read the same books over and over again so that the words become very familiar to them.

Objective 37 Demonstrates progress in listening to and understanding English

Strategies, *continued*

- Supply English words for any object that an English-language learner shows interest in (often they will bring objects to you to identify). Then see if you can elicit what the name for that object is in the child's home language.

- Plan small-group activities so that there are times when an activity is done with only English-language-learning children and all language can be tailored to their needs, and there are times when the group has both English-language-learning children and English-speaking children and the language can be more complex.

- Keep talking. English-language-learning children will need lots and lots of input to hear the sounds of English and to begin to understand what they mean.

Demonstrates progress in speaking English

38

The second task for second-language learners is to begin the process of using their new language. Most children begin by repeating words or phrases, either in one-on-one interactions with adults or in group situations when all of the children are using the same words, for instance, during a group sing-along.

A distinct feature of young children's second-language acquisition is their memorization and use of social interactive terms (Wong Fillmore, 1976, 1979) to help them enter play situations and to have their needs met. Once children have acquired a number of words and socially useful phrases, they can begin to construct original sentences. Eventually second-language learners use the input from speakers of the new language to develop their ability to use questions, negatives, and past and future tenses. Second-language learners make many of the same mistakes made by young children learning their home language. Throughout this process, second-language learners continue to acquire vocabulary so they will have the words they need in order to communicate verbally with other speakers of the new language.

Objective 38 Demonstrates progress in speaking English

1	2	3	4	5	6	7	8	9
	Beginning		Progressing		Increasing		Advancing	

Repeats sounds and words in English, sometimes very quietly • Mouths the words of a song during circle time • Echoes a word or phrase, e.g., says, "Monkey," while group chants "Five Little Monkeys Jumping on the Bed" • After teacher says, "Up," child repeats, "Up." • Repeats, "Mil, mil, mil," after the teacher asks, "Would you like more milk?"	**Uses a few socially interactive terms in English appropriately; uses one or two words in English to represent a whole idea** • Says , "Hi"; "Lookit"; "My turn"; and "Stopit." • Hears someone nearby say, "Be careful!" and repeats phrase as a warning in a similar situation later • Points at snack basket and says, "More crackers." • Looks out the window and says, "Go outside." • Says, "No, mine," when another child takes her toy truck	**Develops multiword phrases by using socially interactive terms in English; adds new words to the phrase** • Says, "I do a ice cream"; "I want my mommy"; and "Lookit this, Teacher." • Says, "How you do this flower?" • Says, "Big. I gotta big." • Says, "How do you gonna make dese?"	**Uses increasingly complex grammar in English; makes some mistakes typical of young children** • Develops entire sentences, e.g., "The door is a square," and "The house has a lot of windows." • Uses questions and negatives, e.g., "Your name is what?" and "You no my mommy." • Uses past and future tenses, e.g., "I goed to the park," and "I'll get it." • Interacts in elaborate play schemes, "I be the mommy and you be the baby. Here's your bottle, Baby."

Objective 38 Demonstrates progress in speaking English

Strategies

- Spend time one-on-one with English-language learners; they may be more likely to start using English if they are not in a group situation.

- Be alert to children beginning to use English very softly, perhaps rehearsing what they want to say.

- Use repetitive songs, games and fingerplays during group times. Children who are English-language learners often say their first words in English when singing familiar songs and fingerplays. Singing in a group helps give children a secure environment in which to try out their emerging English skills.

- Try to have English-language-learning children repeat words as you demonstrate what objects or illustrations they refer to.

- Validate children's language attempts in either language. If English-language-learners use their home language, acknowledge their effort, and if you can guess what they are talking about, respond in English.

- Give English-language-learners lots of time to think about what they want to say. If you ask a question ("what would you like to do?") wait longer than you would normally. It may take longer for the children to think of the words they want to say in English.

- For children who are at the beginning stages of learning English, ask close-ended questions and offer some options for response ("Would you like to paint or would you like to build?")

- When reading books with repetitive refrains, pause and let the children fill in the next word. For example, "Brown bear, brown bear, what do you_____?" This helps children feel successful and builds confidence when they know what comes next and are able to fill in the missing word.

- Intentionally introduce new vocabulary words. Use those words frequently in different contexts throughout the day. Provide visual aids and gestures to illustrate the meaning of the words.

- Give English-language-learners a chance to respond in English in group situations when they can answer in chorus with all of the children.

- Encourage families to bring pictures and objects from home. Children are more likely to talk about things they know and that are familiar to them. Children are also more likely to engage in dramatic play if objects similar to what they see used at home are included in the classroom.

- Engage children in conversations on interesting topics that connect to their daily lives. This provides children opportunities to express ideas and thoughts about things that are relevant and important to them.

- Expand and extend any effort that a child makes to use English. For example, when a child says, "car", you might say, "Yes! That's a racing car."

- Notice which phrases a child uses ("Hey," "OK," "Mine," "Stopit") and help the child build from those phrases ("Hey you," "I'm okay," "That's mine," "Stopit, please.").

- Make learning new vocabulary words in English a primary goal of instruction and all communication. Choose words you want all of the children to know and use them repeatedly in the classroom. Introduce the words using objects or illustrations and develop activities during which the children will need to use these words.

- Help children move from nonverbal responses to productive responses by prompting them with questions. For example, when a child points to her untied shoe ask, "What do you need?" If the child does not respond ask, "Do you need me to tie your shoe?" When the child responds, "Tie...shoe," recognize her effort and say, "Okay! I will tie your shoe."

- Encourage interactions between English-language-learners and English-speaking children by modeling initiations. For example, you might say to a child, "Ask Sally, 'May I play with you?'"

- Model correct English versions of phrases used by English-language learners. For example, if a child says, "I goed to the store," you respond, "You went to the store? What did you get?"

Glossary

/ /: surrounding a letter, diagonal lines indicate the sound (rather than the name) of that letter, e.g., /k/ for the initial consonant sound in *cat* or /s/ for the initial consonant sound in *cell*

abstract symbol: a sign, figure, mark, image, or numeral that is used to represent an object, person, concept, idea, or number

alliteration: the repetition of initial consonant sounds in two or more neighboring words, e.g., *big blue balloons*

alphabetic principle: the fact that written words are composed of letters that represent sounds

areas of development and learning: the broadest domains of development and learning, e.g., *Social–Emotional*

attend: pay attention to an activity or experience

colored bands: in *Objectives for Development & Learning*, the colored bands or lines (red, orange, yellow, green, blue, and purple) that show the age or the class/grade ranges for widely held developmental and learning expectations

compare and contrast: examine the relationship between two items or groups of items to determine how they are alike and how they are different

count on: a strategy by which a child figures out a quantity by beginning with the sum of a small number of objects and then counts the remaining objects until he counts them all. For example, with a group of five objects, the child might say "Three," and then point to the remaining objects, saying, "Four, five. I have five." *Counting on* is a more advanced strategy than *counting all*, in which a child would count "One, two, three, four, five. I have five."

decontextualized language: language that is not tied to the immediate context, e.g., that refers to past events, future events, or imaginary scenarios

dimension: a specific aspect or subskill of an objective, e.g., *Manages feelings* or *Follows limits and expectations*

direction: related to where a person or thing is going or from where a person or thing has come

distance: how near or far away a person or object is located

dual-language learners: children who acquire two or more languages simultaneously, as well as those who learn a second language while continuing to develop their first language

engaged in learning: when children are focused, deeply interested, and involved in experiences through which they gain knowledge and skills. When they are engaged, children attend to and persist with tasks.

engage: interact or become deeply involved with a person or activity

examples: in *Objectives for Development & Learning*, different ways that children show what they know and can do, e.g., *Moves to the sand table at the suggestion of an adult when there are too many at the art table*

explanatory talk: talk that consists of explaining and describing, including definitions of words; discussion of cause-and-effect relationships; and discussion of connections between ideas, events, and actions

"fair share" groups: the result of dividing objects, food, etc. into groups so that each person gets an equal or approximately equal amount

fine-motor skills: small movements that involve the small muscles of the fingers and wrists, such as grasping something with one's thumb and index finger

gallop: a traveling movement that involves leaping (taking a big step forward), keeping the same foot in front of the body at all times, and bringing the rear foot to meet the front foot

genre: a kind or type of art (e.g., folk art and modern art), literature (e.g., picture books and poetry), or music (e.g., classical music and pop music)

gross-motor skills: large movements that involve the large muscles in the arms, legs, torso, and feet, such as running and jumping

growing pattern: a pattern that increases by at least plus one and continues to increase, e.g., a block staircase

home language: a language spoken in the home that is different from the main language spoken in the community

indicators: descriptions of knowledge, skills, or behaviors that children demonstrate at four levels of each developmental progression. In *Objectives for Development & Learning*, these statements are in bold underneath levels 2, 4, 6, and 8, e.g., *Accepts redirection from adults.*

invented spelling (also called *sound spelling* or *developmental spelling*): a child's attempt to spell words by writing a letter for each sound he or she notices. This is an important step toward conventional spelling.

large ball: a beach ball or playground ball

lowercase letters: the letters of the alphabet that are not uppercase (capital) letters, e.g., *a*, *b*, and *c*. Although children often refer to these as "small" letters, adults should use the term *lowercase* when referring to them because their actual size varies from text to text

levels: in *Objectives for Development & Learning*, the rating scale that describes specific points along the progression for each objective

listen (vs. hear): to pay attention to sound, to hear something with thoughtful attention, or to be alert to catch an expected sound

location: relates to positional language that indicates where a person or thing is situated

nonstandard measuring tools: tools that are not formal measuring tools. These may have units of equal length (e.g., same-sized cubes, links, or paper clips) or unequal length (e.g., children's strides).

numeral: the symbol that represents a number, e.g., the number *four* is shown as the numeral *4*

objective: a statement of expectations of knowledge, skills, and behaviors, e.g., *Regulates own emotions and behaviors*

onset: the first consonant sound(s) before the vowel in a one-syllable word, e.g., /k/ in *cat* and /th/ in *think*

parentese: singsong speech and exaggerated facial expressions. This type of communication encourages young infants to listen and focus on what is said.

persist: remain focused on an activity for an adequate length of time

phoneme: the smallest unit of sound in a word

pictorial map: a map that uses drawings or pictures to represent objects in the environment

phonological awareness: the understanding that spoken language can be divided into smaller and smaller units that can be manipulated

position: an indication of where a person or object is located in relation to someone or something else

progress checkpoints: three or four points during the year when teachers determine the progress a child is making toward an objective

progressions of development and learning: paths, or trajectories, that children typically follow when acquiring a skill or behavior

proximity: the closeness or nearness of something, often described as *beside*, *next to*, *touching*, or *alongside*

redirection: guiding children's behavior by restating or providing an attractive alternative

repeating pattern: a pattern in which the core unit repeats a minimum of five times, e.g., red, blue; red, blue; red, blue; red, blue; red, blue

rhyme: words with the same ending sounds but not necessarily the same ending letters.

rime: the vowel sound and all the sounds that follow the vowel in a syllable or one-syllable word, e.g., /at/ in *cat* and /ink/ in *think*

scenario: a series of real or imagined events

secure attachment: the strong emotional bond or trusting relationship between a child and an important person in his or her life

secure base: a familiar, trusted adult to whom a child returns for protection when the child becomes frightened or uneasy in the process of exploring his or her world

self-talk: (sometimes referred to as *private speech*) the language an adult uses with children to describe his or her actions at the time they are being performed, e.g., "Now I am putting milk in the refrigerator."

skip: a traveling movement involving a step and a hop, using alternating feet

sociodramatic play: dramatic play, e.g., role-playing or fantasy play, with the additional component of social interaction with either a peer or an adult

standard measuring tools: tools that mark units of measurement with numerals, e.g., rulers, measuring tapes, and meter sticks

story-related problems: in sophisticated picture books, the difficulties characters face that the reader must infer from the information provided. These problems require the reader to analyze information and make predictions.

subitize: to quickly glance at a small group of objects and identify the quantity without counting the objects one at a time

tally: use marks to keep a record of whatever has been counted

tally marks: one-to-one representations of counted items, usually vertical and diagonal lines arranged in groups of five with four vertical lines in a row "crossed" by one descending diagonal line

teaching strategies: what teachers can do to support and scaffold children's learning as it relates to a particular objective

three-dimensional shape: a figure that has width, height, and depth (thickness), e.g., a sphere, cube, triangular prism, cone, cylinder, or pyramid

two-dimensional shape: a figure that has width and height only, e.g., a circle, square, rectangle, triangle, or pentagon

uppercase letters: the capital letters of the alphabet, e.g., *A*, *B*, and *C*. Although children often refer to these as "big" letters, adults should use the term *uppercase* when referring to them because their actual size varies from text to text

References

Adams, M. J. (1990). *Beginning to read: Thinking and learning about print.* Urbana, IL: University of Illinois Center for the Study of Reading.

Adams, M. J. (2001). Alphabetic anxiety and explicit systematic phonics instruction: A cognitive science perspective. In S. B. Neuman & D. K. Dickinson (Eds.), *Handbook of early literacy research* (pp. 66–80). New York: Guilford Press.

American Academy of Pediatrics (2003). *Baby & Child Health.* Jennifer Shu, M.D., Editor-in-Chief, New York: DK Publishing.

Andress, B. (1991). From research to practice: Preschool children and their movement responses to music. *Young Children, 47*(1), 22–27.

Andress, B. (1995). Transforming curriculum in music. In S. Bredekamp & T. Rosegrant (Eds.), *Reaching potentials: Transforming early childhood curriculum and assessment,* Vol. 2 (pp. 99–108). Washington, DC: National Association for the Education of Young Children.

Anthony, J. L., Lonigan, C., Driscoll, K., Phillips, B. M., & Burgess, S. R. (2003).Preschool phonological sensitivity: A quasi-parallel progression of word structure units and cognitive operations. *Reading Research Quarterly, 38,* 470–487.

Araujo, N., & Aghayan, C. (2006). *Easy songs for smooth transitions in the classroom.* St. Paul, MN: Redleaf Press.

Arnone, M. P. (2003). *Using instructional design strategies to foster curiosity.* Retrieved July 9, 2007, from http://www.marilynarone.com/ERIC%20Digest%20on%20Curiosity%20and%201D.pdf

Arste, J. C., Woodward, V. A. & Burcke, C. I. (1984). *Language stories and literacy lessons.* Portsmouth: Heinemann.

Aubrey, C. (2001). Early mathematics. In T. David (Ed.), *Promoting evidenced-based practice in early childhood education: Research and its implications, Vol. 1,* (pp. 185–210). Amsterdam: Elsevier Science.

August, D., & Hakuta, K. (1998). *Educating language minority children.* New York: National Academy Press.

Ayoub, C. C. & Fischer, K. W. (2006). Developmental pathways and intersections among domains of development. In K. McCartney & D. Phillips (Eds.), *Blackwell handbook of early childhood development* (pp. 62–81).

Bae, J. (2004). Learning to teach visual arts in an early childhood classroom: The teacher's role as a guide. *Early Childhood Education Journal, 31*(1), 247–254.

Baghban, M. (2007). Immigration in childhood: Using picture books to cope. *The Social Studies, 98*(2), 71–76.

Bailey, A. (2008). Assessing the language of young learners. In N. H. Hornberger, P. Clapham, & C. Corson (Eds.), *Encyclopedia of language and education,* Vol. 7., *Language testing and assessment* (2nd ed.), (pp. 379–400). New York: Springer Science Business Media.

Baker, B. L., & Brightman, A. J. (2004). *Steps to independence: Teaching everyday skills to children with special needs* (4th ed.). Baltimore, MD: Paul H. Brookes.

Barbour, A. C. (1999). The impact of playground design on the play behaviors of children with differing levels of physical competence. *Early Childhood Research Quarterly, 14,* 75–98.

Barkley, R. A. (1997). *ADHD and the nature of self-control.* New York: Guilford Press.

Baron-Cohen, S. (1995). *Mindblindness: An essay on autism and theory of mind.* London: MIT Press.

Baroody, A. J. (1987). *Children's mathematical thinking: A developmental framework for preschool, primary, and special education teachers.* New York: Teachers College, Columbia University.

Baroody, A. J. (2000). Research in Review: Does mathematics instruction for three-to five-year-olds really make sense? *Young Children, 55*(4), 61–67.

Baroody, A .J. (2004). The developmental bases for early childhood number and operations standards. In D. H. Clements, J. Sarama, & A. Diabiase (Eds.), *Engaging young children in mathematics: Standards for early childhood mathematics education* (pp. 173–220). Mahway, NJ: Lawrence Erlbaum Associates.

Baroody, A. J., & Wilkins, J. L. M. (1999). The development of informal counting, number, and arithmetic skills and concepts. In J. V. Copley (Ed.), *Mathematics in the early years* (pp. 48–65). Reston, VA: National Council of Teachers of Mathematics.

Barry, E. S. (2006). Children's memory: A primer for understanding behavior. *Early Childhood Education Journal, 33,* 405–411.

Beals, D. E. (2001). Eating and reading: Links between family conversations with preschoolers and later language and literacy. In D. K. Dickenson & P. O. Tabors (Eds.), *Beginning literacy with language: Young children learning at home and school* (pp. 75–92). Baltimore: Paul H. Brookes.

Beckman, M., & Edwards, J. (2000). The ontogeny of phonological categories and the primacy of lexical learning in linguistic development. *Child Development, 71,* 240–249.

Beland, K. R. (1996). A school wide approach to violence prevention. In R. L. Hampton, P. Jenkins, & T. P. Gulatta (Eds.), *Preventing violence in America* (pp. 209–231). Thousand Oaks, CA: Sage Publications.

Benigno, J. P., & Ellis, S. (2004). Two is greater than three: Effects of older siblings on parental support of preschoolers' counting in middle-income families. *Early Childhood Research Quarterly, 19,* 4–20.

Benoit, L., Lehalle, H., & Jouen, F. (2004). Do young children acquire number words through subitizing or counting? *Cognitive development, 19*(3), 291–307.

Bergen, D. (2002). The role of pretend play in children's cognitive development. *Early Childhood Research and Practice, 4*(1). Retrieved May 27, 2007, from http://www.ecrp.uiuc.edu/v4n1/bergen.html.

Berger, S. E., Adolph, K. E., & Lobo, S. A. (2005). Out of the toolbox: Toddlers differentiate wobbly and wooden handrails. *Child Development, 76,* 1294–1307.

Berk, L. E. (2002). *Infants, children, & adolescents* (4th ed.). Boston: Allyn & Bacon.

Berk, L. E. (2006). Looking at kindergarten children. In D. F. Gullo (Ed.), *K today: Teaching and learning in the kindergarten year* (pp. 11–25). Washington, DC: National Association for the Education of Young Children.

Berk, L. E. (2009). *Child development* (8th ed.). Boston: Pearson.

Berk, L. E., & Winsler, A. (1995). *Scaffolding children's learning: Vygotsky and early childhood education.* Washington, DC: National Association for the Education of Young Children.

Bernstein, B. (1971). *Class codes and control. Vol. 1.* London: Routledge and Kegan Paul.

Bialystok, E., & Martin, M. M. (2004). Attention and inhibition in bilingual children: Evidence from the dimensional change card sort task. *Developmental Science, 7,* 325–339.

Bialystok, E., McBride-Chang, C., & Luk, G. (2005). Bilingualism, language proficiency, and learning to read in two writing systems. *Journal of Educational Psychology, 97,* 580–590.

Bialystok, E., & Senman, L. (2004). Executive processes in appearance-reality tasks: The role of inhibition of attention and symbolic representation. *Child Development, 75,* 562–579.

Bilmes, J. (2004). *Beyond behavior management: The six life skills children need to thrive in today's society.* St. Paul, MN: Redleaf Press.

Bilmes, J. (2006). *Common psychological disorders in young children: A handbook for childcare professionals.* St. Paul, MN: Redleaf Press.

Birbili, M. (2006). Mapping knowledge: Concept maps in early childhood education. *Early Childhood Research and Practice. 8*(2). Retrieved June 20, 2007, from http://www.ecrp.uiuc.edu/v8n2/birbili.html

Birch, S., & Ladd, G. (1997). The teacher-child relationship and children's early school adjustment. *Journal of School Psychology, 35,* 61–69.

Bisgaier, C. S., Samaras, T., & Russo, M. J. (2004). Young children try, try again: Using wood, glue, and words to enhance learning. *Young Children, 59*(4), 22–29.

Bjorklund, D. F. (2005). *Children's thinking: Cognitive development and individual differences.* Belmont, CA: Wadsworth Thomson Learning.

Black, B., & Hazen, N. L. (1990). Social status and patterns of communication in acquainted and unacquainted preschool children. *Developmental Psychology, 26,* 379–387.

Blair, C. (2002). School readiness: Integrating cognition and emotion in a neurobiological conceptualization of children's functioning at school entry. *American Psychologist, 57*(2), 111–127.

Blair, C. (2003). *Self-regulation and school readiness.* Retrieved May 24, 2007, from http://www.ericdigests.org/2004-1/self.htm

Blair, C., & Razza, R. P. (2007). Relating effortful control, executive function, and false belief understanding to emerging math and literacy ability in kindergarten. *Child Development, 78,* 647–663.

Blaut, J. M., & Stea, D. (1974). Mapping at the age of three. *Journal of Geography, 73*(7), 5–9.

Bloodgood, J. W. (1999). What's in a name? Children's name writing and literacy acquisition. *Reading Research Quarterly, 34*(3), 342–367.

Bodrova, E., & Leong, D.J. (2001). *The tools of the mind project: A case study of implementing the Vygotskyian approach in American early childhood and primary classrooms.* Geneva, Switzerland: International Bureau of Education, UNESCO.

Bodrova, E., & Leong, D. J. (2004). Chopsticks and counting chips: Do play and foundational skills need to compete for the teacher's attention in an early childhood classroom? In D. Koralek (Ed.), *Spotlight on young children and play* (pp. 4–11). Washington, DC: National Association for the Education of Young Children.

Bodrova E., & Leong, D. J. (2005). Self-regulation as a key to school readiness: How can early childhood teachers promote this critical competency? In M. Zaslow & I. Martinez-Beck (Eds.), *Critical issues in early childhood professional development* (pp. 223–270). Baltimore: Paul H. Brookes.

Bodrova, E., & Leong, D. J. (2008). Developing self-regulation in kindergarten: Can we keep all the crickets in the basket? *Young Children, 63*(2), 56–58.

Bosma, A. Domka, A., & Peterson, J. (2000). Improving motor skills in kindergartners. St. Xavier University (ERIC Document Reproduction Service No. ED453913). Retrieved August 10, 2008 from http://www.eric.ed.gov/contentdelivery/servlet/ERICServlet?accno=ED453913

Bowey, J. A., & Francis, J. (1991). Phonological analysis as a function of age and exposure to reading instruction. *Applied Psycholinguistics, 12*(1), 91–121.

Bowman, B., Donovan, M. S., & Burns, M. S. (Eds.). (2001). *Eager to learn: Educating our preschoolers.* Washington, DC: National Academy Press.

Bowman, B., & Moore, E. K. (2006). *School readiness and social-emotional development: Perspectives on cultural diversity.* Washington, DC: National Black Child Development Institute.

Bowman, B., & Stott, F. (1994). Understanding development in a cultural context: The challenge for teachers. In B. L. Mallory & R. S. New (Eds.), *Diversity and developmentally appropriate practices: Challenges for early childhood education* (pp. 119–133). New York: Teachers College Press.

Bredekamp, S., & Copple, C. (1997). *Developmentally appropriate practice in early childhood programs.* Washington, DC: National Association for the Education of Young Children.

Bredekamp, S., & Rosegrant, T. (1992). *Reaching potentials: Appropriate curriculum and assessment for young children,* Vol. 1. Washington, DC: National Association for the Education of Young Children.

Brenneman, K., & Louro, I. F. (2008). Science journals in the preschool classroom. *Early Childhood Education Journal, 36*(2), 113–119.

Breslin, C. M., Morton, J. R., & Rudisill, M. E. (2008). Implementing a physical activity curriculum into the school day: Helping early childhood teachers meet the challenge. *Early Childhood Education Journal, 35*, 429–437.

Briody, J., & McGarry, K. (2005). Using social studies to ease children's transitions. *Young Children, 60*(5), 38–42.

Bronson, M. B. (2000). *Self-regulation in early childhood.* New York: Guildford Press.

Bronson, M. B. (2006). Developing social and emotional competence. In D. F. Gullo, (Ed.), *K today: Teaching and learning in the kindergarten year* (pp. 47–56). Washington, DC: National Association for the Education of Young Children.

Brophy, J.E. (2004). *Motivating students to learn* (2nd ed.). Mahwah, NJ: Erlbaum.

Brown, V. (1990). Drama as an integral part of the early childhood curriculum. *Design for Arts in Education, 91*(6), 26–33.

Burger, L. K., & Miller, P. J. (1999). Early talk about the past revisited: Affect in working-class and middle-class children's co-narrations. *Journal of Child Language, 26*(1), 133–162.

Burgess, S. R., & Lonigan, C. J. (1998). Bidirectional relations of phonological sensitivity and prereading abilities: Evidence from a preschool sample. *Journal of Experimental Child Psychology, 70*(2), 117–141.

Burhans, K. K., & Dweck, C. S. (1995). Helplessness in early childhood: The role of contingent worth. *Child Development, 66*, 1719–1738.

Burton, R. A., & Denham, S. A. (1998). Are you my friend?: How two young children learned to get along with others. *Journal of Research in Childhood Education, 12*, 210–224.

Bus, A. G., & van IJzendoorn, M. H. (1988). Mother-child interactions, attachment, and emergent literacy: A cross-sectional study. *Child Development, 50*, 1262–1273.

Buysse, V. (1993). Friendships of preschoolers with disabilities in community-based child care settings. *Journal of Early Intervention, 17*, 380–395.

Buysse, V., Goldman, B. D., & Skinner, M. L. (2003). Friendship formation in inclusive early childhood classrooms: What is the teacher's role? *Early Childhood Research Quarterly, 18*, 485–501.

Campbell, F. A., Ramey, C. T., Pungello, E., Sparling, J., & Miller-Johnson, S. (2002). Early childhood education: Young adult outcomes from the Abecedarian project. *Applied Developmental Science, 6*, 42–57.

Campbell, N. E., & Foster, J. E. (1993). Play centers that encourage literacy development. *Early Childhood Education Journal, 21*(2), 22–26.

Campbell, S. B. (1995). Behavior problems in preschool children: A review of recent research. *Journal of Child Psychology and Psychiatry and Allied Disciplines, 36*, 113–149.

Campbell, S. B., Pierce, E. W., March, C. L., Ewing, I. J., & Szumowski, E. K. (1994). Hard-to-manage preschool boys: Symptomatic behavior across contexts and time. *Child Development, 65*, 836–851.

Carroll, J. M., Snowling, J. J., Hulme, C., & Stevenson, J. (2003). The development of phonological awareness in preschool children. *Developmental Psychology, 39*(5), 913–923.

Carruthers, P. (1996). *Autism as mind-blindness: An elaboration and partial defense.* Retrieved July 18, 2007, from http://cogprints.org/1193/00/autism.htm

Casby, M. W. (1997). Symbolic play of children with language impairment: A critical review. *Journal of Speech, Language, and Hearing Research, 40*(3), 468–479.

Cats, H. W., Fey, M. E., Zhang, X., & Tomblin, J. B. (2001). Estimating the risk of future reading difficulties in kindergarten children: A research-based model and clinical implications. *Language, Speech and Hearing Services in School, 32*, 38–50.

Chalufour, I., & Worth, K. (2004). *Building structures with young children: The Young Scientist Series.* St. Paul, MN: Redleaf Press.

Chalufour, I., & Worth, K. (2006). Science in Kindergarten. In D. F. Gullo (Ed.), *K today: Teaching and learning in the kindergarten year* (pp. 95–106). Washington, DC: National Association for the Education of Young Children.

Chaney, C. (1992). Language development, metalinguistic skills, and print awareness in 3-year-old children. *Applied Psycholinguistics, 13*, 485–514.

Chapin, J. R. (2006). The achievement gap in social studies and science starts early: Evidence from the Early Childhood Longitudinal Study (Survey). *The Social Studies, 97*(6), 231–238.

Charlesworth, R. (2005a). *Experiences in math for young children* (5th ed.). Clifton Park, NY: Thomson Delmar Learning.

Charlesworth, R. (2005b). Prekindergarten mathematics: Connecting with national standards. *Early Childhood Education Journal, 32*, 229–236.

Charlesworth, R. (2008). *Understanding child development* (7th ed.). New York: Thomson Delmar Learning.

Charlesworth, R., & Lind, K. K. (2009). *Math and science for young children* (6th ed.). Albany, NY: Delmar.

Chen, S. (1996). Are Japanese young children among the gods? In D. W. Shwalb & B. J. Shwalb (Eds.), *Japanese child rearing: Two generations of scholarship* (pp.31–43). New York: Guilford Press.

Chen, Z., Sanchez, R. P., & Cambell, T. (1997). From beyond to within their grasp: The rudiments of analogical problem solving in 10- and 13-month-olds. *Developmental Psychology, 33*, 790–801.

Christie, J. F. (1983). The effects of play tutoring on young children's cognitive performance. *Journal of Educational Research, 76*, 326–330.

Cillessen, A. H. N., & Bellmore, A. D. (2002). Social skills and interpersonal perception. In P. K. Smith & C. H. Hart (Eds.), *Blackwell handbook of childhood social development* (pp. 355–374). Oxford: Blackwell.

Clay, M. M. (1979a). *The early detection of reading difficulties* (2nd ed.). Auckland, New Zealand: Heinemann.

Clay, M. M. (1979b). *Reading recovery: A guidebook for teachers in training.* Auckland, New Zealand: Heinemann.

Clements, D. H. (1999). Geometry and spatial thinking in young children. In J.V. Copley (Ed.), *Mathematics in the early years* (pp. 66–79). Reston, VA: National Council of Teachers of Mathematics.

Clements, D. H. (2001). Mathematics in the preschool. *Teaching Children Mathematics, 7*(5), 270–275.

Clements, D. H. (2003, September). *Good beginnings in mathematics: Linking a national vision to state action.* New York: Carnegie Corporation.

Clements, D. H. (2004). Geometric and spatial thinking in early childhood education. In D. H. Clements, J. Sarama, & A. Dibiase, (Eds.), *Engaging young children in mathematics* (pp. 267–298). Mahwah, NJ: Lawrence Erlbaum Associates.

Clements, D. H., Battista, M. T., & Sarama, J. (2001). Logo and geometry. *Journal for Research in Mathematics Education, Monograph Series, 10.*

Clements, D. H., Battista, M. T., Sarama, J., & Swaminathan, S. (1997). Development of students' spatial thinking in a unit on geometric motions and area. *Elementary School Journal, 98*(2), 171–186.

Clements, D. H., & Sarama, J. (2000). Young children's ideas about geometric shapes. *Teaching Children Mathematics, 6*(8), 482–488.

Clements, D. H., & Sarama, J. (2003). Young children and technology: What does the research say? *Young Children, 58*(6), 34–40.

Clements, D. H., Sarama, J., & DiBiase, A. (Eds.). (2004). *Engaging young children in mathematics: Standards for early childhood mathematics education.* Mahwah, NJ: Lawrence Erlbaum Associates.

Clements, D. H., & Sarama, J. (2009). *Learning and teaching early math: The learning trajectories approach.* New York: Routledge.

Clements, D. H., Wilson, D. C., & Sarama, J. (2004). Young children's composition of geometric figures: A learning trajectory. *Mathematical thinking and learning, 6*(2), 163–184.

Cohen, L., & Uhry, J. (2007). Young children's discourse strategies during block play: A Bakhtinian approach. *Journal of Research in Childhood Education, 21,* 302–315.

Colbert, C. (1997). Visual arts in the developmentally appropriate integrated curriculum. In C. H. Hart, D. C. Burts, & R. Charlesworth (Eds.), *Integrated curriculum and developmentally appropriate practice: Birth to age eight* (pp. 201–223). Albany, NY: SUNY Press.

Collier, V. (1987). Age and rate of acquisition of second language for academic purposes. *TESOL Quarterly, 21*(4), 617–641.

Collier, V. (1989, September). How long? A synthesis of research on academic achievement in second language. *TESOL Quarterly, 23*(3), 509–531.

Committee for Children. (2002). *Second Step: A violence-prevention curriculum.* Seattle: Author.

Conezio, K., & French, L. (2002). Science in the preschool classroom: Capitalizing on children's fascination with the everyday world to foster language and literacy development. *Young Children, 57*(5), 12–18.

Cook, R. E., Klein, M. D., & Tessier, A. (2004). *Adapting early childhood curricula for children in inclusive settings* (6th ed.). Upper Saddle River, NJ: Pearson Merrill Prentice Hall.

Coplan, R. J., Findlay, L. C., & Nelson, L. J. (2004). Characteristics of preschoolers with lower perceived competence. *Journal of Abnormal Child Psychology, 32,* 399–408.

Coplan, R. J., & Prakash, K. (2003). Spending time with teacher: Characteristics of preschoolers who frequently elicit versus initiate interactions with teachers. *Early Childhood Research Quarterly, 18,* 143–158.

Copley, J. V. (Ed.). (1999). *Mathematics in the early years.* Washington, DC and Reston, VA: National Association for the Education of Young Children and National Council of Teachers of Mathematics.

Copley, J. V. (2000). *The young child and mathematics.* Washington, DC: National Association for the Education of Young Children.

Copley, J. V. (2005). *Measuring with young children.* Paper presented at the International Conference for the Education of the Young Child, Madrid, Spain.

Copley. J. V., & Hawkins, J. (2005). *Interim report of C3 coaching grant: Mathematics professional development.*

Copley, J. V., Jones, C., & Dighe, J. (2007). *Mathematics: The Creative Curriculum* approach.* Washington, DC: Teaching Strategies, Inc.

Copple, C., & Bredekamp, S. (2006). *Basics of developmentally appropriate practice: An introduction for teachers of children 3 to 6.* Washington, DC: National Association for the Education of Young Children.

Copple, C., & Bredekamp, S. (Eds.). (2009). *Developmentally appropriate practice in early childhood programs serving children from birth to age 8* (3rd ed.). Washington, DC: National Association for the Education of Young Children.

Cummins, J. (1984). *Bilingualism and special education: Issues in assessment and pedagogy.* San Diego: College-Hill Press.

Curenton, S. M., & Ryan, S. K. (2006). Oral storytelling: A cultural art that promotes school readiness. *Young Children, 61*(5), 78–89.

Curry, N. E., & Johnson, C. N. (1990). *Beyond self-esteem: Developing a genuine sense of human value.* Washington, DC: National Association for the Education of Young Children.

Curtis, D., & Carter, M. (2003). *Designs for living and learning: Transforming early childhood environments.* St. Paul, MN: Redleaf Press.

Cutler, K. M., Gilderson, D., Parrott, S., & Browne, M. T. (2003). Developing math games based on children's literature. In D. Koralek (Ed.), *Spotlight on young children and math* (pp. 14–18). Washington, DC: National Association for the Education of Young Children.

D'Addesio, J., Grob, B., Furman, L., Hayes, K., & David, J. (2005). Social Studies: Learning about the world around us. *Young Children, 60*(5), 50–57.

Danoff-Burg, J. A. (2002). Be a bee and other approaches to introducing young children to entomology. *Young Children, 57*(5), 42–47.

Day, C. B. (2006). Leveraging diversity to benefit children's social-emotional development and school readiness. In B. Bowman & E. K. Moore (Eds.), *School readiness and social-emotional development: Perspectives on cultural diversity* (pp. 23–32). Washington, DC: National Black Child Development Institute, Inc.

Deak, G. O. (2003). *The development of cognitive flexibility and language abilities.* Retrieved May 25, 2007, from http://cogsci.ucsd.edu/~deak/publications/Deak_Advances03pdf

Deater-Deckard, K., Petrill, S. A., Thompson, L. A., & DeThorne, L. S. (2005). A cross-sectional behavioral genetic analysis of task persistence in the transition to middle childhood. *Developmental Science, 8*(3), F21–F26.

Deci, E. L., Koestner, R., & Ryan, R. M. (2001). Extrinsic rewards and intrinsic motivation in education: Reconsidered once again. *Review of Educational Research, 71*(1), 1–27.

Deli, E., Bakle, I., & Zachopoulou, E. (2006). Implementing intervention movement programs for kindergarten children. *Journal of Early Childhood Research, 4*(1), 5–18.

DeLoache, J. S. (1987). Rapid change in the symbolic functioning of very young children. *Science, 238*(4833), 1556–1557.

DeLoache, J. S. (1991). Symbolic functioning in very young children. Understanding of pictures and models. *Child Development, 62,* 736–752.

DeLoache, J. S. (2000). Dual representation and young children's use of scale models. *Child Development, 71,* 329–338.

DeLoache, J. S. (2004). Becoming symbol-minded. *Trends in Cognitive Sciences, 8*(2), 66–70.

Denac, O. (2008). A case study of preschool children's musical interests at home and at school. *Early Childhood Education Journal, 35*(5), 439–444.

Denham, S. A., Blair, K., Schmidt, M., & DeMulder, E. (2002). Compromised emotional competence: Seeds of violence sown early? *American Journal of Orthopsychiatry. 72*(1), 70–82.

Denham, S. A., & Burton, R. (1996). A social-emotional intervention for at-risk 4-year-olds. *Journal of School Psychology, 34*(3), 225–245.

Denham, S. A., & Burton, R. (2003). *Social and emotional prevention and intervention programming for preschoolers.* New York: Springer.

Denham, S. A., Caverly, S., Schmidt, M., Blair, K., DeMulder, E., Caal, S., et al. (2002). Preschool understanding of emotions: contributions to classroom anger and aggression. *Journal of Child Psychology and Psychiatry, 43*(7), 901–916.

Denham, S. A., & Kochanoff, A. T. (2002). Parental contributions to preschoolers' understanding of emotion. *Marriage and Family Review, 34,* 311–343.

Denham, S. A., McKinley, M., Couchoud, E. A., & Holt, R. (1990). Emotional and behavioral predictors of preschool peer ratings. *Child Development, 61,* 1145–1152.

Denham, S., von Salisch, M., Olthof, T., Kochanoff, A., & Caverly, S. (2002). Emotional and social development in childhood. In P. K. Smith & C. H. Hart (Eds.), *Blackwell handbook of childhood social development* (pp. 307–328). Oxford: Blackwell.

Desouza, J. M. S., & Czerniak, C. M. (2002). Social behaviors and gender differences among preschoolers: Implications for science activities. *Journal of Research in Childhood Education, 16*(2), 175–188.

de Vries, P. A. (2008). Parental perceptions of music in storytelling sessions in a public library. *Early Childhood Education Journal, 35*(5), 473–478.

DeVries, R., Haney, J., & Zan, B. (1991). Sociomoral atmosphere in direct-instruction, eclectic, and constructivist kindergartens: A study of teachers' enacted interpersonal understanding. *Early Childhood Research Quarterly, 6*(4), 449–471.

Diamond, K. E. (2002). Social competence in children with disabilities. In P. K. Smith & C. H. Hart (Eds.), *Blackwell handbook of childhood social development* (pp. 571–587). Oxford: Blackwell.

Diamond, K. E., & Hestenes, L. L. (1996). Preschool children's conceptions of disabilities: The salience of disabilities in children's ideas about others. *Topics in Early Childhood Special Education, 16*(4), 458–475.

Dickinson, D., & Neuman, S., Eds. (2002). *Handbook of Early Literacy Research.* New York: Guildford Press.

Dickinson, D., & Neuman, S., Eds. (2006). *Handbook of Early Literacy Research,* Vol. 2. New York: Guildford Press.

Dickinson, D. K., & Tabors, P. O. (1991). Early literacy: Linkages between home, school, and literacy achievement at age five. *Journal of Research in Childhood Education, 6,* 30–46.

Dickinson, D. K., & Tabors, P. O. (Eds.). (2001). *Building literacy with language: Young children learning at home and school.* Baltimore: Paul H. Brookes.

Dinwiddle, S. A. (1994). The saga of Sally, Sammy, and the red pen: Facilitating children's social problem solving. *Young Children, 49,* 13–19.

Dodd, J. (1992). *Preventing American Indian children from overidentification with learning disabilities: Cultural considerations during the pre-referral process.* Paper presented at the Council for Exceptional Children, Division for Early Childhood, Topical Conference on Culturally and Linguistically Diverse Exceptional Children (Minneapolis, MN, November 12–14, 1992).

Dodge, D. T., Colker, L. J., & Heroman, C. (2002). *The Creative Curriculum˚ for preschool* (4th ed.). Washington, DC: Teaching Strategies.

Dodge, D. T, Rudick, S., & Berke, K. (2006). *The Creative Curriculum˚ for infants, toddlers & twos* (2nd ed.). Washington, DC: Teaching Strategies.

Dodge, K. A., Schlundt, D. C., Schocken, I., & Delugach, J. D. (1983). Social competence in children's sociometric status: The role of peer group strategies. *Merrill-Palmer Quarterly, 29,* 309–336.

Downey, G. & Walker, E. (1989). Social cognition and adjustment in children at risk for psychopathology. *Developmental Psychology, 25,* 835–845.

Drew, W. F., & Rankin, B. (2004). Promoting creativity for life using open-ended materials. *Young Children, 59*(4), 38–45.

Duncan, G. J., Dowsett, C. J., Claessens, A., Magnuson, K., Huston, A. C., Klebanov, P., et al. (2007). School readiness and later achievement. *Developmental Psychology, 43*(6), 1428–1446.

Dunn, J., & Brown, J. (1991). Relationships, talk about feelings, and the development of affect regulation in early childhood. In J. Garber & K. A. Dodge (Eds.), *The development of emotional regulation and dysregulation* (pp. 89–108). New York: Cambridge University Press.

Ehri, L. C., Nunes, S. R., Willows, D. M., Schuster, B. V., Yaghoub-Zadeh, Z., & Shanahan, T. (2001). Phonemic awareness instruction helps children learn to read: Evidence from the national reading panel's meta-analysis. *Reading Research Quarterly, 36,* 250–297.

Eisenberg, A. R. (1985). Learning to describe past experiences in conversation. *Discourse Processes, 8,* 177–204.

Eisenberg, A. R. (1999). Emotion talk among Mexican-American and Anglo-American mothers and children from two social classes. *Merrill-Palmer Quarterly, 45*(2), 267–284.

Eisenberg, N., Fabes, R. A., Shepard, S. A., Murphy, B. C., Guthrie, I. K., Jones, S., et. al. (1997). Contemporaneous and longitudinal predictors of child's social function from regulation and emotionality. *Child Development, 68,* 642–664.

Elbro, C. I., Borstrom, D. K. & Peterson, P. (1998). Predicting dyslexia from kindergarten: The importance of directness of phonological representations of lexical items. *Reading Research Quarterly, 3,* 36–60.

Elias, C. L., & Berk, L. E. (2002). Self-regulation in young children: Is there a role for sociodramatic play? *Early Childhood Research Quarterly, 17,* 216–238.

Elliot, A. J., & Dweck, C. S. (Eds.). (2005). *Handbook of competence and motivation.* New York: Guilford Press.

Ellis, R. (2000). *Second language acquisition.* New York: Oxford University Press.

Engel, B. S. (1995). *Considering children's art: Why and how to value their works.* Washington, DC: National Association for the Education of Young Children.

Epstein, A. S. (2007). *The intentional teacher: Choosing the best strategies for young children's learning.* Washington, DC: National Association for the Education of Young Children.

Epstein, A. S. (2009). *Me, you, us: Social-emotional learning in preschool.* Ypsilanti, MI: HighScope Press.

Eshach, H., & Fried, N. N. (2005). Should science be taught in early childhood? *Journal of Science Education and Technology, 14*(3), 315–336.

Erdley, C. A., & Asher, S. R. (1999). A social goals perspective on children's social competence. *Journal of Emotional and Behavioral Disorders, 7,* 156–167.

Espinosa, L. (2005). Curriculum and assessment considerations for young children from culturally, linguistically, and economically diverse backgrounds. *Psychology in the Schools, 42*(8), 837–853.

Fabes, R. A., Eisenberg, N., Karbon, M., Bernzweig, J., Speer, A. L., & Carlo, G. (1994). Socialization of children's vicarious emotional responding and prosocial behavior: Relations with mothers' perceptions of children's emotional reactivity. *Developmental Psychology, 30,* 44–55.

Fantini, A. (1985). *Language acquisition of a bilingual child.* San Diego: College-Hill Press.

Fantuzzo, J., & McWayne, C. (2002). The relationship between peer-play interactions in the family context and dimensions of school readiness for low-income preschool children. *Journal of Educational Psychology, 94*(1), 79–87.

Fantuzzo, J., Perry, M. A., & McDermott, P. (2004). Preschool approaches to learning and their relationship to other relevant classroom competencies for low-income children. *School Psychology Quarterly, 19*(3), 212–230.

Farver, J. A. M. (1992). Communicating shared meaning in social pretend play. *Early Childhood Research Quarterly, 7,* 501–516.

Feeney, S., & Moravcik, E. (2005). Children's literature: A window to understanding self and others. *Young Children 60*(5), 20–28.

Feldman, R. S., McGee, G., Mann, L. & Strain, P. S. (1993). Nonverbal affective decoding ability in children with autism and in typical preschoolers. *Journal of Early Intervention, 17*(4), 341–350.

Fenson, L., Dale, P. S., Reznick, J. S., Bates, E., Thal, D. J., & Pethick, S. J. (1994). Variability in early communicative development. *Monographs of the Society for Research in Child Development, 59* (5, Serial No. 242).

Ferreiro, E., & Teberosky, A. (1982). Children's metalinguistic knowledge of syntactical constituents: Effects of age and schooling. *Developmental Psychology, 30,* 663–674.

Fisher, E. P. (1992). The impact of play on development: A meta-analysis. *Play and Culture, 5*(2), 159–181.

Fletcher, K. L., & Sabo, J. (2006). Picture book reading experience and toddler's behaviors with photographs and books. *Early Childhood Research and Practice, 8*(1). Retrieved June 20, 2007, from http://ecrp.uiuc.edu/v8n1/fletcher.html

Flynn, L. L., & Kieff, J. (2002). Including everyone in outdoor play. *Young Children, 57*(3), 20–26.

Friedman, S. (2005). Social studies in action. *Young Children, 60*(5), 44–47.

Friel, S. N., Curcio, F. R., & Bright, G. W. (2001). Making sense of graphs: Critical factors influencing comprehension and instructional implications. *Journal for Research in Mathematics Education, 32*, 124–158.

Gabbard, C. (1998). Windows of opportunity for early brain and motor development. *Journal of Physical Education, Recreation & Dance, 69*(8), 54–56.

Gallahue, D. A. (1995). Transforming physical education curriculum. In S. Bredekamp & T. Rosegrant (Eds.), *Reaching potentials: Transforming early childhood curriculum and assessment,* Vol. 2 (pp. 125–144). Washington, DC: National Association for the Education of Young Children.

Gallahue, D.A. (2008). Developmental physical education for all. Champaign, IL: Human Kinetics Publishers.

Gargiulo, R., & Kilgo, J. (2007). *Young children with special needs* (2nd ed). Albany, NY: Thomson Delmar Learning.

Gartrell, D., & Gartrell, J. J. (2008). Guidance matters: Understand bullying. *Young Children, 63*(3), 54–57.

Geist, E. (2001). Children are born mathematicians: Promoting the construction of early mathematical concepts in children under five. *Young Children, 56*(4), 12–19.

Geist, E. (2003). Infants and toddler exploring mathematics. In D. Koralek (Ed.), *Spotlight on young children and math* (pp. 4–6). Washington, DC: National Association for the Education of Young Children.

Geist, E. (2009). *Children are born mathematicians: Supporting mathematical development, birth to age 8.* Upper Saddle River, NJ: Pearson.

Gelman, R., & Brenneman, K. (2004). Science learning pathways for young children. *Early Childhood Research Quarterly, 19*(1), 150–158.

Gelman, R., & Gallistel, C.R. (1978). *The Child's Understanding of Number.* Cambridge, MA: Harvard University Press.

Gelman, S. A. (1998). Categories in young children's thinking. *Young Children, 53*(1), 20–26.

Gelman, S. A., Chesnick, R., & Waxman, S. (2005). Mother-child conversations about pictures and objects: Referring to categories and individuals. *Child Development, 76*, 1129–1143.

Gelman, S. A., & Coley, J. D. (1990). The importance of knowing a dodo is a bird: Categories and inferences in 2-year-old children. *Developmental Psychology, 26*, 796–804.

Gelman, S. A., Coley, J. D., Rosengren, K. S., Hartman, E., & Pappas, A. (1998). Beyond labeling: The role of maternal input in the acquisition of richly structured categories. *Monographs of the Society for Research in Child Development, 63* (1, Serial No. 253).

Genishi, C., & Brainard, M. (1995). Assessment of bilingual children: A dilemma seeking solutions. In E. E. García & B. McLaughlin (Eds.), *Meeting the challenge of linguistic and cultural diversity in early childhood education* (pp. 49–63). New York: Teachers College Press.

George, J., & Greenfield, D. B. (2005). Examination of a structured problem-solving flexibility task for assessing approaches to learning on young children: Relation to teacher ratings and children's achievement. *Applied Developmental Psychology, 26*(1), 69–84.

Ginsburg, H. P., & Baroody, A. J. (2003). *Test of early mathematics ability: Examiner's manual* (3rd ed.). Austin, TX: Pro-Ed.

Ginsburg, H. P. & Golbeck, S. L. (2004). Thoughts on the future of research on mathematics and science learning and education. *Early Childhood Research Quarterly 19*, 190–200.

Ginsburg, H. P., Inoue, N., & Seo, K. (1999). Young children doing mathematics. In J. V. Copley (Ed.), *Mathematics in the early years* (pp. 88–91). Washington, DC and Reston, VA: National Association for the Education of Young Children and National Council of Teachers of Mathematics.

Gober, S. Y. (2002). *Six simple ways to assess young children.* Albany, NY: Delmar Thomson Learning.

Golbeck, S. L. (2005). Research in review: Building foundations for spatial literacy in early childhood. *Young Children, 60*(6), 72–83.

Goldstein, P. (2004). Helping young children with special needs develop vocabulary. *Early Childhood Education Journal, 32,* 1–43.

Gonzalez, V. (1998). *Language and cognitive development in second language learners.* Boston: Allyn & Bacon.

Gonzalez, V., Bauerle, P., & Felix-Holt, M. (1996). Theoretical and practical implications of assessing cognitive and language development in bilingual children with qualitative methods. *Bilingual Research Journal, 20*(1), 93–131.

Gonzalez-Mena, J. (2002). *The child in the family and the community* (3rd ed.). Upper Saddle River, NJ: Merrill Prentice Hall.

Gopnik, A., & Choi, S. (1995). *Beyond names for things: Children's acquisition of verbs.* Hillsdale, NJ: Erlbaum.

Gordon, A. M., & Williams-Brown, K. (1996). *Beginnings and beyond* (4th ed.). Albany, NY: Delmar.

Gould, P., & Sullivan, J. (1999). *The inclusive early childhood classroom: Easy ways to adapt learning centers for all children.* Beltsville, MD: Gryphon House.

Gowen, J. W. (1995). Research in review: The early development of symbolic play. *Young Children, 50*(3), 75–84.

Gullo, D. F. (Ed.). (2006). *K today: Teaching and learning in the kindergarten year.* Washington, DC: National Association for the Education of Young Children.

Gundlach, R., McLane, J., Stott, F. M., & McNamee, G. D. (1985). The social foundations of early writing development. In M. Farr (Ed.), *Advances in writing research:* Vol. 1*: Studies in children's early writing development.* Norwood, NJ: Ablex.

Hair, E., Halle, T., Terry-Humen, E., Lavelle, B., & Calkins, J. (2006). Children's school readiness in the ECLS-K: Predictions to academic, health, and social outcomes in first grade. *Early Childhood Research Quarterly, 21*(4), 431–454.

Hakuta, K. (1978). A report on the development of grammatical morphemes in a Japanese girl learning English as a second language. In E. M. Hatch (Ed.), *Second language acquisition: A book of readings* (pp. 132–147). Rowley, MA: Newbury House Publishers.

Hakuta, K. (1986). *Mirror of language: The debate on bilingualism.* New York: Basic Books.

Halliday, M. A. K. (2002). Relevant models of language. In B. M. Power & R. S. Hubbard (Eds.), *Language development: A reader for teachers* (2nd ed., pp. 49–53). Upper Saddle River, NJ: Merrill.

Hamre, B. K., & Pianta, R. C. (2001). Early teacher-child relationships and the trajectory of children's school outcomes through eighth grade. *Child Development, 72,* 625–638.

Hannust, T., & Kikas, E. (2007). Children's knowledge of astronomy and its change in the course of learning. *Early Childhood Research Quarterly, 22*(1), 89–104.

Harper, L. V., & McCluskey, K. S. (2002). Caregiver and peer responses to children with language and motor disabilities in inclusive preschool programs. *Early Childhood Research Quarterly, 17,* 148–166.

Hart, B., & Risley, T. R. (1995). *Meaningful differences in the everyday experience of young American children.* Baltimore: Paul H. Brookes.

Hart, B., & Risley, T. R. (2003). The early catastrophe. *Education Review, 17*(1), 110–118.

Hart, C. H., McGee, L. M., & Hernandez, S. (1993). Themes in the peer relations literature: Correspondence to outdoor peer interactions portrayed in children's storybooks. In C. H. Hart (Ed.), *Children on playgrounds: Research perspectives and applications* (pp. 371–416). Albany, NY: SUNY Press.

Harter, S. (1998). The development of self-representations. In W. Damon & N. Eisenberg (Eds.), *Handbook of child psychology,* Vol. 3*: Social, emotional, and personality development* (pp. 553–617). New York: John Wiley & Sons.

Harter, S. (1999). *The construction of the self: A developmental perspective*. New York: Guilford Press.

Hartup, W. W., & Abecassis, M. (2002). Friends and enemies. In P. K. Smith & C. H. Hart (Eds.), *Blackwell handbook of childhood social development* (pp. 285–306). Oxford: Blackwell.

Harwood, R. L., Miller, J. G., & Irizarry, N. L. (1995). *Culture and attachment: Perceptions of the child in context*. New York: Guilford.

Haugland, S. W. (2000). What role should technology play in young children's learning? Part 2: Early childhood classrooms in the 21st century: Using computers to maximize learning. *Young Children, 55*(1), 12–18.

Head Start Bureau. (2002). *Identifying strategies to support English language learners in Head Start and Early Head Start programs*. (English Language Learners Focus Group Report.) Washington, DC: Author.

Heath, S. M., & Hogben, J. H. (2004). Cost-effective prediction of reading difficulties. *Journal of Speech, Language, and Hearing Research, 47*(4), 751–765.

Heise-Baigorria, C. & Tabors, P. O. (2004). *Bilingual early language and literacy assessment (BELA)*. Cambridge, MA: Cambridge 0–8 Council/Cambridge Public Schools. Retrieved July 2, 2007, from http://www.cpsd.us/bela

Heisner, J. (2005). Telling stories with blocks: Encouraging language in the block center. *Early Childhood Research and Practice, 7*(2). Retrieved September 23, 2008, from http://ecrp.uiuc.edu/v7n2/heisner.html

Henniger, M. L. (1991). Play revisited: A critical element of the kindergarten curriculum. *Early Child Development and Care, 70*, 63–71.

Henrich, C. C., Wheeler, C. M., & Zigler, E. F. (2005). Motivation as a facet of school readiness in a Head Start sample. *NHSA Dialog, 8*(1), 72–87. Retrieved July 17, 2007, from https://webftp.gsu.edu/~wwwcch/Henrich,%20Wheeler,%20&%20Zigler%20(2005).pdf

Hensen, R. (2005). Real super-hero play. *Young Children, 60*(5), 37.

Herbert, J., Gross, J., & Hayne, H. (2007). Crawling is associated with more flexible memory retrieval by 9-month old infants. *Developmental Science, 10*(2), 183–189.

Heroman, C., & Jones, C. (2004). *Literacy: The Creative Curriculum® approach*. Washington, DC: Teaching Strategies, Inc.

Hesse, P., & Lane, F. (2003). Media literacy starts young: An integrated curriculum approach. *Young Children, 58*(6), 20–26.

Hildreth, G. (1936). Developmental sequences in name writing. *Child Development, 7*, 291–302.

Hirschler, J. A. (1994, Winter). Preschool children's help to second language learners. *Journal of Educational Issues of Language Minority Students, 14*, 227–240.

Hirsch-Pasek, K., Golinkoff, R. M., & Naigles, L. (1996). *The origins of grammar: Evidence from early language comprehension*. Cambridge, MA: MIT Press.

Hoisington, C. (2002). Using photographs to support children's science inquiry. *Young Children, 57*(5), 26–32.

Holowka, S., & Petitto, L.A. (2002, August). Left hemisphere cerebral specialization for babies while babbling. *Science, 297*, 1515.

Honig, A. S. (2005). The language of lullabies. *Young Children, 60*(5), 36, 30–36.

Hooper, S. R., Roberts, J. E., Zeisel, S.A., & Poe, M. (2003). Core language predictors of behavioral functioning in early elementary school children: Concurrent and longitudinal findings. *Behavioral Disorders, 29*, 10–24.

Howes, C. (2000). Social-emotional classroom climate in child care: Child-teacher relationships and children's second grade peer relations. *Social Development, 9*(2), 191–204.

Howes, C., Burchinal, M., Pianta, R., Bryant, D., Early, D., Clifford, R., et al. (2008). Ready to learn? Children's pre-academic achievements in pre-kindergarten programs. *Early Childhood Research Quarterly, 23*, 27–50.

Howes, C., Hamilton, C. E., & Matheson, C. C., (1994). Children's relationships with peers: Differential associations with aspects of the teacher-child relationship. *Child Development, 65,* 253–263.

Howes, C., & James, J. (2002). Children's social development within the socialization context of childcare and early childhood education. . In P. K. Smith & C. H. Hart (Eds.), *Blackwell handbook of childhood social development* (pp. 137–155). Oxford: Blackwell.

Howes, C. & Matheson, C. C. (1992). Sequences in the development of competent play with peers: Social and social pretend play. *Developmental Psychology, 94*(1), 79–87.

Howes, C., & Ritchie, S. (1998). Changes in teacher-child relationships in a therapeutic preschool. *Early Education and Development, 4,* 411–422.

Howse, R. B., Lange, G., Farran, D. C., & Boyles, C. D. (2003). Motivation and self-regulation as predictors of achievement in economically disadvantaged young children. *The Journal of Experimental Education, 71*(2), 151–174.

Huang, J., & Hatch, E. M. (1978). A Chinese child's acquisition of English. In E. M. Hatch (Ed.), *Second language acquisition: A book of readings* (pp. 118–131). Rowley, MA: Newbury House Publishers.

Hubbard, J. A., & Coie, J. D. (1994). Emotional correlates of social competence in children's peer relationships. *Merrill-Palmer Quarterly, 20,* 1–20.

Humphryes, J. (2000). Exploring nature with children. *Young Children, 55*(2), 16–20.

Hurley, D. S. (2000). *Developing fine and gross motor skills: Birth to three.* Austin, TX: PRO-ED.

Hyson, M. (2005). Professional Development. Enthusiastic and engaged: Strengthening young children's positive approaches to learning. *Young Children, 60*(6), 68–70.

Hyson, M. (2008). *Enthusiastic and engaged learners: Approaches to learning in the early childhood classroom.* New York: Teachers College Press.

Hyson, M. C. (2004). *The emotional development of young children: Building an emotion-centered curriculum* (2nd ed.). New York: Teachers College Press.

Hyson, M., Buch, L., Fantuzzo, J., & Scott-Little, C. (2006). *Enthusiastic and engaged: Why are positive approaches to learning so important, and how can we support their development in young children?* Paper presented at the Annual Conference of the National Association for the Education of Young Children, Atlanta, GA.

Itoh, H., & Hatch, E. M. (1978). Second language acquisition: A case study. In E. M. Hatch (Ed.), *Second language acquisition: A book of readings* (pp. 76–88). Rowley, MA: Newbury House Publishers.

Izard, C. E., Fine, S. E., Schultz, D., Mostow, A. J., Acerman, B. P., & Younstrom, E. (2001). Emotion knowledge as a predictor of social behavior and academic competence in children at risk. *Psychological Science, 12,* 18–23.

Jablon, J. R., Dombro, A. L., & Dichtelmiller, M. L. (2007). *The power of observation.* (2nd ed.). Washington, DC: Teaching Strategies, Inc. and National Association for the Education of Young Children.

Jablon, J. R., & Wilkinson, M. (2006). Using engagement strategies to facilitate children's learning and success. *Young Children, 61*(2), 12–16.

Jalongo, M. R. (2008). *Learning to listen, listening to learn: Building essential skills in young children.* Washington, DC: National Association for the Education of Young Children.

Jalongo, M. R., & Isenberg, J. P. (2006). Creative expression and thought in kindergarten. In D. F. Gullo (Ed.), *K today: Teaching and learning in the kindergarten year* (pp. 116–126). Washington, DC: National Association for the Education of Young Children.

Jambunathan, S., Burts, D. C., & Pierce, S. H. (1999). Developmentally appropriate practice as predictors of self-competence among preschoolers. *Journal of Research in Childhood Education, 13,* 167–174.

Jipson, J. L., & Gelman, S. A. (2007). Robots and rodents: Children's inferences about living and nonliving kinds. *Child Development, 78*(6), 1675–1688.

Johnson, M. H. (2008). Developing verbal and visual literacy through experiences in the visual arts. *Young Children, 63*(1), 74–79.

Jones, N. P. (2005). Big jobs: Planning for competence. *Young Children, 60*(2), 86–93.

Jordan, N. C., Kaplan, D., Olah, L. N., & Locuniak, M. N. (2006). Number sense growth in kindergarten: A longitudinal investigation of children at risk for mathematics difficulties. *Child Development, 77,* 153–175.

Jung, M., Kloosterman, P., & McMullen, M.B. (2007). Research in review. Young children's intuition for solving problems in mathematics. *Young Children, 62*(5), 50–57.

Kagan, S. L., Britto, P. R., Kauerz, K., & Tarrant, K. (2005). *Washington state early learning and development benchmarks: A guide to young children's learning and development: From birth to kindergarten entry.* Retrieved March 23, 2009, from http://www.k12.WA.US/ Earlylearning/pubdocs/earlylearningbenchmarks.pdf

Kaiser, B., & Rasminsky, S. (2003). *Challenging behavior in young children: Understanding, preventing, and responding effectively.* Boston: Allyn & Bacon.

Kalmar, K. (2008). Let's give children something to talk about! Oral language and preschool literacy. *Young Children, 63*(1), 88–92.

Kantor, R., Elgas, P. M., & Fernie D. (1993). Cultural knowledge and social competence within a preschool peer-culture group. *Early Childhood Research Quarterly, 8,* 125–148.

Katz, L. F., Kramer, L., & Gottman, J. M. (1992). Conflict and emotions in marital, sibling, and peer relationships. In. C. U. Shantz & W. W. Hartup (Eds.), *Conflict in child and adolescent development* (pp. 122–149). New York: Cambridge University Press.

Katz, L. G. (1999). *Another look at what young children should be learning.* Retrieved June 16, 2007, from http://ecap.crc.uiuc.edu/eecearchive/digests/1999/ katzle99.pdf

Katz, L. G., & Chard, S. C. (1995). *Engaging children's minds: The project approach.* Norwood, NJ: Ablex.

Kelley, S. A., Brownell, C. A., & Campbell, S. B. (2000). Mastery motivation and self-evaluative affect in toddlers: Longitudinal relations with maternal behavior. *Child Development, 71,* 1061–1071.

Kemple, K. M., Batey, J. J., & Hartle, L. C. (2004). Music play: Creating centers for musical play and exploration. *Young Children, 59*(4), 30–37.

Kemple, K. M., & Nissenberg, S. A. (2000). Nurturing creativity in early childhood education: Families are part of it. *Early Childhood Education Journal, 28*(1), 67–71.

Kenney, S. H. (1997). Music in the developmentally appropriate integrated curriculum. In C. H. Hart, D. C. Burts, & R. Charlesworth (Eds.), *Integrated curriculum and developmentally appropriate practice: Birth to age eight* (pp. 103–144). Albany, NY: SUNY Press.

Kerem, E. A., Kamaraj, I., & Yelland, N. (2001). An analysis of Turkish pre-school teachers' ideas about the concept of creativity and the activities that can foster creativity in young children. *Contemporary Issues in Early Childhood, 2*(2), 248–252.

Kilmer, S. J., & Hofman, H. (1995). Transforming science curriculum. In S. Bredekamp & T. Rosegrant (Eds.), *Reaching potentials: Transforming early childhood curriculum and assessment,* Vol. 2 (pp. 43–64). Washington, DC: National Association for the Education of Young Children.

Kilpatrick, J., Swafford, J., & Findell, B. (2001). *Adding it up: Helping children learn mathematics.* Washington, DC: National Academy Press.

Kim, H., Park, E., & Lee, J. (2001). "All done! Take it home." Then into a trashcan?: Displaying and using children's art projects. *Early Childhood Education Journal, 29*(1), 41–50.

Kim, S. D. G. (2005). Kevin: "I gotta get to the market": The development of peer relationships in inclusive early childhood settings. *Early Childhood Education Journal, 33*(3), 163–169.

Kimple, K. M. (1991). Research in Review: Preschool children's peer acceptance and social interaction. *Young Children, 46*(5), 47–54.

Klein, A., & Starkey, P. (2004). Fostering preschool children's mathematical knowledge: Findings from the Berkeley math readiness project. In D. H. Clements, J. Sarama, & A. M. DiBiase (Eds.), *Engaging young children in mathematics: Standards for early childhood mathematics education* (pp. 343–360). Mahwah, NJ: Lawrence Erlbaum Associates.

Klein, M. D., & Chen, D. (2001). *Working with children from diverse backgrounds.* Albany, NY: Delmar.

Klein, T. P., Wirth, D., & Linas, K. (2004). Play: Children's context for development. In D. Koralek (Ed.), *Spotlight on young children and play* (pp. 28–34). Washington, DC: National Association for the Education of Young Children.

Kohn, A. (1993). Choices for children: Why and how to let students decide. *Phi Delta Kappan, 75,* 8–20.

Kopp, C. B. (1982). Antecedent of self-regulation: A developmental perspective. *Developmental Psychology, 18,* 199–214.

Koralek, D. (Ed.). (2003). *Spotlight on young children and math.* Washington, DC: National Association for the Education of Young Children.

Koralek, D. (Ed.). (2004). *Spotlight on young children and play.* Washington, DC: National Association for the Education of Young Children.

Krafft, K. C., & Berk, L. E. (1998). Private speech in two preschools: Significance of open-ended activities and make-believe play for verbal self-regulation. *Early Childhood Research Quarterly, 13,* 637–658.

Kreidler, W. J., & Whittall, S. T. (2003). Resolving conflict. In C. Copple (Ed.), *A world of difference: Readings on teaching young children in a diverse society* (pp. 52–56). Washington, DC: National Association for the Education of Young Children.

Ladd, G. W. (1990). Having friends, keeping friends, making friends, and being liked by peers in the classroom: Predictors of children's early school adjustment? *Child Development, 61,* 1081–1100.

Ladd, G. W. (1999). Peer relationships and social competence during early and middle childhood. *Annual Review of Psychology 50,* 333–359.

Ladd, G. W., Birch, S. H., & Buhs, E .S. (1999). Children's social and scholastic lives in kindergarten: Related spheres of influence? *Child Development, 70,* 1373–1400.

Ladd, G. W., Buhs, E. S., & Seid, M. (2000). Children's initial sentiments about kindergarten: Is school liking an antecedent of early classroom participation and achievement? *Merrill-Palmer Quarterly, 46,* 255–279.

Lamb, M. E., Bornstein, M. H., & Teti, D.M. (2002). *Development in infancy: An introduction.* Mahwah, NJ: Lawrence Erlbaum Associates.

Lanvers, U. (1999). Lexical growth patterns in a bilingual infant: The occurrence of significance of equivalents in the bilingual lexicon. *International Journal of Bilingual Education and Bilingualism, 2.* 30–32.

Larkina, M., Guler, O. E., Kleinknect, E., & Bauer, P. J. (2008). Maternal provision of structure in a deliberate memory task in relation to their preschool children's recall. *Journal of Experimental Child Psychology, 100,* 235–251.

Lenhoff, R., & Huber, L. (2000). Young children make maps. *Young Children, 55*(3), 6–11.

Levin, D. E. (2003). Teaching young children in violent times: Building a peaceable classroom (2nd ed.). Washington, DC: National Association for the Education of Young Children.

Levy, A. K., Wolfgang, C. H., & Koorland, M. A. (1992). Sociodramatic play as a method for enhancing the language performance of kindergarten age students. *Early Childhood Research Quarterly, 7,* 245–262.

Lewis, M., & Michalson, L. (1993). Children's emotions and moods: developmental theory and measurement. New York: Plenum Press.

Lewis, V. (2003). *Development and disability.* (2nd ed.). Malden, MA: Blackwell.

Lin, P., Schwanenflugel, P. J., & Wisenbaker, J. M. (1990). Category typicality, cultural familiarity, and the development of category knowledge. *Developmental Psychology, 26*, 805–813.

Lind, K. K. (1997). Science in the developmentally appropriate integrated curriculum. In C. H. Hart, D. C. Burts, & R. Charlesworth (Eds.), *Integrated curriculum and developmentally appropriate practice: Birth to age eight* (pp. 75–101). Albany, NY: SUNY Press.

Lind, K. K. (2001). *Science in early childhood: Developing and acquiring fundamental concepts and skills.* Presentation handout retrieved October 21, 2008 from www.hsnrc.org/CDI/pdfs/klind1.pdf

Lomax, R. G., & McGee, L. M. (1987). Young children's concepts of print and reading: Toward a model of word reading acquisition. *Reading Research Quarterly, 22,* 237–256.

Lonigan, C. J., Burgess, S. R., & Anthony, J. L. (2000). Development of emergent literacy and early reading skills in preschool children: Evidence from a latent-variable longitudinal study. *Developmental Psychology, 36,* 596–613.

Lonigan, C. J., Burgess, S. R., Anthony, J. L., & Barker, T. A. (1998). Development of phonological sensitivity in 2- to 5-year-old children. *Journal of Educational Psychology, 90*(2), 294–311.

Lorenzo-Lasa, R., Ideishi, R. I., & Ideishi, S. K. (2007). Facilitating preschool learning and movement through dance. *Early Childhood Education Journal, 35*(1), 25–31.

Lu, M. (2000). *Language development in the early years.* Bloomington, IN: ERIC Clearinghouse on Reading, English, and Communication.

Lutz, T. & Kuhlman, W. D. (2000). Learning about culture through dance in kindergarten classrooms. *Early Childhood Education Journal, 28*(1), 35–40.

Macrina, M., Hoover, D., & Becker, C. (2009). The challenge of working with dual language learners: Three perspectives: Supervisor, mentor, and teacher. *Young Children 64*(2), 27–34.

Mallory, B. L., & New, R. S. (Eds.). (1994). *Diversity and developmentally appropriate practices: Challenges for early childhood education.* New York: Teachers College Press.

Manross, M. A. (2000). Learning to throw in physical education class: Part 3. *Teaching Elementary Physical Education, 11*(3), 26–29.

Mantzicopoulos, P., Patrick, H., & Samarapungavan, A. (2008). Young children's motivational beliefs about learning science. *Early Childhood Research Quarterly, 23*(3), 378–394.

Marcus, G. F. (1995). Children's overregularization of English plurals: A quantitative analysis. *Journal of Child Language, 22,* 447–460.

Marcus, G. F., Pinker, S., Ullman, M., Hollander, M., Rosen, T. J., & Xu, F. (1992). Overregularization in language acquisition. *Monographs of the Society for Research in Child Development, 57* (Serial No. 228).

Mason, J. (1980). When do children begin to read? An exploration of four-year-old children's letter and word reading competencies. *Reading Research Quarterly, 15,* 203–227.

Matlock, R., & Hornstein, J. (2004). Sometimes a smudge is just a smudge, and sometimes it's a saber-toothed tiger: Learning and the arts through the ages. *Young Children, 59*(4), 12–17.

McAfee, O., & Leong, D. (2007). *Assessing and guiding young children's development and learning* (4th ed). Boston: Allyn & Bacon.

McAfee, O., Leong, D. J., & Bodrova, E. (2004). *Basics of assessment: A primer for early childhood educators.* Washington, DC: National Association for the Education of Young Children.

McCabe, A. (1997). Developmental and cross-cultural aspects of children's narration. In M. Bamberg (Ed.), *Narrative development: Six approaches* (pp. 137–174). Mahwah, NJ: Erlbaum.

McClelland, M. M., Morrison, F. J., & Holmes, D. L. (2000). Children at risk for early academic problems: The role of learning-related social skills. *Early Childhood Research Quarterly, 15*(3), 307–329.

McCormick, C. E., & Mason, J. M. (1986). Intervention procedures for increasing preschool children's interest in and knowledge about reading. In W. H. Teale & E. Sulzby (Eds.), *Emergent literacy: Writing and reading* (pp. 90–115). Norwood, NJ: Ablex.

McGee, L., Lomax, R., & Head, M. (1988). Young children's written language knowledge: What environmental and functional print reading reveals. *Journal of Reading Behavior, 20,* 99–118.

McGee, L., & Richgels, D. J. (1996). *Literacy's beginnings: Supporting young readers and writers.* Boston: Allyn & Bacon.

McGee, L., & Richgels, D. J. (2003). *Designing early literacy programs: Strategies for at-risk preschool and kindergarten children.* New York: Guilford Press.

McHenry, J. D., & Buerk, K. J. (2008). Infants and toddlers meet the natural world. *Young Children, 63*(1), 40–41.

McKay, P. (2006). *Assessing young language learners.* New York: Cambridge University Press.

McKenzie, T. L., Sallis, J. F., Elder, J. P., Berry, C. C., Hoy, P. L., Nader, P. R., et al. (1997). Physical activity levels and prompts in young children at recess: A two-year study of a bi-ethnic sample. *Research Quarterly for Exercise and Sport, 68*(3), 195–202.

McLaughlin, B., Blanchard, A., & Osanai, Y. (1995, June). *Assessing language development in bilingual preschool children* [National Clearinghouse for Bilingual Education Rep. No. 22]. Washington, DC: George Washington University. Retrieved August 16, 2007, from http://www.ncela.gwu.edu/pubs/pigs/pig22.htm

McWilliams, R. A., Scarborough, A. A., & Kim, H. (2003). Adult interactions and child engagement. *Early Education and Development, 14*(1), 7–28.

Meisel, J. (1989). Early differentiation of languages in bilingual children. In K. Hylterstam & L. Obler (Eds.), *Bilingualism across the lifespan: Aspects of acquisition, maturity, and loss* (pp. 13–54). Cambridge, England: Cambridge University Press.

Meisels, S. (1994). Designing meaningful measurements for early childhood. In B. L. Mallory & R. S. New (Eds.), *Diversity and developmentally appropriate practices: Challenges for early childhood education* (pp. 202–222). New York: Teachers College Press.

Menn, L., & Stoel-Gammon, C. (2001). Phonological development: Learning sounds and sound patterns. In J. B. Gleason (Ed.), *The development of language* (pp. 39–100). Boston: Allyn & Bacon.

Metsala, J. L., & Walley, A. C. (1998). Spoken vocabulary growth and the segmental restructuring of lexical representations: Precursors to phonemic awareness and early reading ability. In J. L. Metsala & L. C. Ehri (Eds.), *Recognition in beginning literacy* (pp. 89–120). Mahwah, NJ: Lawrence Erlbaum Associates.

Meyer, C. (1989). *The role of peer relationships in the socialization of children to preschool: A Korean example.* Unpublished doctoral dissertation, Ohio State University, Columbus.

Miller, P. J., Fung, H., & Mintz, J. (1996). Self-construction through narrative practices: A Chinese and American comparison of early socialization. *Ethos, 24*(2), 237–280.

Miller, S. E. (1999). Balloons, blankets, and balls: Gross-motor activities to use indoors. *Young Children, 54*(5), 58–63.

Mindes, G. (2005a). Resources for teaching and learning about social studies. *Young Children 60*(5), 58–60.

Mindes, G. (2005b). Social studies in today's early childhood curricula. *Young Children, 60*(5), 12–18.

Mindes, G. (2006). Social studies in kindergarten. In D. F. Gullo (Ed.), *K today: Teaching and learning in the kindergarten year* (pp. 107–115). Washington, DC: National Association for the Education of Young Children.

Mitchell, L. C. (2004). Making the most of creativity in activities for young children with disabilities. *Young Children* 59(4), 46–49.

Mix, K. S., Huttenlocher, J., & Levine, S. C. (2002). *Quantitative development in infancy and early childhood.* New York, NY: Oxford University Press.

Miyakawa, Y., Kamii, C., & Nagahiro, M. (2005). The development of logico-mathematical thinking at ages 1–3 in play with blocks and an incline. *Journal of Research in Childhood Education, 19*, 292–301.

Monhardt, L., & Monhardt, R. (2006). Creating a context for the learning of science process skills through picture books. *Early Childhood Education Journal, 34*(1), 67–71.

Mooney, C. (2005). *Use your words: How teacher talk helps children learn.* St. Paul, MN: Redleaf Press.

Moore, S. G. (1985). Social effects of peers on curiosity. *Early Report, 12*(3), 1–2.

Morrow, L. (2005). *Literacy development in the early years: Helping children read and write* (5th ed.). Boston: Allyn & Bacon.

Morrow, L. M. (1985). Retelling stories: A strategy for improving children's comprehension, concept of story structure, and oral language complexity. *The Elementary School Journal, 85*, 647–661.

Morrow, L. M. (1990). Preparing the classroom environment to promote literacy during play. *Early Childhood Research Quarterly, 5*, 537–554.

Mostow, A. J., Izard, C. E., Fine, S., & Trentacosta, C. J. (2002). Modeling emotional, cognitive, and behavioral predictors of peer acceptance. *Child Development, 73(6)*, 1775–1788.

Murphey, D. A., & Burns, C. E. (2002). Development of a comprehensive community assessment of school readiness. *Early Childhood Research and Practice, 2.* Retrieved June 16, 2007, from http://ecrp.uiuc.edu/v4n2/murphey.html

Murphy, K. L., DePasquale, R., & McNamara, E. (2003). Meaningful connections: Using technology in primary classrooms. *Young Children, 58*(6), 12–18.

Mussen, P. H., Conger, J. J., Kagan, J., & Huston, A. C. (1990). *Child development and personality* (7th ed.). New York: Harper and Row.

National Association for the Education of Young Children. (1996). NAEYC position statement: Responding to linguistic and cultural diversity—Recommendations for effective early childhood education. *Young Children, 52*(2), 4–12.

National Association for the Education of Young Children. (2005a). *Screening and assessment of young English-language learners: Supplement to the NAEYC position statement on early childhood curriculum, assessment, and program evaluation.* Washington, DC: Author.

National Association for the Education of Young Children. (2005b). *Where we stand on the screening and assessment of young English-language learners.* Washington, DC: Author.

National Center for Education Statistics (NCES). (1993). *Public school kindergarten teachers' views on children's readiness for school.* Washington, DC: Author. Retrieved July 6, 2007, from http://nces.ed.gov/surveys/frss/publications/93410/index.asp?sectionID=3

National Center for Education Statistics (NCES). (2000). *Special analysis 2000. Entering kindergarten: A portrait of American children when they begin school.* Retrieved September 12, 2007, from http://nces.ed.gov/programs/coe/2000/essay/e03g.asp

National Center for Education Statistics (NCES). (2002). *Children's reading and mathematics achievement in kindergarten and first grade.* Washington, DC: Author. Retrieved July 6, 2007, from http://nces.ed.gov/pubs2002/kindergarten/24.asp?nav=4

National Committee on Science Education Standards and Assessment, National Research Council (1996). *National Science Education Standards.* Retrieved October 20, 2008, from http://books.nap.edu/openbook. php?record_id=4962&page=105

National Council of Teachers of Mathematics (NCTM). (2000). *Principles and standards for school mathematics.* Reston, VA: Author.

National Council of Teachers of Mathematics (NCTM). (2006). *Curriculum focal points for prekindergarten through grade 8 mathematics: A quest for coherence.* Reston, VA: Author.

National Early Literacy Panel. (2004). *A synthesis of research on language and literacy.* Retrieved June 2004, from http://www.famlit.org/ProgramsandInitiatives/ FamilyPartnershipinReading/index.cfm

National Early Literacy Panel. (2008). *Developing early literacy: Report of the National Early Literacy Panel.* Retrieved January 2009, from http://www.nifl.gov/nifl/ publications/pdf/NELPReport09.pdf

National Institute of Child Health and Human Development. (2000). *Report of the national reading panel. Teaching children to read: An evidence-based assessment of the scientific research literature on reading and its implications for reading instruction* (NIH Publication No. 00-4769). Washington, DC: U.S. Government Printing Office.

National Institute on Deafness and Other Communication Disorders (NIDCD). (2000, April). *Speech and language developmental milestones.* Retrieved July 21, 2007, from http://www.nidcd.nih.gov/health/ voice/speechandlanguage.asp/

National Reading Panel. (2000). *Teaching children to read: An evidence-based assessment of the scientific research literature on reading and its implications for reading instruction.* NIH Publication No. 00-4769. Washington, DC: National Institute of Child Health and Human Development.

National Research Council. (1998). *Preventing reading difficulties.* Washington, DC: National Academy Press.

National Research Council. (1998). *Starting out right.* Washington, DC: National Academy Press.

National Research Council. (2009). *Mathematics learning in early childhood: Paths toward excellence and equity.* Committee on Early Childhood Mathematics, C. T. Cross, T. A. Woods, and H. Schweingruber, Eds. Center for Education, Division of Behavioral and Social Sciences and Education. Washington, DC: The National Academies Press.

National Scientific Council on the Developing Child. (2004). *Children's emotional development is built into the architecture of their brain: Working paper no. 2.* Retrieved August 31, 2007, from www.developingchild.net/pubs/ wp/emotional_development_is_built.pdf

Neuman, S., & Roskos, K. (1990). Play, print and purpose: Enriching play environments for literacy development. *Reading Teacher, 44*(3), 214–221.

Neuman, S., & Roskos, K. (1993). Access to print for children of poverty: Differential effects of adult mediation and literacy-enriched play settings on environmental and functional print tasks. *American Educational Research Journal, 30,* 95–122.

Neuman, S., Copple, C., & Bredekamp, S. (2000). *Learning to read and write: Developmentally appropriate practices for young children.* Washington, DC: National Association for the Education of Young Children.

Neuman, S. B. (2003). From rhetoric to reality: The case for high-quality compensatory prekindergarten programs. *Phi Delta Kappan, 85*(4), 286–291.

Newman, L. S. (1990). Intentional and unintentional memory in young children: Remembering vs. playing. *Journal of Experimental Child Psychology, 50,* 243–258.

Nicolopoulou, A., & Richner, E. S. (2007). From actors to agents to persons: The development of character representation in young children's narratives. *Child Development, 78,* 412–429.

Nilges, L., & Usnick, V. (2000). The role of spatial ability in physical education and mathematics. *Journal of Physical Education, Recreation & Dance, 71*(6), 29–35.

Nobes, G., Moore, D. G., Martin, A. E., Clifford, B. R., Butterworth, G., Panagiotaki, G., et al., (2003). Children's understanding of the earth in a multicultural community: Mental model or fragments of knowledge? *Developmental Science, 6*(1), 72–85.

Normandeau, S., & Guay, F. (1998). Preschool behavior and first-grade school achievement: The mediational role of cognitive self-control. *Journal of Educational Psychology, 90*, 111–121.

Northwest Educational Technology Consortium, Northwest Regional Educational Laboratory. (2002). 5 effective ways for young children to use technology. Portland, OR: Author.

Nourot, P. M., & Van Hoorn, J. L. (1991). Research in review: Symbolic play in preschool and primary settings. *Young Children, 46*(6), 40–50.

O'Reilly, A. W., & Bornstein, M. H. (1993). Caregiver-child interaction in play. *New Directions in Child Development, 59*, 55–66.

Ohman-Rodriquez, J. (2004). Music from inside out: Promoting emergent composition with young children. *Young Children, 59*(4), 50–55.

Oller, D. K., & Eilers, R. E. (Eds.). 2002. *Language and literacy in bilingual children.* Bristol, UK: Multilingual Matters.

Ontai, L. & Thompson, R. A. (2002). Patterns of attachment and maternal discourse effects on children's emotion understanding from 3 to 5 years of age. *Social Development, 11*(4), 433–450.

Ostrov, J. M., Woods, K. E., Jansen, E. A., Casas, J. F., & Crick, N. R. (2004). An observational study of delivered and received aggression, gender, and social-psychological adjustment in preschool: "This white crayon doesn't work…" *Early Childhood Research Quarterly, 19*, 355–371.

Owens, C. V. (1999). Conversational science 101A: Talking it up! *Young Children, 54*(5), 4–9.

Páez, M. M., Tabors, P. O., & López, L. M. (2007). Dual language and literacy development of Spanish-speaking preschool children. *Journal of Applied Developmental Psychology, 28*(2), 85–102.

Palermo, F., Hanish, L. D., Martin, C. L., Fabes, R. A., & Reiser, M. (2007). Preschoolers' academic readiness: What role does the teacher-child relationship play? *Early Childhood Research Quarterly, 22*, 407–422.

Palmer, H. (2001). The music, movement, and learning connection. *Young Children, 56*(5), 13–17.

Parish-Morris, J., Hennon, E. A., Hirsh-Pasek, K., Golinkoff, R. M., & Tager-Flusberg, H. (2007). Children with autism illuminate the role of social intention in word learning. *Child Development, 78*, 1265–1287.

Parker, J. G. & Asher, S. R. (1987). Peer relations and later personal adjustment: Are low-accepted children at risk? *Psychological Bulletin, 102*, 357–389.

Pauen, S. (2002). The global-to-basic level shift in infants' categorical thinking: First evidence from a longitudinal study. *International Journal of Behavioral Development, 26*, 492–499.

Payne, J. N., & Huinker, D. M. (1993). Early number and numeration. In R. J. Jensen (Ed.), *Research ideas for the classroom: Early childhood mathematics* (pp. 43–71). New York: Macmillan.

Payne, V. G., & Rink, J. E. (1997). Physical education in the developmentally appropriate integrated curriculum. In C. H. Hart, D. C. Burts, & R. Charlesworth (Eds.), *Integrated curriculum and developmentally appropriate practice: Birth to age eight*, pp. 145–170. Albany, New York: SUNY Press.

Pearson, B., & Fernández, S. (1994). Patterns of interaction in the lexical growth in two languages of bilingual infants and toddlers. *Language Learning, 44*(4), 617–653.

Pearson, B., Fernández, S., Lewedeg, V., & Oller, D. K. (1997). The relation of input factors to lexical learning by bilingual infants. *Applied Psycholinguistics, 18*, 41–58.

Peisner-Feinberg, E. S., Burchinal, M. R., Clifford, R. M., Culkin, M. L., Howes, C., & Kagan, S. L., et al. (1999). The children of the cost, quality, and outcomes study go to school: Technical report. Chapel Hill: University of North Carolina at Chapel Hill, Frank Porter Graham Child Development Center.

Pellegrini, A. D., & Galda, L. (1982). The effects of theme-fantasy play training on the development of children's story comprehension. *American Educational Research Journal, 19,* 443–452.

Peña, E. D., & Mendez-Perez, A. (2006). Individualistic and collectivistic approaches to language learning. *Zero to Three, 27*(1), 34–41.

Perry, M. W. (2006). A splash of color. *Young Children, 61*(2), 83.

Petersen, S., & Wittmer, D. (2008). Relationship-based infant care: Responsive, on demand, and predictable. *Young Children, 63*(3), 40–42.

Peterson, S. M., & French, L. (2008). Supporting young children's explanations through inquiry science in preschool. *Early Childhood Research Quarterly, 23*(3), 395–408.

Pettit, G. S., & Harrist, A. W. (1993). Children's aggressive and socially unskilled playground behavior with peers: Origins in early family relations. In C. H. Hart (Ed.), *Children on playgrounds: Research perspectives and applications.* Albany, NY: SUNY Press.

Piaget, J., & Inhelder, B. (1967). *The child's conception of* space (F. J. Langdon & J. L Lunzer, Trans.). New York: Norton.

Pianta, R. C. (1999). *Enhancing relationships between children and teachers.* Washington, DC: American Psychological Association.

Pianta, R. C., & Stuhlman, M. W. (2004). Teacher-child relationships and children's success in the first years of school. *School Psychology Review, 33,* 444–458.

Pica, R. (1997). Beyond physical development: Why young children need to move. *Young Children, 52*(6), 4–11.

Pica, R. (2006). Physical fitness and the early childhood curriculum. *Young Children, 61*(3), 12–19.

Pickett, L. (1998). Literacy learning during block play. *Journal of Research in Childhood Education, 12*(2), 225–230.

Pierce, K. L., & Schreibman, L. (1994). Teaching daily living skills to children with autism in unsupervised settings through pictorial self-management. *Journal of Applied Behavioral Analysis 27*(3), 471–481.

Piker, R. A., & Rex, L. A. (2008). Influences of teacher-child interactions on English language development in a Head Start classroom. *Early Childhood Education Journal, 36,* 187–193.

Pinciotti, P. (1993). Creative drama and young children: The dramatic learning connection. *Arts Education Policy Review, 94*(6), 24–28.

Plumert, J. M., & Hawkins, A. M. (2001). Biases in young children's communication about spatial relations: Containment versus proximity. *Child Development, 72,* 22–36.

Ponitz, C. E. C., McLelland, M. M., Jewkes, A. M., Conner, C. M., Farris, C. L., & Morrison, F. J. (2008). Touch your toes! Developing a direct measure of behavioral regulation in early childhood. *Early Childhood Research Quarterly, 23*(2), 141–158.

Poole, C., & Miller, S. A. (n.d.) *Problem solving in action.* Retrieved February 1, 2009, from http://www2.scholastic.com/browse/article.jsp?id=3746479

Pope, C. E., & Springate, K. W. (1995). Creativity in early childhood classrooms. *ERIC Digest.* ED389474 1995-12-00. Retrieved July 16, 2007, from www.eric.ed.gov

Preissler, M. A., & Carey, S. (2004). Do both pictures and words function as symbols for 18- and 24-month old children? *Cognition and development, 5*(2), 185–212.

Public Broadcasting System. (n.d.) *Child Development and Early Child Development Advice/PBS parents: Child development tracker.* Retrieved September 7, 2007, from www.pbs.org/parents/childdevelopment/

Putallaz, M. & Gottman, J.M. (1981). Social skills and group acceptance. In S. R. Asher & J. M. Gottman (Eds.), *The development of children's friendships* (pp. 116–149). New York: Cambridge University Press.

Putallaz, M., & Wasserman, A. (1990). Children's entry behavior. In S. R. Asher & J. D. Coie (Eds.), *Peer rejection in childhood* (pp. 60–89). New York: Cambridge University Press.

Ramsey, P. G. (2003). Growing up with the contradictions of race and class. In C. Copple (Ed.), *A world of difference: Readings on teaching young children in a diverse society* (pp. 24–28). Washington, DC: National Association for the Education of Young Children.

Ratner, N. B. (2001). Atypical language development. In J. B. Gleason (Ed.), *The development of language* (pp. 369–406). Boston: Allyn & Bacon.

Raver, C. C., & Zigler, E. F. (1997). Social competence: An untapped dimension in evaluating Head Start's success. *Early Childhood Research Quarterly, 12,* 363–385.

Rawson, R. M., & Goetz, E. M. (1983). *Reading-related behavior in preschoolers: Environmental factors and teacher modeling.* Unpublished manuscript.

Ray, A., Bowman, B., & Brownell, J. O. (2006). Teacher-child relationships, social-emotional development, and school achievement. In B. Bowman & E. K. Moore (Eds.), *School readiness and social-emotional development: Perspectives on cultural diversity* (pp. 7–22). Washington, DC: National Black Child Development Institute, Inc.

Reio, T. G., Jr., Petrosko, J. M., Wiswell, A. K., & Thongsukmag, J. (2006). The measurement and conceptualization of curiosity. *The Journal of Genetic Psychology, 16*(2), 117–135.

Resources for exploring the creative arts with young children. (2004). *Young Children, 59*(4), 58–59.

Richard, B. A., & Dodge, K. A. (1982). Social maladjustment and problem-solving in school aged children. *Journal of Consulting and Clinical Psychology, 50,* 226–233.

Richardson, K., & Salkeld, L. (1995). Transforming mathematics curriculum. In S. Bredekamp & T. Rosegrant (Eds.), *Reaching potentials: Transforming early childhood curriculum and assessment,* Vol. 2. Washington, DC: National Association for the Education of Young Children.

Richgels, D. J. (1986). An investigation of preschool and kindergarten children. *Journal of Research and Development in Education, 19*(4), 41–47.

Riley, D., San Juan, R. R., Klinkner, J., & Ramminger, A. (2008). *Social & emotional development: Connecting science and practice in early childhood settings.* St. Paul, MN and Washington, DC: Redleaf Press and National Association for the Education of Young Children.

Riley, J. (1996). *The Teaching of Reading.* London: Paul Chapman.

Rimm-Kaufman, S., Pianta, R. C., & Cox, M. (2000). Teachers' judgments of problems in the transition to school. *Early Childhood Research Quarterly, 15*(2), 147–166.

Robert, D. L. (1999). *The effects of a preschool movement program on motor skill acquisition, movement concept formation, and movement practice behavior.* (Doctoral dissertation, West Virginia University). Retrieved August 10, 2008 from http://eidr.wvu.edu/files/1193/Robert_D_Diss.pdf

Roberts, J. E., Burchinal, M., & Durham, M. (1999). Parents' report of vocabulary and grammatical development of African American preschoolers: Child and environmental associations. *Child Development, 70,* 92–106.

Robinson, C. C., Anderson, G. T., Porter, C. L., Hart, C. H., & Wouden-Miller, M. (2003). Sequential transition patterns of preschoolers' social interactions during child-initiated play: Is parallel-aware play a bidirectional bridge to other play states? *Early Childhood Research Quarterly, 18,* 3–21.

Robinson, L. (2003). Technology as a scaffold for emergent literacy: Interactive storybooks for toddlers. *Young Children, 58*(6), 42–48.

Rodger, L. (1996). Adding movement throughout the day. *Young Children, 51*(3), 4–7.

Rodriguez, R. (1983). *Hunger of memory: The education of Richard Rodriguez.* New York: Bantam Books.

Rogoff, B., Mistry, A., Goncu, A., & Mosier, C. (1993). Guided participation in cultural activity by toddlers and caregivers. *Monographs of the Society for Research in Child Development, 58,* Serial No. 236.

Rosenow, N. (2008). Learning to love the Earth… and each other. *Young Children, 63*(1), 10–13.

Roskos, K., Tabors, P., & Lenhart, L. (2004). *Oral language and early literacy in preschool.* Newark, DE: International Reading Association.

Ross, M. E. (2000). Science their way. *Young Children, 55*(2), 6–13.

Rowe, M. B. (1987). Wait time: Slowing down may be a way of speeding up. *American Educator, 11,* 38–43, 47.

Rubin, K. H., Bukowski, W., & Parker, J. G. (1998). Peer interactions, relationships, and groups. In W. Damon & N. Eisenberg (Eds.), *Handbook of child psychology,* Vol. 3: *Social, emotional, and personality development* (pp. 619–700). New York: John Wiley & Sons.

Rule, A. C. (2007). Mystery boxes: Helping children improve their reasoning. *Early Childhood Education Journal, 35*(1), 13–18.

Rule, A. C., & Stewart, R. A. (2002). Effects of practical life materials on kindergartners' fine motor skills. *Early Childhood Education Journal, 30*(1), 9–13.

Russell, S. J. (1991). Counting noses and scary things: Children construct their ideas about data. In D. Vere-Jones (Ed.), *Proceedings of the third international conference on teaching statistics* (pp. 158–164). Voorburg, Netherlands: International Statistical Institute.

Russo, M. (with Colurciello, S. G. & Kelly, R.). (2008). For the birds! Seeing, being, and creating the bird world. *Young Children, 63*(1), 26–30.

Sacha, T. J., & Russ, S. W. (2006). Effects of pretend imagery on learning dance in preschool children. *Early Childhood Education Journal, 33*(5), 341–345.

Salmon, M., & Akaran, S. E. (2005). Cross-cultural e-mail connections. *Young Children, 60*(5), 36.

Saltz, E., Dixon, D., & Johnson, H. (1997). Training disadvantaged preschoolers on various fantasy activities: Effects on cognitive functioning and impulse control. *Child Development, 48,* 367–380.

Saltz, E., Dixon, D., & Johnson, H. (1997). Training disadvantaged preschoolers on various fantasy activities: Effects on cognitive functioning and impulse control. *Child Development, 48,* 367–380.

Sanders, S. W. (2002). *Active for life: Developmentally appropriate movement programs for young children.* Washington, DC: National Association for the Education of Young Children.

Sanders, S. W. (2006). Physical education in kindergarten. In D. F. Gullo (Ed.), *K today: Teaching and learning in the kindergarten year* (pp. 127–137). Washington, DC: National Association for the Education of Young Children.

Sarama, J., & Clements, D. H. (2003). Early childhood corner: Building blocks of early childhood mathematics. *Teaching Children Mathematics, 9*(8), 480–484.

Sarama, J., & Clements, D. H. (2004). *Building Blocks* for early childhood mathematics. *Early Childhood Research Quarterly, 19,* 181–189

Sarama, J., & Clements, D. H. (2006). Mathematics in kindergarten. In D. F. Gullo (Ed.), *K Today: Teaching and learning in the kindergarten year* (pp. 85–94). Washington, DC: National Association for the Education of Young Children.

Satchwell, L. (1994). Preschool physical education class structure. *Journal of Physical Education, Recreation, and Dance, 65*(6), 34–36.

Saunders, G. (1988). *Bilingual children: From birth to teens.* Philadelphia: Multilingual Matters.

Saville-Troike, M. (1987). Dilingual discourse: The negotiation of meaning without a common code. *Linguistics, 25,* 81–106.

Saville-Troike, M. (1988). Private speech: Evidence for second language learning strategies during the "silent" period. *Journal of Child Language, 15*(3), 567–590.

Scarborough, H., & Dobrich, W. (1994). On the efficacy of reading to preschoolers. *Developmental Review, 14,* 245–302.

Scharmann, M. W. (1998). We are friends when we have memories together. *Young Children, 53*(2), 27–29.

Schickedanz, J. A. (1999). *Much more than the abc's: The early stages of reading and writing.* Washington, DC: National Association for the Education of Young Children.

Schickedanz, J. A., & Casbergue, R. M. (2009). *Writing in preschool: Learning to orchestrate meaning and marks.* (2nd ed.). Newark, DE: International Reading Association.

Schickedanz, J. A., Schickedanz, D. I., Forsyth, P. D., & Forsyth, G. A. (2001). *Understanding children and adolescents* (4th ed.). Boston: Allyn & Bacon.

Schmidt, D. (1985). Adult influences on curiosity in children. *Early Report, 12*(3), 2–3.

Schmidt, H. M., Burts, D. C., Durham, R. S., Charlesworth, R., & Hart, C. H. (2007). Impact of developmental appropriateness of teacher guidance strategies on kindergarten children's interpersonal relations. *Journal of Research in Childhood Education, 21,* 290–301.

Schultz, D., Izard, C. E., & Ackerman, B. P. (2000). Children's anger attribution bias: Relations to family adjustment and social adjustment. *Social Development, 9,* 284–301.

Seefeldt, C. (1995). Transforming curriculum in social studies. In S. Bredekamp & T. Rosegrant (Eds.), *Reaching potentials: Transforming early childhood curriculum and assessment,* Vol. 2. (pp. 109–124). Washington, DC: National Association for the Education of Young Children.

Seefeldt, C. (1997). Social studies in the developmentally appropriate integrated curriculum. In C. H. Hart, D. C. Burts, & R. Charlesworth (Eds.), *Integrated curriculum and developmentally appropriate practice: Birth to age eight* (pp. 171–199). Albany, NY: SUNY Press.

Segatti, L., Brown-DuPaul, J., & Keyes, T. L. (2003). Using everyday materials to promote problem solving in toddlers. *Young Children, 58*(5), 12–16, 18.

Seo, K. (2003). What children's play tells us about teaching mathematics. *Young Children, 58*(1), 28–33.

Share, D. L., & Jaffe-Gur, T. (1999). How reading begins: A study of preschoolers' print identification strategies. *Cognition and Instruction, 17,* 177–213.

Shipman, K. L., & Zeman, J. (2001). Socialization of children's emotion regulation in mother-child dyads: A developmental psychopathology perspective. *Development and Psychopathology, 13,* 317–336.

Shonkoff, J. P., & Phillips, D. A. (Eds). (2000). *From neurons to neighborhoods: The science of early childhood development.* Washington, DC: National Academy Press.

Shore, R. & Strasser, J. (2006). Music for their minds. *Young Children, 61*(2), 62–67.

Shure, M. B. (1997). Interpersonal cognitive problem solving: Primary prevention of early high-risk behaviors in the preschool and primary years. In G. W. Albee & T. P. Gullota (Eds.), *Primary prevention works* (pp. 167–190). Thousand Oaks, CA: Sage Publications.

Sigman, M. & Ruskin, E. (1999). Continuity and change in the social competence of children with autism, Down syndrome, and developmental delay. *Monographs of the Society for Research in Child Development,* 64 (1, Serial No. 256).

Silvern, S., Williamson, P., & Waters, B. (1983). Play as a mediator of comprehension: An alternative to play training. *Educational Research Quarterly, 7,* 16–21.

Slaby, R. G., Roedell, W. C., Arezzo, D., & Hendrix, K. (1995). *Early violence prevention: Tools for teachers of young children.* Washington, DC: National Association for the Education of Young Children.

Smetana, J. G. (1984). Toddlers' social interactions regarding moral and conventional transgressions. *Child Development, 55,* 1767–1776.

Smidts, D. P., Jacobs, R., & Anderson, V. (2004). The object classification task for children (OCTC): A measure of concept generation and mental flexibility in early childhood. *Developmental Neuropsychology, 26*(1), 385–401.

Smilansky, S., & Shefatya, L. (1990). *Facilitating play: A medium for promoting cognitive, socio-emotional, and academic development in young children.* Gaithersburg, MD: Psychosocial and Educational Publications.

Smith, H., & Heckman, P. (1995). The Mexican-American war. In E. García & B. McLaughlin (Eds.), *Meeting the challenge of linguistic and cultural diversity in early childhood education* (pp. 64–84). New York: Teachers College Press.

Smith, P. K., & Hart, C. H. (2002). Blackwell handbook of childhood social development. Oxford: Blackwell Publishers.

Smith, S. P. (2006). *Early childhood mathematics* (3rd ed.). Boston: Pearson.

Snow, C. E. (1983a). Age differences in second language acquisition: Research findings and folk psychology. In K. Bailey, M. Long, & S. Peck (Eds.), *Second language acquisition studies* (pp. 141–150). Rowley, MA: Newbury House.

Snow, C. E. (1983b). Literacy and language: Relationships during the preschool years. *Harvard Educational Review, 53*(2), 165–189.

Snow, C. E. (1991). The theoretical basis for relationships between language and literacy development. *Journal of Research in Childhood Education, 6*(1), 5–10.

Snow, C. E., Burns, M. S., & Griffin, P. (Eds.). (1998). *Preventing reading difficulties in young children.* Washington, DC: National Academy Press.

Snow, C. E., & Hoefnagel-Hohle, M. (1977). Age differences in the pronunciation of foreign sounds. *Language and Speech, 20,* 357–365.

Snow, C. E., & Van Hemel, S. B. (Eds.). (2008). *Early childhood assessment: Why, what, and how? Report of the National Research Council of the National Academies.* Washington, DC: National Academies Press. http://www.nap.edu/catalog/12446.html

Son, S. H., & Meisels, S. J. (2006). The relationship of young children's motor skills to later school achievement. *Merrill-Palmer Quarterly, 52,* 755–778.

Spaulding, C., Gottlib, N. H., & Jensen, J. (2008). Promoting physical activity in low-income preschool children. *Journal of Physical Education, Recreation & Dance, 79*(5), 42–47.

Spivak, G., & Shure, M. B. (1974). *Social adjustment of young children: A cognitive approach to solving real-life problems.* San Francisco: Jossey-Bass.

Stadler, M. A., & Ward, G. C. (2005). Supporting the narrative development of young children. *Early Childhood Education Journal, 33*(2), 73–80.

Staley, L., & Portman, P. A. (2000). Red Rover, Red Rover, it's time to move over. *Young Children, 55*(1), 67–72.

Stark, R. (1978). Features of infant sounds: The emergence of cooing. *Journal of Child Language, 5,* 1–12.

Starkey, P., Klein, A., & Wakely, A. (2004). Enhancing young children's mathematical knowledge through a pre-kindergarten mathematics intervention. *Early Childhood Research Quarterly, 19,* 99–120.

Steglin, D. A. (2005). Making the case for play policy: Research-based reasons to support play-based environments. *Young Children, 60*(2), 76–85.

Stetson, C., Jablon, J., & Dombro, A. L. (2009). *Observation: The key to responsive teaching.* Washington, DC: Teaching Strategies, Inc.

Stevenson, H. W., & Newman, R. S. (1986). Long-term prediction of achievement and attitudes in mathematics and reading. *Child Development 57*, 646–659.

Stewart, R. A., Rule, A. C., & Giordano, D. A. (2007). The effect of fine motor skill activities on kindergarten student attention. *Early Childhood Education Journal, 35*, 103–109.

Stipek, D. (2002). *Motivation to learn: Integrating theory and practice* (4th ed.). Boston: Allyn & Bacon.

Stipek, D., Recchia, S, & McClintic, S. (1992). Self-evaluations in young children. *Monographs of the Society for Research in Child Development, 57*(1), Serial No. 226.

Stipek, D. J., Feiler, R., Byler, P., Ryan, R., Milburn, S., & Salmon, J. M. (1998). Good beginnings: What difference does the program make in preparing young children for school? *Journal of Applied Psychology, 19*(1), 41–66.

Stoel-Gammon, C., & Menn, L. (2004). Phonological development: Learning sounds and sound patterns. In J. B. Gleason (Ed.), *The development of language* (7th ed.). Boston: Allyn & Bacon.

Strickland, D. S. (2006). Language and literacy in kindergarten. In D. F. Gullo (Ed.), *K today: Teaching and learning in the kindergarten year* (pp. 73–84). Washington, DC: National Association for the Education of Young Children.

Strickland, D. S., & Riley-Ayers, S. (2007). *Literacy leadership in early childhood: The essential guide.* New York: Teacher's College Press.

Strickland, D. S., & Schickedanz, J. A. (2004). *Learning about print in preschool: Working with letters, words, and beginning links with phonemic awareness.* Newark, DE: International Reading Association.

Strickland, D. S., & Shanahan, T. (2004). Laying the groundwork for literacy. *Educational Leadership, 61*(6), 74–77.

Stuart, M. (1995). Prediction and qualitative assessment of five- and six-year-old children's reading: A longitudinal study. *British Journal of Educational Psychology, 65*, 287–296.

Sulzby, E. (1985).Children's emergent reading of favorite storybooks: A developmental study. *Reading Research Quarterly, 20*(4), 464.

Sutterby, J. A., & Frost, J. L. (2002). Making playgrounds fit for children and children fit on playgrounds. *Young Children, 57*(3), 36–42.

Szechter, L. E., & Liben, L. S. (2007). Children's aesthetic understanding of photographic art and the quality of art-related parent–child interactions. *Child Development, 78*(3), 879–894.

Tabors, P. O. (1998, November). What early childhood educators need to know: Developing effective programs for linguistically and culturally diverse children and families. *Young Children, 53*(6), 20–26.

Tabors, P. O. (2002). Language and literacy for *all* children. *Head Start Bulletin, 74,* 10–14.

Tabors, P. O. (2008). *One child, two languages: A guide for early childhood educators of children learning English as a second language* (2nd ed.). Baltimore: Paul H. Brookes.

Tabors, P. O., Aceves, C., Bartolomé, L., Páez, M., & Wolf, A. (2000). Language development of linguistically diverse children in Head Start classrooms: Three ethnographic portraits. *NHSA Dialog, 3*(3), 409–440.

Tabors, P. O., Beals, D. E., & Weizman, Z. O. (2001). "You know what oxygen is?" Learning new words at home. In D. K. Dickinson & P. O. Tabors (Eds.), *Beginning literacy with language: Young children learning at home and school* (pp. 93–110). Baltimore: Paul H. Brookes.

Tabors, P. O., & López, L. M. (2005). How can teachers and parents help young children become (and stay) bilingual? *Head Start Bulletin, 78,* 14–17.

Tabors, P. O., Páez, M., & López, L. (2003). Dual language abilities of bilingual four-year olds: Initial findings from the Early Childhood Study of Language and Literacy Development of Spanish-speaking Children. *NABE Journal of Research and Practice, 1*(1), 70–91. Retrieved August 16, 2007, from http://www.uc.edu/njrp/pdfs/Tabors.pdf

Tabors, P. O., & Snow, C. (1994). English as a second language in preschools. In F. Genesee (Ed.), *Educating second language children: The whole child, the whole curriculum, the whole community* (pp. 103–125). New York: Cambridge University Press.

Tabors, P. O., & Snow, C. E. (2001). Young bilingual children and early literacy development. In S. B. Neuman & D. K. Dickinson (Eds.), *Handbook of early literacy research,* Vol. 1 (pp. 159–178). New York: Guilford.

Taeschner, T. (1983). *The sun is feminine: A study of language acquisition in bilingual children.* New York: Springer-Verlag.

Taylor, D. (1983). *Family literacy.* Exeter, NH: Heinemann.

Taylor, I. (1981). Writing systems and reading. In G. E. Mackinnon & T. G. Waller (Eds.), *Reading research: Advances in theory and practice* (Vol. 2), New York: Academic Press.

Taylor-Cox, J. (2003). Algebra in the early years? Yes. In D. Koralek (Ed.), *Spotlight on young children and math* (pp. 7–13). Washington, DC: National Association for the Education of Young Children.

Teaching and learning about science [Special section]. (2002). *Young Children, 57*(5), pp. 10–47.

Teaching and learning about social studies [Special section]. (2005). *Young Children, 60*(5), pp. 10–60.

Teale, W., & Yokota, J. (2000). Beginning reading and writing: Perspectives on instruction. In D. S. Strickland & L. M. Morrow (Eds.), *Beginning reading and writing: Language and literacy series* (pp. 3–21). Newark, DE: International Reading Association.

Tenenbaum, H. R., & Callanan, M. A. (2008). Parents' science talk to their children in Mexican-descent families residing in the United States. *International Journal of Behavioural Development, 32*(1), 1–12.

Tenenbaum, H. R., Rappolt-Schlichtmann, G., & Zanger, V. V. (2004). Children's learning about water in a museum and in the classroom. *Early Childhood Research Quarterly, 19*(1), 40–58.

Thatcher, D. H. (2001). Reading in the math class: Selecting and using picture books for math investigations. *Young Children, 56*(4), 20–26.

Thompson, C. M. (1995). Transforming curriculum in the visual arts. In S. Bredekamp & T. Rosegrant (Eds.), *Reaching potentials: Transforming early childhood curriculum and assessment,* Vol. 2 (pp. 81–98). Washington, DC: National Association for the Education of Young Children.

Thompson, R. A., & Lagattuta, K. H. (2006). Feeling and understanding: Early emotional development. In K. McCartney & D. Phillips (Eds.), *Blackwell handbook of early childhood development* (pp. 317–337). Malden, MA: Blackwell Publishing.

Thompson, S. C. (2005). *Children as illustrators: Making meaning through art and language.* Washington, DC: National Association for the Education of Young Children.

Torquati, J., & Barber, J. (2005). Dancing with trees: Infants and toddlers in the garden. *Young Children, 60*(3), 40–47.

Trawick-Smith, J. (1998). An analysis of metaplay in the preschool years. *Early Childhood Research Quarterly, 13,* 433–452.

Trawick-Smith, J. (1998). Why play training works: An integrated model for play intervention. *Journal of Research in Childhood Education, 12,* 117–129.

Trawick-Smith, J. (2006). *Early childhood development: A multicultural perspective* (4th ed.). Upper Saddle River, NJ: Pearson.

Tsybina, I., Girolametto, L. E., Weitzman, E., & Greenberg, J. (2006). Recasts used with preschoolers learning English as their second language. *Early Childhood Education Journal, 34*, 177–185.

Tu, T. (2006). Preschool science environment: What is available in a preschool classroom? *Early Childhood Education Journal, 33*(4), 245–251.

Ulrich, B. D., & Ulrich, D. (1985). The role of balancing ability in performance of fundamental motor skills in 3-, 4-, 5-year-old children. In J. E. Clark & J. H. Humphrey (Eds.), *Motor development: Current selected research* (Vol. 1), pp. 87–97. Princeton: Princeton Book Company.

Van Hiele, P. M. (1986). *Structure and insight: A theory of mathematics education.* Orlando, FL: Academic Press.

Varol, F., & Farran, D. C. (2006). Early mathematical growth: How to support young children's mathematical development. *Early Childhood Education Journal, 33*, 381–387.

Verschueren, K., Buyck, P., & Marcoen, A. (2001). Self-representations and socioemotional competence in young children: A 3-year longitudinal. *Developmental Psychology, 37*, 126–134.

Vlach, H. A., & Carver, S. M. (2008). The effects of observation coaching on children's graphic representations. *Early Childhood Research and Practice, 10*(1). Retrieved April 7, 2009 from http://ecrp.uiuc.edu/v10n1/vlach.html

VORT Corporation. (2004). *HELP for preschoolers—Assessment strands: Ages 3–6 years.* Palo Alto, CA: Author.

VORT Corporation. (2004). *Revised HELP Checklist: Birth to three years.* Palo Alto, CA: Author.

Vukelich, C. (1990). Where's the paper? Literacy during dramatic play. *Childhood Education, 55*(4), 205–209.

Vygotsky, L. (1997). *The history of the development of higher mental functions.* In R. W. Rieber (Ed.), *The collected works of L. S. Vygotsky* (M. J. Hall, Trans., Vol. 4). New York: Plenum Press.

Wagner, R. K., Torgesen, J. K., Laughon, P., Simmons, K., & Rashotte, C. A. (1993). The development of young readers' phonological processing abilities. *Journal of Educational Psychology, 30*, 73–87.

Wagner, R. K., Torgesen, J. K., Rashotte, C. A., Hecht, S. A., Barker, T. A., Burgess, S. R., et al. (1997). Changing causal relations between phonological processing abilities and word-level reading as children develop from beginning to fluent readers: A 5-year longitudinal study. *Developmental Psychology, 33*, 468–479.

Wang, J. H. T. (2004). A study of gross motor skills of preschool children. *Journal of Research in Childhood Education, 19*(1), 32–43.

Wang, W. Y., & Ju, Y. H. (2002). Promoting balance and jumping skills in children with Down syndrome. *Perceptual Motor Skills, 94*, 443–438.

Washington state early learning and development benchmarks (2005). Retrieved May 23, 2007, from http://www.k12.wa.us/EarlyLearning/pubdocs/EarlyLearningBenchmarks.pdf

Webster-Stratton, C., & Herbert, M. (1994). *Troubled families—Problem children: Working with parents: A collaborative process.* Chichester, England: Wiley.

Weitzman, E., & Greenberg, J. (2002). *Learning language and loving it.* Toronto, Ontario: The Hanen Centre.

Wells, G. (1985). Preschool literacy-related activities and success in school. In D. R. Olance, N. Torrance, & A. Hildyard (Eds.), *Literacy, language, and learning* (pp. 229–255). Cambridge, England: Cambridge University Press.

Wells, G. (1986). *The meaning makers: Children learning language and using language to learn.* Portsmouth, NH: Heinemann.

Wentzel, K., & Asher, S. (1995). The academic lives of neglected, rejected, popular, and controversial children. *Child Development, 66*, 754–763.

West, J., Denton, K., & Germino-Hausken, E. (2000). *America's kindergartners: Findings from the early childhood longitudinal study, kindergarten class of 1998–99, Fall 1998.* Retrieved July 16, 2007, from http://ceep.crc.uiuc.edu/eecearchive/digests/ed-cite/ed438089.html

Whitehurst, G. J., & Fischel, J. (1994). Practitioner review: Early developmental language delay: What, if anything, should the clinician do about it? *Journal of Child Psychology and Psychiatry, 35*, 613–648.

Whitin, P. (2001). Kindness in a jar. *Young Children, 56*(5), 18–22.

Whitin, P., & Whitin, D. J. (2003). Developing mathematical understanding along the yellow brick road. In D. Koralek (Ed.), *Spotlight on young children and math* (pp. 25–28). Washington, DC: National Association for the Education of Young Children.

Whiting, B. B., & Edwards, C. P. (1988). *Children of different worlds.* Cambridge, MA: Harvard University Press.

Whiting, B. B., & Whiting, J. W. M. (1975). *Children of six cultures: A psycho-cultural analysis.* Cambridge, MA: Harvard University Press.

Wien, C. A., Keating, B., Coates, A., & Bigelow, B. (2008). Moving into uncertainty: Sculpture with three- to five-year-olds. *Young Children, 63*(4), 78–86.

Wiggins, D. G. (2007). Pre-K music and the emergent reader: Promoting literacy in a music-enhanced environment. *Early Childhood Education Journal, 35*(1), 55–64.

Williams, A. E. (2008). Exploring the natural world with infants and toddlers in an urban setting. *Young Children, 63*(1), 22–25.

Williams, K. C., & Cooney, M. H. (2006). Young children and social justice. *Young Children, 61*(2), 75–82.

Wishard, A. G., Shivers, E. M., Howes, C., & Ritchie, S. (2003). Child care program and teacher practices: Associations with quality and children's experiences. *Early Childhood Research Quarterly, 18*, 65–103.

Wong Fillmore, L. (1976). *The second time around: Cognitive and social strategies in second language acquisition.* Unpublished doctoral dissertation, Stanford University, Palo Alto.

Wong Fillmore, L. (1979). Individual differences in second language acquisition. In C. J. Fillmore, D. Kempler, & W. S-Y. Wang (Eds.), *Individual differences in language ability and language behavior* (pp. 203–228). New York: Academic Press.

Wong Fillmore, L. (1985). *Second language learning in children: A proposed model.* In *English Language Development. Proceedings of a conference on issues in English language development for minority language education.* Washington, DC: ERIC Clearinghouse on Languages and Linguistics. (ERIC Document Reproduction Service No. ED273149)

Wong Fillmore, L. (1991a). Language and cultural issues in the early education of language minority children. In S. Kagan (Ed.), *The care and education of America's young children: Obstacles and opportunities. 90th yearbook of the National Society for the Study of Education, Part I* (pp. 30–49). Chicago: University of Chicago Press.

Wong Fillmore, L. (1991b). When learning a second language means losing the first. *Early Childhood Research Quarterly, 6*(3), 323–346.

Woodard, C., Haskins, G., Schaefer, G., & Smolen, L. (2004). Let's talk: A different approach to oral language development. *Young Children, 59*(4), 92–95.

Worden, P. E., & Boettcher, W. (1990). Young children's acquisition of alphabet knowledge. *Journal of Reading Behavior, 20*(3), 277–295.

Wright, C., Bacigalupa, C., Black, T., & Burton, M. (2008). Windows into children's thinking: A guide to storytelling and dramatization. *Early Childhood Education Journal, 35*(4), 363–369.

Wu, P., Robinson, C. C., Yang, C, Hart, C. H., Olsen, S. F., Porter, C. L., et al. (2002). Similarities and differences in mothers' parenting of preschoolers in China and the United States. *International Journal of Behavioral Development, 26*, 481–491.

Yamamoto, J., & Kubota, M. (1983). Emotional development of Japanese-American children. In G. J. Powell (Ed.), *The psychosocial development of minority children* (pp. 237–247). New York: Brunner/Mazel.

Yeats, K. O., Schultz, L. H., & Selman, R. L. (1991). The development of interpersonal negotiation strategies in thought and action: A social-cognitive link to behavioral adjustment and social status. *Merrill-Palmer Quarterly, 37,* 369–405.

Yoon, J., & Onchwari, J. A. (2006). Teaching young children science: Three key points. *Early Childhood Education Journal, 33*(6), 419–423.

Young, D., & Behounek, L. M. (2006). Kindergartners use PowerPoint to lead their own parent–teacher conferences. *Young Children, 61*(2), 24–26.

Youngblade, L. M., & Dunn J. (1995). Individual differences in young children's pretend play with mother and sibling: Links to relationships and understanding of other people's feelings and beliefs. *Child Development, 66,* 1472–1492.

Younger, B. A., & Johnson, K. E. (2004). Infants' comprehension of toy replicas as symbols for real objects. *Cognitive Psychology, 18,* 207–242.

Youngstrom, E., Wolpaw, J. M., Kogos, J. L., Schoff, K., Ackerman, B., & Izard, C. (2000). Interpersonal problem solving in preschool and first grade: Developmental change and ecological validity. *Journal of Clinical Child Psychology, 29,* 589–602.

Yuzawa, M., Bart, W. M., Yuzawa, M., & Junko, I. (2005). Young children's knowledge and strategies for comparing sizes. *Early Childhood Research Quarterly, 20,* 239–253.

Zachopoulou, E., Tsapakidou, A., & Derri, V. (2004). The effects of a developmentally appropriate music and movement program on motor performance. *Early Childhood Research Quarterly, 19,* 631–642.

Zaslow, M., & Martinez-Beck, I. (Eds.). (2005). *Critical issues in early childhood professional development.* Baltimore: Paul H. Brookes.

Zill, N., Collins, M., West, J., & Hausken, E.G. (1995). *Approaching kindergarten: A look at preschoolers in the United States.* Washington, DC: U.S. Department of Education, Office of Education.

Zimmerman, E., & Zimmerman, L. (2000). Art education and early childhood education: The young child as creator and meaning maker within a community context. *Young Children, 55*(6), 87–92.

Zur, O., & Gelman, R. (2004). Young children can add and subtract by predicting and checking. *Early Childhood Research Quarterly, 19,* 121–137.

KAFFE FASSETT'S BOLD BLOOMS

KAFFE FASSETT'S BOLD BLOOMS

Quilts and Other Works Celebrating Flowers

KAFFE FASSETT WITH LIZA PRIOR LUCY

PHOTOGRAPHY BY DEBBIE PATTERSON

ABRAMS | NEW YORK

INTRODUCTION *7*

PART ONE

Designing with Bold Blooms

INSPIRATION *13*
*In Pursuit of Bold Blooms
in Decorative Arts*

THE SINGLE BLOSSOM *19*
Stitching Needlepoint Blooms

FABRICS IN BLOOM *21*
*Drawing Blossoms for
Quilting Cottons*

FLOWERS ON RIBBONS *26*
Designing Strips of Abstract Flowers

FLORAL PATCHWORK *29*
Lush Arrangements of Flower Prints

LIVE FLOWERS *34*
Arranging Fresh Blossoms

BOUQUET STILL LIFES *36*
Painting Cut Flowers

PART TWO

*Bold Bloom Quilts
and Needlepoints*

NEUTRALS & SOFT PASTELS *40*
Gray Random Strips Quilt 44
Gray Blocks Quilt 46
White Dahlia Needlepoint Pillow 48

BRIGHT PASTELS *50*
Radiating Bubbles Quilt 54
Yellow Sunlight Quilt 56
Basket Quilt 58
Bouquet Needlepoint Pillow 60

BRILLIANT HIGHS *62*
Attic Window On-Point Quilt 66
Seed Packet Quilt 68
Round and Round Quilt 70
Carlton Ware Needlepoint Pillow 72

SMOLDERING DEEP TONES *74*
Hexagon Florets Quilt 78
Tawny Hatboxes Quilt 80
Pink Peonies Needlepoint Pillow 82

CONTENTS

LEAFY GREENS & FLOWERS *84*
Leafy Appliqué Quilt 88
Leafy Medallion Quilt 90
Lattice with Vases Quilt 92
Tulip Vase Needlepoint Pillow 94

RICH, DARK TONES *96*
Blue Ohio Star Quilt 100
Millefiore Snowball Quilt 102
String Stripes Quilt 104
Dark Peony Needlepoint Pillow 106

HIGH CONTRAST *108*
Floral Octagons Quilt 112
High-Contrast Squares Quilt 114
Carnations Needlepoint Pillow 116

PART THREE
How To

INSTRUCTIONS *120*
Quilting Basics 204
Needlepoint Basics 210

TEMPLATES *211*

SOURCES *221*

ACKNOWLEDGMENTS *221*

INTRODUCTION

———

For many years I've dreamed of doing a book celebrating my passion for flowers in the decorative arts. I've been privileged to travel to all corners of the globe to see inspiring uses of flowers in everything from embroidery to wall decoration to architectural details.

My love of live flowers is no less passionate and never far from my color-processing thoughts. Realizing my love of blooms, my great friend photographer Steve Lovi taught me to explore gardens at different seasons and to draw people's attention to the intense beauty of flower forms and colors. When I was planning my book *Glorious Knitting* in the 1980s, he encouraged me to have garments of certain color schemes knitted to coincide with the seasons at the gardens and parks where he planned to do our fashion shoots. During the last creative phase of his life, he would hit the flower markets of San Francisco at their dawn opening and be home ready to shoot a beautifully composed still life as the light became strong enough in his studio. I could easily do a whole book on the inspiration I gained from his photographs of flowers, so great is my admiration for his ingenious eye.

While creating this book, I focused on my desire to bring others a little closer to seeing flowers the way I do. Color is the starting point, and I've arranged the projects into color moods. Few other objects on this earth capture and reflect color the way flower petals do. From delicate pale subtleties to brilliant saturated primary hues to the smoldering depths of the darkest purples and bronze tones, flowers and foliage have it all.

Shape, of course, is vital to communicating the flower's powerful beauty. What has always grabbed me are large-scale shapes that create the wow factor in nature. Perhaps it is my theatrical side that prefers florals that "read" from a stage or pop out of a textile design. There are plenty of people in the world who dissolve with delight over lilies of the valley, snowdrops, or tiny forget-me-nots, and I love them, too, but mostly I want to celebrate the extoverts of the plant world. The lacy delicate sprays we can leave aside for now as we plunge into the dramatic, full-blown, bold blooms of this world—blooms that aren't shy, that stand out with punch and pizzazz, that sing opera not lullabies.

In addition to giving you flower-inspired projects to work on here, I share a behind-the-scenes look into the simple processes I go through when designing and painting bold blooms—from inspiration to color palettes to the final renderings in the forms of fabrics, quilts, needlepoints, ribbons, and live displays. I show you my designs and ideas as they "bloom."

When designing the quilts included, I had at my disposal so many outspoken blooms in the array of super-large-scale floral prints in the Kaffe Fassett Collective fabric collection and in other knockout floral fabrics I have gathered over the years. "Fussy-cutting" very large flowers and smaller strong ones out of the fabrics allowed me to focus attention on their boldness. It also enabled me to cherry-pick colors from fabrics to create my specific color schemes. With needlepoint, of course, I was able to create any pronounced flower I desired.

While the projects included here feature the crafts of patchwork and needlepoint, the ideas I present translate to any discipline that uses pattern and color, including mosaics, embroidery, beading, knitting, rag rugs, furniture and wall decoration, and the display of live flowers. In producing a study of the bold flower element in the arts and nature, my desire is to inspire makers of many disciplines to use this floral excitement in their own way. By dedicating this book to the bold blooms, I hope to be sending you off on a passion-filled creative journey.

I design fabrics as part of the Kaffe Fassett Collective along with Brandon Mably and Philip Jacobs. The large florals on the table at right are two of Philip's designs—*Japanese Chyrsanthemum* and *Gloxinia*. Philip beautifully paints his designs based on classic vintage florals and other archival materials. I choose all of the colors for his fabrics, and it is one of my joyous tasks.

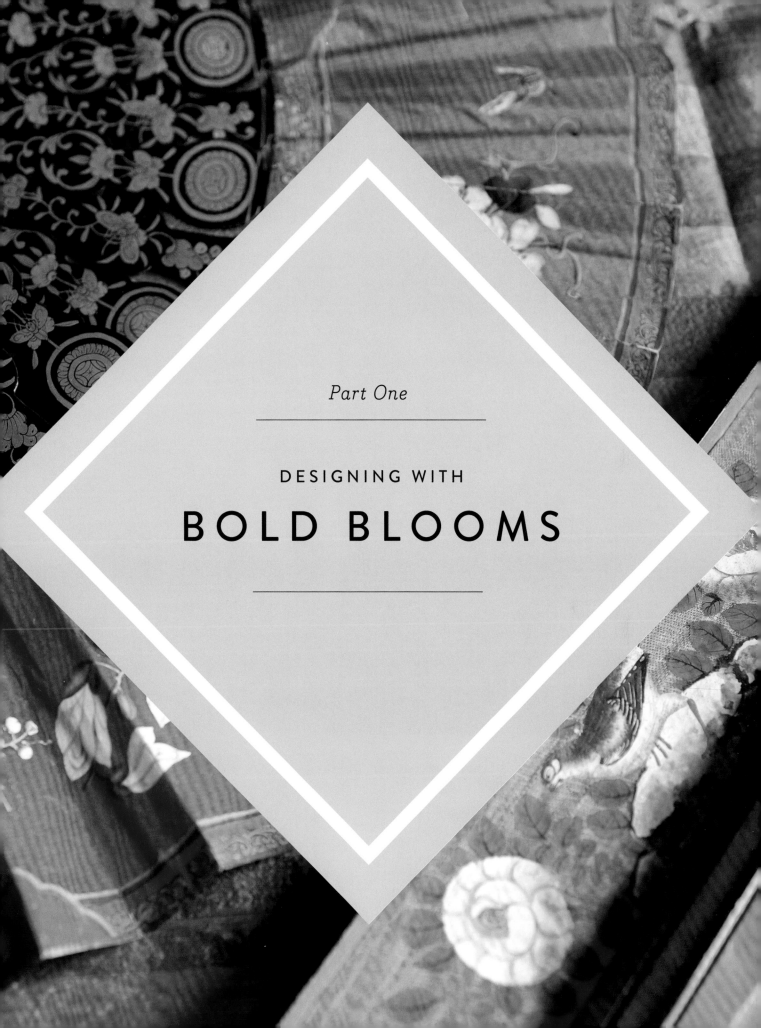

Part One

DESIGNING WITH

BOLD BLOOMS

INSPIRATION

In Pursuit of Bold Blooms in Decorative Arts

Flowers have been a focus in my work for nearly as long as I can remember. They are a fragile, ephemeral element that seems born to delight us and help us realize that there is more to life than mere survival. The glow of pure color in flowers is my essential attraction to them. Of course, I am not alone. Flowers have been inspiring artists and craftspeople in nearly all creative media throughout time, in weaving, embroidery, mosaic, painting, jewelry, pottery, and wallpapers. The way flowers are depicted in decorative arts is endlessly fascinating to me.

To be sure, there are many moods and scales to floral depiction, from delicate sprays through riotous wildflower meadows. But my main obsession is with large-scale, articulate blooms with a pronounced shape, such as spiky dahlias, voluptuous peonies, and facelike pansies.

Much of my inspiration comes from East Asia. China and especially Japan are treasure troves when it comes to bold flower forms. From the most realistic flower paintings to the most abstracted simplified forms in unusual colorings, Japanese culture must be the most fertile on earth for flowers in decorative arts. The Japanese have entire festivals dedicated to individual blooms as they come into season, such as morning glories, chrysanthemums, and hydrangeas. As I write this, I'm looking at a gigantic weaving of a flaming orange chrysanthemum on a kimono sash probably made for the kabuki theater. The massive explosion of fiery petals shows half a flower that is the size of a large watermelon. How that must have glowed from the kabuki stage!

My full-on conscious search for floral inspiration started when I arrived in London from California in the 1960s as an aspiring fine artist. The wondrous

Some of the many source books that inform my floral designs.

13

Collecting decorative china has been my passion since arriving in England in the 1960s. The Chinese ginger jar in the center at right is one of my all-time favorites.

halls of the Victoria and Albert Museum became my home away from home, a place where I began filling sketchbooks with inspiring florals of all sorts to be depicted later in my paintings. In the grand English houses I visited, I discovered eclectic furnishings that had been collected by world travelers and handed down from one generation to the next. Inlaid marble tables, huge oriental fans, massive printed and woven drapes and tapestries, wallpapers, and porcelains, all decorated with florals, lit up my imagination.

At the same time I found a treasure trove of flea markets and antique shops in London. I began collecting textiles and ceramics laden with floral motifs, pieces that continue to inspire me to this day, some of which appear in this book. After my first few years in England, keen to explore blossoms in media other than painting, I started working on my first needlepoints and fabric designs. To find subjects for my designs, I looked at my collections of objects depicting flowers and searched for books that showed clear, large-scale images of flowers on textiles, pottery, and in classic paintings. Rather than creating detailed, botanically accurate representation of a flower, I wanted to exaggerate and highlight certain shapes and colors, and seeing how other artists had done this was more helpful to me than photographs or even live specimens. In fact, I continue to use this technique in many of my projects today. My collecting isn't as constant as it was years ago—my shelves are overstuffed—but I still pick up the occasional floral ceramic, beaded piece, or textile when I just can't resist it.

FOR INFORMATION ABOUT THESE IMAGES, see page 223

THE SINGLE BLOSSOM

---

*Stitching
Needlepoint
Blooms*

Once an inspiring bloom sparks my imagination, I am anxious to use it right away in my work. Needlepoint is perfect for this type of quick gratification because I am a fast stitcher and I love creating a bloom using a palette of colored wool threads. And, conveniently, I can easily carry needlepoint around wherever I go. With a lightweight piece of canvas, small skeins of many colors, a blunt-tipped tapestry needle, and a tiny pair of scissors, I am happily busy whenever and wherever, watching a colorful composition unfold at my fingertips.

When I'm dreaming up a needlepoint pillow on a floral theme, I always search for a large, bold rendering of a flower or flowers that I can use for reference. That rendering might be in a painting or on a ceramic piece, wallpaper design, or even a seed packet.

Although I sometimes do large panels, for most of my needlepoints I stick to pillow-size. A pillow is a relatively small object that could get lost or reduced to a bit of texture in a room if too understated, so I design my pillows as bright jewels meant to lift a furnishing scheme. For an even more emphatic statement, I make lots of pillows and place them all together. I have stacks of them in my studio.

With my source material in front of me, I begin by drawing the simple outlines of my bold bloom onto canvas with a waterproof pen. When picking colors I try to focus on hues that are radiant and a bit lighter than you might at first suppose. This is because each stitch on the canvas is surrounded by a slight shadow that tends to deepen whatever tone I have chosen. I also try to limit the number of colors I select—mostly to about fourteen to sixteen per design, or even to as few as ten. If I don't go crazy with colors, my needlepoint can be

In a typically crowded corner of my studio, I stitch on the white dahlia needlepoint for this book.

made into a kit (or chart) that others can work from. These color boundaries are where creativity comes into play in a big way because they encourage me to figure out how to make fourteen colors feel like twenty-five. It is amazing how this magic happens once you get used to the discipline.

I begin the needlepoint by stitching color inside my drawn outlines, introducing details and highlights stitch by stitch. As the bloom grows, I work little bits of the background color I've chosen around it to see how it will affect the shades within the flower. Then I can strengthen or temper the bloom colors if necessary. I don't slavishly follow the outlines if I see where I can improve them, and I almost never take out any stitches, but instead just keep building on them.

If I have several needlepoints on the go at once, I complete everything until only the background needs finishing, then I hand off the remaining stitching to someone else in the studio while I turn my attention to my next creation.

For me, the joy of needlepointing is not just the end result. I deeply enjoy the process of sitting still—back to the window with the daylight pouring in over my shoulder—dabbing colored stitches like paint onto my canvas while I listen to plays on the radio.

A single line drawing of the white dahlia from a seed catalog. This was later traced onto canvas for stitching.

FABRICS IN BLOOM

*Drawing Blossoms
for Quilting Cottons*

Before discovering textiles I saw myself as a fine-art painter. I painted still lifes so I could create indoor "landscapes" and not allow bad weather to deter me from painting every day. In my early years in London these paintings were filled with decorative china on patterned cloth. When I was painting I would wonder how these patterned cloths came about.

Stephen Sheard and Ken Bridgewater, who founded Westminster Fibers (then known as Westminster Patchwork and Quilting), asked me to design my first quilting cottons in the 1990s, so I reached into my imagination for the fabrics I had loved in the past—those chintzy big-scale florals on drapes and bed covers I'd encountered in grand English country houses in the 1990s. Having studied old patchwork and noticed that most of the prints were small-scale, I decided I should start by making some small-scale texture-type prints, like dots, pebbles, artichokes, and smaller flowers. I call them "texture-type" prints because, seen at a distance, the motifs of small-scale prints tend to blur together with their background to create a textured color tone. Stripes and paisleys also became favorite themes because they are great to cut and arrange in patchwork and add sparks of movement within the whole. After these initial explorations, inspired by my memory of quilts made with furnishing fabrics with large-scale motifs, I started designing prints with large-scale flowers and, nearly instantly, I realized I had found my specialty. I loved designing large blooms, and they definitely set my collection apart in the world of quilting fabric, where bitty prints were (and still are) the norm.

When I started designing prints, first I learned the art of the repeat from a textile designer—how to draw only one section of the design, a section that fits together with itself so it can be repeated over and over across yards (meters) of fabric. I also learned how to design with a limited number of colors as each color added makes the fabric more expensive to produce. I realized quickly—and with great joy—that designing floral fabric was bringing back my painting and drawing skills. At the same time, it gave me the chance to design the sort of fabrics that thrilled me in museum collections, antique shops, and old country houses.

My florals got even bigger when I painted a fabric design called *Bekah*. I was painting the design twice as large as it would be printed in order to get in the detail and so that when printed at a reduced size, it would look sharp. The finished design looked so good large that the manufacturer—to my delight—decided to print it that way. From then on, I never hesitated to paint huge blooms and have them printed at the same size as the artwork.

When designing floral fabrics, first I do my usual search through my own sketchbooks and my collection of decorative art books for inspiration. I usually already have ideas for what I am looking for—things that sparked my imagination in the past that I haven't yet had a chance to work on. Several different blooms from different sources often find their way into a single design.

Gouache is my preferred medium for fabric designs because it is opaque, making it easy for the fabric printers to reproduce the painted strokes. My paint palette is nothing grand—frosted plastic tops from restaurant takeout containers or a plain white china plate. If the repeat size of the painted design is going to be fairly small, I paint it onto a pad of white watercolor paper about 12" × 17" (30 cm × 43 cm). For really big designs, I cut pieces off a roll of drawing paper that is 5 feet (1.5 m) wide. I tape the paper to a large plywood board that rests on my painting table. My paints in small tubes sit on a card table to the side.

My brushes are generally limited to three sizes: a very fine brush for outlines, dots, and stripes; a slightly larger brush for almost everything else; and a medium-size brush for filling in largish backgrounds. To rinse them, I set up a few empty jam jars with fresh water. The most important ingredients of all while I am painting fabric designs are lots of daylight and BBC Radio 4 as company in the background, churning out interesting interviews, news on current events, and plays.

Fabric prints from the Kaffe Fassett Collective (CLOCKWISE FROM TOP LEFT): *Kirman, Japanese Chrysanthemum, Bekah, Lake Blossoms,* and *Zinnias.*

As I draw out my repeat and paint in the colors, I register each new color in a grid outside the artwork. When the original is complete I photocopy it and paint my different colorways for the design on top of the printed photocopy in grids that match the original colorway grid. The printer can then see what color to substitute for each color in the original when making each new colorway of the design.

I mail off my completed designs and colorway information directly to the printer and wait for a month or two for fabric samples, called strike-offs, to arrive back in the studio for approval. If there are changes to be made, I make careful note of them and return the strike-offs to the printer for the changes. It's an exciting day when the fabric is finally delivered and placed on my shelves, ready to become my next quilts.

LEFT: More floral fabric prints from the Kaffe Fassett Collective (CLOCKWISE FROM TOP LEFT): *Lake Blossoms*, *Big Blooms*, *Lake Blossoms*, *Tree Peony*, and *Gloxinia*. ABOVE: Painting a new fabric design called *Corsage* and a page from my archive.

FLOWERS ON RIBBONS

---

*Designing Strips
of
Abstract Flowers*

In 2004 Renaissance Ribbons asked me to design for them. I think I may have turned them down three times before—convinced I didn't have the time—until I finally succumbed to the tempation. Their jacquard ribbons are so exquisite and woven in such stunning detail that I couldn't resist having a go at them. That first season they gave me free rein to design five ribbons in any pattern or color palette without having to create a "collection" per se. Not surprisingly, I was quickly hooked, and since then I have designed about ten sets (and counting) of four to seven ribbons in all sorts of patterns, including stripes, circles, squares, dots, florals, and abstract designs.

I approach ribbon design similarly to fabric design and paint the designs in gouache. But in this case, I'm limited to six or seven colors per ribbon and a repeat width of about 1–4" (2.5–10 cm), which are interesting challenges. Sometimes I hit on designs when looking through my decorative arts books and other times Renaissance Ribbons will ask me to adapt a design from one of my fabrics.

For floral ribbons, the blooms have to stand out from a distance and, at the same time, be detailed enough to look superb when viewed up close. After I send my designs to Renaissance, they make up samples for me to color-correct. They go to great pains to reproduce my artwork with amazing accuracy, sometimes going through several proofs, which I appreciate immensely. I have used my ribbons on cushions and on the button bands and cuffs of my shirts. Spools of all my ribbons are displayed in a colorful array on a shelf at eye level in the office in my studio, where they catch my eye every time I pass by.

Painting colors on a printout of a Philip Jacobs design. Some of Philip's actual ribbons and a box of mine.

FLORAL PATCHWORK

Lush Arrangements
of
Flower Prints

It's always hard for me to analyze the process I go through when I am designing a quilt because it is totally instinctive. But, since I'm often asked about my process, I will try.

It all starts off with a request for a quilt from a craft magazine or from a private client for a unique piece. Or I may have just begun a collection of quilts for a book. The reason it's hard for me to explain what happens next is because from the time I think, oh, I need to design a quilt, my imagination is a whirl of activity. Sometimes I recall a vintage quilt from memory that I have been longing to reinterpret. Or, if that isn't the case, I might look through my books of vintage quilts to see if something there draws my attention. Or I might refer to my newest fabrics, which are always begging to find their way into an assemblage of patchworked shapes.

When designing for a magazine or book, I work within certain boundaries. I try to limit myself to twenty fabrics per quilt. This is difficult sometimes because I produce scraplike quilts that need to have a lot of variety. I also try to do layouts that are easy for the instruction writer to break down into manageable steps and for quilters to sew.

Of course, designing a quilt for a private client is always a joy—I can use any fabrics I want, from those in my own extensive collections of stripes, prints, and solids to any scraps I have collected over the years of other designers' work, including pieces of vintage fabric. Anything that suits my chosen palette can find its way into a quilt when there are no constraints at all. But the challenge of having to use only the fabrics from my latest collections doesn't dim my enthusiasm—they are bursting with colors and motifs I love.

My flannel work wall allows me to arrange a quilt without pins before sewing.

LEFT: A mockup of the center of a quilt I designed for an Australian magazine. RIGHT: Blocks for Leafy Appliqué (page 88) collaged on paper (and later appliquéd).

Deciding on a palette for a quilt just comes to me as I look over my newest prints and my classics. I start to pile up fabric pieces on the floor—all in either soft neutrals, brilliant jewel tones, or something in between. I arrange the pieces next to each other so they enhance or harmonize with each other. Seeing the fabrics spread out can lead my palette in a slightly different direction as I find out how the prints and colors react with and against each other. Having chosen some starting fabrics, I can begin to cut my patches. If it's a format I've used before, such as a Tumbling Blocks or Snowball quilt, I can look it up in one of my previous books and use the templates or measurements there. If the format is new to me, I'll ask my collaborator, Liza Prior Lucy, to send me the templates I need.

As I cut my fabric pieces I stick them up on my gray cotton flannel design wall so I can stand back and view from a distance. I used to try to guess what fabrics would look like combined by simply folding and arranging them on the floor, then standing on tiptoes on a bed or chair to view. When I realized that cut pieces of cotton would stick (without even a single pin) to a piece of flannel hung on my studio wall, my entire workflow changed. With the design wall, I can stand back as far as needed to really see the composition. Instead of making my best guess of what I want and then sending instructions to a sewer to test, I can now make my choices with much more certainty that the end result will be successful. Many hours of unpicking stitches and revising are saved.

When I look at a design on a wall, I can clearly see how the fabrics are interacting. The gray color of the flannel is very important; it enhances colors and makes them easier to work with. In constrast, using a white flannel ground would be like looking at colors against a snow bank, which is very hard on the eyes and distracts from the colors' innate hue and intensity. Sometimes colors I thought would work stop my eye from moving pleasantly around the whole arrangement. Quickly I take them down and replace them with fabrics that have a level of color more in keeping with the rest of the work.

At this point, usually I sit down and knit a few rows or stitch on a project on the go next to my chair, which is across the room from my work wall. From there I can quietly study the new composition I'm creating. If I'm not quite satisfied, I'll wait until the next day to come into my studio after a good night's sleep and catch it afresh. That is the point when I can usually see what is amiss and correct it.

Next I photograph the fabrics arranged on the design wall to see how the composition looks on camera. By reducing the image down in scale, I can spot discrepancies in the color balance more easily. When I see the photo on the computer screen the design also gains a professional shine that is encouraging. I then make any necessary last-minute changes and take a final photo before carefully taking down the pieces and packing them up to send to Liza. Following the photo, Liza machine-sews the pieces together. At this point, although I have selected all of my fabrics, I may have only arranged one section of the quilt top on my design wall—if the rest of the arrangement is self-evident and can be intuited by Liza. Occasionally, I sew all the patches together myself, which I love to do; in these cases, I compose the whole quilt on my design wall and then stitch the pieces by hand. The slight wonkiness of a hand-stitched quilt adds a delightful human texture to the whole.

When working on this book, I would pass on a large section of the quilt pieces to Liza. She would then arrange the entire quilt on her design wall and send me photos so that I could see the whole before the sewing began.

Sometimes, everything would be just right; other times, I would tweak or even replace a fabric. Sometimes Liza would see something wasn't working and try out other options before getting back to me.

For many of the quilts in this book, I used the technique of fussy-cutting flowers out of fabrics. This involves selecting a motif and positioning it exactly as I want it inside a patchwork square. I hate wasting fabric so I always look carefully at the edges of my yardage to find the biggest, boldest blooms. I place a transparent plastic template or a cardboard cutout of the shape I want to cut over the flower I want to use. Then I outline the template onto the fabric with a pencil. Sometimes this will enclose only the center of a really large fabric bloom or, if the fabric bloom is a medium size, it will encompass surrounding background and some foliage. I am careful as I choose which flowers to fussy-cut not to get too close to another really good flower and spoiling its chance to be used as well. This fussy-cutting can be like cropping a so-so photo to make it come alive in a dynamic way.

The most satisfying type of collaboration is when Liza and I can get together at her home in Pennsylvania, which we did for several of the quilts in this collection, including Basket (page 58), Tawny Hatboxes (page 80), and Attic Window On-Point (page 66). First we discuss the quilt I want to work on, then Liza pulls out a pile of fabrics from her huge stash. As we cut and position pieces on her design wall, Liza can tell me right away if a block is or isn't reading as it should aesthetically. Every morning that I wake up at Liza's, I'm instantly filled with anticipation and excitement for the day ahead. Once a quilt top is completed on the design wall, we photograph it and carefully put the pieces away for Liza to stitch together later. Then we rush on to the next quilt.

I don't always have the border for a quilt decided in my mind before the quilt center is sewn together, so Liza will send me a photo of the quilt center once it's done and I will make a suggestion. Sometimes it's only after a failed border attempt that I, or Liza and I together, hit on the answer. Then with the quilt top finally completed, off it goes to the machine quilter with the backing fabric. The backing fabric is chosen very carefully to either complement or contrast with the quilt front, and it is always a fabric that makes a bold statement on its own. I don't like over-quilting, so the quilting on my patchworks is usually not obvious over the busy patterned surface seen at a distance. If I am doing a quilt entirely by myself, I choose a thread thick enough to show up nicely, but not obtrusively, and weave simple parallel lines of running stitches over the entire piece—a technique influenced by the enticing surface texture of Indian quilts.

Each of my quilts is returned to me after it has been machine-quilted for me to sew on the binding, which I always do in a low chair in a quiet corner of my studio. There is something so mysteriously satisfying about sewing down the finishing frame of a quilt in careful near-invisible stitches that I always try to reserve this task for myself. I usually use a bias-cut stripe or polka dot-like fabric to ensure a sharp, defined edge. Once I am done, I can't wait till the next quilt reaches my greedy fingers. But, in the meantime, my enthusiasm is rushing toward the delights of starting my next design.

LEFT: Starting to mock up Attic Window On-Point (page 66) on my work wall. RIGHT: The layout of Tawny Hatboxes (page 80) almost complete.

LIVE FLOWERS

—

Arranging Fresh Blossoms

There are few things in life more inspiring than stepping into a flower shop or garden arranged by someone with a good eye. Because of the way light plays on and through them and their fragile, translucent quality, flower petals bring us an intense purity of color. Whatever I happen to be going through in life, being in the presence of masses of flowers in full bloom always lifts my spirit. For me, it is like being in the presence of a very complex paint box.

When I was growing up on the California coast I was all for gathering as many wild blooms as I could find on the hilly meadows around my home. My goal was usually to make a multicolored splash with as much variety as possible—a complexity of yellows, reds, pinks, lavenders, and greens thrilled me.

Nowadays I arrange flowers for photo shoots, for my home, and for still lifes, and I usually stick to one color group, such as all shades of reds, magentas, and deep orange—or purples, blues, and dark lavenders—for an undiluted impact. To place a deep purple next to magenta or chestnut brown and surround that with dark green or plum red leaves is to plunge into the most distinct color mood. Keeping all the tones on the same level of intensity seems to really unlock their deep beauty.

To echo the different color moods of the projects I designed for this book, I set out to make a flower arrangement for each of them. For example, for my Rich, Dark Tones color theme, I selected the deepest purple sweetpeas at the flower shop that day. They ranged from magenta to dark violet and were a stunning base to show off some maroon peonies I found alongside them at the florist. I was also delighted to find bronze foliage, as often these deep arrangements are watered down by too bright a green leaf. The pot I chose from my extensive collection was the darkest I could find that had several colors within it. I have black teapots, but they would have been too monochrome for my needs. I love the accidental arrangement of glazes in jade greens, deep ochers, and dark brown that occurred in the firing of this pot. It all came together for me when I found the African indigo and turquoise batik cloth that gives us such a tapestry-like deep ground. The finishing touch was the addition of purple cabbage and the darkest of all vegetables—eggplant. You can see me working on the arrangement below right and the final result on page 96. This setup is a perfect example of how all deep tones can set each other off if there are no light colors to distract from the mysterious twilight mood.

LEFT: Happily shopping for flowers at Achillea, a flower shop I love in my London neighborhood. RIGHT: Arranging a bouquet in rich, dark tones (page 96).

BOUQUET STILL LIFES

---

*Painting
Cut Flowers*

Most of my colorwork when designing textiles explores the world of low contrast, almost camouflage, but when creating a painting I like the blooms to stand out and be the fresh focal point. Most of the time I begin by setting up a still life tableau in my painting studio, which is a peaceful room with very good natural light reserved solely for this purpose in my house.

For the painting I worked on while writing this book, I placed a bunch of peonies in yellow and bright pink from my local flower shop in an antique jug with birds and flowers on it on a taupe surface. I set up my arrangement on top of the large table in my studio that I use for all my still lifes. Daylight floods into the room over the table and the wall behind it. After placing my bouquet at the center of the table, I started trying out various textiles to place behind it on the wall. In the end I opted for a vintage hand-painted kimono with dusty pink and magenta peonies on blue-green leaves against a lavender and pink sky, which creates a rather tapestry-like effect. For the floor of the arrangement, I chose one of Philip Jacobs's fabrics, *Begonia Leaf,* in shades of aqua and jade green.

As with all my creative work, when I paint, I try out several different color combinations before selecting just the right one, but this process happens with great speed as I am dying to start painting so I can begin to see the colors all come to life on the canvas.

One thing I'd forgotten to calculate when setting out this still life was the opening and expanding of the blooms in my arrangement; as the studio heated up with shafts of sun from the window, the peonies tripled in size, and so I felt compelled to repaint them.

I work in acrylic paints because I am impatient and they dry faster than oil paints. I work on whatever size canvas makes sense for the still life—from a miniature of a few inches up to 3 feet × 4 feet (1 m × 1.4 m) or even larger. Before I had a car, I always limited the sizes to what would fit in a London taxi to get the works to my gallery shows.

For me it takes a very special kind of energy to finish a painting. I need to have a clear, uninterrupted block of time—say three days or so. I may speed up in a heat of inspiration and finish a canvas in half that time, but I need to know I can have that time if necessary. If I get distracted, I lose my original drive. Textile work, such as knitting or needlepoint, I can pick up and leave frequently and my passion stays alight, but I do not feel the same way about painting.

LEFT: Painting a flower arrangement in my studio. RIGHT: The backdrop is a painted kimono; the fabric print on the table is Philip Jacobs's *Begonia Leaf*.

Part Two

BOLD BLOOM QUILTS

AND

NEEDLEPOINTS

NEUTRALS & SOFT PASTELS

Time and again I have been drawn to the silver world of bleached driftwood and dried flowers all but devoid of color and to the many fascinating tones of neutral marbles and granite in the stone world. Starting in this subtle realm makes sense to me, before the eye is lured by the sensual excitement of more pronounced color. My flower arrangement of silver leaves and gray-lavender and dusty pink petals against a backdrop of a pebbled cloth and my pastel cabbage fabric elicit just the color mood I am after here.

Many of my early knits were in shades of gray and off white, but after I started exploring more full-blooded pools of color, it took a while for me to return to this whispering world. Once I did, however, I again felt its restrained allure. I like finding ancient wreaths of faded flowers in graveyards or end-of-season plants with blooms that have been bleached and browned in the sun, revealing only the faintest hint of their former glow of high color.

I am often relieved when one of the students in a patchwork workshop produces a quilt design of only pearly gray prints—it really stands out in a room full of high-color offerings.

FOR INFORMATION ABOUT THESE IMAGES, see page 223

GRAY RANDOM STRIPS

For this quilt I picked all the muted prints in my stash, digging out lots of old pieces from my fabric collection, including Souleiado prints I bought in the south of France in the 1970s and bits of flea market kimonos sent to me by good friends in Japan.

I made the quilt in the improvisational style and entirely by hand. Working from the center outward, I added on rectangles and strips of random widths and lengths. My main palette was muted soft grays, with shades of lavender, dusty pink, and green to spice up and merge with these gray tones.

At the last moment, by which time I had already reached the outer edges, I felt the quilt needed a more dramatic center. I found an old piece of marbled fabric in my fat quarter drawer (a piece I had purchased the very first time I attended the Houston Quilt Festival in 1997) and appliquéd it on top rather than trying to redo the center. If I didn't tell you, you'd never notice.

see instructions on page 120

ABOVE: A close-up showing the blue-and-green marbled fabric that I appliquéd around the *Brassica* print after the rest of the stitching was complete. The lively border makes a perfect center for this complex of neutral tones. **OPPOSITE**: The finished quilt blends beautifully into this vintage-style room.

GRAY BLOCKS

As I was placing pieces of fabric I had designed in gray colorways on my design wall for this quilt, I was struck by how much the fabrics combined looked like marble paving. Even the fussy-cut flowers at the centers of the blocks looked as if they were made of stone tiles. If I had collected all blue fabrics, it might have looked like lapis lazuli, and deep greens could have been malachite.

The layout of this quilt is a basic one. It is made up of simple blocks constructed from the center outward. Each block starts with a central square that contains a fussy-cut flower that fills the square. Then two or three rings of borders are added around this square, each ring cut from a different fabric. What keeps the composition from looking static and blandly repetitive is the number of different fabrics used and the fact that almost every block has slightly different-sized central squares and borders. All the finished blocks need to be the same size, but you don't have to make them precisely the same size to start. Instead you can press them really well and trim them down to the correct size, like I did.

see instructions on page 124

LEFT: The *Brassica* print is available in multiple colorways, but this gray one is my favorite. **OPPOSITE:** In this shot you can really see how using all of the neutral patterns together created a marble-like effect. I especially like the way the softly colored flowers emerge gently from the squares.

WHITE DAHLIA NEEDLEPOINT

KEY

▨	963
■	104
▨	101
▨	884
▨	251A
▨	873
▨	401
▨	403
▨	961
□	991B

There are many white flowers I could have chosen for the subject of this needlepoint. Somehow the lavender tips of the dahlia seemed the perfect quiet drama to sum up the mood I was aiming for. The pearly gray background created the ideal misty mood. The beautiful iron bench on which we photographed this piece made the pale dahlia glow.

see instructions on page 200

BRIGHT PASTELS

Many children think of Easter as a time to indulge in chocolate eggs and bunnies, but my most vivid childhood memories of this holiday are of the bright, high color scheme—canary yellow, candy pink, duck egg blue, lime green, and warm lavender tones. To this day I think of it as a time when the baskets, ribbons, eggs, and fluffy yellow chicks vie with cupcake frosting and flowery dresses to celebrate the coming of spring. This is also the time of year when banks of brilliant yellow daffodils, meadows of wildflowers, and branches festooned with pink cherry blossoms replace the dark tones and bareness of the winter earth. Each spring I am amazed all over again that nature still knows how to create this light-filled brilliance.

In addition to this outdoor magnificence, one of the key markers of the season in London is the annual Chelsea Flower Show in May. This internationally renowned event features staggering displays of floral abundance, often with wit and style. It is the most powerful demonstration I have ever seen of the British love of color, which has broadened widely since my arrival here in the '60s.

Many of the florals in my fabric collections are in sweet bright pastels because I am so fond of painting in this joyful palette. My fascination with it also extends into my collection of decorative objects, vintage ceramics, and antique textiles.

FOR INFORMATION ABOUT THESE IMAGES, see page 223

RADIATING BUBBLES

Two-color radiating stripes are as dramatic as you can get—the Japanese sunrise flag has long been a favorite of mine, with its contrasting scarlet and white stripes radiating out from the center to the edge. The idea of taking many pastel flowers, fussy-cutting them into circles, and floating them on pink and cream stripes was irresistible because of the tantalizing contrast between the soft bubbles of flowers and the linear geometry of the stripes. The sharp black-and-white polka-dot ground at the center of this quilt gives a zingy base for the flowers to bloom on. The pink and white morning glories are most effective at echoing the pink and white radiating stripes.

This quilt layout could be done in a high-contrast palette rather than a bright pastel one or anything in between these two extremes. If I were to use black-and-white in my radiations, I would choose brilliant scarlets, blues, and sharp lemon yellows in my flowers.

see instructions on page 128

Probably the biggest thrill for me after creating a quilt on my design wall is placing the finished work in a setting that brings it to life. I enjoy seeing Radiant Bubbles in the marble-floored sunroom **ABOVE**, but I think it truly shines on the bed in the room at **OPPOSITE**; the peeling paint on the wall, the floral painting, and the flowery cushion really make it glow. The quilt's flower "bubbles" are doing a lively dance, and all the colors are in harmony.

YELLOW SUNLIGHT

I originally made this quilt in deep autumnal tones, blacks, and scarlets, then became curious to see how it would look in high pastels. It appears complex, but it is easy to construct using four different-sized squares. I got the idea originally from an antique religious patchwork made of old brocades and damasks. My finished quilt makes me think of English cottage gardens, wildflower meadows in early summer, and the bright Easter-egg-toned flowers that you find in most florist shops year-round.

This quilt could be more "modern quilter" if you used all-white-based fabric prints including an equal amount of graphic geometrics and two-color brocades with white grounds. It would make the whole piece a lot airier.

see instructions on page 134

Yellow can be a difficult color to get right. Here the sunny yellow tones in the quilt are tempered by the grass (**ABOVE**) and in the colors in the room (**OPPOSITE**). I love the wonderful play of scale between the gigantic tumbling-blocks carpet and the jaunty red-and-white stripes on the sofa cushion at right. The hot magenta pinks add to the lively color scheme.

BASKET

I've always been intrigued by the classic basket quilts I see in vintage quilt books. Here I put a different spin on the concept by using Brandon Mably's *Mad Plaid* print for the baskets and placing each basket and its individually fussy-cut Gloxinia blooms on a polka-dot soft mint green ground.

I'd like to try this one again, putting the baskets on a pastel polka dot with a paler ground so they would be more predominate. The *Gloxinia* print flowers in each basket, being larger than life, work perfectly as appliqué pieces, so those I wouldn't change, though any large-scale floral would work. Big pink roses on a duck egg blue ground could be another idea to try in this way.

see instructions on page 138

BELOW AND OPPOSITE: I have grown to love English gardens since arriving in London in the '60s. The vegetable gardens on old estates (like the one shown here) have a special place in my heart because they remind me of childhood stories like Peter Rabbit. Those old rhubarb-forcing covers of lichen-covered terracotta blend so well with the subtle coloring of the quilt.

BOUQUET NEEDLEPOINT

KEY	
■	742
■	421
■	831
■	354
■	833
■	447
■	504
■	624
■	942
■	751
□	991B
■	471
■	844

This needlepoint design was inspired by a bouquet of yellow and soft red flowers on a powder blue ground on the border of a nineteenth-century French wallpaper pattern. Wallpaper designs can become great subjects for needlepoint because they often depict simplified flowers that are easy to translate into stitches. Try this idea as a cross stitch if that is something you enjoy. I'd love to see this pillow in a room with the original wallpaper.

see instructions on page 200

BRILLIANT HIGHS

I have great respect for all the variations of color that exist in the flower world, but I am partial to deep jewel hues. As a result, brilliant high tones is the palette many associate with my work.

Brilliant reds, purples, and golds are exciting to arrange to grab people's attention and make pulses quicken. My Seed Packet quilt (page 68) for this color mood was a joy to construct and made everyone who saw it on the design wall gasp as they entered the studio. This is a world of saturated, no-nonsense color that doesn't sit on the fence.

When I am painting flowers for fabric designs, I like to place deep magenta or scarlet blooms on burnt orange or maroon to intensify and extend the redness of the flowers. Purple flowers can be magnified by a cobalt blue background so the fabrics are as saturated as possible to cut up and add punch to a quilt. Often when I see bright flowers growing, the amount of bright green foliage lessens the impact of the color for me. So sometimes I isolate a blossom from its greenery and place it on a plain ground to make it glow.

To create and maintain a brilliant high palette, it's important not to have your brights muddied or grayed down, while acknowledging that some neutral elements in leaves or on grounds can help intensify the pure colors.

FOR INFORMATION ABOUT THESE IMAGES, see page 223

ATTIC WINDOW ON-POINT

The boldness of Attic Window On-Point made it an exciting project to work on. I love the way my *Kim* striped fabric makes such a dramatic border. Fussy-cutting big flowers was fun for the blocks. Any collection of big florals could be used this way. You could also create an equally dramatic effect by sewing together contrasting solid fabrics, like my shot cottons. Color combos like purple and apple green, maroon and gold, and forest green and lavender could give you the same drama.

This is the kind of quilt that could serve as the centerpiece in a stark modern room, lighting up a wall or the bed. The layout would also be marvelous as a patchwork coat with a red velvet collar.

see instructions on page 142

At **LEFT**, the creeper and the old stones beautifully set off the jewel tones of the quilt hanging on the gate. **OPPOSITE**, we see how these bold tones light up a vintage room, relating so well with a magenta velvet stool and scarlet and cream dressing gown. The soft neutrals of the bed, wall, and carpet lend a sophisticated quality to the bright colors in the quilt. The Oriental lamp with its deep pink shade completes the arrangement.

SEED PACKET

This quilt design needs a really big selection of super-large-scale blooms to fussy-cut for the center squares and large-scale florals for the squares for the two borders. I used some fabrics I designed for early collections, some fabrics from Philip Jacobs, and oriental and vintage fabrics I've collected over the years. I even threw in a few patches cut from old clothes.

You could have fun for months on a treasure hunt selecting just the right bold blooms for your squares. The trick is to look for flowers about 7½" (19 cm) in diameter for the large squares at the center of the quilt and flowers about 3¾" (9.5 cm) in diameter for the small border squares. You want the flowers to tightly fill most of the squares to achieve an exuberant concoction.

Though I have incorporated lavenders and blues within the color scheme, I love the predominant redness of this palette. Any rich or pastel colors could do to create another sort of mood. I long to see what you come up with using this simple squares concept.

see instructions on page 147

ABOVE: When we took this photograph in an Italian-style garden in Somerset, England, the only red around was a creeper dropping crimson leaves from a yew tree. Fortunately, the leaves were the perfect shade to reflect the red notes in the fussy-cut flowers in the quilt. **LEFT AND OPPOSITE:** This room set, on the other hand, gave us a stunning rosy base upon which to bring the flowers to life. The red-and-white inlaid mirror echoes the quilt perfectly, and I love the pink roses with black foliage on the couch.

ROUND AND ROUND

Like Gray Random Strips (page 44), I hand-stitched Round and Round in an improvisational manner. I've done a few quilts in this simple Trip Around the World layout, but this is the version with which I'm most pleased. I used Liberty and other designer prints, and it's the mix that gives this scrappy quilt its fizz. I particularly enjoy the odd changes of print in each layer as it progresses.

My aim was to have enough contrast in the prints to separate the layers but to encourage a certain amount of cross-blending within them. Perhaps I have a bit too much contrast. You could try for more intermingling between the rings of borders by choosing prints that are a little more alike in tone.

see instructions on page 150

CARLTON WARE NEEDLEPOINT

KEY

■	824
□	552
▨	474
▨	696
▨	443
▨	884
▨	451
▨	421
▨	432
▨	831
■	529
■	643

It was only a matter of time before I'd depict my Carlton ware vase in needle-point. I love its bold, high colors, which are hard to come by in the porcelain world (believe me, I'm always on the look out for such strong work). How brave to place orange and lemon yellow exploding flowers on cobalt blue!

see instructions on page 201

SMOLDERING DEEP TONES

When I came to this color mood, I was thinking of the glow of color combinations that are closer in tone than those in the brilliant highs mood, which are more sharply contrasting. The palette here is more tonal, as my flower arrangement shows. The color is still high but deeper in quality so it smolders.

Many of the fabrics I design have colorways in these close, glowing tones. They make me think of elegant Victorian interiors with rich velvet furnishings and brocade wallpaper and tapestries in deep, rich purples, reds, rusts, and moss greens. Or more brocade tonal stories—dark orange on maroon, turquoise, and dark cobalt, dark reds on black, deep magenta on dark olive.

My flower arrangement sets the color mood so much better than words ever could. First I chose my cloisonné vase in turquoise with maroon patterned in a way the Japanese do so well. Sweet William in magenta tones and white echoed the cloisonné patterns. My huge red-orange poppy, with its black center, crowned the arrangement with high drama. Lastly, I placed my bouquet on a luscious maroon cut-velvet cloth. The deep gunmetal ground on the cut-velvet demonstrates perfectly the smolder achieved by combining this deep neutral tone with the radiant maroon.

FOR INFORMATION ABOUT THESE IMAGES, see page 223

HEXAGON FLORETS

A skirt in hexagons separated by plaid that I found in one of my vintage textile books inspired this quilt. The husky hexagon florets, with their sky blue and gold centers, evoke bold blooms; Brandon Mably's *Mad Plaid* fabric sets them off with just the right graphicness.

This quilt makes a handsome throw for a couch. It is also a good design for a large bolster on a bed or for a rich covering for a small round table in a Victorian sitting room.

I like the abstract feel of these flowers boldly playing with striped dots and zigzag prints to make the childlike florets. Since hexagons are so popular these days, I'm sure I'm going to see many color variations on this quilt. It could be handsome, indeed, in Civil War prints in many shades of mustard, plum tones, and teal blues.

see instructions on page 154

My Victorian beaded bag (**BELOW LEFT**) and weaving from Guatemala (**BELOW RIGHT**) reflect the deep tones in Hexagon Florets.

TAWNY HATBOXES

The concept for this quilt came to me after seeing the wonderfully decorated hatboxes at the American Museum in Bath, England. I did an earlier version in vintage fabrics and soft pastel prints for my book *Passionate Patchwork*. Here I've gone for a huskier, more bronze palette that suits this smoldering chapter. You could do one with many different stripes on the floors of the blocks and different prints—paisleys perhaps—for the blocks' side walls. The boxes themselves need the biggest, boldest prints you can find. I've used florals here but geometrics or leafy prints could do, or toiles de Jouy like I used in my first version. I've seen this quilt done with bright rose prints on black grounds. Stunning!

see instructions on page 159

PINK PEONIES NEEDLEPOINT

KEY

994
311
696
244
643
647
505
504
946
944
942

It was risky putting these deep pink blooms on the burnt orange ground, but they hold their own and glow wonderfully. I took the idea for these floral shapes from a vintage wallpaper. This needlepoint is relatively simple to stitch with the big areas of each tone. The pillow would make a dramatic focal point in a colorful room or a dark wood-paneled one.

Changing the background of this type of design will throw it into a totally different mood—imagine the peonies on a brilliant purple or ultramarine blue. Of course, black grounds are always dramatic, but I would then deepen all the flower tones, making the lightest one about the medium magenta tone and going darker to almost black maroon for the deepest color—it could be exciting!

see instructions on page 201

LEAFY GREENS & FLOWERS

In this book I'm focusing mainly on the larger floral forms for their color impact, but there is a whole world of possibilities in flowers nestled in a leafy setting. Many charming floral prints bear an equal share of leaves to flowers. Oriental pots, where I get so much inspiration, often depict flowers in a dense pattern of leaves. I'm also moved by trellises of leafy vines with flowers sprinkled among them on old Italian murals and on French and English wallpaper and chintz fabrics. Primitive Haitian and Indian paintings often show forests of flowering trees overlapping in a carpetlike effect, all the shades and shapes of green leaves like a mosaic punctuated by bright blooms.

As I write this, I'm sitting on a porch in Toowoomba, Australia, surrounded by big flowering trees, dots of color on a mass of greenery. The dappled effect of colorful blooms among a pattern of leaves is an exciting addition to our flower design choices.

Leaves are, of course, in and of themselves, a brilliantly varied source of color, scale, and shape possibilities. Often they rival flowers in their various patterns and color changes. I could do a whole book on leaves, especially when it comes to the vegetable kingdom, which I grow more and more attracted to as I get older—but that will have to wait for now.

FOR INFORMATION ABOUT THESE IMAGES, see page 222

LEAFY APPLIQUÉ

Leafy Appliqué was an amazing collaboration experience for me—a room full of expert appliquérs helping me put together a massive quilt extravaganza. For years I've loved other quilters' expressive and amazing uses of patterned cloth cut into shapes and sewn carefully onto patchwork quilts. For this book, I wanted to include this appliqué method to add to the variety of approaches I was taking with flowers in quilts. The design is based on a vintage quilt called Bird of Paradise.

Liza introduced me to a group of expert appliquers headed by Bekah, Sylvi, and Anita, who did most of the actual sewing and selecting of prints for each section. To have quilters of this caliber was the single most fortuitous thing to happen while making this entire book. (When you see this quilt in person, you will understand my enthusiasm.) We met in a room at the Houston Quilt Market in autumn 2013; I had a few ideas about the scale of each block and a great bag of possible fabrics for my leaves and flowers. With only a day to sort out the whole layout and choose fabrics, the pressure was most definitely on! My extraordinary crew of talented ladies rolled up their sleeves and formed a production line to help me out, and I acquainted them with my plan.

Twelve different appliqué blocks make up the entire quilt, some repeated, some not. During the collaboration process I would draw the shapes, leaves, flowers, vases, etc., onto a square of paper matching each lifesize block, then pass it on to one of the appliquérs. She traced my drawing and cut templates for every leaf, stem, and flower petal in the block design. Then I traced the shapes onto the prints I had chosen, and another talented volunteer cut them for me to glue down on a mock-up drawing. These collages were wasted fabric but essential for me to visualize the allover design and allowed the appliquéers to see what I wanted and where. Later they would cut fresh pieces with seam allowances and sew them into place on a cloth background—often adding their own touches of wit to the choices of fabric placement.

This one-day event had me rushing to keep up with the appliquérs as I drew my blocks, cut out individual vases for many of the vase blocks, chose fabrics, and tweaked the fabric selection and the positioning of the blocks. By the end of the day there were twelve perfect blocks, each with its own envelope full of numbered templates organized by the expert appliquérs. I explained that with the repetition of the blocks, no block should have the fabrics positioned in exactly the same way so that each would be unique.

This collaboration was a dream. Though exhausted by the end of the day, I was inspired by the creative buzz in the room. To have good will and sheer talent so lovingly offered is what the quilt world is all about for me, and why I still love teaching. There are often times in classes when everyone feels such a creative high that it is like an old-time revival.

see instructions on page 164

LEAFY MEDALLION

With all the green leafy prints we produce for the Kaffe Fassett Collective fabric collections, this sort of garden medallion was a given for this section. I'm really pleased with how the fussy-cut blooms settle into the foliage.

This would make a gorgeous tablecloth in a sunroom or a room lined with William Morris wallpaper. I love the play of different scales in this quilt, from the tiny dots in the *Guinea Flower* print to the medium-scale center panel to the really bold begonia leaves and the *Peony* print borders. I like the way the two-by-two patches in the third border almost merge with the *Brassica* print.

The same patchwork layout could be done in red or yellow colorways for a glowing summery effect.

see instructions on page 168

OPPOSITE: Leafy Medallion found a perfect home in this garden in the west of England, becoming an extension of the garden greenery reflected in the pond. The way the florals appear in this quilt, almost hidden in the foliage, is exactly what this chapter is all about: how greenery becomes a fertile, almost camouflage, setting for blooms.

LATTICE WITH VASES

I've long been a lover of small oriental vases with floral themes. Often they are in blue and white, but I do come across wonderful versions with yellow or lavender or sometimes even deep red grounds. The slender neck and potbelly of the vase shape on this quilt was ideal for creating a lattice and showing flowers in a different way. Our classic *Brassica* print creates the right leafy texture for the lattice sashing. Backgrounds of lime green, turquoise, and lavender work well in achieving an overall effect of soft spring greenness.

I can also imagine making this quilt with all blue and white vases, keeping the leafy delicate green sashing, with maybe soft silver gray behind each vase. If you try this, be sure at least some of the vases have large-scale florals on them.

see instructions on page 173

ABOVE: This greenhouse entrance is such a perfect setting for Lattice with Vases. The verdant wisteria creates just the leafy atmosphere I was after in this quilt. **OPPOSITE:** This room—with its striking display of mostly dusty-toned ceramics—complements the quilt also. **LEFT:** The classic tobacco-leaf pattern on this china plate echoes the color palette of the quilt.

TULIP VASE NEEDLEPOINT

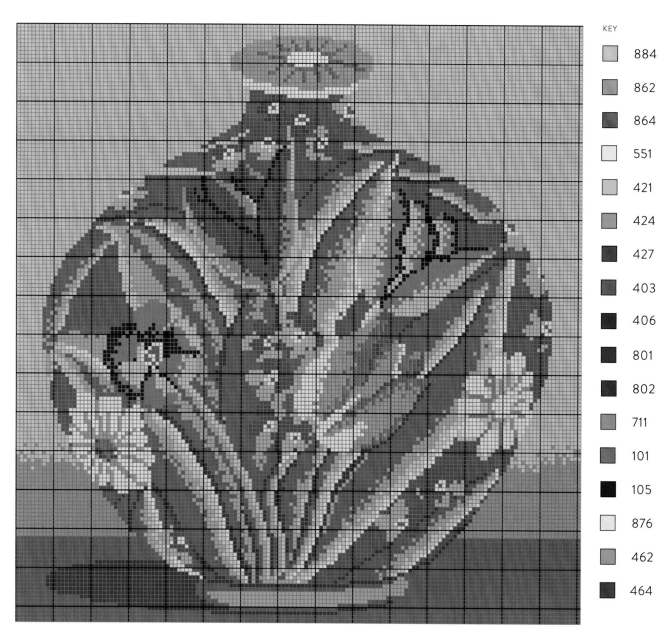

KEY	
■	884
■	862
■	864
■	551
■	421
■	424
■	427
■	403
■	406
■	801
■	802
■	711
■	101
■	105
■	876
■	462
■	464

Years ago, somewhere in the world (was it Venice?), I purchased a small, magical, painted vase with carved flowers. I was attracted to the delicious way its sumptuous green leaves highlighted the flowers. It never occurred to me to make a needlepoint of it until I came to this section of my floral book. I loved stitching the blooms and leaves into a vase shape for the pillow.

This pillow is perfect for a rattan chair in a sunroom or a room with leafy wallpaper. Its bold colors and soft ground would also add a rich note in a minimal, modern room.

see instructions on page 202

RICH, DARK TONES

One of a creative designer's most powerful tools is taking color schemes to extremes. I am always excited when a student in one of my workshops goes to the extreme of paleness: delicate, almost colorless tones on a base of pearly grays and off whites. But I am even more thrilled when a student tries the darkest arrangements, where black, navy blue, bottle green, and the deepest sienna browns play together to create a velvety depth. It takes courage to remove all of the contrast from a work and let it stand on subtle, close, dark tones.

In the plant world I am deeply moved by almost black in flowers or leaves. Begonias and coleus leaves can give us maroons that have the depth of dark chocolate. When looking for more rich dark tones in the flower kingdom, I also think of burgundy cosmo blooms, deep brown lilies, and claret-colored roses that are so dark they look burnt.

I once came across an unforgettable grave planted with a bed of dark primulas—it was a large rectangle of such intense purple that it took my breath away. It looked like someone had scattered dark violet jewels that glowed like moonlight. It was the lack of anything light to break the spell of the intense glow that made such an impression on me.

The Australian interior designer Anouska Hempel used to create high drama by placing large spotlight bowls of purple ranunculus with black centers in a room painted charcoal. What fun I had arranging live flowers for this color theme, rummaging through my darkest ceramics and antique fabrics to go with the palette.

FOR INFORMATION ABOUT THESE IMAGES, see page 223

BLUE OHIO STAR

I picked out all my current deep bluish fabrics to create this quilt, a variation of one I did years ago in very Victorian browns, golds, and reds, which was itself an interpretation of the classic Ohio Star of the 1800s. The deep coloring shown here should go well on a dark wood bed or perhaps in a red room. Of course, periwinkle or deep green sheets would go wonderfully with these colors.

In my workshops I am always trying to get people to make their colors sparkle more. One of the first steps is to remove anything too contrasting in the arrangement. Immediately the colors start to breathe and become more themselves. I made this quilt in just that way: constantly subtracting anything too light or bright that lessened the impact of the cobalt-teal-purple story. I'm sure there are many who would prefer shades of red and maroons. Be my guest and send pictures of your results.

see instructions on page 177

ABOVE: Here we have our Blue Ohio Star in an English garden with lavender blue flowers complementing it. **OPPOSITE:** And now our quilt glows on a blue-green couch with purple rosettes.

MILLEFIORE SNOWBALL

The dark color mood of this easy-to-sew quilt has the power to move me more than almost any other. Perhaps it is because I prefer to wear dark colors. There is something so mysterious and exciting about tones that are almost black—aubergines, purple plums, and cabbages, all so richly splendid.

This quilt shows off my *Millefiore* classic print in Dark. The deep *Shot Cottons* spark off the fussy-cut flowers. The concept is a good one for experimenting with different color versions—deep reds or cobalt blues would be good, and *Millefiore* comes in those tones. Or golden brown marquetry tones would be handsome. Or try very pastel and lacy if you like.

see instructions on page 181

BELOW AND OPPOSITE: The black wall in this drawing room is so perfect for Millefiore Snowball—its dark tones make the florals sing out—that it looks like it was made for it. I've always been partial to dark blue delphiniums but this setting really heightens their purple depth. The vase on the table next to the couch is one of my experiments for Highland Stoneware in Scotland.

STRING STRIPES

This is the easiest quilt in this book. The dark floral prints make it move and shine. The dark chocolate *Aboriginal Dots* print strips set off those florals perfectly. This will make a handsome throw for your couch or easy chair, especially in dark, rich colors. How amazing it looks with dark grape leaves.

Do try it in other combinations and color moods—reds, or silvery gray tones with pastel florals and white highlights. I'll bet you anything that deep cobalt blues turns out to be a favorite for this graphic quilt.

see instructions on page 185

BELOW AND OPPOSITE: The dark prints used to make the string patches in this quilt really glow under the dark grapevine. **BELOW LEFT:** This close-up photo of stunning blue-black grapes against gunmetal leaves with a single red-orange leaf could spark a whole new quilt idea.

DARK PEONY NEEDLEPOINT

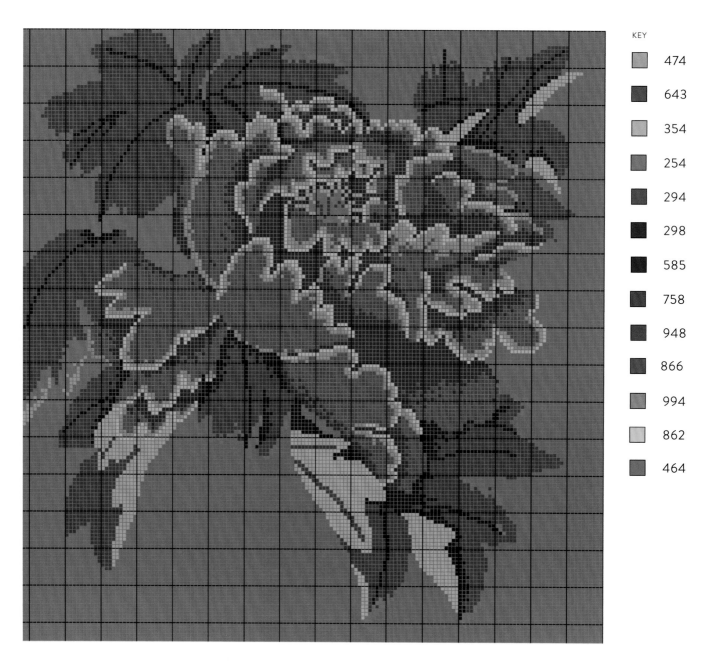

KEY

■	474
■	643
■	354
■	254
■	294
■	298
■	585
■	758
■	948
■	866
■	994
■	862
■	464

The inspiration for this needlepoint came from a peony in an Oriental painting;
its deep maroon tones caught my eye and made me shiver with delight. The deep
blue ground gives it the dark midnight feel I wanted. This would be great on a
dark velvet chair against a dark teal or black wall. A vivid deep purple ground
could be even more intriguing. This is such a good example of the power of the
glow you can achieve by putting deep tones on a dark ground.

see instructions on page 202

HIGH CONTRAST

Though I often work my textile designs in low-contrast harmonies, high contrast is always exciting to turn to for dramatic effect.

As I observe life in the various countries I travel to, many bold patterns grab my eye. The yellow and white lines on dark roads, massive red and white stripes on buildings in India and Africa, and blue and white awnings and deck chairs in many European countries. The most eye-catching to me in England are the large-scale diagonal stripes of golden yellow and black on trucks and trains and on police warning tapes. Zebras, pandas, and skunks all sport black and white contrasting markings.

The flower kingdom produces some thrilling examples of contrast—yellow and purple pansies, tulips striped in bold tones, and petunias in pinwheels of jaunty white and purple.

There are some quilts that I find too simplistic for my overactive mind, such as the classic red and white ones that so many admire. But now and then I come across a strongly contrasting quilt that draws me in and holds my attention and makes me want to play with the drama of contrast.

FOR INFORMATION ABOUT THESE IMAGES, see page 223

FLORAL OCTAGONS

Inspired by Marie-Christine Flocard's brilliant hexagon quilt (page III), Floral Octagons is one of the most contrasting quilts of my career so far. Marie-Christine's original consisted of toile de Jouy hexagons with very contrasting dark frames all floating on a white background. Each hexagon contained a scene drawn in dark lines of various shades on a cream ground that unified all the blocks. I used flowers in mine—neatly framed bouquets of a sort. Framing florals in dark octagons on a pale ground makes this quite a strong arrangement. The flowers are fussy-cut for impact as are the little accent blooms between them. I chose deep plum instead of black as my outlines. I also used a pastel polka dot as a ground or sashing and included a fussy-cut flower at each junction of the sashing.

I could see this quilt in a room with striped wallpaper and maybe a black-and-white checkerboard floor. This could also be done reversed—very dark sashing with medium tones for the outlined octagons.

see instructions on page 188

LEFT: The beginnings of Floral Octagons on my design wall. **ABOVE:** This stylized quilt plays well against the graphic wallpaper and Victorian-style radiator. **OPPOSITE:** The small stained-glass circles in the windows echo the bordered hexagons in the quilt. The graphic printed cushion furthers the contrast theme.

HIGH-CONTRAST SQUARES

I started this concept with log cabin squares of brilliant high-color contrasts like maroon and gold, and lime and purple. As Liza and I played with the idea, the more neutral contrasts of gray and almost black seemed better. It now has a more Art Deco feel, and the flowers shine out a bit more than in the first attempt.

I particularly like the checkerboard inner border; making it neutral gray and dark maroon or shades of blue helped the flowers to hum a bit more than they would have if they were framed in black and white. I still like the idea of high colors in contrasts for the borders. I hope one of you will try it and surprise me.

This is a quilt that even tough, anti-floral men wouldn't mind sleeping under. It would be handsome in a room with gray tones or stone floors.

see instructions on page 194

BELOW AND OPPOSITE: This formal garden was such a perfect setting for this quilt. I love the way the Italianate carved doorway dramatically frames it. Did you notice how the little pebble dividers for the box hedge garden relate to the quilt's gray tones?

CARNATIONS NEEDLEPOINT

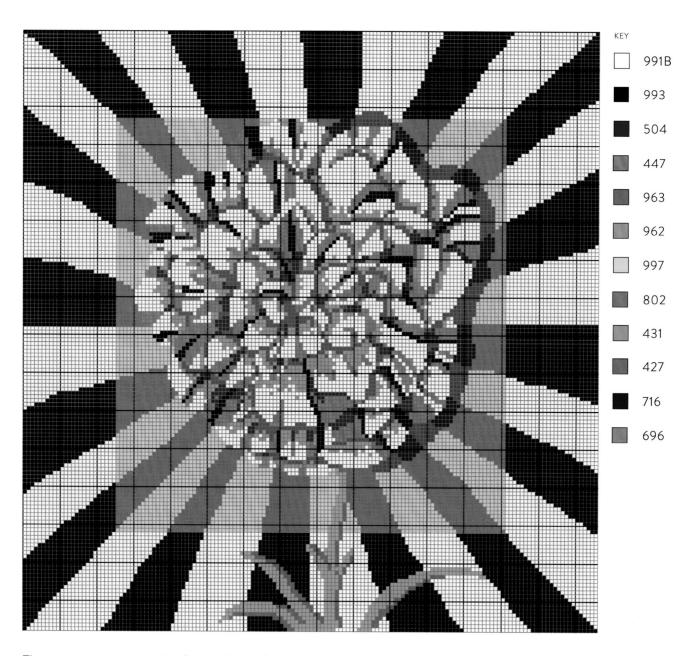

KEY

□	991B
■	993
■	504
■	447
■	963
■	962
■	997
■	802
■	431
■	427
■	716
■	696

There are many contrasting flowers in the floral world, but this jaunty carnation reached out to me as I perused my flower books. The design makes use of the fresh stripes of the carnation and the bold radiations found in Japanese flags and some advertising layouts. High contrast is fun to stitch, particularly this black-and-white radiating border.

This jazzy pillow will be a great accent in a room full of saturated color or a plain white one. I can imagine it on a bold checkerboard bedcover, perhaps in traditional red and white. Of course it will show up on any color scheme.

see instructions on page 203

Part Three

HOW TO

GRAY RANDOM STRIPS

Making a quilt using the improvisational method is very rewarding. In this example I worked from the center outward, first creating a large center with rectangles of various sizes, then adding border strips. Guidelines are given here for piece sizes, but feel free to improvise like I did.

FINISHED SIZE

62" × 62" (156.5 cm × 156.5 cm)

PATCHWORK FABRICS

Use quilting cottons 44–45" (112–115 cm) wide

Fabric A (center rectangle): ¼ yard (25 cm) of a light-toned large-scale floral print in predominantly grays and gray-pinks; OR, as used here, Kaffe Fassett Collective *Brassica* in Pastel

Fabric B (pieces 2, 3, 4, and 5): ¼ yard (25 cm) of a light-medium-toned marbled print in turquoise blues

Fabric C (random rectangles and strips): ¼–¾ yard (25-70 cm) of each of an assortment of at least 14 different prints (including large- and medium-scale florals, a paisley, a polka dot) all in predominantly grays, gray pinks, gray-greens, and gray-blues, with one accent large-scale floral print of white and gray flowers with turquoise leaves on a gray-pink ground (I have included the Kaffe Fassett Collective *Brassica* in Gray in this mix)

OTHER INGREDIENTS

Backing fabric: 4 yards (3.7 m) of desired fabric

Binding fabric: ¾ yard (70 cm) of a black and gray stripe or desired fabric

Cotton batting: 69" × 69" (175 cm × 175 cm) piece of batting

Quilting thread: Medium gray

SIZES OF RECTANGLES AND STRIPS

Exact sizes are given for the quilt center pieces and only strip widths for the surrounding strips, which are added outward around the quilt center. Follow the instructions in Cutting the Pieces when working from the chart.

QUILT CENTER WIDTH × HEIGHT		RANDOM BORDER STRIPS WIDTH OF STRIP	
Piece 1:	5½" × 20½" (13.7 cm × 51.7 cm)	**Strip 18:**	3" (7.2 cm)
Piece 2:	2½" × 20½" (6.2 cm × 51.7 cm)	**Strip 19:**	3" (7.2 cm)
Piece 3:	2½" × 20½" (6.2 cm × 51.7 cm)	**Strip 20:**	3" (7.2 cm)
Piece 4:	9½" × 2½" (23.7 cm × 6.2 cm)	**Strip 21:**	4" (10.2 cm)
Piece 5:	9½" × 2½" (23.7 cm × 6.2 cm)	**Strip 22:**	4½" (11.7 cm)
Piece 6:	4¼" × 9½" (10.7 cm × 23.7 cm)	**Strip 23:**	6" (15.2 cm)
Piece 7:	4¼" × 9½" (10.2 cm × 23.7 cm)	**Strip 24:**	5" (12.7 cm)
Piece 8:	8" × 4" (19.7 cm × 10.2 cm)	**Strip 25:**	4" (10.2 cm)
Piece 9:	8" × 3½" (19.7 cm × 8.7 cm)	**Strip 26:**	6" (15.2 cm)
Piece 10:	8" × 3½" (19.7 cm × 8.7 cm)	**Strip 27:**	4" (10.2 cm)
Piece 11:	8" × 6" (19.7 cm × 15.2 cm)	**Strip 28:**	4" (10.2 cm)
Piece 12:	2" × 24½" (5.2 cm × 61.7 cm)	**Strip 29:**	6" (15.2 cm)
Piece 13:	5½" × 13" (13.7 cm × 32.7 cm)	**Strip 30:**	4" (10.2 cm)
Piece 14:	4½" × 13" (11.2 cm × 32.7 cm)	**Strip 31:**	4" (10.2 cm)
Piece 15:	9½" × 3½" (23.7 cm × 8.7 cm)	**Strip 32:**	4" (10.2 cm)
Piece 16:	9½" × 3½" (23.7 cm × 8.7 cm)	**Strip 33:**	2" (5.2 cm)
Piece 17:	9½" × 6" (23.7 cm × 15.2 cm)	**Strip 34:**	2" (5.2 cm)
		Strip 35:	2" (5.2 cm)
		Strip 36:	2" (5.2 cm)
		Strip 37:	3" (7.2 cm)
		Strip 38:	3" (7.2 cm)
		Strip 39:	3" (7.2 cm)
		Strip 40:	3" (7.2 cm)

CUTTING THE PIECES

This quilt is constructed in an improvisational manner. You can vary the size of the quilt and the width of the strips as desired. You can also piece together fabrics to reach the required sizes of the fabric strips.

Working using the improvisational technique means building up your design on your design wall one piece at a time, adding colors and prints at random and in an intuitive way. (See more about design walls on page 205.) To get you started, the exact cutting sizes for pieces in the quilt center are given in the Sizes of Rectangles and Strips chart (see above).

QUILT CENTER

Piece 1 (center rectangle): From fabric A, fussy-cut the rectangular center of the quilt, carefully positioning a column of flowers as a focal point at the center of the quilt. Place the rectangle on your design wall.

Pieces 2, 3, 4, and 5: From fabric B, cut pieces 2, 3, 4, and 5 as borders for the center rectangle and place them around your center rectangle on your design wall.

Pieces 6–17: From an assortment of C fabrics, cut pieces 6–17; these rectangles form the columns on either side of the center rectangle (see the Quilt Center diagram). As you cut the pieces, place them on your design wall to achieve the desired color arrangement. If you like, you can use two or more different fabrics for a single "piece." For example, I used more than one fabric for my pieces 6, 9, and 14, so that I could introduce small sections of polka dots into them.

RANDOM BORDER STRIPS

All the border strips are cut from fabric C. The widths for the strips are given in the Sizes of Rectangles and Strips chart (page 120). Because the border strips are cut in lengths to fit the quilt center, cut the lengths as you need them while you are adding on the borders.

ASSEMBLING THE QUILT CENTER

Following the Quilt Center diagram and using a ¼" (6 mm) seam allowance for all seams, sew pieces 2 and 3 to the long side edges of the center rectangle (1). Press. Then sew pieces 4 and 5 to the top and bottom of the quilt center piece. Press.

Next, sew together pieces 6 and 7. Add piece 8 to the top of joined 6–7 and then add on pieces 9, 10, and 11, in the order of the piece numbers. Sew piece 12 to the right side of this section. Sew this pieced column to the quilt center piece and press.

Sew together pieces 13 and 14, then add on pieces 15, 16, and 17. Sew this pieced column to the other side of the quilt center piece and press.

ADDING ON THE RANDOM BORDERS

Following the Gray Random Strips Assembly diagram, begin adding the borders to the quilt center piece in the order of the strip numbers. First, measure the edge that the strip will be stitched to. Then choose a fabric C for strip 18 and cut a strip 3" (7.2 cm) wide and trim its length to fit the edge you have just measured. Sew the strip in place and press.

Continue adding the strips in this way, following the sequence of the numbers and cutting all the strips from the C fabric. You can create rings of different colors or tones around the center or select strip fabrics at random. Piece strips together end-to-end to achieve a long enough length if necessary, or piece them to add interest to the strip. Once you get going, feel free to improvise and abandon the designated strip widths and sequence, just working outward randomly until the quilt is the desired size. After completing each ring of strips, always make sure the corners of the quilt top are perfect right angles. If this is not done, the top will lose its square corners as it grows outward.

FINISHING THE QUILT

Prepare the backing. Press the quilt top. Layer the quilt top, batting, and backing, then baste the layers together (page 208).

Machine quilt as desired, or hand quilt as I did, working simple parallel lines of running stitch across the quilt, about 1½" (4 cm) apart.

Trim the quilt edges. Then cut the binding strips on the bias and sew the binding on around the edge of the quilt (page 209).

Note: It is tempting to cut each border strip to a random length and then trim off the end after stitching it in place, but this method tends to make the quilt wonkier as you work outward. For straighter edges, always measure the edge first and cut the strip to the correct length before sewing it on.

Quilt Center

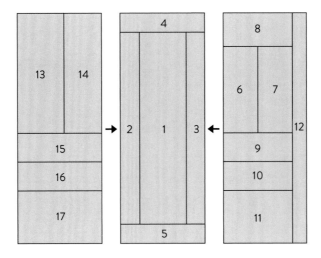

Gray Random Strips Assembly

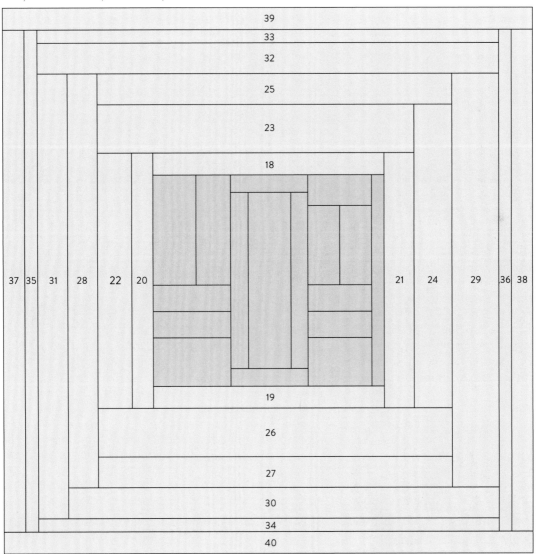

GRAY BLOCKS

Your goal for this design is to make each of the 20 blocks in the quilt look different. To do this, choose a different flower for each center square and vary the strip choices and strip widths as much as you can. The irregularity creates the charm of the composition.

FINISHED SIZE

72½" × 89½" (183 cm × 226 cm)

PATCHWORK FABRICS

Use quilting cottons 44–45" (112–115 cm) wide

Fabric A (outer border and sashing strips): 2½ yards (2.3 m) of a pale-toned floral circles print in pastels and pale gray; OR, as used here, Kaffe Fassett Collective *Millefiore* in Grey

Fabric B (small sashing squares): ¼ yard (25 cm) of a light-toned medium-scale floral print with pink, yellow, and aqua-blue flowers, approximately 2" (5 cm) in diameter, and white dots on a gray ground; OR, as used here, Kaffe Fassett Collective *Guinea Flower* in Grey

Fabric C (block center squares and block strips): ½ yard (50 cm) each of at least 8 different pale-toned and light-toned super-large-scale floral prints, in predominantly pinks with some pale blues and pale greens; OR, as used here, the following 8 Kaffe Fassett Collective fabrics: *Brassica* in Green and Pastel, *Brocade Peony* in Mauve, *Gloxinia* in Frost, *Japanese Chrysanthemum* in Pastel, *Lake Blossoms* in Sky, *Tree Peony* in Peach and Aqua

Fabric D (block strips): ½ yard (50 cm) each of at least 9 different pale-toned, light-toned, and light-medium-toned wavy and ombré stripes, and dot, circle, swirl, and medium-scale floral prints, in predominantly pinks, mauves, and grays with some blues and greens; OR, as used here, the following 9 Kaffe Fassett Collective fabrics: *Antwerp Flowers* in Soft, *Brassica* in Grey, *Curly Baskets* in Silver, *Gertrude* in Grey, *Joy* in Mauve, *Jupiter* in Stone, *Kim* in Mauve, *Ombre* in Purple, *Paperweight* in Grey

OTHER INGREDIENTS

Backing fabric: 6 yards (5.5 m) more of fabric B or desired fabric

Binding fabric: ¾ yard (70 cm) of a small-scale circles print in grays, pinks, and blues; OR, as used here, Kaffe Fassett Collective *Paperweight* in Grey

Cotton batting: 80" × 97" (200 cm × 250 cm) piece of batting

Quilting thread: Pale gray thread

CUTTING THE PIECES

This quilt is constructed in an improvisational manner. You can vary the size of the quilt and the width of the strips as desired.

Working using the improvisational technique means building up your design on your design wall one piece at a time, adding colors and prints at random and in an intuitive way. (See more about design walls on page 205.) To get you started, the exact cutting sizes for pieces in the quilt center are given below.

BORDER PIECES

4 border strips: From fabric A, cut two strips 3½" × 83½" (8.7 cm × 211.2 cm) for the side borders; then cut two strips 3½" × 72½" (8.7 cm × 183.2 cm) for the top and bottom borders.

SASHING PIECES

31 sashing strips: From fabric A, cut 31 strips 2½" × 15½" (6.2 cm × 39.2 cm) for the sashing strips.

12 small cornerstone squares: From fabric B, fussy-cut 12 squares 2½" × 2½" (6.2 cm × 6.2 cm), carefully framing a single flower at the center of each square.

BLOCK PIECES

20 squares: From fabric C, fussy-cut one square for each block, carefully centering a large flower in each square. Cut the squares in different sizes, between 4¼" (10.7 cm) and 8½" (21.6 cm) square. Use the remainder of fabric C for block strips.

Block strips: Each center square in block no. 1 is bordered by two rings of strips and each center square in block no. 2 is bordered by three rings of strips. Do not cut the strips now, but wait to cut them from the D fabrics and the remainder of fabric C as you construct each block.

MAKING THE BLOCKS

There are a total of 20 blocks. Make one block no. 1 and one block no. 2 to start and then continue making the two blocks randomly until you have a total of 20 blocks.

BLOCK NO. 1

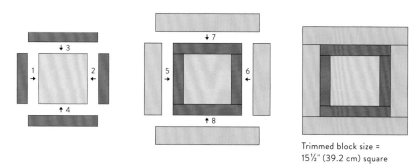

Trimmed block size =
15½" (39.2 cm) square

Choose one of the larger center squares, then choose a fabric C or fabric D for the first ring of strips to border the square. Cut a strip from the strip fabric 2–3½" (5–8.9 cm) wide and long enough to form the first ring border around the center square. With right sides together align one end of the strip with one side edge of the square and sew the strip to the square (arrow 1), using a ¼" (6 mm) seam allowance for all seams. Press. Trim the strip to the same length as the square. Sew the strip to the opposite side edge of the square in the same way (arrow 2), press, and trim. Next, sew the strip to the top (arrow 3) and bottom (arrow 4) in the same way. Press.

Choose a second strip fabric and cut a strip long enough to form the last ring of strips around the block and wide enough so that the finished block will measure at least 15½" (39.2 cm) square. Sew the side strips and the top and bottom strips to the block as before (arrows 5–8).

If necessary, trim the finished block to 15½" (39.2 cm) square.

BLOCK NO. 2

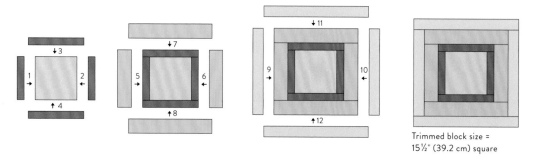

Trimmed block size =
15½" (39.2 cm) square

Choose one of the smaller center squares, then choose a fabric C or fabric D for the first ring of strips to border the square. Cut a strip from the strip fabric 1½–3½" (4–8.9 cm) wide and long enough to form the first ring border around the center square. Sew the first strip border around the center square as for block no. 1 (arrows 1–4).

Choose a second strip fabric and cut a strip of fabric 1½–3½" (4–8.9 cm) wide and long enough to form the second ring border around the block. Sew on the second strip border as before (arrows 5–8).

Choose a third strip fabric and cut a strip wide enough so that the finished block will measure at least 15½" (39.2 cm) square. Sew the third strip border as before (arrows 9–12).

If necessary, trim the finished block to 15½" (39.2 cm) square.

Gray Blocks Assembly

KEY

▢ Fabric A
▨ Fabric B
▢ Fabric C
▨ Fabric D
▢
▢

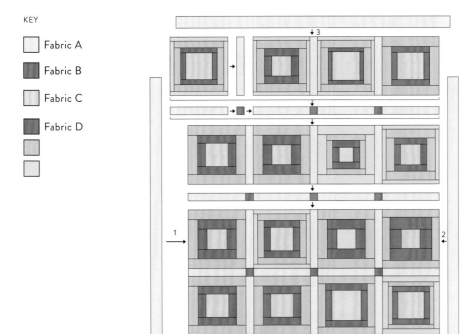

ASSEMBLING THE QUILT TOP

Arrange the 20 blocks for the quilt center, lining them up on the floor or on a design wall (page 205). Make sure the blossoms are upright in the center squares. The blocks are separated by the sashing, so allow gaps between them to position the sashing, as well. The quilt center consists of five horizontal rows of four blocks each (see Gray Blocks Assembly diagram). Position the sashing cornerstones at the ends of the sashing strips as shown.

Take the pieces for the top row—four blocks and three sashing strips—and sew them together (see diagram). Sew the remaining four rows of blocks together in the same way. Press.

Next, sew together a horizontal row of sashing strips and three cornerstones. Make a total of four horizontal rows of sashing strips in this way.

Sew together the block rows and sashing rows following the diagram. Press.

Sew the side borders to the quilt center, then sew on the top and bottom borders to complete the quilt top. Press.

FINISHING THE QUILT

Prepare the backing. Press the quilt top. Layer the quilt top, batting, and backing, then baste the layers together (page 208).

Machine-quilt around each center flower. Then meander machine-quilt over the rest of the quilt.

Trim the quilt edges. Then prepare the binding and sew it on around the edge of the quilt (page 209).

RADIATING BUBBLES

For a lively design, choose a different flower for each of your appliqué bubbles. You'll need a variety of fabric flower sizes in a range of bright pastel colors, so choose your floral fabrics carefully.

FINISHED SIZE

64½" × 76½" (162 cm x 192 cm)

PATCHWORK FABRICS

Use quilting cottons 44–45" (112–115 cm) wide

Fabric A (quilt center background): ¾ yard (70 cm) of a polka-dot fabric with black dots on a white ground; OR, as used here, Kaffe Fassett Collective *Spot* in White

Fabric B (lilac-pink radiating stripes): 1½ yards (1.4 m) of a light-medium-toned large-scale ovals print in lilac-pink; OR, as used here, Kaffe Fassett Collective *Aboriginal Dots* in Lilac

Fabric C (cream radiating stripes): 1½ yards (1.4 m) of a large-scale ovals print in very pale blue; OR, as used here, Kaffe Fassett Collective *Aboriginal Dots* in Cream

Fabric D (outer borders): 1¾ yards (1.6 m) of a light-toned multicolored wavy stripe in mostly pinks, blues, and greens; OR, as used here, Kaffe Fassett Collective *Jupiter* in Pastel

Fabric E (border corner squares): ¾ yard (70 cm) of a light-toned super-large-scale floral print with pink-and-white and orange-and-white flowers about 8" (20.3 cm) in diameter; OR, as used here, Kaffe Fassett Collective *Kimono* in Orange/Pink

Fabric F (appliqué circles): ¼–½ yard (25–50 cm) each of at least 11 different light-toned and medium-toned medium-scale to super-large-scale floral prints, in predominantly reds, pinks, blues, and lilacs, with a few greens and yellows; OR, as used here, the following 11 Kaffe Fassett Collective fabrics: *Asian Circles* in Green, *Big Blooms* in Green, *Bouffant* in Green, *Brassica* in Pastel, *Camellia* in Pink, *Floating Mums* in Duckegg, *Grandiflora* in Old Rose, *Lacy* in Cool, *Painted Daisies* in Turquoise, *Petunias* in Pastel, *Picotte Poppies* in Pastel

OTHER INGREDIENTS

Backing fabric: 5 yards (4.6 m) of desired fabric

Binding fabric: ½ yard (50 cm) more of fabric B

Cotton batting: 72" × 84" (180 cm × 210 cm) piece of batting

Quilting thread: Pink thread

Template materials: Four large sheets of paper at least 15" × 36" (38 cm × 92 cm) for radiating stripes templates, and heat-resistant template plastic (or stiff cardboard) for circles templates

MAKING THE TEMPLATES

Before cutting any pieces, make your own templates for the radiating stripes and for the circles appliqué, using paper for the radiating-stripes templates and heat-resistant plastic or stiff cardboard for the circle templates.

RADIATING STRIPE TEMPLATES

Make the five templates for the radiating stripe side pieces first. Cut out a rectangle 12" × 30" (30 cm × 75 cm) from a large sheet of paper, then mark the lines for the radiating stripes widthwise across the rectangle, following the diagram for the measurements. Label the templates G, H, J, K, and L and cut away the excess paper below template L. Turn the trimmed paper over and mark the reverse of each template with the same letter and "rev" (reverse) after it—G rev, H rev, J rev, K rev, and L rev. Carefully cut the template pieces apart along the marked lines. These templates DO NOT include the seam allowances, so if you use them as they are, cut each fabric piece ¼" (6 mm) from the edge of the template. (Alternatively, trace each template you have made onto paper, add a ¼" [6 mm] seam allowance all around it, and cut out.)

Make the four templates for the radiating stripe top and bottom pieces in the same way, starting with a rectangle measuring 12" × 24" (30 cm × 60 cm) and following the diagram for templates M, N, O, and P. Remember to mark the back of each template as well, for templates M rev, N rev, O rev, and P rev.

CIRCLES TEMPLATES

For the appliqué circles, cut out perfect circles from heat-resistant plastic or stiff cardboard. Make a variety of sizes of template circles; the sizes will depend on the sizes of the floral motifs in the prints you are using for the circles. (The templates do not include the seam allowance, so your flowers should fit snugly inside the outline of the circle.) For example, the quilt here has circles ranging from 2½" (6.4 cm) to 8" (20.3 cm) in diameter and 11 sizes were used: 2½" (6.4 cm), 2¾" (7 cm), 3" (7.6 cm), 3½" (9 cm), 4" (10.1 cm), 4½" (11.4 cm), 4¾" (12 cm), 5½" (14 cm), 5¾" (14.6 cm), 7½" (19 cm), and 8" (20.3 cm).

Note that the circle templates need to be stiff, but thin, as the seam allowance of each fabric circle is pressed to the wrong side over the template.

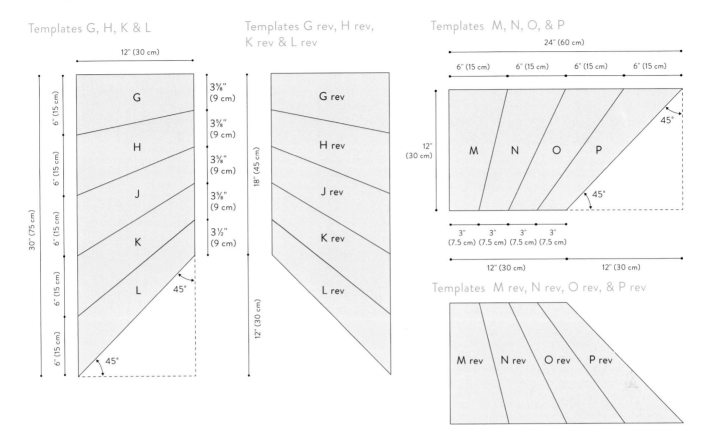

Templates G, H, K & L

Templates G rev, H rev, K rev & L rev

Templates M, N, O, & P

Templates M rev, N rev, O rev, & P rev

CUTTING THE PIECES

QUILT CENTER

1 large rectangle: From fabric A, cut a rectangle 27" × 39" (67.7 cm × 97.7 cm) for the quilt center. This piece will be trimmed down to 24½" × 36½" (61.2 cm × 91.2 cm) after most of the circles have been appliquéd in place as appliqué can shrink the background fabric a little.

RADIATING-STRIPE PIECES

18 fabric-B pieces: From fabric B, cut two pieces each using these nine templates: G, J, L, M, O, H rev, K rev, N rev, and P rev. If you are using templates without the seam allowance, don't forget to cut out each piece ¼" (6 mm) from the edge of the template (See Making the Templates, opposite). Pin a label to the right side of each piece as you cut it.

18 fabric-C pieces: From fabric C, cut two pieces each using these nine templates: G rev, J rev, L rev, M rev, O rev, H, K, N, and P. If you are using templates without the seam allowance, don't forget to cut out each piece ¼" (6 mm) from the edge of the template (See Making the Templates, opposite). Pin a label to the right side of each piece as you cut it.

OUTER BORDER PIECES

4 outer-border strips: From fabric D, cut two strips 8½" × 60½" (21.5 cm × 151.2 cm) for the side borders; then cut two strips 8½" × 48½" (21.5 cm × 121.2 cm) for the top and bottom borders. Make sure the stripes run parallel to the short edge so they appear to radiate from the quilt center.

4 outer-border corner squares: From fabric E, fussy-cut four squares each 8½" × 8½" (21.5 cm × 21.5 cm), carefully centering a large flower in each square.

APPLIQUÉ CIRCLE PIECES

80 circles: From fabric F, fussy-cut a total of 80 circles of various sizes, carefully centering a flower in each circle. To cut each flower, use a template circle that is the size of the flower you are cutting. With the fabric wrong side up, place the template so that the flower is centered inside the circle and draw around the template using a chalk pencil, then cut approximately ⅜" (1 cm) outside the outline to allow for a generous seam allowance. Make sure you have a variety of sizes. For example, this quilt has three circles 7½" (19 cm) to 8" (20.3 cm) in diameter, four circles 4¾" (12 cm) to 5¾" (14.6 cm) in diameter, 33 circles 3½" (9 cm) to 4½" (11.4 cm) in diameter, and 40 circles 2½" (6.4 cm) to 3" (7.6 cm) in diameter.

MAKING THE FLOWER APPLIQUÉ CIRCLES

To prepare each flower appliqué circle, with the right side facing, baste around the circle approximately ⅛–¼" (3–6 mm) from the raw edge, leaving a long thread tail at each end of the hand stitching. Place the template used for the circle on the wrong side of the circle and, holding the template firmly in place, pull the ends of the basting thread to gather the edge of the fabric over the template. Tie the ends of the thread together. Using spray starch, press both sides of the fabric circle, taking care not to destroy the template so you can use it again. When the fabric is cool, remove the basting thread and the template.

APPLIQUÉING THE CIRCLES TO THE QUILT CENTER PIECE

The majority of the appliqué circles are sewn to the fabric-A quilt center before the radiating stripe border is added. Begin by basting a line around the fabric-A quilt center piece, 2¾" (7.1 cm) from the edge, to indicate the position of the seam line around the quilt center. Using your design wall (see page 205) or the floor, arrange the circles all over the quilt center inside the seam line, over the seam line, and to about 5" (13 cm) outside the seam line. To create a "bubble" effect, position the biggest circles closer to the bottom and more of the smallest circles near the top. If the blossoms have a "direction," position them facing upward to further enhance the bubble effect.

Once you are happy with your appliqué arrangement, pin in place the circles that are inside the basted seam line and remove all the others. (You might want to take a photo of your arrangement before you remove the outer circles as a reminder of their positions.)

Appliqué in place the circles that are pinned to the quilt center piece. Press.

Trim the quilt center piece to 24½" × 36½" (61.2 cm × 91.2 cm).

MAKING THE RADIATING-STRIPE BORDERS

Sew the radiating-stripe border pieces together to form two side borders and top and bottom borders using a ¼" (6 mm) seam allowance for all seams.

SIDE BORDERS

For the left side border, arrange the following 10 fabric pieces as shown in the Side Bordrs diagram: L rev, K rev, J rev, H rev, G rev, G, H, J, K, and L. Sew the G, H, J, K, and L pieces together to form the bottom section of the border panel, then sew the five reverse pieces together to form the top section. Sew the top and bottom sections together to complete the left border panel.

Sew together the right side border in the same way, using the same fabric pieces and following the diagram when arranging them.

TOP AND BOTTOM BORDERS

For the top border, arrange the following eight fabric pieces as shown in the Top and Bottom Borders diagram: P rev, O rev, N rev, M rev, M, N, O, and P. Sew the M, N, O, and P pieces together to form the right section of the border panel, then sew the five reverse pieces together to form the left section. Sew the right and left sections together to complete the top border panel.

Sew together the bottom border in the same way, using the same fabric pieces and following the diagram when arranging them.

ASSEMBLING THE QUILT TOP

Follow the Radiating Bubbles Assembly diagram when assembling the quilt top. First, sew the radiating-stripe side panels to the left and right edges of the trimmed quilt center, stopping each seam ¼" (6 mm) from each end. Sew on the top and bottom radiating-stripe panels in the same way, again stopping each seam ¼" (6 mm) from each end. Sew the diagonal corner seams together, stitching from the outside edge toward the quilt center and making a reverse stitch where it joins the quilt center. Press the diagonal corner seams open.

Top and Bottom Borders

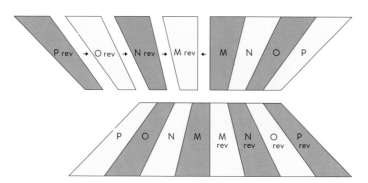

Side Borders

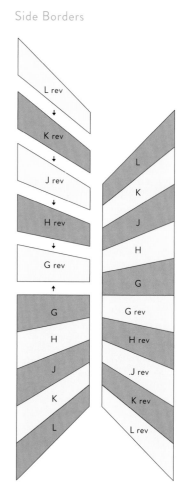

FINAL APPLIQUÉ

Now complete the appliqué before adding the outer border. Arrange the remaining circles on the quilt top, so that they overlap the quilt center seam and spill onto the radiating-stripe panels, referring to your earlier arrangement photo if you took one. Complete the appliqué and press.

OUTER BORDER

Sew the two fabric-D outer side borders to the quilt top. Then sew one fabric-E fussy-cut flower square to each end of the top and bottom borders. Sew on the top and bottom borders.

FINISHING TOUCHES ON THE APPLIQUÉ

Carefully trim away the background fabric behind the circle appliqués, leaving a seam allowance approximately ¼" (6 mm) wide.

FINISHING THE QUILT

Prepare the backing. Press the quilt top. Layer the quilt top, batting, and backing, then baste the layers together (page 208).

Machine-quilt around each circle appliqué, just inside the outer edge of the circle. Machine-quilt circles in the borders as though they were invisible bubbles. Stitch-in-the-ditch on the radiating-stripe border. Then meander machine-quilt over the outer border, following some of the wavy stripe lines.

Trim the quilt edges. Then prepare the binding and sew it on around the edge of the quilt (page 209).

Radiating Bubbles Assembly

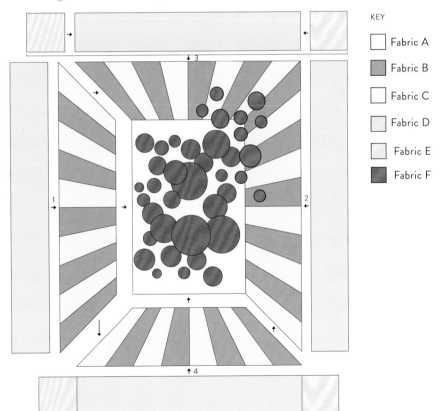

KEY

☐ Fabric A
▨ Fabric B
☐ Fabric C
☐ Fabric D
☐ Fabric E
▨ Fabric F

YELLOW SUNLIGHT

Made from simple squares of different sizes, this is a perfect quilt for a beginner. Most of the squares feature blossoms, but for a touch of variety I have thrown in some stripes and plaids. Enjoy composing the whole quilt on your design wall before stitching.

FINISHED SIZE

87½" x 93½" (219 cm x 234 cm)

PATCHWORK FABRICS

Use quilting cottons 44–45" (112–115 cm) wide

Fabric A (inner border): 1 yard (1 m) of a light-toned polka-dot ombré stripe in golds and greens; OR, as used here, Kaffe Fassett Collective *Ombre* in Moss

Fabric B (outer border): 2 yards (1.9 m) of a medium-toned large-scale floral print with pink flowers and lime green and turquoise leaves on a golden orange ground; OR, as used here, Kaffe Fassett Collective *Gertrude* in Yellow

Fabric C (outer border): ½ yard (50 cm) of a light-medium-toned large-scale floral print in pale green, gold, and pink; OR, as used here, Kaffe Fassett Collective *Lotus Stripe* in Gold

Fabric D (quilt center squares): ¼–½ yard (25–50 cm) each of at least 16 different light-toned medium-scale to super-large-scale floral prints, predominantly in yellows, but including blues, mauves, pinks, and greens; OR, as used here, the following 16 Kaffe Fassett Collective fabrics: *Big Blooms* in Green, *Brassica* in Moss and Yellow, *Brocade Peony* in Green, Mauve, Yellow, and Pink, *Dianthus* in Blue and White, *Gertrude* in Grey and Yellow, *Guinea Flower* in Mauve, *Joy* in Mauve, *Lake Blossoms* in Yellow, *Lavinia* in Mauve, *Lotus Stripe* in Gold

Fabric E (quilt center squares): ¼ yard (25 cm) each of at least 4 different bright pastel geometric prints; OR, as used here, the following 5 Kaffe Fassett Collective fabrics: *Antwerp Flowers* in Soft, *Jupiter* in Stone, *Mad Plaid* in Mauve, *Millefiore* in Pastel, *Zig Zag* in Mauve

OTHER INGREDIENTS

Backing fabric: 9 yards (8.3 m) of desired fabric

Binding fabric: ¾ yard (70 cm) of desired fabric

Cotton batting: 95" x 101" (235 cm x 250 cm) piece of batting

Quilting thread: Yellow thread

CUTTING THE PIECES

INNER-BORDER PIECES

4 border strips: From fabric A, cut eight strips 3½" (8.7 cm) wide, cutting from selvage to selvage. Cut off the selvages and sew the eight strips together end-to-end. From this long pieced strip, cut two strips 75½" (188.7 cm) long for the side borders; then cut two strips 69½" (173.7 cm) long for the top and bottom borders.

4 corner squares: From fabric D, fussy-cut four squares from different fabrics each 3½" × 3½" (8.7 cm × 8.7 cm), carefully centering a flower in each square.

OUTER-BORDER PIECES

4 top- and bottom-border strips: From fabric B, cut four strips 6½" × 34" (16.2 cm × 84.2 cm). Pin a label to each of these strips to identify them as the main sections of the top and bottom outer borders.

2 top- and bottom-border rectangles: From fabric C, cut two rectangles 6½" × 8½" (16.2 cm × 22.7 cm). Pin a label to these rectangles to identify them as the rectangles at the center of the top and bottom outer borders.

4 side-border strips: From fabric B, cut four strips 6½" × 40" (16.2 cm × 101.2 cm). Pin a label to each of these strips to identify them as the main sections of the side outer borders.

2 side-border rectangles: From fabric C, cut two rectangles 6½" × 14½" (16.2 cm × 33.7 cm). Pin a label to these rectangles to identify them as the rectangles at the center of the side outer borders.

QUILT CENTER PIECES

Use the largest flower prints for the largest quilt center squares and cut these first. Fussy-cut most of the quilt center squares so that a single flower is centered in each one. Where the flowers are not big enough to fill a whole square, position them carefully to show off several flowers to their best advantage within the square.

8 extra-large squares: From fabric D, fussy-cut a total of eight squares 12½" × 12½" (31.2 cm × 31.2 cm).

15 large squares: From fabric D, fussy-cut a total of 15 squares 9½" × 9½" (23.7 cm × 23.7 cm).

54 medium-sized squares: From fabrics D and E, fussy-cut a total of 54 squares 6½" × 6½" (16.2 cm × 16.2 cm).

96 small squares: From fabrics D and E, fussy-cut a total of 96 squares 3½" × 3½" (8.7 cm × 8.7 cm).

MAKING THE OUTER BORDERS

TOP AND BOTTOM OUTER BORDERS

For the top border, sew one fabric-B strip to each end of a fabric-C rectangle, using a ¼" (6 mm) seam allowance for all seams. Press. Make the bottom border in the same way.

SIDE OUTER BORDERS

For each side border, sew one fabric-B strip to each end of a fabric-C rectangle. Press.

Quilt Center Assembly

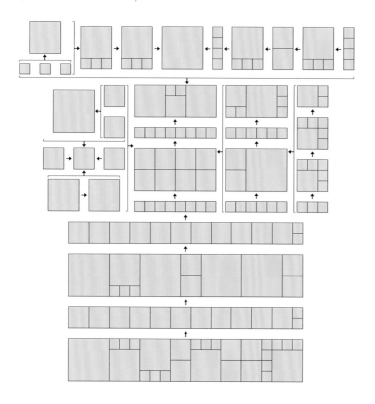

Yellow Sunlight Assembly

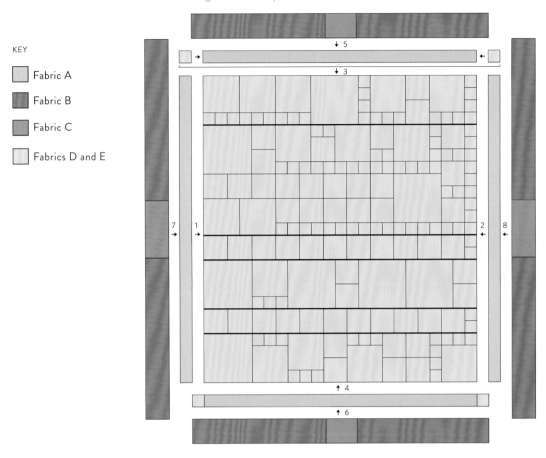

KEY

Fabric A

Fabric B

Fabric C

Fabrics D and E

ASSEMBLING THE QUILT TOP

Follow the Quilt Center Assembly diagram when arranging the flower squares for the quilt top. Take your time arranging the squares, lining them up on the floor or on a design wall (page 205). If the prints are directional, make sure the flowers are upright.

Once you have achieved the desired effect for the quilt center, sew the squares together in units then in horizontal sections while following the quilt center diagram.

INNER BORDER

Following the Yellow Sunlight Assembly diagram, sew the two fabric-A inner side borders to the sides of the quilt top. Then sew one fabric-D fussy-cut-flower square to each end of the top and bottom inner borders. Sew on the top and bottom borders.

OUTER BORDER

Sew the pieced top and bottom outer borders to the quilt. Then sew on the pieced side outer borders to complete the quilt top.

FINISHING THE QUILT

Prepare the backing. Press the quilt top. Layer the quilt top, batting, and backing, then baste the layers together (page 208).

Machine-quilt around the flower shapes. Machine-quilt leaf shapes in the inner border.

Trim the quilt edges. Then prepare the binding and sew it on around the edge of the quilt (page 209).

BASKET

If you like doing primitive appliqué, this is the quilt for you. Choose a floral fabric with distinctive blossoms for the appliqué and arrange the flowers differently in each basket to keep it interesting. For a quick project, make a single block for a pillow cover.

FINISHED SIZE

71½" × 91¼" (181.5 cm × 232 cm)

PATCHWORK FABRICS

Use quilting cottons 44–45" (112–115 cm) wide

Fabric A (border): 3¼ yards (3 m) of a dark-medium-toned large-scale directional floral print in grapes, blues, and gold; OR, as used here, Kaffe Fassett Collective *Joy* in Mauve (if the fabric is not directional, 2½ yards [2.3 m] is sufficient)

Fabric B (large squares and edge "setting" triangles): 3 yards (2.8 m) of a medium-toned super-large-scale directional fruit print; OR, as used here, Kaffe Fassett Collective *Market Basket* in Frost

Fabric C (block "background"): 3½ yards (3.2 m) of a light-toned polka-dot fabric with white dots on a mint green ground; OR, as used here, Kaffe Fassett Collective *Spot* in Mint

Fabric D (baskets): 1 yard (1 m) of a light-medium-toned plaid; OR, as used here, Kaffe Fassett Collective *Mad Plaid* in Mauve

Fabric E (appliqué flowers): 2 yards (1.9 m) of a medium-toned super-large-scale floral print in reds, pinks, and blues; OR, as used here, Kaffe Fassett Collective *Gloxinia* in Natural (you may need more fabric, depending on which flowers you choose to fussy-cut)

OTHER INGREDIENTS

Backing fabric: 5¾ yards (5.3 m) of desired fabric

Binding fabric: ¾ yard (70 cm) more of fabric D

Cotton batting: 79" × 99" (200 cm × 250 cm) piece of batting

Appliqué blanket-stitch edging thread: Bright yellow-gold sewing thread

Quilting thread: Gray-green thread

Appliqué materials: Iron-on lightweight fusible adhesive web

Template materials: Heat-resistant template plastic (or stiff cardboard) for templates

Templates: XX, YY, YY rev, and ZZ (page 211)

Fabric B Cutting Guide

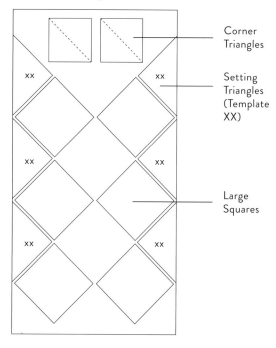

Corner Triangles

Setting Triangles (Template XX)

Large Squares

CUTTING THE PIECES

BORDER PIECES

4 border strips: From fabric A, cut two strips 6½" × 79¾" (16.5 cm × 202.6 cm) for the side borders, cutting these strips lengthwise (parallel to the selvage). If your fabric is directional like *Joy* and you want the flowers in the top and bottom outer borders to be upright, next cut six 6½" (16.5 cm) strips from selvage to selvage from fabric A, lining up the patterns in the strips so you can match them. Cut off the selvages and sew these strips together end-to-end, matching the pattern as well as possible. Then from this long pieced strip, cut two strips 6½" × 71⅞" (16.5 cm × 182.6 cm) for the top and bottom borders.

LARGE SQUARES AND EDGE "SETTING" TRIANGLES

If using directional fabric, follow the Fabric B Cutting Guide when cutting these pieces.
6 large squares: From fabric B, cut six squares 14½" × 14½" (36.8 cm × 36.8 cm), positioning them on-point (with one corner pointing upward) as shown in the cutting guide.
6 large edge "setting" triangles: From fabric B, cut six triangles, using template XX and positioning them with the long edge on the straight grain of the fabric as shown in the cutting guide.
4 corner triangles: From fabric B, cut two squares 10¾" × 10¾" (27.3 cm × 27.3 cm), positioning them on the straight grain as shown in the cutting guide. Then cut each of these squares in half diagonally from corner to corner to make two half-square triangles from each square, for a total of 4 triangles.

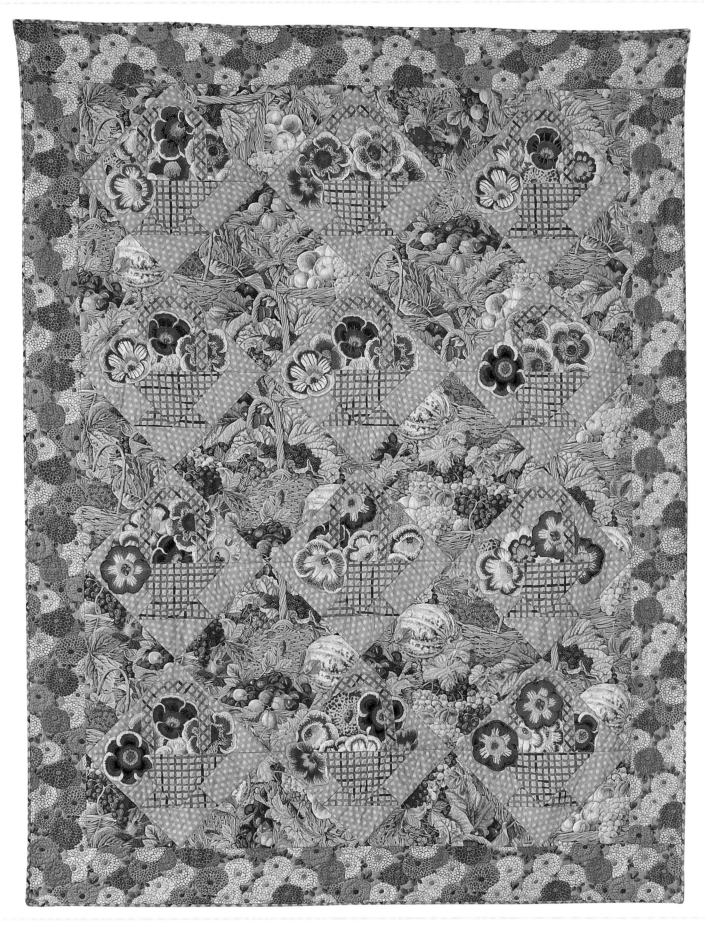

BLOCK PIECES

Block "background" pieces: From fabric C, cut six squares 14⅞" × 14⅞" (37.8 cm × 37.8 cm) and cut each of these squares in half diagonally from corner to corner to make two half-square triangles from each square, for a total of 12 large triangles. Next, from fabric C, cut six squares 6⅞" × 6⅞" (17.5 cm × 17.5 cm) and cut each of these squares in half diagonally from corner to corner to make two half-square triangles from each square, for a total of 12 small triangles. Lastly, from fabric C, cut 12 pieces using template YY and 12 pieces using template YY rev (reverse).

Block basket pieces: From plaid fabric D, cut six squares 8⅞" × 8⅞" (22.5 cm × 22.5 cm) and cut each of these squares in half diagonally from corner to corner to make two half-square triangles from each square, for a total of 12 triangles for the baskets. Next, from plaid fabric D, cut 12 squares 3⅞" × 3⅞" (9.8 cm × 9.8 cm) and cut each of these squares in half diagonally from corner to corner to make two half-square triangles from each square, for a total of 24 small triangles for the basket bases.

APPLIQUÉ PIECES

12 basket handles: Iron fusible adhesive web to the wrong side of the remaining plaid fabric D. Using handle template ZZ, cut out 12 basket handles. If you can't make 12 complete handles, that is alright, as partial handles will do for some of the baskets where flowers obscure them.

12 single flowers and 12 flower clusters: From fabric E, fussy-cut a flower cluster and one single large blossom for each basket. When you find the section of fabric that you wish to use, iron fusible adhesive web to the wrong side in a ring around just the edges of the flower shape. Cut out the 12 selected clusters and the 12 single blossoms, making sure that the adhesive goes all the way to the outer edge of each blossom. Trim the bottom of each cluster so that it has a straight edge that will run along the top of the basket. Cut out a few extra single blossoms. (Do not remove the paper backing on the appliqué pieces until you are ready to fuse them to the blocks.)

MAKING THE BASKET BLOCKS

For each basket block, you will need one large polka-dot fabric-C triangle, one small polka-dot fabric-C triangle, one polka-dot fabric-C piece cut using template YY and one using template YY rev; plus one plaid fabric-D basket and two small fabric-D triangle base pieces. Following the diagram and using a ¼" (6 mm) seam allowance for all seams, sew the pieces together. Press.

Make all 12 basket blocks in the same way.

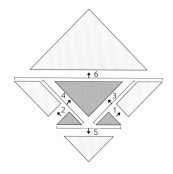

ADDING THE APPLIQUÉ

For the first basket block, select a prepared floral cluster, a prepared large single blossom, and a prepared basket handle. Remove the backing papers. Place the straight edge of the cluster on the seam line at the top of the plaid basket and place the basket handle in front of the cluster. Place the single blossom so it overlaps the handle and hangs over the basket on the left side of the block. Move all three pieces around until the composition is pleasing, then fuse the appliqué in place.

Fuse the appliqué in place on the remaining 11 blocks, making each one different—some with the handle behind the cluster, some with the handle in front on one side and in back on the other, and each with a different flower arrangement.

Using bright yellow-gold thread, machine buttonhole stitch all around the cluster, the single blossom, and the handle on each block.

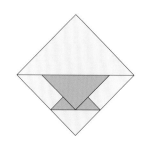

ASSEMBLING THE QUILT TOP

Following the Basket Assembly diagram, arrange the large fabric-B squares and the basket blocks on-point in four vertical rows of three basket blocks each. Alternate with three vertical rows of three large squares, lining them up on the floor or on a design wall (page 205). Position the fabric-B edge "setting" triangles along each outer edge of the quilt center and one fabric-B corner triangle at each corner.

Once you have achieved the desired effect, sew together the blocks and other pieces in diagonal rows as shown on the diagram. Press. Then sew the rows together. Press.

BORDER

Sew the two border side strips to the sides of the quilt top, press, then sew on the top and bottom strips. Press.

FINISHING THE QUILT

Prepare the backing. Press the quilt top. Layer the quilt top, batting, and backing, then baste the layers together (page 208).

Machine-quilt around each appliqué piece just inside the buttonhole stitch. Quilt wavy horizontal lines in each basket. Stitch in the ditch around the other pieces in the blocks. On the plain blocks and the border, quilt around the details in the prints.

Trim the quilt edges. Then cut the binding strips on the bias and sew the binding on around the edge of the quilt (page 209).

Basket Assembly

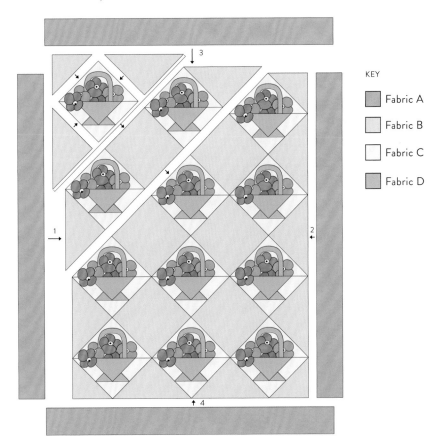

KEY

Fabric A
Fabric B
Fabric C
Fabric D

ATTIC WINDOW ON-POINT

Sewing quilts with on-point blocks is more time-consuming than those with simple rows of blocks, but I love how interesting the layouts look. When fussy-cutting the huge blooms inside the on-point squares, position the flowers so they are "looking" upward.

100¾" × 100¾" (256 cm × 256 cm)

PATCHWORK FABRICS

Use quilting cottons 44–45" (112–115 cm) wide

Fabric A (outer border and block borders): 3 yards (2.8 m) of a light-medium-toned broad stripe in blues and mauve; OR, as used here, Kaffe Fassett Collective *Kim* in Blue

Fabric B (block borders): 1 yard (1 m) each of 4 different light-medium-toned broad stripes, one in browns and terra-cotta, one in greens and blue, one in mauve, beige, and green, and one in red, orange, and raspberry; OR, as used here, the following 4 Kaffe Fassett Collective fabrics: *Kim* in Brown, Green, Mauve, and Red.

Fabric C (floral prints): 1–1½ yards (1–1.4 m) each of 7 different medium-toned super-large-scale floral print in pinks, reds, aqua greens, and mauves; OR, as used here, the following 7 Kaffe Fassett Collective fabrics: 1½ yards (1.4 m) each of *Brocade Peony* in Green, Natural, and Red; 1½ yards (1.4 m) of *Japanese Chrysanthemum* in Pink; 1 yard (1 m) each of *Lavinia* in Mauve, Natural, and Red

OTHER INGREDIENTS

Backing fabric: 9 yards (8.3 m) of desired fabric

Binding fabric: ¾ yard (70 cm) more of Fabric A

Cotton batting: 108" × 108" (275 cm × 275 cm) piece of batting

Quilting thread: Medium gray thread

Template materials: Heat-resistant template plastic, for making templates

Templates: N, N rev, P, P rev, Q, Q rev, R, S, T, T rev, and U on pages 212 and 213 (mark each template on the right side and flip over for the reverse)

CUTTING THE PIECES

OUTER-BORDER PIECES

4 border strips: From fabric A, cut two matching pairs of strips 8½" × 85⅜" (21.6 cm × 216.9 cm)—a total of 4 strips. One matching pair will be used for the top and bottom borders and the other for the side borders. (Use the remaining fabric A for block border pieces.)

4 corner squares: From fabric C, fussy-cut four squares 8½" × 8½" (21.6 cm × 21.6 cm), carefully centering a different flower in each square.

BLOCK PIECES

It is not necessary to exactly match the blocks to the original quilt. Cut more of your favorite fabrics and fewer of others. When cutting border pieces, refer to the block diagrams to check the direction of the stripes and how to position the flowers in the on-point squares (squares pointing upward).

41 whole blocks: From fabric C, fussy-cut 41 M on-point squares 8½" × 8½" (21.6 cm × 21.6 cm) each, carefully positioning a flower at the center of each *on-point* square. (The cut edges will probably be on the bias so it is best to starch the fabric before cutting and keep these squares flat.) Next, for each of the 41 whole blocks, cut a pair of striped border pieces from a single fabric B (or fabric A), using templates N (and N rev). To cut the pairs of borders pieces so the stripes will match up when sewn together, first cut a strip 4½" × 27" (11.4 cm × 68.6 cm) with the stripes running parallel to the long edge of the strip. Then fold the strip in half widthwise, place template N on top of the folded fabric, and cut the two matching pieces—one will be an N piece and one an N rev (reverse) piece. Pin labels to all your block pieces as you cut them, and keep matching border pairs pinned together.

8 side-edge half blocks: From fabric C, fussy-cut a total of four on-point squares each 8⅞" × 8⅞" (22.6 cm × 22.6 cm), carefully positioning the flowers in each on-point square. Cut each of the squares in half diagonally from corner to corner for a total of eight O half-square triangles. For the single border on each of these eight partial blocks, cut four pairs of N/N rev pieces from different B (or A) fabrics as you cut them for the whole blocks.

2 top-corner quarter blocks: From fabric C, cut one template P piece and one template P rev piece (no need to fussy-cut these). For the partial border pieces, cut one template Q piece and one template Q rev piece from fabric B (or fabric A), with the stripes running parallel to a different short edge on each.

For 4 top-edge half blocks: From fabric C, fussy-cut four template R pieces. For each of the template R pieces, cut a pair of border pieces from a single fabric B (or fabric A)—one template Q piece and one template Q rev piece, with the stripes running parallel to a different short edge on each.

For 2 bottom-corner quarter blocks: From fabric C, cut two template S pieces. For the partial border pieces, cut one template T rev piece and one template T piece from fabric B (or fabric A), with the stripes running parallel to the longest edge.

For 4 bottom-edge half blocks: From fabric C, cut four template U pieces. For each of the template U pieces, cut a pair of border pieces from a single fabric B (or fabric A)—one template T piece and one template T rev piece, with the stripes running parallel to the longest edge.

MAKING THE BLOCKS

41 WHOLE BLOCKS

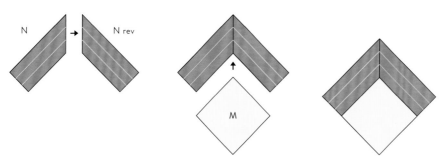

Choose one floral M square and one pair of border pieces (one N and one N rev) for each of the 41 whole blocks (see diagram). These three pieces are sewn together with a set-in or Y-seam. With right sides together and using a ¼" (6 mm) seam allowance for all seams, first sew the N and N rev pieces together along the angled edge, starting at the pointy end and stopping ¼" (6 mm) from the blunt end. Make a backstitch before removing these border pieces from the machine so the seam is well secured at the inside edge. Press the seam *open*.

  With right sides together, align one of the top edges of the M square with one of the inside edges of the striped border. With the floral square on top, sew the seam from the outside edge of the border toward the center of the border (the top of the on-point square), stopping ¼" (6 mm) from the end—this should meet exactly with the center seam on the border. With the machine needle down and still piercing the fabric layers, lift the presser foot and swivel the fabrics so that the other inside edge of the border is aligned with the next edge of the floral square—this takes a bit of poking and pulling to achieve. When the edges are aligned, put the presser foot down again and sew the seam to the end. Open the block and press the floral square seam toward the striped border. Make the remaining 40 whole blocks in the same way.

8 SIDE-EDGE HALF BLOCKS

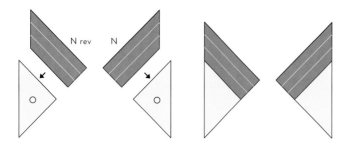

Choose one floral O triangle and one N border piece for each of four side-edge half blocks. Choose one floral O triangle and one N rev border piece for each of the remaining four side-edge half blocks. Sew one border piece to each O triangle as shown in the diagram. Press.

2 TOP-CORNER QUARTER BLOCKS

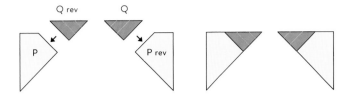

Following the diagram, sew the floral P piece to the Q rev border piece for the top left corner block, and sew the floral P rev piece to the Q border piece for the top right corner block. Press.

4 TOP-EDGE HALF BLOCKS

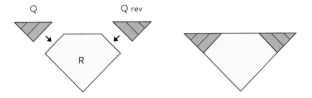

For each of these four half blocks, choose one floral R piece and a pair of Q and Q rev border pieces. Sew the border pieces to each R piece as shown in the diagram. Press.

2 BOTTOM-CORNER QUARTER BLOCKS

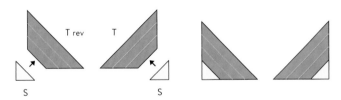

Following the diagram, sew one floral S piece to the T rev border piece for the bottom left corner block, and sew one floral S piece to the T border piece for the bottom right corner block. Press.

4 BOTTOM-EDGE HALF BLOCKS

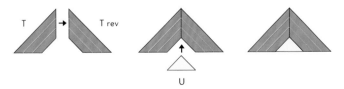

For each of these four half blocks, choose one floral U piece and a pair of T and T rev border pieces. Sew the border pieces together (see diagram) and then sew in the U piece using a set-in seam as for the whole blocks. Press as for the whole blocks.

Attic Window On-Point Assembly

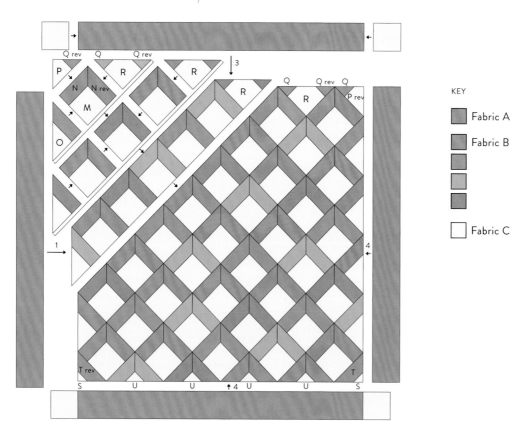

KEY

Fabric A

Fabric B

Fabric C

ASSEMBLING THE QUILT TOP

Follow the Attic Window On-Point Assembly diagram when arranging the on-point whole blocks for the quilt top. Take your time arranging the blocks, lining them up on the floor or on a design wall (page 30). Start with a horizontal row of five on-point blocks, then nestle a horizontal row of four blocks into the V-shapes left along the bottom edge of the first row. Continue in this way, arranging a row of five blocks and four blocks alternately and ending with a row of five blocks.

Once you have achieved the desired effect, position one corner block at each of the four corners, then the half blocks along the edges. Sew the blocks together in diagonal rows as shown, press, then sew the rows together. Press.

BORDER

Following the diagram, sew the two fabric-A side borders to the sides of the quilt top. Press. Then sew one fabric-C fussy-cut flower square to each end of the top and bottom borders. Press. Sew on the top and bottom borders. Press.

FINISHING THE QUILT

Prepare the backing. Press the quilt top. Layer the quilt top, batting, and backing, then baste the layers together (page 208).

Machine-quilt each flower around most of the petals. Machine-quilt between the colors on the stripes in the block borders and the outer border of the quilt.

Trim the quilt edges. Then cut the binding strips on the bias and sew the binding on around the edge of the quilt (page 209).

SEED PACKET

Collect as many different florals as you can for this quilt; the aim is to fussy-cut a different flower for each square in the quilt center and the border. When arranging your squares, pay attention to the subtle tonal differences so you can alternate "darks" and "lights." This is a dream project for a beginner.

FINISHED SIZE

68" × 83" (172 cm × 210 cm)

PATCHWORK FABRICS

Use quilting cottons 44–45" (112–115 cm) wide

Fabric A (large center squares):
Large scrap or ½ yard (50 cm) each of at least 15–20 different super-large-scale light-medium-toned and medium-toned floral prints, in predominantly reds, strong pinks, and lavenders, with a smattering of blues and greens

Fabric B (small inner-border squares):
½ yard (50 cm) each of at least 8–10 different large-scale medium-toned floral prints, in the same colors as fabric A

Fabric C (small outer-border squares):
½ yard (50 cm) each of at least 8 different large-scale light-medium-toned floral prints, predominantly in strong pinks, blues, lavenders, and greens

OTHER INGREDIENTS

Backing fabric: 6 yards (5.5 m) of desired fabric

Binding fabric: ¾ yard (70 cm) of a mostly red stripe

Cotton batting: 75" × 90" (190 cm × 225 cm) piece of batting

Quilting thread: Red thread

CUTTING THE PIECES

Fussy-cut all the squares, carefully framing the flowers in each square. For most of the squares, choose one flower to fill the entire square. For fabrics that have sprays of flowers rather than single blooms, frame the sprays just as carefully to give the same generous feel a single bloom gives.

63 large fabric-A squares: From fabric A, cut 63 squares, each 8" × 8" (20.2 cm × 20.2 cm), for the quilt center.

68 small fabric-B squares: From fabric B, cut 68 squares, each 4¼" × 4¼" (10.7 cm × 10.7 cm), for the inner border.

76 small fabric-C squares: From fabric C, cut 76 squares, each 4¼" × 4¼" (10.7 cm × 10.7 cm), for the outer border.

ASSEMBLING THE QUILT TOP

Arrange the 63 large squares for the quilt center, lining them up on the floor or on a design wall (page 205). The quilt center consists of nine horizontal rows of seven squares each (see Seed Packet Assembly diagram on page 149).

Using a ¼" (6 mm) seam allowance for all seams, sew together each of the nine rows of seven large squares, press, then sew the rows together to form the quilt center. Press.

Once you have sewn the quilt center together, take the 68 fabric-B squares and arrange them in a single row all around the quilt center. Then arrange the 76 fabric-C squares around these.

Sew the squares of the two side borders together in pairs, press, then sew the pairs together so each border is 18 squares long by two squares wide. Press. Sew the side borders to the quilt center. Press.

Sew the top and bottom border squares together in the same way, press, and sew them on to complete the quilt top. Press.

FINISHING THE QUILT

Prepare the backing. Press the quilt top. Layer the quilt top, batting, and backing, then baste the layers together (page 208).

Machine-quilt in the ditch around each square. Then machine-quilt around the petals of the individual flower in each square.

Trim the quilt edges. Then cut the binding strips on the bias and sew the binding on around the edge of the quilt (page 209).

Seed Packet Assembly

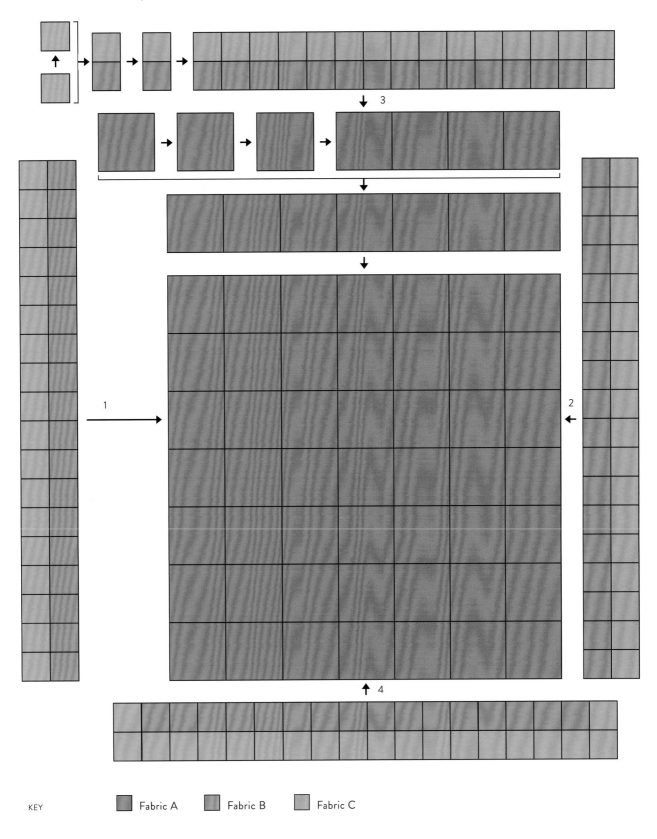

KEY | Fabric A | Fabric B | Fabric C

ROUND AND ROUND

You can easily improvise this quilt like I did. I stitched it entirely by hand, adding on borders outward from the rectangular center piece. Keep to the palette of brilliant highs, or choose your own palette. If you want to introduce a few larger-scale florals, make the borders wider to show them off.

FINISHED SIZE

Approximately 70½" × 75½" (177 cm × 190 cm)

PATCHWORK FABRICS

Use quilting cottons 44–45" (112–115 cm) wide

Fabric A (center rectangle): 4½" × 9½" (11.2 cm × 24.2 cm) piece of medium-toned fabric featuring a flower, a vase, or any other vertical flower design, for the centerpiece

Fabric B (strips): ⅓–½ yard (35–50 cm) each of at least 16 different light-toned to medium-toned floral prints in predominantly warm colors with splashes of greens and teals

Fabric C (last ring of strips): ¾ yard (70 cm) of a light-medium-toned large-scale floral print

OTHER INGREDIENTS

Backing fabric: 5 yards (4.6 m) of desired fabric

Binding fabric: ¾ yard (70 cm) of a warm-colored dots print

Cotton batting: 78" × 83" (195 cm × 210 cm) piece of batting

Quilting thread: Red thread

CUTTING THE PIECES

This quilt is constructed in an improvisational manner. You can vary the size of the quilt and the width of the strips as desired.

Center rectangle: From fabric A, fussy-cut a rectangle measuring 4½" × 9½" (11.2 cm × 24.2 cm), carefully centering the vertical centerpiece motif.

4 strips for first ring of strips: Using a fabric B that contrasts with fabric A, cut a long strip 1½" (3.7 cm) wide, cutting from selvage to selvage of the fabric. From this strip, cut two strips 9½" (24.2 cm) long and two strips 6½" (16.2 cm) long.

Strips for the 2nd–16th rings of strips: Cut the strips for each of the remaining rings of strips as you add them on in an improvisational manner, using a different fabric B for each ring. Cut the strips for most of the rings 2½" (6.2 cm) wide and a few of them 2¼" (5.7 cm) wide, but make sure the strips are the same width for each individual ring of strips. To achieve the given finished size, make eleven of these 15 rings 2½" (6.2 cm) wide and four of them 2¼" (5.7 cm) wide.

Use your shorter lengths of fabric B for the beginning rings of strips and the longer lengths of fabric for the rings nearer the outside edge of the quilt top. As the rings get longer, you will have to cut the strips selvage to selvage and then piece the strips together end-to-end for a long enough strip to ring the entire quilt center. If you run out of a fabric when cutting your strips for a ring, add in another fabric similar in color and tone, but try to keep the majority of each ring in the same fabric.

Last ring of strips: From fabric C, cut seven long strips each 3½" (8.7 cm) wide, cutting from selvage to selvage. Sew the strips together end-to-end. Press the seams to one side.

ASSEMBLING THE QUILT TOP

FIRST RING OF STRIPS

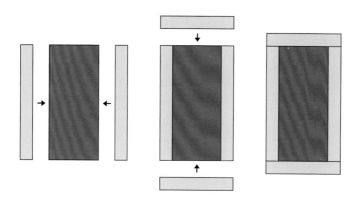

Note: It is tempting to cut each strip to a random length and then trim off the end after stitching it in place, but this method tends to make the quilt wonkier as you work outward. For straighter edges, always measure the edge first and cut the strip to the correct length before sewing it on.

With right sides together and using a ¼" (6 mm) seam allowance for all seams, sew one strip 1½" × 9½" (3.7 cm × 24.2 cm) to each long side of the center rectangle as shown in the diagram. Press. Then sew one strip 1½" × 6½" (3.7 cm × 16.2 cm) to the top of the quilt top and one to the bottom. Press. After completing each ring of strips always make sure the corners of the quilt top are perfect right angles. If this is not done, the top will lose its square corners as it grows outward.

SECOND RING OF STRIPS

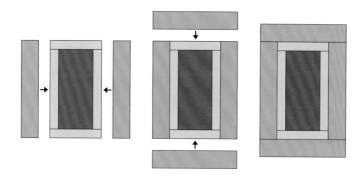

From a fabric B in a different color and different type of floral print, cut a long strip 2½" (6.2 cm) wide, cutting from selvage to selvage. Measure the side edges of the quilt center and cut two strips this length from the strip. As shown in the diagram, sew one cut strip to each side of the quilt center and press. Next, measure the top edge of the quilt center and cut two strips this length—one for the top and one for the bottom. Then, as shown in the diagram, sew a strip to the top edge and the bottom edge and press. (If you run out of strip at any stage, cut a new strip.)

THIRD RING OF STRIPS

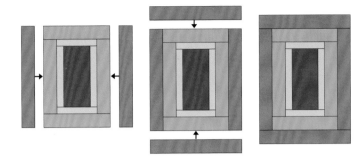

From a fabric B in a different color and different type of floral print, cut strips 2½" (6.2 cm) wide for the third ring, making sure you measure the strip length needed each time as for the second ring of strips. Sew a strip to each side edge and then the top and bottom of the quilt center as shown in the diagram. Press.

4TH–16TH RINGS OF STRIPS

Cutting strips as explained in the cutting instructions and sewing each ring of strips to the quilt center as before, add 13 more rings of strips, using a different fabric B for each ring.

LAST RING OF STRIPS

Using the 3½" (8.7 cm) fabric C strip prepared earlier, sew on a ring of strips as for the previous rounds to complete the quilt top. Press.

FINISHING THE QUILT

Prepare the backing. Press the quilt top. Layer the quilt top, batting, and backing, then baste the layers together (page 208).

Machine-quilt in the ditch between the strips.

Trim the quilt edges. Then prepare the binding and sew it on around the edge of the quilt (page 209).

HEXAGON FLORETS

This quilt is made using the English paper-piecing method, and all the hexagons are hand-stitched together. You will need a paper hexagon for each of the 400 fabric hexagons. To save time, purchase the papers at a quilt store, as they are a standard size.

FINISHED SIZE

63" × 70" (160 cm × 178 cm)

PATCHWORK FABRICS

Use quilting cottons 44–45" (112–115 cm) wide

Fabric A (outer border): 2¼ yards (2.1 m) of a dark-toned medium-scale floral print with circular red floral motifs on a black ground; OR, as used here, Kaffe Fassett Collective *Surrey* in Black

Fabric B (hexagon floret centers): ¾ yard (70 cm) each of 2 different light-toned medium-scale floral prints, one in blues and one in yellows; OR, as used here, the 2 following Kaffe Fassett Collective fabrics: *Dianthus* in Blue and Yellow

Fabric C (hexagon floret "petals"): ¾ yard (70 cm) each of at least 8 different medium-toned to dark-toned nonfloral prints, including stripes, all in reds, pinks, purples, and a splash of blue and gold; OR, as used here, the following 8 Kaffe Fassett Collective fabrics: ¾ yard (70 cm) of *Broad Stripe* in Bliss, ½ yard (50 cm) of *Mad Plaid* in Red, ¾ yard (70 cm) of *Multi Stripe* in Pimento, ½ yard (50 cm) of *Roman Glass* in Red, ½ yard (50 cm) of *Spot* in Fuchsia, Purple, and Royal, ½ yard (50 cm) of *Zig Zag* in Warm

Fabric D ("background" hexagons): 1¼ yards (1.2 m) of a medium-toned plaid with red, green, and blue crossed stripes on a pale curry ground; OR, as used here, Kaffe Fassett Collective *Mad Plaid* in Curry

OTHER INGREDIENTS

Backing fabric: 4 yards (3.7 m) of desired fabric

Binding fabric: ¾ yard (70 cm) of a red plaid; OR, as used here, Kaffe Fassett Collective *Mad Plaid* in Red

Cotton batting: 70" × 77" (175 cm × 195 cm) piece of batting

Quilting thread: Red thread

Template materials: Heat-resistant template plastic to make the template for the fabric hexagons and the template for the paper hexagons; stiff, thin paper (cardstock) to make the 400 paper hexagons needed (Note: If you prefer to buy ready-made papers, purchase 1¾" [4.5 cm] paper hexagons; the size refers to the length of each of the six sides of the hexagon.)

Template: E (page 220)

Fabric glue: Temporary glue stick (optional)

PREPARING THE TEMPLATES AND PAPER HEXAGONS

This quilt is made entirely by hand using the English paper-piecing method.

TEMPLATE FOR THE FABRIC HEXAGONS

Use the outer dotted outline of template E to make a plastic template. This template will be used to cut the fabric hexagons. It allows for a ⅜" (1 cm) seam allowance around each hexagon.

TEMPLATE FOR THE PAPER HEXAGONS

The seam allowance on each fabric hexagon is folded to the wrong side over a paper hexagon that is the size of the finished hexagon. This paper is removed only as the quilt top blocks are pieced together. If you are making your own paper templates, use the inner solid outline of template E to make a plastic template to trace the papers. Then trace and cut out a total of 400 papers.

CUTTING THE PIECES

OUTER-BORDER PIECES

4 border strips: From fabric A, cut four strips 10" (25.5 cm) wide and 2 yards (1.9 m) long for the borders. These will be trimmed to fit when they are stitched on.

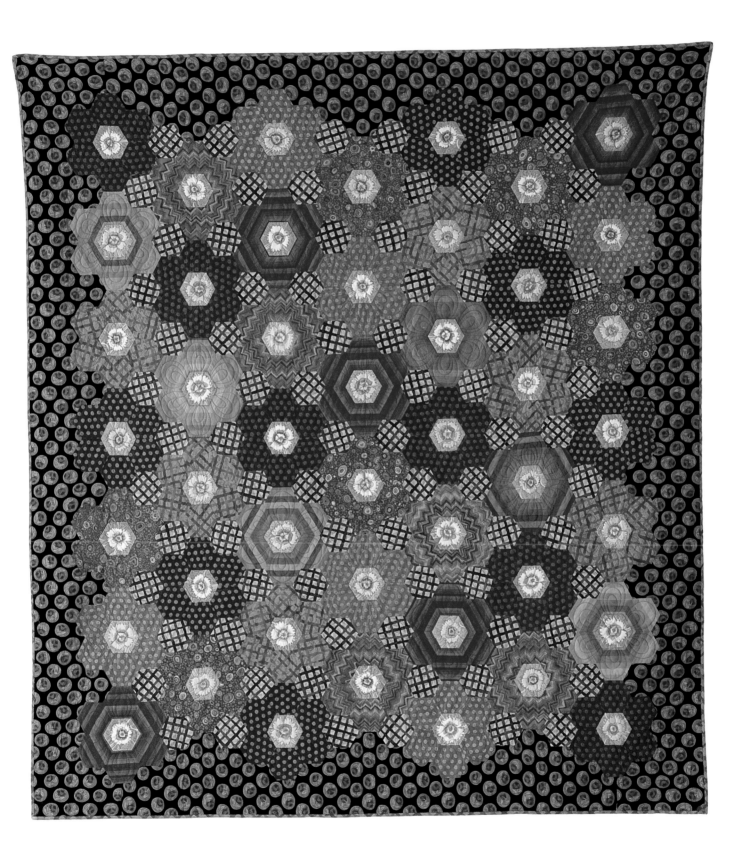

FLORET-BLOCK PIECES

46 floret blocks: For each of the 46 floret blocks, fussy-cut one center hexagon from fabric B, centering a flower in the hexagon, and six "petal" hexagons from a single fabric C. Use each of the two B center fabrics for 23 of the blocks, and use each of the eight C petal fabrics for five or six floret blocks. Trace the hexagon shapes onto the wrong side of the fabric, using the hexagon template that includes the seam allowance, and cut out. When cutting petals from one of the stripe fabrics, be sure to cut six identical pieces.

"BACKGROUND" PIECES

78 "background" hexagons: From fabric D, cut 78 hexagons. Trace the shapes onto the wrong side of the fabric, using the hexagon template that includes the seam allowance, and cut out.

PREPARING THE HEXAGONS

Prepare each hexagon before you start sewing the hexagons together. Place a paper hexagon in the center of the wrong side of a fabric hexagon and fold the fabric seam allowances neatly and snugly to the wrong side over the paper hexagon. Then either sew-baste or glue-baste the seam allowance in place.

Prepare all 400 fabric hexagons in the same way.

MAKING THE FLORET BLOCKS

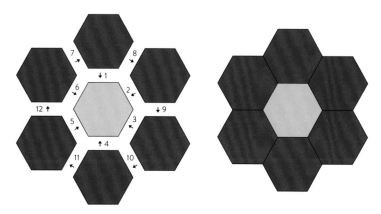

Each floret block is made up of a set of six "petal" hexagons cut from the same C fabric and one center hexagon cut from a B fabric. Start the block by sewing all six petals to the center hexagon. Using whip stitch and with right sides together, first sew each petal hexagon to one edge of the center hexagon as shown by arrows 1–6 on the block diagram. When stitching, be sure to catch just the edges of the fabric and not the paper. Then sew the petals to each other (arrows 7–12 on the diagram). When the floret block is complete, remove the paper from only the center hexagon.

Make a total of 46 blocks in the same way, remembering to keep the papers in all the petals.

ASSEMBLING THE QUILT TOP

QUILT CENTER

Following the Hexagon Florets Assembly diagram, arrange the blocks on the floor or on a design wall (page 205). Arrange them in four vertical rows of seven blocks each, and between these seven-block rows, three vertical rows of six blocks. Position the 78 fabric-D "background" blocks in the spaces left between the blocks.

Hexagon Florets Assembly

KEY

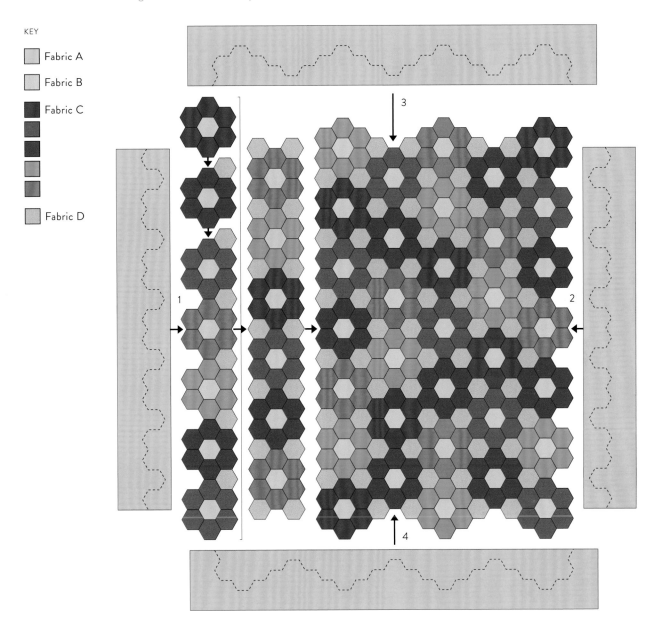

Fabric A

Fabric B

Fabric C

Fabric D

Once you have achieved the desired effect, sew together the vertical rows of blocks, then sew the vertical rows together. Once a hexagon has been sewn on all its sides to other hexagons, the paper can be removed. It is much easier to handle the quilt top if you remove the paper as soon as possible. By the time all the vertical rows of hexagons have been sewn together, the only papers still in hexagons should be those around the edge of the quilt top.

BORDER

With the papers still inside the outside edge hexagons, iron the hexagons along the left side edge of the quilt very well using starch. Carefully remove the papers of the hexagons along this edge and place the edge on top of one strip of border, making sure that the border fills in the empty space between the floret blocks and measures about 8½" (21.6 cm) wide from the deepest valley to the outer edge of the strip. Manipulate the fabric so that the border extends well beyond both ends of the quilt top and the hexagons sit evenly along the border. Baste the hexagons in place on the border strip. Then using an appliqué stitch, sew the outer edge of the hexagons to the border, but do not sew down the first or last floret blocks—leave them loose.

Sew each of the other three edges to a border strip in the same way.

Next, overlap the side borders on top of the top and bottom borders. At each corner, fold about ¼" (6 mm) of the overlapping edge of the side border to the wrong side and press. Appliqué stitch the side borders at the corners to the top and bottom borders. Trim away the excess top and bottom border fabric from the back. Baste and then appliqué stitch the corner florets to the border fabric. Press well.

Trim the border to 8" (20.3 cm) beyond the valleys, or to any desired width, making sure the corners are square.

FINISHING THE QUILT

Prepare the backing. Press the quilt top. Layer the quilt top, batting, and backing, then baste the layers together (page 208).

Machine-quilt around each circular motif in the border fabric. Machine-quilt petal shapes in the flower hexagons.

Trim the quilt edges. Then cut the binding strips on the bias and sew the binding on around the edge of the quilt (page 209).

TAWNY HATBOXES

The background blocks for the hatboxes on this quilt are made from three simple pieces—a square and two trapezoids—which require a set-in seam. Once the appliqué pieces have been secured in place with a machine blanket stitch, the background behind it is cut away to eliminate the excess bulk, so your set-in seams don't have to be perfect.

FINISHED SIZE

92" × 92" (234 cm × 234 cm)

PATCHWORK FABRICS

Use quilting cottons 44–45" (112–115 cm) wide

Fabric A (outer border): 2¾ yards (2.6 m) of a medium-toned large-scale nonfloral swirl print predominantly in rich orangey browns with splashes of blues; OR, as used here, Kaffe Fassett Collective *Curly Baskets* in Antique

Fabric B (floor stripes): 2½ yards (2.3 m) of a subtle dark-medium-toned broad stripe in browns and grays with a hint of purple; OR, as used here, Kaffe Fassett Collective *Kim* in Dark

Fabric C (side walls): 2 yards (1.9 m) of a medium-toned plaid with red, green, and blue crossed stripes on a pale curry ground; OR, as used here, Kaffe Fassett Collective *Mad Plaid* in Curry

Fabric D (back walls): ½ yard (50 cm) each of at least 5 different dark-toned medium-scale circles and zigzag stripe prints; OR, as used here, the following 5 Kaffe Fassett Collective fabrics: *Flame Stripe* in Brown, *Millefiore* in Brown, *Paperweight* in Algae, *Roman Glass* in Byzantium and Red

Fabric E (sashing strips): 2 yards (1.9 m) of a subtly shaded light-toned dots print in golds and browns; OR, as used here, Kaffe Fassett Collective *Ombre* in Brown

Fabric F (sashing squares): ½ yard (50 cm) of a medium-scale floral print of yellow and red flowers (approximately 1½" [4 cm] in diameter) and yellow dots on a dark red ground; OR, as used here, Kaffe Fassett Collective *Guinea Flower* in Yellow

Fabric G (floral hatboxes): ¼ yard (25 cm) each—or ½ yard (50 cm) each if you want to fussy-cut the boxes—of at least 18 different medium-toned and dark-toned large-scale to super-large-scale floral (and leaf) prints in predominantly pinks, reds, and blues; OR, as used here, the following 18 Kaffe Fassett Collective fabrics: *Big Blooms* in Emerald and Turquoise, *Big Leaf* in Mint and Pink, *Gertrude* in Black and Orange, *Gloxinia* in Blue, *Joy* in Blue, *Kimono* in Crimson, *Lake Blossoms* in Black, Magenta, and Red, *Lazy Daisy* in Red, *Lilacs* in Plum and Red, *Lotus Stripe* in Black, *Tree Peony* in Blue and Orange

Fabric H ("ribbon" box lid rims): ¼ yard (25 cm) each of at least 12 different light-medium-toned to medium-toned stripe-like and dots prints; OR, as used here, the following 12 Kaffe Fassett Collective fabrics: *Antwerp Flowers* in Blue, Brown, and Green, *Guinea Flower* in Yellow, *Flame Stripe* in Red, *Kim* in Blue, Brown, and Red, *Victoria* in Antique and Hot, *Zig Zag* in Jade and Multi

OTHER INGREDIENTS

Backing fabric: 8¼ yards (7.6 m) of desired fabric

Binding fabric: ¾ yard (70 cm) more of fabric E

Cotton batting: 99" × 99" (250 cm × 250 cm) piece of batting

Appliqué blanket-stitch edging thread: Bright turquoise sewing thread

Quilting thread: Medium warm brown thread

Appliqué materials: Heat-resistant template plastic, for making appliqué templates, and iron-on lightweight fusible adhesive web, for securing edges of the appliqué

Block templates: J, J rev, and K (page 219)

Appliqué templates: Box lid, box bottom, box lid rim (page 219)

PREPARING THE TEMPLATES

BLOCK TEMPLATES

Use templates J, J rev (reverse), and K to cut the three pieces of each block.

APPLIQUÉ TEMPLATES

Use the box appliqué pieces to trace the box lid, box lid rim, and box bottom shapes onto template plastic. Cut out the shapes carefully and label each one. These shapes are *not* symmetrical so it is important to label them on the *right side*.

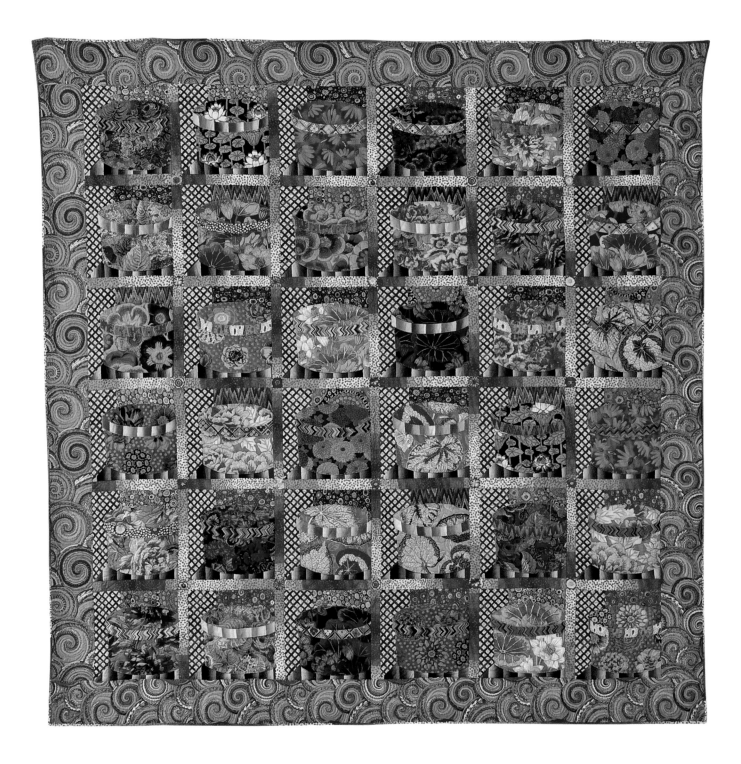

CUTTING THE PIECES

OUTER-BORDER PIECES

4 border strips: From fabric A, cut two strips 6½" × 80" (16.2 cm × 204.2 cm) for the side borders and two strips 6½" × 92" (16.2 cm × 234.2 cm) for the top and bottom borders.

BLOCK PIECES

36 striped floors: From fabric B, cut 36 floor pieces, using template J rev and cutting the pieces one at a time—*do not* cut them in layers. Be sure to cut these shapes with the long side perpendicular to the selvage so that the stripes run widthwise across the shape (up and down in the block).

36 plaid side walls: From fabric C, cut 36 side wall pieces, using template J and cutting the pieces one at a time—*do not* cut them in layers. It is most efficient to cut these with the long side of the shape parallel to the selvage.

36 back walls: From fabric D, cut a total of 36 back wall pieces, using template K; this square template measures 8½" × 8½" (21.6 cm × 21.6 cm), including the seam allowances. Make sure you use all of your different D fabrics for the walls, cutting 7 or 8 from each of the five fabrics.

SASHING PIECES

60 sashing strips: From fabric E, cut 60 strips 2" × 12½" (5.2 cm × 31.7 cm), paying attention to the ombré effect so that the color changes in each strip.

25 sashing squares: From fabric F, fussy-cut 25 squares 2"× 2" (5.2 cm × 5.2 cm), carefully centering a flower in each square.

APPLIQUÉ PIECES

36 floral boxes: For each of the 36 boxes, cut a box lid and a box bottom piece from the same fabric G. Cut pieces for two boxes from each of the 18 G fabrics. To begin, using a pencil and leaving at least 1" (2.5 cm) between the pieces, trace the box lid shape and the box bottom shape onto the *right side* of the fabric. Make sure that the templates are right side up. Then cut out each shape appoximately ½" (12 mm) outside the drawn outline. On the wrong side of each shape, iron on a strip of fusible web approximately ½" (12 mm) wide along the top edge and the left side edge of the lid shape and along the left edge and bottom edge of the bottom shape, positioning the strip ¼" (6 mm) from the raw edge (so that it is centered on the drawn lines on the other side of the fabric). The fusible web stops edges A/B and C/D from fraying (see Adding the Appliqué diagram, page 162). Always follow the manufacturer's instructions when using fusible web. Cut out the shapes along the drawn lines.

36 "ribbon" box lid rims: From fabric H, cut 36 box lid rim pieces. First, iron the fusible web onto the wrong side of the fabrics you are going to use. Then draw several lid rims onto the right side of each fabric. Cut out the lid rims along the drawn line.

MAKING THE BLOCKS

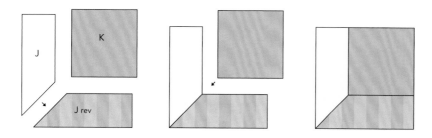

Each block is a traditional Attic Window with a hatbox appliquéd on top of the pieced block. For each block, select one side wall piece, one floor piece, and one square back wall piece. Using the ¼" (6 mm) seam allowance marked on the templates for all seams, sew the floor and side wall together along the angled edges as for the block on page 144. Then sew the back wall to the side wall and floor with a set-in seam. Don't be too concerned about stitching a perfect set-in as it will be covered by the appliqué.

Make a total of 36 blocks in the same way.

ADDING THE APPLIQUÉ

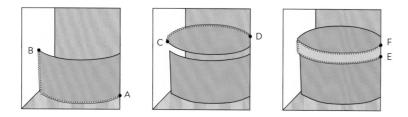

For each block, select a lid and bottom cut from the same fabric, then select a fabric box lid rim. Peel off the paper backing from the fusible web. Place the box bottom on the right side of a block, aligning the right edge of the box with the edge of the block and positioning the box as shown on the box templates on page 219. Fuse the piece in place. Then using a blanket stitch setting on your sewing machine and a bright turquoise thread, sew from A to B along the bottom edge of the box and up the left side edge as shown on the diagram.

Position the lid above the box as shown on the templates, fuse it in place, and blanket stitch from C to D along the left and top edges of the lid as shown on the diagram.

Position the lid rim piece so it overlaps the box lid and the box bottom—note that the rim sticks out about ¼" (6 mm) beyond the box bottom on the left. Fuse the rim in place, then blanket stitch around the edge from E to F as shown on the diagram.

After the appliqué has been applied to each of the 36 blocks, carefully cut away the block background behind each of the boxes, leaving a ¼" (6 mm) seam allowance. It will not be possible to cut behind the fused rim band, and that is okay.

Tawny Hatboxes Assembly

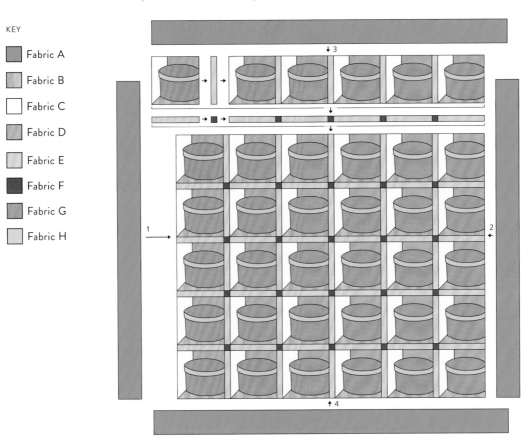

KEY

■ Fabric A

■ Fabric B

□ Fabric C

■ Fabric D

□ Fabric E

■ Fabric F

■ Fabric G

□ Fabric H

ASSEMBLING THE QUILT TOP

Follow the Tawny Hatboxes Assembly diagram when arranging the blocks for the quilt top. Take your time arranging six horizontal rows of six blocks each, lining them up on the floor or on a design wall (page 205). Lay the vertical sashing strips in place between the blocks on each of the six horizontal rows. Then arrange the sashing strips between the rows with the sashing squares at each juncture of the strips as shown.

Once you have achieved the desired effect, sew together the horizontal rows of blocks, alternating them with a sashing strip. Press. Sew together the five horizontal rows of sashing strips and sashing squares. Press. Then sew together the rows of blocks alternating with the rows of sashing strips and squares. Press.

BORDER

Following the quilt assembly diagram, sew the two fabric-A side borders to the sides of the quilt top. Press. Then sew on the fabric-A top and bottom borders. Press.

FINISHING THE QUILT

Prepare the backing. Press the quilt top. Layer the quilt top, batting, and backing, then baste the layers together (page 208).

Machine-quilt each box inside the blanket stitching and outline the blossoms in the boxes. Meander machine-quilt in the side and back walls. Outline the stripes in the floors. Meander quilt on the sashing strips. Outline the shapes on the border.

Trim the quilt edges. Then cut the binding strips on the bias and sew the binding on around the edge of the quilt (page 209).

LEAFY APPLIQUÉ

This is a challenging project for appliqué enthusiasts. It would be a great quilt to make with a group of stitchers for a special event. For an energetic design, do not use exactly the same leaf fabrics for each leaf in the matching blocks—each block should be unique.

FINISHED SIZE

96½" × 112½" (245 cm × 286 cm)

PATCHWORK FABRICS

Use quilting cottons 44–45" (112–115 cm) wide

Fabric A (background fabric): 12 yards (11 m) of a light-toned polka-dot fabric with light blue dots on a white ground; OR, as used here, Kaffe Fassett Collective *Spot* in Sky

Fabric B (stems): 1 yard (1 m) each of 2 ombré-stripe fabrics, one mostly in pinks with an accent of yellow and covered with light blue dots and the other mostly in reds and pinks with an accent of blue and covered with light turquoise dots; OR, as used here, Kaffe Fassett Collective *Ombre* in Pink and Red

Fabric C (18 border pots—block No. 10): ¼ yard (25 cm) each of at least 8 different light-medium-toned to medium-toned predominantly blue prints, including mostly small-scale and medium-scale florals, with 1 or 2 geometrics

Fabric D (border-blossom petals—block No. 10): ½ yard (50 cm) of a dark-medium-toned bright red print

Fabric E (border-blossom centers—block No. 10): ¼ yard (25 cm) of a solid light green; OR, as used here, Kaffe Fassett Collective *Shot Cotton* in Apple

Fabric F (4 corner vases—block No. 11): ½ yard (50 cm) of a medium-toned large-scale bright aqua floral print with red highlights

Fabric G (leaves and stems): ¼–½ yard (25–50 cm) each of a large variety of light-toned and medium-toned prints in greens and blue-greens, including dots, stripes, circles, and small-scale to medium-scale florals; some of the most useful used here are the following 9 Kaffe Fassett Collective fabrics: *Brassica* in Green, *Guinea Flower* in Green, *Kim* in Green, *Oriental Trees* in Green, *Paperweight* in Algae, *Roman Glass* in Leafy, *Spot* in Apple, Moss, and Pond

Fabric H (flowers, flower buds, radishes, and tomatoes): Up to ¼ yard (25 cm) each of a large variety of light-toned and medium-toned prints in reds, pinks, and yellows, including dots, stripes, and ombrés; some of the most useful used here are the following 5 Kaffe Fassett Collective fabrics: *Alternating Stripe* in Yellow, *Flame Stripe* in Yellow, *Kim* in Mauve and Red, *Spot* in Yellow

OTHER INGREDIENTS

Backing fabric: 9 yards (8.3 m) of desired fabric

Binding fabric: 1 yard (1 m) of an ombré stripe in greens and blue-greens; OR, as used here, Kaffe Fassett Collective *Kim* in Green

Cotton batting: 104" × 120" (260 cm × 305 cm) piece of batting

Quilting thread: Green, blue, and white threads

Template materials: Heat-resistant template plastic, cardstock, or thick, stiff paper, for making your appliqué templates

Appliqué materials: If you are using the fused raw-edge appliqué technique, you will need iron-on lightweight fusible adhesive web (for the quilt shown, the edges of the appliqué pieces were turned under, so no adhesive web was used)

Appliqué block templates: Block Nos. 1–11 (pages 213–218)

PREPARING THE APPLIQUÉ TEMPLATES

Enlarge each of the eleven block designs as instructed. Once enlarged the designs are the exact size of the *finished* blocks, i.e., 16" × 16" (40.7 cm × 40.7 cm). No. 10 Leaves & Buds in a Pot is for the 18 borders blocks; No. 11 Vase is for the four quilt corner blocks; and No. 9 Radishes is for the four inner corners. All the other blocks (Nos. 1–8) are used twice, once as per the block drawing and once in reverse for a reversed image.

For each block design, trace each shape (each leaf, bud, flower petal, flower center, stem, etc.) and prepare a template of it, using template plastic, cardstock, or thick, stiff paper. Note that there are no seam allowances on the individual shapes, so these will need to be added when you cut out the fabric pieces unless you are using the fused raw-edge appliqué technique. To organize the individual templates, write a number on each appliqué shape on the block design and, as you make your templates, number them on the right side (the front) with the design number, design name, and the shape number—for example, "No. 1 Dahlia; 1," "No. 1 Dahlia; 2," "No. 1 Dahlia; 3," and so on. Make sure you put the labels on the right side (the front) of each template, as you will need to reverse the shapes for the reverse designs for block Nos. 1–8.

Prepare the templates for one block at a time and put them in a large envelope labeled with the block name and number.

CUTTING THE BACKGROUND SQUARES

42 background squares: From fabric A, cut 42 squares 18" × 18" (45.7 cm × 45.7 cm). The background squares are cut bigger than needed as appliqué can shrink the overall size of the square. The squares will be trimmed to 16½" × 16½" (41.9 cm × 41.9 cm) once the appliqué is complete, which allows for the ¼" (6 mm) seam allowances. The finished blocks will be 16" × 16" (40.7 cm × 40.7 cm).

CUTTING THE APPLIQUÉ PIECES

Follow the photograph of the quilt (and the fabric list) for guidance when making fabric choices for your appliqué pieces. Trace the template shapes, right side up, onto the right side of the fabric, allowing room around the edges for the seam allowances if you are turning under the raw edges. As you cut out the fabric pieces, label each one with the template identification number.

TIPS FOR FUSSY-CUTTING THE SHAPES

Fussy-cut the fabrics (C and F) for the border pots and corner vases, carefully positioning the floral motifs.

When cutting pieces from the ombré fabrics (*Kim* and *Ombre*) try to use the shading to get the best effect for the particular shape. Try to cut pieces from all the other prints and stripes with careful thought, so that they are used to get the best effect for each individual petal, bud, leaf, and stem.

Do not attempt to use exactly the same fabrics for the leaves in the matching blocks (the block and its reverse). The more variety in the leaves, the better. Do, however, use the same fabrics for the blossoms in the matching blocks.

Keep the labeled pieces for each individual block together in a group.

PREPARING THE BACKGROUND SQUARES

To mark the center of each fabric-A background square and divide it in quarters, fold each square in half in both directions and press a visible crease. OR, using long basting stitches and a contrasting thread, sew down the center in both directions. Then, using long basting stitches, sew a line along each side of the square 2" (5 cm) in from the raw edges to mark a 16" × 16" (40.7 cm × 40.7 cm) square in the center of the piece—the finished block size. The outline and the dividing marks will help you position the individual appliqué pieces.

APPLIQUÉING THE BLOCKS

Using your preferred method, sew the appliqué pieces to each block. Be sure to keep the pieces within the 16" (40.7 cm) perimeter, except where the leaves disappear into the seam as on the sides of No. 5 Sunflower.

After the appliqué has been applied to each of the 42 blocks, press well and trim each block to 16½" × 16½" (41.9 cm × 41.9 cm).

Leafy Appliqué Assembly

BLOCKS KEY

No. 1 Dahlia—make 2,
one of which is reversed
No. 2 Tulip—make 2,
one of which is reversed
No. 3 Tomato—make 2,
one of which is reversed
No. 4 Daisy—make 2,
one of which is reversed
No. 5 Sunflower—make 2,
one of which is reversed
No. 6 Marigold—make 2,
one of which is reversed
No. 7 Geranium—make 2,
one of which is reversed
No. 8 Foxglove—make 2,
one of which is reversed
No. 9 Radish—make 4
No. 10 Leaves & Buds in Pot—
make 18, for the borders
No. 11 Vase—make 4,
one for each border corner

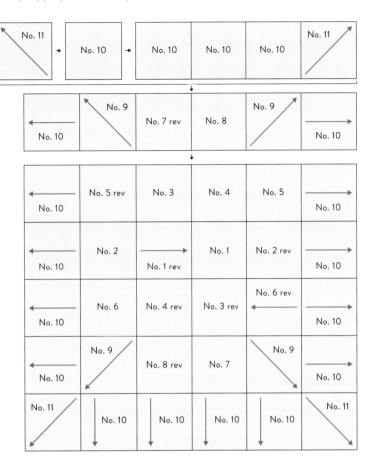

ASSEMBLING THE QUILT TOP

Follow the Leafy Appliqué Assembly diagram when arranging the blocks for the quilt top. Arrange the blocks in seven horizontal rows of six blocks each as shown, lining them up on the floor or on a design wall (page 205). All the blocks (and reverse blocks) are positioned upright except those with arrows. On the blocks with arrows, the arrowhead points to the top of the block, so turn these blocks as indicated—for example, the border blocks (No. 10 Leaves & Buds in a Pot) all point outward from the quilt center, and all the corner blocks (No. 11 Vase) and the Radish blocks (No. 9) point toward the quilt corners.

Sew together the horizontal rows of six blocks each. Press. Then sew together the seven horizontal rows. Press.

FINISHING THE QUILT

Prepare the backing. Press the quilt top. Layer the quilt top, batting, and backing, then baste the layers together (page 208).

Using green thread, machine-quilt veins in the bigger leaves. Using blue thread, outline quilt details in the border pots. Using white thread, echo quilt around the appliqué shapes.

Trim the quilt edges. Then cut the binding strips on the bias and sew the binding on around the edge of the quilt (page 209).

LEAFY MEDALLION

The center square of this quilt is surrounded by eight simple borders added from the center outward. One of the borders is made up of on-point blocks, which means this is a good quilt for an intermediate-level quilter.

90½" × 90½" (230 cm x 230 cm)

PATCHWORK FABRICS

Use quilting cottons 44–45" (112–115 cm) wide

Fabric A (center square): ¾ yard (70 cm) of a medium-toned large-scale leaf print in greens, pinks, reds, and yellows on a blue ground; OR, as used here, Kaffe Fassett Collective *Lilacs* in Turquoise

Fabric B (border no. 1 strips): ¼ yard (25 cm) of a dark-medium-toned ombré stripe in pinks, orange, and yellow; OR, as used here, Kaffe Fassett Collective *Ombre* in Pink

Fabric C (border no. 2 strips): 1 yard (1 m) of a light-medium toned super-large-scale leaf print in blue greens with purple accents; OR, as used here, Kaffe Fassett Collective *Big Leaf* in Mint

Fabric D (border no. 3 strips and border no. 8 corner squares): ¾ yard (70 cm) of a light-toned super-large-scale floral print in pinks and greens; OR, as used here, Kaffe Fassett Collective *Tree Peony* in Aqua

Fabric E (border no. 4 strips): 1½ yards (1.4 m) of a dark-medium-toned medium-scale floral print with pink, yellow, blue, and green flowers and green dots on a black ground; OR, as used here, Kaffe Fassett Collective *Guinea Flower* in Green

Fabric F (border no. 5 flower block): 1 yard (1 m) of a medium-toned large-scale floral print with pink, yellow, and purple flowers on a green ground; OR, as used here, Kaffe Fassett Collective *Big Blooms* in Green

Fabric G (border no. 5 flower block): ½ yard (50 cm) of a dark-toned polka-dot print with lime green dots on a purple-blue ground; OR, as used here, Kaffe Fassett Collective *Spot* in Periwinkle

Fabric H (border no. 5 squares block): ½ yard (50 cm) of a light-medium-toned polka-dot print with orange dots on a turquoise ground; OR, as used here, Kaffe Fassett Collective *Spot* in Turquoise

Fabric J (border no. 5 squares block): ½ yard (50 cm) of a light-toned polka-dot print with light blue dots on a lime green ground; OR, as used here, Kaffe Fassett Collective *Spot* in Apple

Fabric K (border no. 5 block backgrounds): 2 yards (1.9 m) of a medium-toned large-scale leaf print in greens and blues, with accents of purple; OR, as used here, Kaffe Fassett Collective *Brassica* in Green

Fabric L (border no. 6 strips): ⅔ yard (65 cm) of a light-toned ombré stripe in greens, blue-greens, and golds; OR, as used here, Kaffe Fassett Collective *Ombre* in Moss

Fabric M (border no. 7 strips and border no. 3 corner squares): 2 yards (1.9 m) of a light-medium-toned large-scale floral print in greens, pinks, creams, and turquoise; OR, as used here, Kaffe Fassett Collective *Lake Blossoms* in Green

Fabric N (border no. 6 and no. 7 corner squares): ½ yard (50 cm) of a medium-toned floral circles print in predominantly yellows, greens, and pinks; OR, as used here, Kaffe Fassett Collective *Millefiore* in Green

Fabric O (border no. 8 strips): 1½ yards (1.4 m) of a medium-toned broad stripe in mauve, green, and dusty pink; OR, as used here, Kaffe Fassett Collective *Kim* in Mauve

OTHER INGREDIENTS

Backing fabric: 8½ yards (7.8 m) of desired fabric

Binding fabric: ¾ yard (70 cm) more of fabric B

Cotton batting: 98" × 98" (245 cm × 245 cm) piece of batting

Quilting thread: Green thread

CUTTING THE PIECES

Cut the pieces in the sequence given here. Pin labels to the pieces as you cut them and keep the pieces for each border together.

Center square: From fabric A, fussy-cut a square 16½" × 16½" (41.9 cm × 41.9 cm), carefully positioning a cluster of flowers as a focal point at the center of the quilt.

Border no. 1 strips: From fabric B, cut two strips 2" x 16½" (5.1 cm × 41.9 cm) for the side borders and two strips 2" × 19½" (5.1 cm × 49.5 cm) for the top and bottom borders. Cut these pieces so that the stripes run widthwise across the strips.

Border no. 2 strips: From fabric C, cut two strips 8" × 19½" (20.3 cm × 49.5 cm) for the side borders and two strips 8" × 34½" (20.3 cm × 87.6 cm) for the top and bottom borders.

Border no. 3 strips: From fabric D, cut four strips 6½" × 34½" (16.5 cm × 87.6 cm). (Do not cut the corner squares yet.)

Border no. 4 strips: From fabric E, fussy-cut two strips 2½" × 46½" (6.4 cm × 118.1 cm) for the side borders and two strips 2½" × 50" (6.4 cm × 127 cm) for the top and bottom borders, cutting so that a row of blooms is centered in each strip.

Border no. 5—center of flower block: From fabric F, fussy-cut one square 4¹¹⁄₁₆" × 4¹¹⁄₁₆" (11.9 cm × 11.9 cm) for each of the 14 flower blocks, centering a flower in each square. From fabric G, cut a total of 28 strips 1⁵⁄₁₆" × 4¹¹⁄₁₆" (3.4 cm × 11.9 cm) and a total of 28 strips 1⁵⁄₁₆" × 6⁵⁄₁₆" (3.4 cm × 16.1 cm).

Border no. 5—center of squares block: From fabric H, cut 28 squares 3⁷⁄₁₆" × 3⁷⁄₁₆" (8.8 cm × 8.8 cm). From fabric J, cut 28 squares 3⁷⁄₁₆" × 3⁷⁄₁₆" (8.8 cm × 8.8 cm).

Border no. 5—block backgrounds: From fabric K, cut 56 squares 5" × 5" (12.7 cm × 12.7 cm). Then cut each square in half diagonally from corner to corner to make a total of 112 half-square triangles. (If any of these fabric-K triangles are mostly purple, do not use them; instead, cut more to replace them.)

Border no. 6 strips: From fabric L, cut seven strips 2½" (6.4 cm) wide, cutting from selvage to selvage of the fabric. Cut off the selvages and sew the strips together end-to-end. From the long strip, cut four strips 66½" (169 cm) long. (Do not cut the corner squares yet.)

Border no. 7 strips and corner squares: From fabric M, cut four strips 6½" × 70½" (16.5 cm × 179.1 cm). From fabric N, fussy-cut four squares 6½" × 6½" (16.5 cm × 16.5 cm), centering an orb in each square.

Border no. 6 corner squares: From the leftover fabric N, fussy-cut four squares 2½" × 2½" (6.4 cm × 6.4 cm), centering an orb in each square.

Border no. 3 corner squares: From the leftover fabric M, cut four squares 6½" × 6½" (16.5 cm × 16.5 cm).

Border no. 8 strips and corner squares: From fabric O, cut eight strips 4½" (11.4 cm) wide, cutting from selvage to selvage of the fabric. Cut off the selvages and sew the strips together end-to-end. From the long strip, cut four strips 82½" (209.6 cm) long. From the leftover fabric D, fussy-cut four squares 4½" × 4½" (11.4 cm × 11.4 cm), centering a blossom in each square.

MAKING THE FLOWER BLOCKS FOR BORDER NO. 5

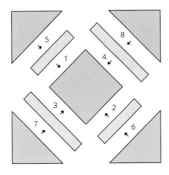 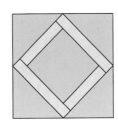

Each of the 14 flower blocks in border no. 5 is made up of a fabric-F flower square center, two fabric-G strips $1\frac{5}{16}$" × $4\frac{11}{16}$" (3.4 cm × 11.9 cm), two fabric-G strips $1\frac{5}{16}$" × $6\frac{5}{16}$" (3.4 cm × 16.1 cm), and four fabric-K block-background half-square triangles. Following the diagram and using a ¼" (6 mm) seam allowance for all seams, sew the strips to the flower center, then sew on the background triangles at the corners. Make all 14 blocks in this way.

MAKING THE SQUARES BLOCKS FOR BORDER NO. 5

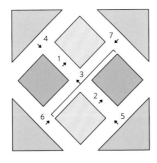 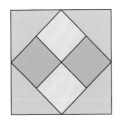

Each of the 14 squares blocks in border no. 5 is made up of two fabric-H squares, two fabric-J squares, and four fabric-K block-background half-square triangles. Following the diagram, sew the squares together in pairs, then sew the pairs of squares together, and lastly sew on the background triangles at the corners. Make all 14 blocks in this way.

ASSEMBLING THE BORDER NO. 5 BORDER STRIPS

Alternating the two different blocks for border no. 5, sew six blocks together for each of the side borders and sew eight blocks together for the top and bottom borders.

ADDING ON THE BORDER CORNERS

For borders no. 3, no. 6, no. 7, and no. 8, sew a border corner to each end of two of the strips.

Leafy Medallion Assembly

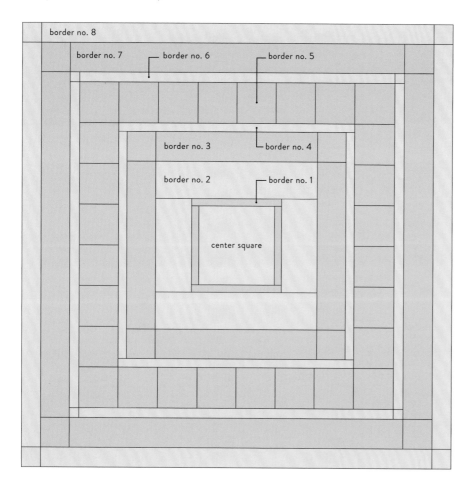

ASSEMBLING THE QUILT TOP

The top is assembled from the center outward. Following the Leafy Medallion Assembly diagram, start by sewing the shorter border no. 1 strips to the sides of the quilt center, press, then sew the longer strips to the top and bottom. Following the diagram, add on the remaining borders in the same way.

FINISHING THE QUILT

Prepare the backing. Press the quilt top. Layer the quilt top, batting, and backing, then baste the layers together (page 208).

Machine-quilt around most leaves and blossoms. Meander quilt in the remainder of the spaces.

Trim the quilt edges. Then cut the binding strips on the bias and sew the binding on around the edge of the quilt (page 209).

LATTICE WITH VASES

Fussy-cutting the floral appliqué vases on this quilt is done differently than on my other quilts. Instead of centering the flowers on each vase, they are positioned slightly to one side, which makes them look more three-dimensional.

FINISHED SIZE

84¼" × 99" (214 cm × 251.4 cm)

PATCHWORK FABRICS

Use quilting cottons 44–45" (112–115 cm) wide

Fabric A (outer border and sashing strips): 5 yards (4.6 m) of a medium-toned large-scale leaf print in greens and blues with accents of purple; OR, as used here, Kaffe Fassett Collective *Brassica* in Green (3¼ yards [3 m] is sufficient if you are not using *Brassica* and trying to avoid the deep purple sections when cutting the pieces)

Fabric B (small sashing squares): ¾ yard (70 cm) of a dark-medium-toned medium-scale floral print of green, blue, and pink flowers and green dots on a black ground; OR, as used here, Kaffe Fassett Collective *Guinea Flower* in Green

Fabric C (block "background" squares): ¾ yard (70 cm) each of at least 6 different light-medium-toned dots, ovals, and circles prints in greens, blues, and ochres; OR, as used here, the following 6 Kaffe Fassett Collective fabrics: *Aboriginal Dots* in Lime, *Paperweight* in Lime, *Spot* in Apple, Mint, Pond, and Turquoise

Fabric D (vases and border corners): ½ yard (50 cm) each of at least 12 different medium-toned large-scale floral prints in predominantly pinks, reds, and blues; OR, as used here, the following 12 Kaffe Fassett Collective fabrics: *Big Blooms* in Duckegg, *Guinea Flower* in Turquoise, *Lake Blossoms* in Magenta and Red, *Lavinia* in Natural, Mauve, and Red, *Lilacs* in Turquoise and Yellow, *Lotus Stripe* in Pastel and Red, *Tree Peony* in Orange

Fabric E (edge "setting" triangles and vases): 1 yard (1 m) of a light-medium-toned large-scale floral print in predominantly greens, with accents of cream, pink, and turquoise; OR, as used here, Kaffe Fassett Collective *Lake Blossoms* in Green

OTHER INGREDIENTS

Backing fabric: 8 yards (7.4 m) of desired fabric

Binding fabric: ¾ yard (70 cm) of a light-medium-toned circles print in predominantly lime; OR, as used here, Kaffe Fassett Collective *Paperweight* in Lime

Cotton batting: 92" × 106" (230 cm × 270 cm) piece of batting

Quilting thread: Green thread

Template materials: Heat-resistant template plastic, for making templates

Templates: Template F and appliqué vase template (page 215)

PREPARING THE TEMPLATES

TRIANGLE TEMPLATE

Trace the triangle template F onto template plastic and cut out.

APPLIQUÉ TEMPLATE

Enlarge the vase appliqué on as instructed and use this to trace the vase shape onto template plastic. Cut out the shape.

CUTTING THE PIECES

OUTER-BORDER PIECES

Be sure to cut the biggest pieces first from fabric A, following the sequence here. If you are using the *Brassica* print for your fabric-A border, try to avoid the dense purple areas—some purple is okay, but avoid cutting pieces that are mostly purple.

4 outer-border strips: From fabric A, cut two strips 5½" × 89½" (14 cm × 227 cm) for the side borders and two strips 5½" × 74¾" (14 cm × 190 cm) for the top and bottom borders.

4 outer-border corner squares: From fabric D, fussy-cut four squares 5½" × 5½" (14 cm × 14 cm), carefully centering a different flower in each square.

SASHING PIECES

120 sashing strips: From fabric A, cut 120 strips 3" × 8½" (7.6 cm × 21.6 cm).
49 small sashing squares: From fabric B, fussy-cut 49 squares 3" × 3" (7.6 cm × 7.6 cm), carefully centering a flower in each square.
22 small sashing edge triangles: From fabric B, cut 22 triangles, using template F. Try to cut from only the background areas, avoiding the flowers.

EDGE "SETTING" TRIANGLES

18 large edge triangles: From fabric E, cut five squares 12½" × 12½" (31.8 cm × 31.8 cm). Then cut each of these squares diagonally from corner to corner in both directions to make four quarter-square triangles from each square. You will only need 18 of these quarter-square triangles, so you can discard two.
4 corner edge triangles: From fabric E, cut two squares 6½" × 6½" (16.5 cm × 16.5 cm). Then cut each of these squares in half diagonally from corner to corner to make two half-square triangles from each square—for a total of four triangles. Use the remaining fabric E for the vases.

BLOCK PIECES

50 block "background" squares: Cut a total of 50 squares 8½" × 8½" (21.6 cm × 21.6 cm), cutting eight or nine squares from each of the six C fabrics.
50 appliqué vases: Cut a total of 50 floral vases, cutting about four vases from each of the 12 different D fabrics and from the leftover E fabric. First trace the vase shape onto the right side of the floral fabric, using the vase template. Position the flowers on the vases so they are slightly to one side of each vase, not directly in the center of it. Cut out each vase shape at least ¼" (6 mm) from the drawn outline to allow for the seam allowance.

MAKING THE VASE BLOCKS

Appliqué a vase onto the center of each of the 50 block "background" squares, positioning it in the square on-point—with one of the corners of the square pointing upward. Using your preferred appliqué technique, turn the seam allowance to the wrong side along the drawn outline and sew in place. When the appliqué is complete, carefully cut the background away from behind the vase, leaving a ¼" (6 mm) seam allowance.

ASSEMBLING THE QUILT TOP

Following the Lattice with Vases Assembly diagram (page 176), arrange the blocks on-point in five vertical rows of six blocks each, alternating with four vertical rows of five blocks each. Line them up on the floor or on a design wall (page 205). Lay the sashing strips in place between the blocks. Then arrange the sashing cornerstone squares at each juncture of the strips as shown, positioning the cornerstone triangles where the sashing meets the quilt edge. Lastly position the fabric-E edge "setting" triangles around the outer edge of the quilt center and one fabric-E corner triangle at each corner.

Once you have achieved the desired effect, sew together the blocks and other pieces in diagonal rows as shown on the diagram, using a ¼" (6 mm) seam allowance for all seams. Press. Then sew the diagonal rows together. Press.

BORDER

Sew the two side border strips to the sides of the quilt top. Press. Then sew a border corner square to each end of the top and bottom border strips, making sure that the flowers are upright. Press. Sew the top and bottom borders to the quilt top. Press.

FINISHING THE QUILT

Prepare the backing. Press the quilt top. Layer the quilt top, batting, and backing, then baste the layers together (page 208).

Machine-quilt swirls in the background of each vase block. Machine-quilt cross-hatched straight lines on the sashing. Outline-quilt the leaves on the outer borders.

Trim the quilt edges. Then prepare the binding and sew it on around the edge of the quilt (page 209).

Lattice with Vases Assembly

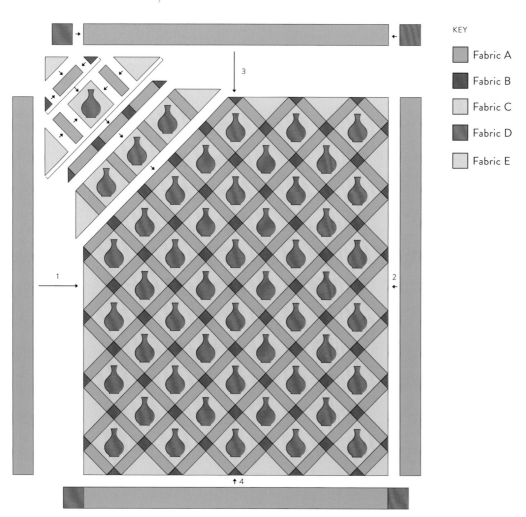

KEY

Fabric A
Fabric B
Fabric C
Fabric D
Fabric E

BLUE OHIO STAR

Even though this layout is on-point, it is not too difficult to make. There are only 20 star blocks in the quilt center, and the remainder is comprised of simple large squares and triangles. The fun part is positioning the floral motifs to achieve the best effect.

FINISHED SIZE

78½" × 93¾" (199.5 cm × 238 cm)

PATCHWORK FABRICS

Use quilting cottons 44–45" (112–115 cm) wide

Fabric A (outer border, stars, and large squares): 2½ yards (2.3 m) of a dark-medium-toned large-scale non-directional floral print in blues; OR, as used here, Kaffe Fassett Collective *Joy* in Blue (if the fabric is directional like *Joy*, you will need 4 yards [3.7 m])

Fabric B (inner border): ¾ yard (70 cm) of a dark-toned stripe in blues with purple accents; OR, as used here, Kaffe Fassett Collective *Ribbon Stripe* in Blue

Fabric C (stars and large squares): ½ yard (50 cm) each of at least 10 different medium-toned and dark-medium-toned large-scale and super-large-scale floral prints in predominantly blues, emerald greens, and plums; OR, as used here, the following 10 Kaffe Fassett Collective fabrics: *Big Blooms* in Emerald, *Brassica* in Blue, *Brocade Peony* in Blue, *Dahlia Blooms* in Cool, *Gloxinia* in Blue, *Japanese Chrysanthemum* in Green, *Kimono* in Cobalt, *Lake Blossom* in Black and Blue, *Lilacs* in Plum

Fabric D (star-block backgrounds): ¼ yard (25 cm) each of at least 10 different small-scale prints or near solids in predominantly dark tones (and a few dark-medium tones) of blues, blue-greens, and plums; OR, as used here, the following 10 Kaffe Fassett Collective fabrics: *Aboriginal Dots* in Charcoal, Chocolate, Iris, Plum, and Periwinkle, *Paper Fans* in Blue, *Paperweight* in Jewel and Purple, *Spots* in Green and Sapphire

OTHER INGREDIENTS

Backing fabric: 7½ yards (6.9 m) of desired fabric; OR, as used here, Kaffe Fassett Collective *Oriental Trees* in Blue

Binding fabric: ¾ yard (70 cm) more of fabric B

Cotton batting: 86" × 101" (215 cm × 255 cm) piece of batting

Quilting thread: Medium blue thread

Template materials: Heat-resistant template plastic, for making templates

Templates: G and H (page 220)

CUTTING THE PIECES

Be sure to cut the biggest pieces from each fabric first, following the cutting sequence here.

OUTER-BORDER PIECES

4 outer-border strips: From fabric A, cut two strips 6" × 83¼" (15.2 cm × 211.5 cm) for the side borders, cutting these strips lengthwise (parallel to the selvage). If your fabric is directional like *Joy* and you want the flowers in the top and bottom outer borders to be upright, next cut four 6" (15.2 cm) strips from selvage to selvage from fabric A, lining up the patterns in the strips so you can match them. Cut off the selvages and sew these strips together end-to-end for a strip 160" (406.4 cm) long, matching the pattern as well as possible. Then from this long pieced strip, cut two strips 78¾" (200 cm) long for the top and bottom borders.

INNER-BORDER PIECES

4 inner-border strips: From fabric B, cut eight 3" (7.6 cm) strips from selvage to selvage (so the stripes run widthwise). Cut off the selvages and sew these strips together end-to-end. Then cut this long strip into two strips each 78¼" (198.8 cm) long for the side borders and two strips 67¾" (172.1 cm) long for the top and bottom borders.

QUILT CENTER

12 large squares: From fabric C (and any leftover fabric A), fussy-cut 12 squares 11½" × 11½" (29.2 cm × 29.2 cm), carefully framing the flowers in each square.

20 star-block centers: From fabric C, fussy-cut 20 squares 6" × 6" (15.2 cm × 15.2 cm), carefully positioning a flower in the center of each square.

14 large edge "setting" triangles: From fabric C (and the remainder of fabric A), cut 14 triangles using template G, paying attention to the grainline arrow on the template.

4 corner edge triangles: From fabric C, cut four triangles using template H, paying attention to the grainline arrow on the template.

160 star-block star points: For each of the 20 star blocks, cut four squares 3⅝" × 3⅝" (9.2 cm × 9.2 cm) from the same fabric C, and cut each one in half diagonally from corner to corner to make a total of eight half-square triangles. Cut eight star points like this for each of the 20 star-block centers, using the same fabric C as the center square. Pin each set of four star points to its matching center square.

Block-star backgrounds: For each of the 20 star blocks, cut four squares 3¼" × 3¼" (8.3 cm × 8.3 cm) for the corners and one square 6¾" × 6¾" (17.2 cm × 17.2cm) all from the same fabric D; then cut the large square diagonally from corner to corner in each direction to make four quarter-square edge triangles. Cut enough sets of background pieces for all 20 blocks. Pin each set of background pieces together.

MAKING THE STAR BLOCKS

For each star block, select one block center square and its matching eight small star-point triangles, plus a set of background pieces—four small corner squares and four large quarter-square edge triangles. Using a ¼" (6 mm) seam allowance for all seams, sew the pieces together in three diagonal rows following the diagram. Press. Then sew the three diagonal rows together. Press. Make all 20 star blocks in the same way.

Blue Ohio Star Assembly

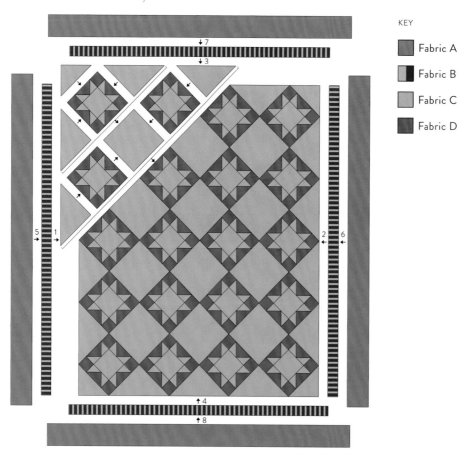

KEY

Fabric A

Fabric B

Fabric C

Fabric D

ASSEMBLING THE QUILT TOP

Following the Blue Ohio Star Assembly diagram, arrange the large fabric-C squares and the star blocks on-point in four vertical rows of five star blocks each, alternating with three vertical rows of four large squares, lining them up on the floor or a design wall (page 205). Position the fabric-C edge "setting" triangles along each outer edge and one fabric-C corner triangle at each corner. Once you have achieved the desired effect, sew together the blocks and other pieces in diagonal rows as shown on the diagram. Press. Then sew the rows together. Press.

BORDERS

Sew the two inner-border side strips to the sides of the quilt top, press, then sew on the inner-border top and bottom strips. Press. Next, sew on the two outer-border side strips to the sides of the quilt top, press, and lastly sew the outer-border top and bottom strips. Press.

FINISHING THE QUILT

Prepare the backing. Press the quilt top. Layer the quilt top, batting, and backing, then baste the layers together (page 208).

Machine-quilt around each blossom in the large squares, the star block center pieces, and the outer border. Stitch in the ditch around each star block and around each of the star-block pieces. Machine-quilt straight lines in the inner border to emphasize the stripe.

Trim the quilt edges. Then cut the binding strips on the bias and sew the binding on around the edge of the quilt (page 209).

MILLEFIORE SNOWBALL

When choosing fabrics for this quilt, be sure to select floral prints and a circles print with very large motifs—about 6" (15 cm) in diameter. You will fussy-cut these flowers and circles in dark, rich tones so they are centered in their blocks and squares.

FINISHED SIZE

75½" × 90½" (192 cm × 230 cm)

PATCHWORK FABRICS

Use quilting cottons 44–45" (112–115 cm) wide

Fabric A (large squares): 3½ yards (3.2 m) of a dark-toned super-large-scale circles print with at least two distinct circle motifs in predominantly deep maroon and gray-blues; OR, as used here, Kaffe Fassett Collective *Millefiore* in Dark

Fabric B (block centers): ¾–1 yard (70–100 cm) each of at least 6 different medium-toned and dark-medium-toned super-large-scale floral prints in blues, blue-greens, pinks, and reds; OR, as used here, the following 6 Kaffe Fassett Collective fabrics: ¾ yard (70 cm) of *Big Blooms* in Emerald, ¾ yard (70 cm) of *Japanese Chrysanthemum* in each of Green and Red, ¾ yard (70 cm) of *Lake Blossoms* in each of Black and Blue 1 yard (1 m) of *Lilacs* in Plum

Fabric C (block frames): ½ yard (50 cm) each of at least 11 different dark-medium-toned and dark-toned solids and dot prints (almost solids) in mostly blues, reds, and grapes; OR, as used here, the following 11 Kaffe Fassett Collective fabrics: *Shot Cotton* in Aegean, Bordeaux, Cobalt, Grape, Mulberry, Prune, and Thunder; *Aboriginal Dots* in Charcoal, Chocolate, Periwinkle, and Purple

Fabric D (border): 3¼ yards (3 m) of a medium-dark-toned medium-scale directional print in predominantly reds and grapes with a green accent; OR, as used here, Kaffe Fassett Collective *Oriental Trees* in Maroon (if the fabric is not directional, 2½ yards [2.3 m] is sufficient)

OTHER INGREDIENTS

Backing fabric: 6 yards (5.5 m) of desired fabric; OR, as used here, Kaffe Fassett Collective *Lake Blossoms* in Black

Binding fabric: ¾ yard (70 cm) of a solid prune fabric; OR, as used here, Kaffe Fassett Collective *Shot Cotton* in Prune

Cotton batting: 83" × 98" (210 cm × 245 cm) piece of batting

Quilting thread: Very dark gray or black thread

CUTTING THE PIECES

44 large squares: From fabric A, fussy-cut 44 squares 8" × 8" (20.3 cm × 20.3 cm), carefully centering a circles motif in each square. Cut 22 with the same distinct motif and 22 with another distinct motif. If you are using *Millefiore*, you will see it has three distinct motifs—use the two smaller ones.

40 floral block centers: From fabric B, fussy-cut 40 squares 6½" × 6½" (16.5 cm × 16.5 cm), carefully centering a flower in each square. Avoid the palest flowers and cut mostly blue and blue-green flowers. If using *Lilacs* in Plum, cut only the roses.

40 sets of block-frame pieces: For each of the 40 blocks, choose a fabric C for framing the floral block center. From this fabric C, for each block cut four small squares 2" × 2" (5.1 cm × 5.1 cm), two strips 1¼" × 6½" (3.2 cm × 16.5 cm), and two strips 1¼" × 8" (3.2 cm × 20.3 cm). Cut a total of 40 sets of these pieces and pin each set to one of the 40 block centers.

4 border strips: From fabric D, cut two strips 8" × 75½" (20.3 cm × 191.8 cm) for the side borders, cutting the pieces lengthwise (parallel to the selvage). Then, as the fabric is directional, you need to cut the top and bottom borders so that the print points upward. First, cut four strips 8" (20.3 cm) wide, cutting from selvage to selvage and lining up the patterns in the strips so you can match them. Sew these strips together end-to-end, matching the pattern as well as possible. Then from this long pieced strip, cut two strips 60½" (153.7 cm) long for the top and bottom borders.

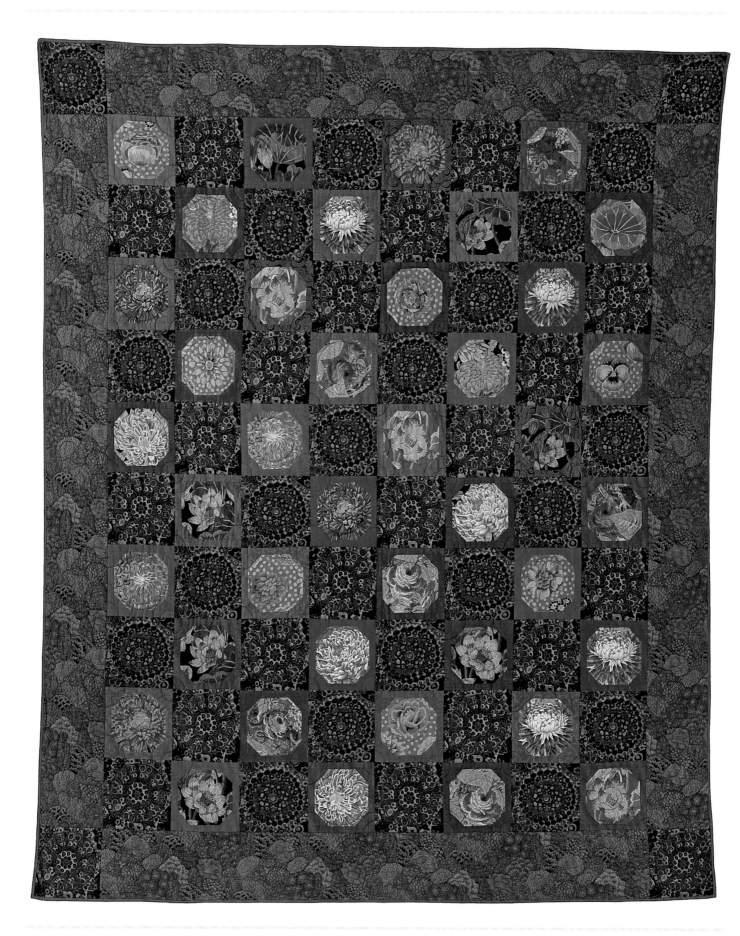

MAKING THE FRAMED SNOWBALL BLOCKS

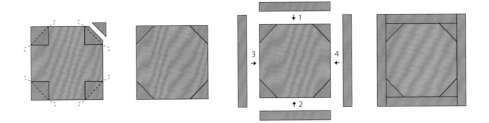

Each of the 40 framed snowball blocks is made up of a fabric-B flower-square center and a set of block-frame pieces cut from the same fabric C—four small squares, two short strips for the top and bottom borders, and two longer strips for the side borders. To assemble each block, first draw a diagonal line from corner to corner on the wrong side of each of the four small squares. With right sides together, place one small square on the corner of the flower square, carefully aligning the raw edges and with the diagonal line on the small square running from one edge of the flower square to the adjacent edge as shown in the diagram. Sew the small square to the flower square, stitching along the drawn diagonal line. Trim the seam allowance to ¼" (6 mm), thereby cutting off the corner of both layers. Press the fabric-C triangle away from the center of the flower square. Sew a small square to the remaining three corners of the flower square in the same way. Using a ¼" (6 mm) seam allowance for all seams, sew the two shorter fabric-C strips to the top and bottom of the flower square, press, and then sew the two longer strips to the sides. Press. Make all 40 blocks in the same way.

ASSEMBLING THE QUILT TOP

Following the Millefiore Snowball Assembly diagram (page 184), arrange the large fabric-A squares and the framed snowball blocks in ten horizontal rows. Each row is made up of four snowball blocks and four large fabric-A squares. Alternate the blocks and fabric-A squares so that the two distinct fabric-A motifs form alternating diagonal rows of matching motifs as shown in the diagram by the two colors representing the two different motifs of fabric A.

Once you have achieved the desired effect, sew together the horizontal rows, press, then sew together the ten rows to form the quilt center. Press.

BORDER

Sew the two longer strips to the sides of the quilt top. Press. Next, sew a large fabric A square to each end of the top and bottom border strips, continuing the alternating positions of the motifs (see diagram, page 184). Press. Lastly, sew the top and bottom strips to the quilt top. Press.

Millefiore Snowball Assembly

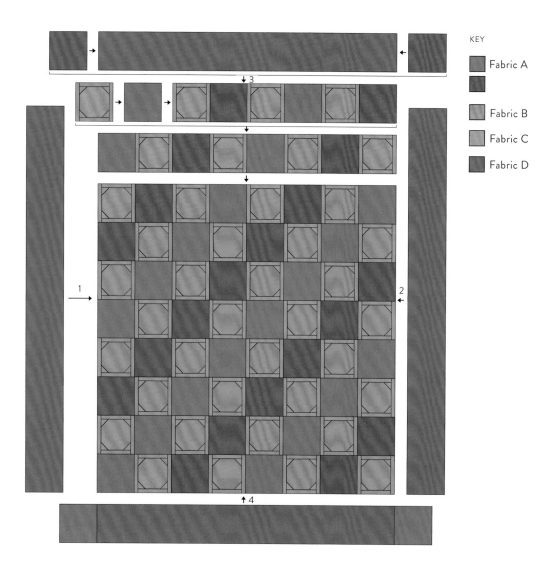

KEY

Fabric A

Fabric B

Fabric C

Fabric D

FINISHING THE QUILT

Prepare the backing. Press the quilt top. Layer the quilt top, batting, and backing, then baste the layers together (page 208).

Machine-quilt around around the circle motifs in the large squares. Quilt a circle shape in the center of each snowball block. Stitch in the ditch between each block. Quilt around the motifs in the border print.

Trim the quilt edges. Then prepare the binding and sew it on around the edge of the quilt (page 209).

STRING STRIPES

Even an absolute beginner will be able to make this quilt. It is composed of six long chocolate brown strips and five long pieced strips full of dark rich blossoms. Compose it on your design wall so you can stand back to see where you need to add a new color.

FINISHED SIZE

61½" × 72½" (157 cm × 184 cm)

PATCHWORK FABRICS

Use quilting cottons 44–45" (112–115 cm) wide

Fabric A (dark panels): 2¼ yards (2.1 m) of a very dark-toned ovals print in chocolate brown; OR, as used here, Kaffe Fassett Collective *Aboriginal Dots* in Chocolate

Fabric B (pieced panels): ¼ yard (25 cm) each of at least 11 different dark-medium-toned to dark-toned large-scale and super-large-scale floral prints in predominantly cobalt blues, reds, pinks, emeralds, plums, and blue-greens; OR, as used here, the following 11 Kaffe Fassett Collective fabrics: *Big Blooms* in Emerald, *Dahlia Blooms* in Fig, *Gloxinia* in Blue, *Guinea Flower* in Purple, *Japanese Chrysanthemum* in Red, *Kimono* in Cobalt, *Lake Blossoms* in Black, *Lazy Daisy* in Charcoal, *Lilacs* in Plum, *Oriental Trees* in Maroon, *Tree Peony* in Blue

OTHER INGREDIENTS

Backing fabric: 4 yards (3.7 m) of desired fabric

Binding fabric: ¾ yard (70 cm) of a dark-toned large ovals print in periwinkle blue; OR, as used here, Kaffe Fassett *Aboriginal Dots* in Periwinkle

Cotton batting: 69" × 80" (175 cm × 200 cm) piece of batting

Quilting threads: Brown and dark blue

CUTTING THE PIECES

6 dark fabric-A panels: From fabric A, cut six panels 6½" × 72½" (16.5 cm × 184 cm).

5 fabric-B pieced floral panels: From the B fabrics, cut pieces all 5½" (14 cm) wide and in varying lengths—from 3" (7.6 cm) to 10½" (26.7 cm). You can cut long strips 5½" (14 cm) from the various fabrics and then cut pieces off these strips as you build up the pieced panels.

MAKING THE PIECED FLORAL PANELS

Using a ¼" (6 mm) seam allowance for all seams, sew floral fabric-B pieces of varying lengths together to make five panels, each measuring 5½" (14 cm) wide by at least 72½" (184 cm) long. Press. Then, if necessary, trim each panel to 72½" (184 cm) long.

ASSEMBLING THE QUILT TOP

Following the String Stripes Assembly diagram (page 189), arrange the six dark fabric-A panels and the five fabric-B pieced floral panels alternately, lining them up on the floor or on a design wall (page 205). Once you have achieved the desired effect, sew together the vertical rows. Press.

FINISHING THE QUILT

Prepare the backing. Press the quilt top. Layer the quilt top, batting, and backing, then baste the layers together (page 208).

Using brown thread, machine-quilt around the large ovals in the dark fabric-A panels. Using dark blue thread, meander quilt around the various blossoms in the floral panels.

Trim the quilt edges. Then prepare the binding and sew it on around the edge of the quilt (page 209).

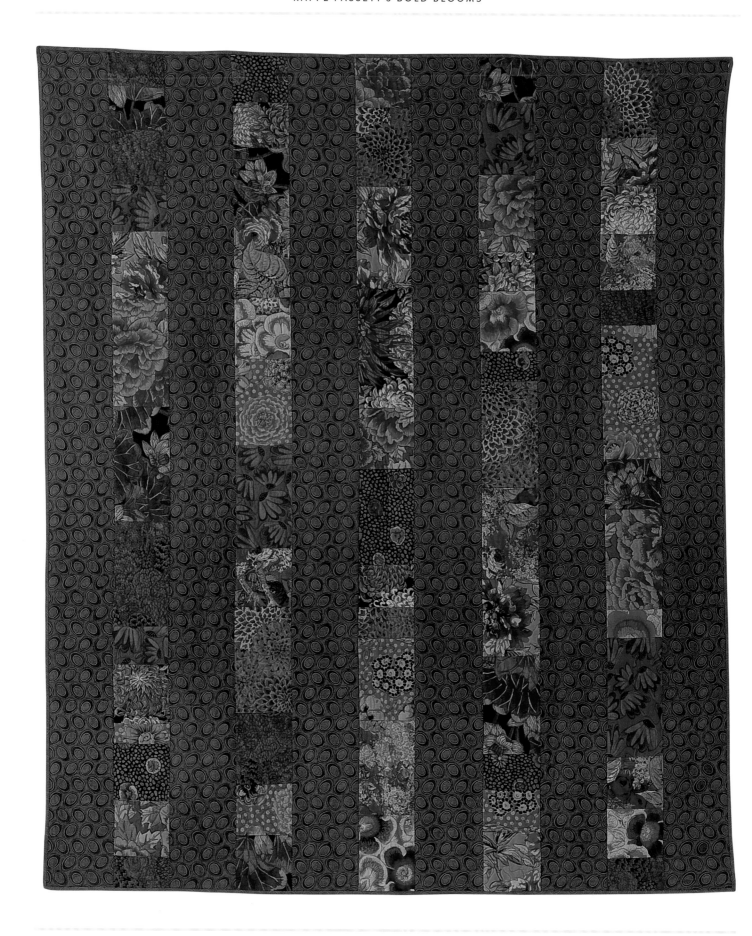

String Stripes Assembly

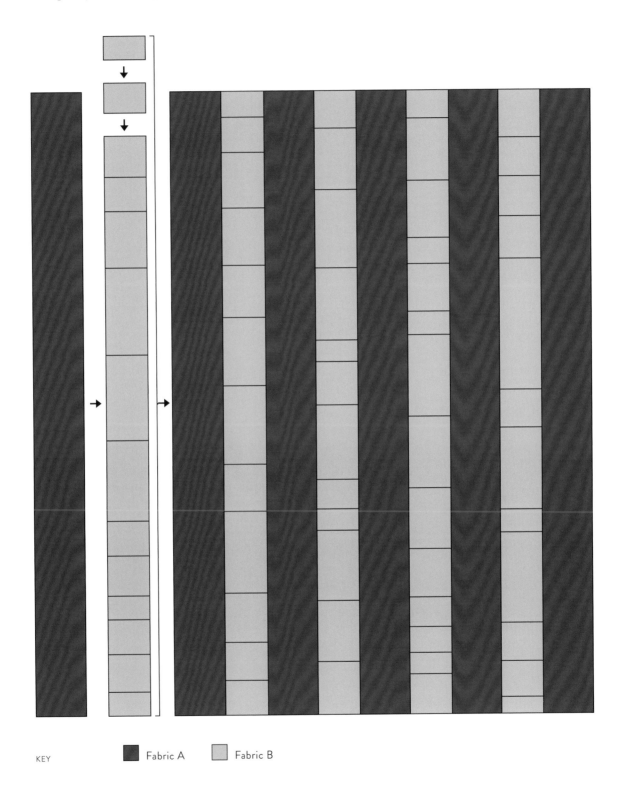

KEY   ■ Fabric A   □ Fabric B

FLORAL OCTAGONS

The large octagons on this quilt are actually made using a simple "snowball" and framing technique. Only the small octagons are cut as octagon shapes and applied with the English paper-piecing method. To fill the large octagons, make sure you choose some fabrics with super-large motifs.

FINISHED SIZE

77¼" × 77¼" (196 cm × 196 cm)

PATCHWORK FABRICS

Use quilting cottons 44–45" (112–115 cm) wide

Fabric A (sashing and block "background"): 3½ yards (3.2 m) of a light-toned polka-dot fabric with pink dots on a white ground; OR, as used here, Kaffe Fassett Collective *Spot* in Magnolia

Fabric B (outer border and octagon frames): 4 yards (3.7 m) of a dark-toned solid maroon; OR, as used here, Kaffe Fassett Collective *Shot Cotton* in Bordeaux

Fabric C (octagons): ¾ yard (70 cm) each of at least 8 different medium-toned large-scale and super-large-scale floral prints in pinks, yellows, oranges, greens, and blues; OR, as used here, the 8 following Kaffe Fassett Collective fabrics: *Big Blooms* in Duckegg and Green, *Brassica* in Natural, *Brocade Peony* in Natural and Yellow, *Gertrude* in Yellow, *Lake Blossoms* in Green, *Lavinia* in Natural

Fabric D (edge "setting" triangles): ½ yard (50 cm) of a solid light blue; OR, as used here, Kaffe Fassett Collective *Shot Cotton* in Ice

OTHER INGREDIENTS

Backing fabric: 5½ yards (5.1 m) of desired fabric

Binding fabric: ¾ yard (70 cm) more of fabric B

Cotton batting: 85" × 85" (215 cm × 215 cm) piece of batting

Quilting thread: Pale pink and burgundy threads

Template materials: Heat-resistant template plastic to make the various templates; stiff, thin paper (cardstock) for the 40 paper octagons needed

Templates: V, X, Y, and Z (pages 216–217)

Fabric glue: Temporary glue stick (optional)

PREPARING THE TEMPLATES AND PAPER OCTAGONS

The small octagons on this quilt are appliquéd in place after the quilt top is complete. These appliqué pieces are prepared in the same way as hexagons are prepared when using the English paper-piecing method.

TEMPLATE FOR THE FABRIC OCTAGONS

Use the outer dotted outline of the octagon template (V) to make a plastic template. This template will be used to cut the fabric octagons. It allows for a ⅜" (1 cm) seam allowance around each octagon.

TEMPLATE FOR THE PAPER OCTAGONS

The seam allowance on each fabric octagon is folded to the wrong side over a paper octagon that is the size of the finished octagon. Use the inner solid outline of the octagon template (V) to make a plastic template to trace the papers. Then trace and cut out a total of 40 papers.

CUTTING THE PIECES

Cut out the pieces in the order given here.

SASHING PIECES

After cutting the following sashing pieces from fabric A, the remainder of fabric A is used for the blocks and edging triangles.

100 sashing strips: From fabric A, cut 100 strips 1½" × 10" (3.7 cm × 25.3 cm).

40 small sashing squares: From fabric A, cut 40 squares 1½" × 1½" (3.7 cm × 3.7 cm).

20 small sashing edge triangles: From fabric A, cut 5 squares 2⅝" × 2⅝" (6.7 cm × 6.7 cm), then cut each of these squares in half diagonally from corner to corner in both directions to make four quarter-triangles from each square, for a total of 20 small triangles.

OUTER-BORDER PIECES

After cutting the following border pieces from fabric B, the remainder of fabric B is used for the blocks and edging triangles.

4 border strips: From fabric B, cut two strips 1¾" × 74¾" (4.4 cm × 189.9 cm) for the side borders; then cut two strips 1¾" × 77¼" (4.4 cm × 196.3 cm) for the top and bottom borders.

FRAMED-OCTAGON-BLOCK PIECES

41 floral centers: For each of the 41 framed octagon blocks, fussy-cut one on-point center square 8" × 8" (20.3 cm × 20.3 cm) from fabric C, carefully centering a blossom in each square and making sure it is on-point (with one corner pointing upward). Because cutting on-point squares means all four sides of the square will be bias cuts, it is advisable to starch the fabric before cutting. Use the largest blooms from fabric C for these squares; the remainder of fabric C will be used for the much smaller appliqué octagons.

Octagon-frame pieces: From fabric B, cut the pieces for the dark octagon frames. Cut 164 squares 2¾" × 2¾" (6.9 cm × 6.9 cm), 82 strips 1½" × 8" (3.7 cm × 20.3 cm), and 82 strips 1½" × 10" (3.7 cm x 25.3 cm).

164 "background" corners: From fabric A, cut 164 squares 3¼" × 3¼" (8.2 cm × 8.2 cm).

EDGE "SETTING" TRIANGLES

36 W triangle corners: From fabric A, cut 9 squares 3⁹⁄₁₆" × 3⁹⁄₁₆" (9.1 cm × 9.1 cm), then cut each of these squares in half diagonally from corner to corner in both directions to make four quarter-triangles from each square, for a total of 36 W triangles.

36 X strips: From fabric B, cut 36 pieces using template X.

36 Y strips: From fabric D, cut 36 pieces using template Y.

36 Z strips: From fabric B, cut 36 pieces using template Z.

OCTAGON APPLIQUÉ PIECES

40 appliqué octagons: From floral fabric C, fussy-cut 40 octagons, using the octagon template you prepared for the fabric octagons and carefully centering a flower in each piece. To do this, trace the octagon onto the right side of the fabric and cut along the drawn outline.

Note: If using a fabric other than *Shot Cottons* for strips X, Y, and Z, cut 18 pieces using each template and 18 pieces using the reverse of each template.

MAKING THE FRAMED OCTAGON BLOCKS

Each framed octagon block is made up of one floral fabric-C on-point square, four fabric-B squares 2¾" × 2¾" (6.9 cm × 6.9 cm), two fabric-B strips 1½" × 8" (3.7 cm × 20.3 cm), two fabric-B strips 1½" × 10" (3.7 cm × 25.3 cm), and four fabric-A squares 3¼" × 3¼" (8.2 cm × 8.2 cm).

To assemble each block, first draw a diagonal line from corner to corner on the wrong side of each of the four small fabric-B squares. With right sides together, place one small square on the corner of the flower square, carefully aligning the raw edges and with the diagonal line on the small square running from one edge of the flower square to the adjacent edge as shown in the diagram. Sew the small square to the flower square, stitching along the drawn diagonal line. Trim the seam allowance to ¼" (6 mm), thereby cutting off the corner of both layers. Press the fabric-B triangle away from the center of the flower square. Sew a small square to the remaining three corners of the flower square in the same way.

Using a ¼" (6 mm) seam allowance for all seams, sew the two shorter fabric-B strips to two opposite sides of the flower square, press, and then sew the two longer strips to the remaining sides. Press. Next, sew the fabric-A squares to the corners of the block in the same way as the first four squares to add "background" corners to the block and complete the "frame." Press.

Make all 41 blocks in the same way.

Framed Octagon Block

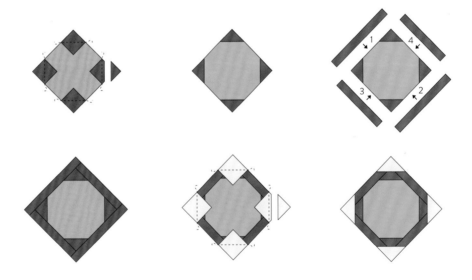

MAKING THE EDGE "SETTING" TRIANGLES

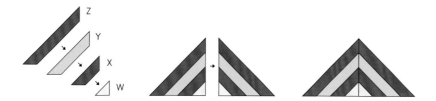

Each half of each edge triangle is made up of one fabric-A W triangle, one fabric-B X piece, one fabric-D Y piece, and one fabric-B Z piece. Following the diagram, sew the W, X, Y, and Z pieces together to complete one half of a triangle. Make a total of 36 half triangles in the same way.

Then make 16 full triangles by sewing 32 half triangles together in pairs as shown. These full triangles are for the edges of the quilt. The remaining four half triangles are for the quilt corners.

ASSEMBLING THE QUILT TOP

QUILT CENTER

Following the Floral Octagon Assembly diagram, arrange the blocks on the floor or on a design wall (page 205). Arrange the blocks on-point in five vertical rows of five blocks each, and between these five-block rows, four vertical rows of four blocks each. Position the sashing strips between the blocks and the sashing squares at the junctions between the strips. Position the tiny sashing triangles at the ends of the sashing strips along the edge of the quilt. Place the full edge triangles along the edge of the quilt and one half triangle at each corner.

Once you have achieved the desired effect, sew the blocks, sashing, and edge triangles together in diagonal rows, press, then sew the diagonal rows together as shown on the diagram. Press.

BORDER

Sew the two fabric-B side borders to the sides of the quilt top. Press. Then sew on the fabric-B top and bottom borders. Press.

Floral Octagons Assembly

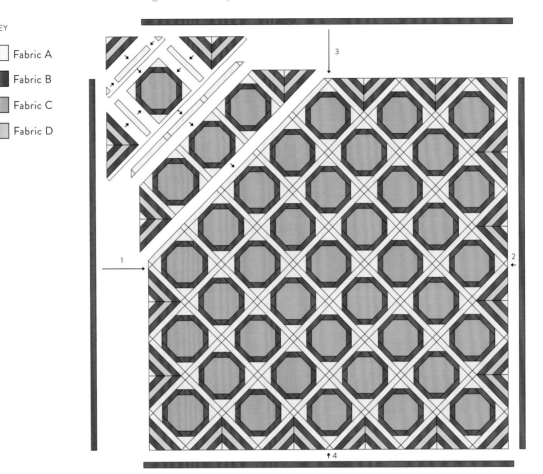

ADDING THE APPLIQUÉ OCTAGONS

To prepare each appliqué octagon, first place a paper octagon in the center of the wrong side of a fabric octagon and fold the fabric seam allowances neatly and snugly to the wrong side over the paper octagon. Either sew-baste or glue-baste the seam allowance in place. Next, iron on both sides, using starch. When the fabric is cool, carefully remove the paper. Prepare all 40 fabric octagons in the same way.

Hand appliqué a flower octagon on top of each intersection of the sashing (over the small sashing square). Carefully cut away the fabric behind the octagon appliqué, leaving a seam allowance at least ¼" (6 mm) wide.

FINISHING THE QUILT

Prepare the backing. Press the quilt top. Layer the quilt top, batting, and backing, then baste the layers together (page 208).

Machine-quilt around each blossom and stitch in the ditch around each block and in the edge setting triangles. Meander quilt in the border and around each appliquéd flower.

Trim the quilt edges. Then prepare the binding and sew it on around the edge of the quilt (page 209).

HIGH-CONTRAST SQUARES

This quilt is less difficult to make than it looks. It is made up entirely of simple strips and squares. Look for super-large-scale floral motifs for most of the large squares, but add variety by using a cluster of flowers or even leaves for some of them.

FINISHED SIZE

85" × 95½" (214 cm × 240.5 cm)

PATCHWORK FABRICS

Use quilting cottons 44–45" (112–115 cm) wide

Fabric A (outer border): 2½ yards (2.3 m) of a dark-toned medium-scale ovals print with black ovals on a pale gray ground; OR, as used here, Kaffe Fassett Collective *Labels* in Black

Fabric B ("light" fabric for blocks): 3¼ yards (3 m) of a light-toned almost solid-looking ovals print in pale gray; OR, as used here, Kaffe Fassett Collective *Aboriginal Dots* in Silver

Fabric C ("dark" fabrics for blocks): ½ yard (50 cm) each of 7 solid fabrics in black, dark blue, deep grape, dark brown-black, dark maroon, deep brown, and dark violet, and of 4 almost solid-looking ovals prints in charcoal, dark brown, periwinkle blue, and purple; OR, as used here, the following 11 Kaffe Fassett Collective fabrics: *Shot Cotton* in Coal, Eucalyptus, Grape, Moor, Mulberry, Nut, and Prune; *Aboriginal Dots* in Charcoal, Chocolate, Periwinkle, and Plum

Fabric D (florals for angle blocks): ½ yard (50 cm) each of at least 9 different medium-toned large-scale and super-large-scale floral prints in a range of bright colors; OR, as used here, the following 11 Kaffe Fassett Collective fabrics: *Big Blooms* in Duckegg and Green, *Gertrude* in Orange, *Gloxinia* in Frost and Natural, *Japanese Chrysanthemum* in Green and Red, *Kimono* in Crimson, *Lake Blossoms* in Magenta and Red, *Lilacs* in Red

OTHER INGREDIENTS

Backing fabric: 7½ yards (6.8 m) of desired fabric

Binding fabric: ¾ yard (70 cm) of a dark-toned almost solid-looking ovals print in charcoal; OR, as used here, Kaffe Fassett Collective *Aboriginal Dots* in Charcoal

Cotton batting: 92" × 103" (230 cm × 255 cm) piece of batting

Quilting thread: Medium gray thread

CUTTING THE PIECES

Follow the cutting sequence in the order given, cutting the pieces for the angle blocks first.

42 large floral squares: From floral fabric D, fussy-cut 42 squares 6" × 6" (15.1 cm × 15.1 cm), carefully framing the flowers in each square. Cut three to five of these squares from each of the D fabrics.

Light strips: From fabric B, cut strips 1½" (3.7 cm) wide. Cutting them as you need them, cut the strips from selvage to selvage and trim the selvages off the ends. From these 1½" (3.7 cm) wide strips, cut 21 strips 11" (27.6 cm) long, 42 strips 10" (25.1 cm) long, 42 strips 9" (22.6 cm) long, 42 strips 8" (20.1 cm) long, 42 strips 7" (17.6 cm) long, and 21 strips 6" (15.1 cm) long. Keep each length in a separate pile of strips and label each pile.

Dark strips: Cut the dark strips from the different C fabrics. Cutting them as you need them, cut the strips from selvage to selvage and trim the selvages off the ends. From these 1½" (3.7 cm) wide strips, cut the strips for each block one bock at a time and use a single "dark" C fabric for each block, making sure you use all the different C fabrics. There are 42 blocks in total, 21 angle blocks no. 1 and 21 angle blocks no. 2. For each of the 21 no. 1 blocks, cut one each of the following lengths of strips—10" (25.1 cm), 9" (22.6 cm), 8" (20.1 cm), and 7" (17.6 cm). For each of the 21 no. 2 blocks, cut one each of the following lengths of strips—11" (27.6 cm), 10" (25.1 cm), 9" (22.6 cm), 8" (20.1 cm), 7" (17.6 cm), and 6" (15.1 cm). Keep the strips together in sets and mark them as for no. 1 or no. 2 blocks.

OUTER-BORDER PIECES

4 outer-border strips: From fabric A, cut two strips 6" × 84½" (15.2 cm × 212.4 cm) for the side borders and two strips 6" × 85" (15.2 cm × 214 cm) for the top and bottom borders. The borders are very similar in length so label them as you cut them.

INNER-BORDER NINE-PATCH BLOCK PIECES

252 small light squares: From fabric B, cut 252 squares 2¼" × 2¼" (5.7 cm × 5.7 cm).
252 small dark squares: Using each of the 11 C fabrics, cut a total of 252 squares, cutting them in sets from the same fabric. For each of the 28 nine-patch blocks no. 1, cut a set of five squares taken from the same fabric. For each of the 28 nine-patch blocks no. 2, cut a set of four squares taken from the same fabric.

MAKING THE ANGLE BLOCKS

21 angle blocks no. 1: For each block, select a large floral square, a set of the four dark strips cut from the same fabric, and the light strips required for block no. 1 as shown on the Angle Block Strip Chart. Following the diagram and using a ¼" (6 mm) seam allowance for all seams, add the strips to the large square from the center outward, in log cabin style and in the sequence of the strip numbers, pressing after each seam. Make sure the flowers in the large square are upright with the logs across the top and down the left side. Make a total of 21 blocks in this way.

21 angle blocks no. 2: For each block, select a large floral square, a set of the six dark strips cut from the same fabric, and the light strips required for block no. 2 as shown on the Angle Block Strip Chart. Following the diagram, add the strips as explained for the no. 1 blocks. Make a total of 21 blocks in this way.

Angle Block No. 1

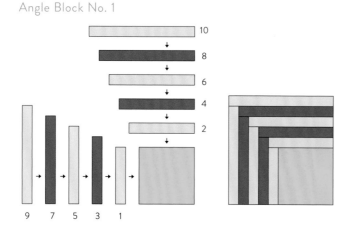

Angle Block No. 2

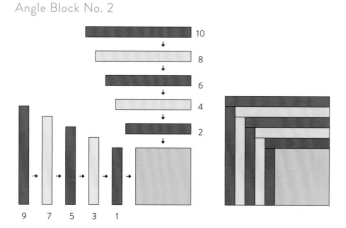

	Strip size	Block no. 1	Block no. 2
Strip 1	1½" × 6" (3.7 cm × 15.1 cm)	light fabric	dark fabric
Strip 2	1½" × 7" (3.7 cm × 17.6 cm)	light fabric	dark fabric
Strip 3	1½" × 7" (3.7 cm × 17.6 cm)	dark fabric	light fabric
Strip 4	1½" × 8" (3.7 cm × 20.1 cm)	dark fabric	light fabric
Strip 5	1½" × 8" (3.7 cm × 20.1 cm)	light fabric	dark fabric
Strip 6	1½" × 9" (3.7 cm × 22.6 cm)	light fabric	dark fabric
Strip 7	1½" × 9" (3.7 cm × 22.6 cm)	dark fabric	light fabric
Strip 8	1½" × 10" (3.7 cm × 25.1 cm)	dark fabric	light fabric
Strip 9	1½" × 10" (3.7 cm × 25.1 cm)	light fabric	dark fabric
Strip 10	1½" × 11" (3.7 cm × 27.6 cm)	light fabric	dark fabric

MAKING THE NINE-PATCH BLOCKS

Nine-patch Block No. 1

Nine-patch Block No. 2

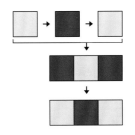

28 nine-patch blocks no. 1: For each block, select a set of five small squares cut from the same dark fabric and four small light fabric-B squares. Following the diagram, arrange these nine squares in three horizontal rows of three squares each, alternating the colors. Sew the squares together in three horizontal rows, press, then sew the rows together. Press. Make a total of 28 blocks in this way.

28 nine-patch blocks no. 2: For each block, select a set of four small squares cut from the same dark fabric and five small light fabric-B squares. Following the diagram, sew together as for the no. 1 blocks. Make a total of 28 blocks in this way.

High-Contrast Squares Assembly

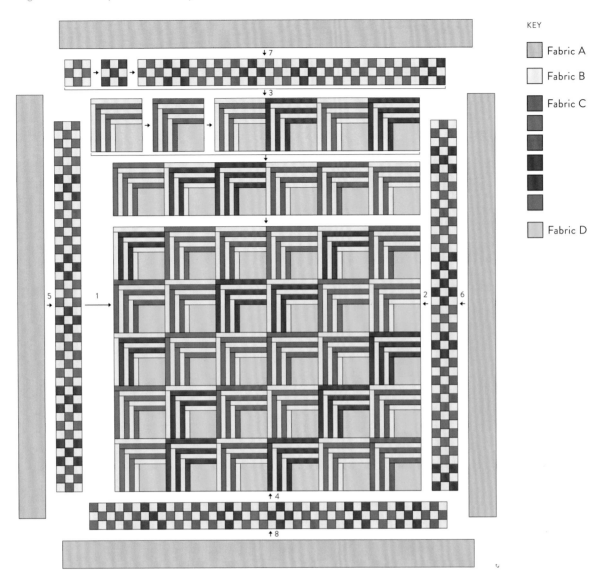

KEY

Fabric A

Fabric B

Fabric C

Fabric D

ASSEMBLING THE QUILT TOP

Following the High-Contrast Squares Assembly diagram, arrange 42 angle blocks in seven horizontal rows of six blocks each, alternating the no. 1 blocks and the no. 2 blocks and lining them up on the floor or on a design wall (page 205). Rearrange the blocks until you have a pleasing mix of colors and make sure the blocks are upright.

Next, arrange the 56 nine-patch inner-border blocks all around the quilt center, alternating the no. 1 and the no. 2 blocks.

QUILT CENTER

Sew together the horizontal rows of six angle blocks each (leaving the inner-border blocks where they are on your design wall). Press. Then sew together the seven horizontal rows. Press.

BORDERS

Sew together the 14 nine-patch blocks for each of the two side inner borders, press, then sew together the 14 nine-patch blocks for the top and bottom inner borders. Press. Sew the two inner-border side stripes to the sides of the quilt top, press, then sew on the top and bottom inner-borders. Press.Next, sew on the two outer-border side strips to the sides of the quilt top, press, and lastly sew the outer-border top and bottom strips. Press.

FINISHING THE QUILT

Prepare the backing. Press the quilt top. Layer the quilt top, batting, and backing, then baste the layers together (page 208).

Machine-quilt in the ditch around each angle block, between the log strips, and around each floral square. Outline-quilt the blossoms. Quilt diagonal lines in both directions across the small squares in the inner border. Meander quilt in the outer border around each oval.

Trim the quilt edges. Then prepare the binding and sew it on around the edge of the quilt (page 209).

WHITE DAHLIA NEEDLEPOINT PILLOW

FINISHED SIZE

The finished needlepoint measures 16¼" (41 cm) wide by 16" (40.5 cm) tall.

MATERIALS NEEDED

- 10-stitches-to-the-inch (2.5 cm) interlock needlepoint canvas, 23" (59 cm) square
- Appleton wool tapestry yarn (11 yard [10 m] skeins) in 10 colors (see below)
- Size 18 tapestry needle
- ½ yard (50 cm) of a 44" (112-cm) wide cotton fabric, for pillow backing, and matching sewing thread
- 2 yards (1.9 m) of ready-made decorative cord (optional)
- Pillow form to fit finished cover

YARN COLORS AND AMOUNTS

A	963	8 skeins
B	104	1 skein
C	101	3 skeins
D	884	3 skeins
E	251A	1 skein
F	873	2 skeins
G	401	1 skein
H	403	1 skein
J	961	1 skein
K	991B	5 skeins

EMBROIDERY NOTES

The chart on page 48 is 162 stitches wide by 161 stitches tall. Follow the chart using tent stitch and one strand of yarn. Fill in the background, color **A** (963), last.

See page 210 for basic needlepoint and finishing instructions.

BOUQUET NEEDLEPOINT PILLOW

FINISHED SIZE

The finished needlepoint measures 17" (43 cm) wide by 17½" (44.5 cm) tall.

MATERIALS NEEDED

- 10-stitches-to-the-inch (2.5 cm) interlock needlepoint canvas, 24" (61 cm) square
- Appleton wool tapestry yarn (11 yard [10 m] skeins) in 13 colors (see below)
- Size 18 tapestry needle
- ½ yard (50 cm) of a 44" (112-cm) wide cotton fabric, for pillow backing, and matching sewing thread
- 2¼ yards (2 m) of ready-made decorative cord (optional)
- Pillow form to fit finished cover

YARN COLORS AND AMOUNTS

A	742	12 skeins
B	421	1 skein
C	831	1 skein
D	354	1 skein
E	833	1 skein
F	447	2 skeins
G	504	1 skein
H	624	2 skeins
J	942	2 skeins
K	751	1 skein
L	991B	1 skein
M	471	1 skein
N	844	3 skeins

EMBROIDERY NOTES

The chart on page 60 is 169 stitches wide by 175 stitches tall. Follow the chart using tent stitch and one strand of yarn. Fill in the background, color **A** (742), and then the 1-stitch inner border, color **M** (471), and the 4-stitch outer border, color **N** (844), last.

See page 210 for basic needlepoint and finishing instructions.

CARLTON WARE NEEDLEPOINT PILLOW

FINISHED SIZE

The finished needlepoint measures 16¾" (42.5 cm) wide by 16½" (42 cm) tall.

MATERIALS NEEDED

• 10-stitches-to-the-inch (2.5 cm) interlock needlepoint canvas, 23" (59 cm) square
• Appleton wool tapestry yarn (11 yard [10 m] skeins) in 12 colors (see below)
• Size 18 tapestry needle
• ½ yard (50 cm) of a 44" (112-cm) wide cotton fabric, for pillow backing, and matching sewing thread
• 2 yards (1.9 m) of ready-made decorative cord (optional)
• Pillow form to fit finished cover

YARN COLORS AND AMOUNTS

A	824	6 skeins
B	552	2 skeins
C	474	3 skeins
D	696	2 skeins
E	443	1 skein
F	884	2 skeins
G	451	2 skeins
H	421	6 skeins
J	432	2 skeins
K	831	2 skeins
L	529	1 skein
M	643	1 skein

EMBROIDERY NOTES

The chart on page 72 is 168 stitches wide by 166 stitches tall. Follow the chart using tent stitch and one strand of yarn. Fill in the background, colors **A** (824) and **H** (421), last.

See page 210 for basic needlepoint and finishing instructions.

PINK PEONIES NEEDLEPOINT PILLOW

FINISHED SIZE

The finished needlepoint measures 16½" (42 cm) wide by 16¼" (41 cm) tall.

MATERIALS NEEDED

• 10-stitches-to-the-inch (2.5 cm) interlock needlepoint canvas, 23" (59 cm) square
• Appleton wool tapestry yarn (11 yard [10 m] skeins) in 11 colors (see below)
• Size 18 tapestry needle
• ½ yard (50 cm) of a 44" (112-cm) wide cotton fabric, for pillow backing, and matching sewing thread
• 2 yards (1.9 m) of ready-made decorative cord (optional)
• Pillow form to fit finished cover

YARN COLORS AND AMOUNTS

A	994	7 skeins
B	311	1 skein
C	696	1 skein
D	244	2 skeins
E	643	3 skeins
F	647	2 skeins
G	505	1 skein
H	504	4 skeins
J	946	2 skeins
K	944	2 skeins
L	942	3 skeins

EMBROIDERY NOTES

The chart on page 82 is 165 stitches wide by 163 stitches tall. Follow the chart using tent stitch and one strand of yarn. Fill in the background, color **A** (994), last.

See page 210 for basic needlepoint and finishing instructions.

TULIP VASE
NEEDLEPOINT PILLOW

FINISHED SIZE

The finished needlepoint measures 15" (38 cm) wide by 15½" (39.5 cm) tall.

MATERIALS NEEDED

- 10-stitches-to-the-inch (2.5 cm) interlock needlepoint canvas, 22" (56 cm) square
- Appleton wool tapestry yarn (11 yard [10 m] skeins) in 17 colors (see below)
- Size 18 tapestry needle
- ½ yard (50 cm) of a 44" (112-cm) wide cotton fabric, for pillow backing, and matching sewing thread
- 2 yards (1.9 m) of ready-made decorative cord (optional)
- Pillow form to fit finished cover

YARN COLORS AND AMOUNTS

A	884	6 skeins
B	862	1 skein
C	864	1 skein
D	551	1 skein
E	421	1 skein
F	424	2 skeins
G	427	2 skeins
H	403	4 skeins
J	406	1 skein
K	802	1 skein
L	801	1 skein
M	711	1 skein
N	101	1 skein
O	105	1 skein
P	876	1 skein
Q	462	1 skein
R	464	1 skein

EMBROIDERY NOTES

The chart on page 94 is 151 stitches wide by 154 stitches tall. Follow the chart using tent stitch and one strand of yarn. Fill in the background last.

See page 210 for basic needlepoint and finishing instructions.

DARK PEONY
NEEDLEPOINT PILLOW

FINISHED SIZE

The finished needlepoint measures 16½" (42 cm) wide by 16¼" (41 cm) tall.

MATERIALS NEEDED

- 10-stitches-to-the-inch (2.5 cm) interlock needlepoint canvas, 23" (59 cm) square
- Appleton wool tapestry yarn (11 yard [10 m] skeins) in 13 colors (see below)
- Size 18 tapestry needle
- ½ yard (50 cm) of a 44" (112-cm) wide cotton fabric, for pillow backing, and matching sewing thread
- 2 yards (1.9 m) of ready-made decorative cord (optional)
- Pillow form to fit finished cover

YARN COLORS AND AMOUNTS

A	474	1 skein
B	643	3 skeins
C	354	1 skein
D	254	1 skein
E	294	2 skeins
F	298	1 skein
G	585	1 skein
H	758	2 skeins
J	948	2 skeins
K	866	2 skeins
L	994	2 skeins
M	862	1 skein
N	464	9 skeins

EMBROIDERY NOTES

The chart on page 106 is 165 stitches wide by 162 stitches tall. Follow the chart using tent stitch and one strand of yarn. Fill in the background, color **N** (464), last.

See page 210 for basic needlepoint and finishing instructions.

CARNATIONS NEEDLEPOINT PILLOW

FINISHED SIZE

The finished needlepoint measures 15½" (39.5 cm) wide by 15¾" (40 cm) tall.

MATERIALS NEEDED

• 10-stitches-to-the-inch (2.5 cm) interlock needlepoint canvas, 22" (56 cm) square
• Appleton wool tapestry yarn (11 yard [10 m] skeins) in 12 colors (see below)
• Size 18 tapestry needle
• ½ yard (50 cm) of a 44" (112-cm) wide cotton fabric, for pillow backing, and matching sewing thread
• 2 yards (1.9 m) of ready-made decorative cord (optional)
• Pillow form to fit finished cover

YARN COLORS AND AMOUNTS

A	991B	8 skeins
B	993	6 skeins
C	504	1 skein
D	447	1 skein
E	963	1 skein
F	962	1 skein
G	997	2 skeins
H	802	2 skeins
J	431	1 skein
K	427	1 skein
L	716	1 skein
M	696	1 skein

EMBROIDERY NOTES

The needlepoint is 156 stitches wide by 158 stitches tall, but the chart on page 116 is 112

stitches wide by 138 stitches tall as not all the background "rays" are shown. Begin by marking the outer outline of the design onto your canvas so that it is 156 stitches wide by 158 stitches tall. Then mark out the area of the chart; the first row of the chart sits on the bottom edge of the design outline and should be centered on this line so that there are 22 stitches between the chart and the left- and right-hand edges of the design outline. Follow the chart using tent stitch and one strand of yarn. Draw lines on the canvas in the empty area of the design to extend the black and white rays outward to the outer outline and fill in this background area, using colors **A** (991A) and **B** (993), last.

See page 210 for basic needlepoint and finishing instructions.

QUILTING BASICS

Here are some useful tips to follow when making your quilts. If you are an absolute beginner at patchwork but are proficient at using the sewing machine, you will have little trouble in tackling most of the quilts in the book. Beginners may like to take a simple beginner's course or have an experienced quilt maker guide them through their first project.

This chapter can't begin to cover all the many quilting shortcuts, but the tips provided will make the quilt-making process easier and more fun. Don't get too worried about technique when you begin. Some of the most wonderful museum quilts have imperfect stitching lines, and these just add to their home-made charm. Concentrate instead on the beautiful colors you are using and on composing them into a spectacular quilt.

PATCHWORK FABRICS

There are lightweight one-hundred-percent cotton fabrics specially produced for quilts, and these are the best materials to use. As they are firmly woven, they are easy to cut, crease, and press, but slow to fray. They also come in a seemingly endless range of colors and prints, which means you can create a quilt with any palette you like.

Choosing fabric colors and prints

The fabrics used for many of the quilts in this book are from the Kaffe Fassett Collective, but each set of instructions gives you guidelines for finding suitable substitutes. Feel free to select your own color palette instead of the one suggested. The most fun part of patchwork, I believe, is playing with and mixing fabric colors and finding a palette that really sings!

When choosing fabrics, pay particular attention to the lightness or darkness of the colors, which accentuate the geometry of the patterns. My quilts usually have a fairly subtle contrast in the lights and darks used. Closeness in tone, rather than sharp tonal contrast, creates a composition of great richness and hidden depths. If you study your favorite antique quilts, you will see they often use very restrained contrasts.

Always look carefully at the photograph of the quilt when choosing your fabric palette. Choose prints with care. Notice the scale of the prints. Very small-scale prints can look like solids at a distance, but they provide more interest and visual "texture" than solids. Large-scale and super-large-scale floral prints are particularly useful because you can cut completely different colors from different areas of the same fabric. Dots and stripes, even used in only a few areas of a quilt, add amazing movement to the composition.

When choosing multicolored prints, study them at a distance. Looking at them up close, you may think you are choosing a particular color, but at a distance they turn into something totally different. For example, you may think you are choosing a "red" because there are bright red small-scale motifs on a white ground, but at a distance it looks pink! Similarly, motifs in two different colors will blend together at a distance to make a totally new color, for example separate blues and yellows on the same print will make it look green.

If you are in doubt, buy small amounts of fabrics and test them by cutting and arranging some patches and then standing back to see the effect at a distance.

Determining how much fabric you need

Deciding on fabric amounts for my designs is not a very exact science, because I use so many different fabrics. The quantities in the instructions are sometimes only an approximate guide, but they tend to be generous. Of course, it is better to have too much fabric than too little, and you can use the leftovers for future projects.

If you do run out of fabric, it is not a tragedy. I think of it as a design opportunity! The replacement you find may make the quilt look even better. After all, quilt making was a craft designed to use up scraps, and chance combinations of fabrics sometimes resulted in antique masterpieces.

When calculating exact fabric amounts for borders, bindings, or backings on your own designs, remember that although specially made cotton patchwork fabrics are usually 44" (about 112 cm) wide, the usable width is sometimes only about 40" (101.5 cm) due to slight shrinkage and the removal of selvages.

Preparing patchwork fabric

Be sure to prewash your cotton patchwork fabrics before use, especially if they are vintage. This will confirm colorfastness and preshrink the fabric just in case it may be prone to this. Wash the darks and lights separately and rinse them well. Then press the fabric with a hot iron while it is still damp. After pressing, cut off the selvages; you can do this quickest with a rotary cutter.

TOOLS AND EQUIPMENT

If you have a sewing machine, you probably already have most of the other tools necessary in your sewing box. Aside from the sewing machine, you'll need fabric scissors, pins, needles, a ruler, lead and chalk pencils, a tape measure, an ironing board, and an iron. These are the bare necessities for making a simple patchwork entirely in squares.

However, to make the quilting process easier, it is also essential, I think, to have template plastic, a rotary cutter, a cutting mat, and an assortment of rotary-cutting rulers. Template plastic is perfect for making durable and precise template and appliqué shapes to trace around. And with the rotary-cutting tools, you can cut your patches quickly and in accurate straight lines. Having a range of large and small cutting mats and rotary-cutting rulers is handy, but if you want to start out with just one mat and one ruler, buy a 12" × 18" (30 cm × 46 cm) mat and a 6" × 12" (15 cm × 30 cm) ruler. The ruler will have measurement markings on it as well as 90-, 60-, and 45-degree angles.

Design wall and reducing glass

The other two items I strongly recommend for successful patchwork are a design wall and a reducing glass. A full-size quilt can be arranged on the floor, but it is much easier to view when on a wall. Our design wall is large enough for a queen-size bed cover and is made with two sheets of insulation board each measuring 4 feet × 8 feet (122 cm × 244 cm). Insulation board is a very light board about ¾" (2 cm) thick; it has a foam core that is covered on one side with paper and on the other with foil. Any sturdy, lightweight board like this would do, but insulation board is especially handy as it can be cut with a craft knife.

To make a design wall, cover one side of each of the two boards with a good-quality cotton flannel in a neutral color. I have designed the ideal flannel for this purpose—it is light gray and has printed on it a pale-colored 2" (5-cm) grid (see Sources on page 221). The grid helps me align my quilt pieces on the wall and gives me an instant idea of the size of the pieces.

After covering the two design boards with flannel, join them with three "hinges" of strong adhesive tape, sticking the hinges to the back of the boards so that you can fold the flannel sides together. The tape hinges will also allow you to bend the design wall slightly so it will stand by itself. If you want to put the wall away with a design in progress on it, just place paper over the arranged patches, fold the boards together, and slide them under a bed.

A quilter's reducing glass looks like a magnifying glass, but instead of making things look larger, it makes them look smaller. By looking at a fabric or a design in progress through a reducing glass, you can see how the fabric print or even a whole patchwork layout will look at a distance. Seeing your quilt layout reduced makes the errors in color or pattern in the design just pop out and become very obvious. Reducing glasses are usually available in shops that sell patchwork supplies. A camera isn't quite as good, but it is an acceptable substitute.

PATCH PREPARATION

Once you have prepared all the fabrics for your patchwork, you are ready to start cutting patches. Squares, rectangles, and simple half-square or quarter-square triangles can be cut quickly and accurately with a rotary cutter, but you will need to use scissors for more complicated shapes, such as curved appliqué pieces.

Using a rotary cutter

Get someone to demonstrate how to use a rotary cutter if you have never used one before, paying particular attention to safety advice. Always use the cutter in conjunction with a cutting mat and a rotary-cutting ruler. You press down on the ruler and the cutter and roll the cutter away from you along the edge of the ruler.

With a little practice, you will be able to cut patches very quickly with a rotary cutter. Long strips can be cut from folded fabric, squares from long strips, and half-square triangles from squares. Just remember to change the cutter blade as soon as it shows the slightest hint of dulling.

Making templates

Templates are not always required for patchwork projects; simple squares, rectangles, strips, and half-square or quarter-square triangles can be cut with a rotary cutter. But some of the patchworks in this book do need templates, and these are provided on pages 211–220. Photocopy any templates to the size you need and cut them out before you begin your quilt. If the shapes can be cut quickly with a rotary

cutter, use the template as a guide to your rotary cutting. If not, you can make a plastic or cardboard template from them and use it to trace around.

Special clear template plastic makes the best templates. It is easy to cut, is very durable, and will retain its shape despite being repeatedly traced around. It is also handy because of its transparency—you can see through it to frame fabric motifs such as flowers.

It is a good idea to punch a hole in each corner of your template at each pivot point on the seam line, using a ⅛" (3 mm) hole punch. This will increase the accuracy of your seam lines, especially on diamonds and triangles.

Before going on to cut all your patches, make a patchwork block with test pieces to check the accuracy of your templates.

Cutting template patches

To cut patches using a template, place the template face up on the right side of the fabric and align the fabric grainline arrow with the straight grain of the fabric (the crosswise or the lengthwise grain). Pressing the template down firmly with one hand, draw around it with a sharp lead or chalk pencil in the other hand. To save fabric, position the patches close together or even touching.

Cutting reverse template patches

A reverse template is the mirror image of the patch shape. A template that is marked as a template and a reverse template can be used for both shapes. For the reverse shape, lay the template face down (instead of face up) on the right side of the fabric, and draw around it in the usual way.

SEWING PATCHES TOGETHER

Quilt instructions give a layout diagram for how to arrange the various patch shapes to form the quilt design. Often several patches are joined together to form small blocks and then the finished blocks are sewn together to form the whole quilt. Whether you are arranging a block or a whole quilt, lay the patches out on the floor or stick them to a design wall. Then study the effect of your arrangement carefully, stepping back to look at it or looking at it through a reducing glass.

Stitch pieces together only once you are sure the color arrangement is just right. If you are unsure, leave it for a few days and come back to it and try another arrangement, or try replacing colors that do not seem to work together with new shades. Remember that an unpredictable arrangement will have more energy and life than one that follows a strict light/dark geometry.

Machine-stitching straight seams

Sew, or piece, patches together using a ¼" (6 mm) seam allowance and following the order specified in the quilt instructions. Use the same neutral-colored thread to piece the entire patchwork. I find that medium taupe or gray thread will work for most patchworks. But when the overall palette is very light, use ecru thread.

Pin the patches together with right sides facing and match the seam lines and corner points carefully. (If you are proficient at the sewing machine, you will be able to stitch small squares together without pinning.) As you machine-stitch the seam, remove each pin before the needle reaches it. (Never stitch over pins with your sewing machine; if the sewing-machine needle and/or a pin break, a metal splinter can shoot up and injure you or someone else nearby.) Always stitch from raw edge to raw edge, except on set-in seams. There is no need to work backstitches at the beginning and end of each patch seam because the stitches will be secured by crossing seam lines as the pieces are joined together.

To save time and thread, you can chain-piece the patches. To do this, feed through the paired together pieces one after another without lifting the presser foot; the machine will stitch through nothing a few times before it reaches the next pair of patches. Simply clip the pairs of patches apart when you're finished.

Pressing seams

Press all seams flat first, to imbed the stitches. Then open out the patches and press the seam allowances to one side, or press open if many fabrics meet in one spot (to reduce bulk) or if sewing set-in seams. As you continue stitching patches into blocks, then the blocks into rows as instructed, press the seam allowances in each row (of patches or blocks) in the same direction. Press the seam allowances in every alternate row in the opposite direction to avoid having to stitch through two layers of seam allowances at once when joining the rows together.

Stitching set-in seams

Most of the projects in this book are made with simple, easy-to-stitch straight seams. However, Attic Window On-Point (page 142) and Tawny Hatboxes (page 159) both require set-in seams, also called inset seams or Y-seams; these are seams that turn a corner. Press these seams open. See page 144 for an explanation of how to sew this type of seam.

APPLIQUÉ

A few of the quilts in this book use the appliqué technique. Appliqué is the addition of shaped fabric pieces on top of a backing fabric. Templates are provided for the shapes. The edges of the appliqué motifs are usually either turned under, as on Lattice with Vases on page 173, or the raw edges are covered with machine stitching, as on Tawny Hatboxes on page 159.

Whichever method you are using for your appliqué, be sure to cut the shapes from well-pressed fabric. Applying spray starch to the fabric makes cutting easier and keeps the fabric from fraying too much. Use very sharp scissors when cutting appliqué pieces. Do not handle them too much once they are cut and keep them flat until you need them.

If you are using machine blanket, buttonhole, or satin stitch to cover the raw edges of the appliqué and secure it to the backing, pin or baste the fabric shapes in place first. You may want to place sewing stablizer paper behind the backing to help it slide neatly through the machine. The same applies to other machine-stitch methods for applying appliqué.

On appliqué where the raw edges are turned under, a seam allowance of ¼" to ¼" (3 mm to 6 mm) is added all around the finished shape. This allowance is then notched or clipped where necessary along curves or at corners and turned to the wrong side. As an aid to turning under the seam allowance, you can use freezer paper. Just cut a piece of freezer paper to the size of the finished appliqué shape and press the shiny side of the paper to the wrong of the fabric appliqué piece. Then press the seam allowance to the wrong side over the paper, using starch, and remove the paper. The appliqué is then ready to be pinned and basted and then stitched in place by hand or machine.

Once you have stitched your appliqué, carefully cut away the backing fabric behind the appliqué to within ¼" (6 mm) of the seam. This keeps the fabric from becoming too bulky and keeps the color of the backing from showing through.

QUILTING AND FINISHING

After you have finished piecing your patchwork, press it carefully. It is now ready to be quilted. Quilting is the allover stitching that joins together the three layers of the quilt sandwich—patchwork top, batting, and backing.

Preparing the quilt backing and batting

Before you quilt your patchwork, you need to prepare the two other layers. Choose a backing fabric that will not do a disservice to the quilt top. Liza likes using sale fabrics for backings, but they still have to have a certain charm of their own and go well with the patchwork top.

Cut the selvages off the backing fabric, then seam the pieces together to form a backing at least 4" (10 cm) bigger all around than the patchwork top. Join the pieces so that the seam lines run lengthwise if possible.

Batting comes in various thicknesses. Pure cotton or mixed cotton and polyester batting, which are both fairly thin, are good choices for most quilts. Thicker batting is usually only suitable when the quilt layers are being tied together with little knots rather than quilting. I prefer thin one-hundred-percent cotton batting because it gives a quilt the attractive, relatively flat appearance of an antique patchwork.

If the batting has been rolled, unroll it and let it rest before cutting it to about the same size as the backing.

Basting together the quilt layers

To keep the three layers of the quilt firmly in place during the quilting process, baste them together.

Lay the backing wrong side up and place the batting on top of it. Lay the finished, pressed patchwork right side up on top of the batting.

Beginning at the center for each stitching line, baste two diagonal lines from corner to corner through the layers of the quilt. Work stitches about 3" (7.5 cm) long and try not to lift the layers too much as you stitch. Always beginning at the center and working outward, baste horizontal and vertical lines about 4" (10 cm) apart across the layers.

Choosing a quilting pattern

Personally, I love to hand quilt, and I usually hand quilt patchworks that I have stitched together completely by hand. Simple parallel rows of stitches are my preferred quilting pattern in these instances, as I like quilting that does not overshadow the play of the patchwork fabrics. For this reason, when my quilts are machine quilted I often choose stitch-in-the-ditch quilting; in this type of quilting the stitching lines are worked very close to the patch seams and are invisible on the right side of the quilt. Echo quilting is another simple quilting pattern that suits many patchwork designs; it is worked by stitching ¼" (6 mm) inside the patch seam lines to echo the shape of the patch. A third favorite machine quilting pattern is outlining motifs on large-scale prints, such as individual flowers, with quilting stitches.

More complicated quilting patterns can be marked on the quilt before you machine-stitch them. Quilting stores sell quilting stencils for these.

Test your chosen quilting on a spare pieced block, stitching through all three quilt layers. This is also a good way to check whether the color of the quilting thread is suitable. The thread color should usually blend invisibly into the overall color of the patchwork quilt when it is viewed from a distance.

Machine quilting

For machine quilting, use a walking foot for straight lines and a darning foot for curved lines. Choose a color that blends with the overall color of the patchwork for the top thread and one that matches the backing for the bobbin thread. Follow the sewing machine manual for tips on using the walking and darning feet.

Binding quilt edges

When the quilting is finished, remove the basting threads that held the layers together. Then trim away the excess batting and backing right up to the edge of the patchwork, straightening the edge of the patchwork at the same time if necessary.

Cut binding strips either on the bias or on the straight grain of the fabric, 2–2½" (5–6 cm) wide. To make a strip long enough to fit around the edge of the quilt, sew these strips together end-to-end, joining bias strips with diagonal seams. Next, fold the strip in half lengthwise with the wrong sides together and press.

Place the doubled binding on the right side of the quilt, with the right sides facing and the raw edges of both layers of the binding aligned with the raw edges of the quilt. Machine stitch ¼" (6 mm) from the edge and stitch up to ¼" (6 mm) from the first corner. Make a few backstitches and cut the thread ends. With the edge just stitched at the top, fold the binding upward so that it makes a 45-degree angle at the corner of the quilt. Keeping the diagonal fold just made in place, fold the binding back down and align the edges with the next side of the quilt. Beginning ¼ (6mm) from the top and side of the corner, stitch down the next side to within ¼" (6 mm) of the next corner, and so on. When you reach the beginning of the binding, turn under the edge of one end and tuck the other end inside it.

Turn the folded edge of the binding to the back of the quilt and hand stitch it in place, folding a miter at each corner.

NEEDLEPOINT BASICS

BUYING CANVAS AND YARNS

Use the recommended canvas. The amount of canvas specified in the instructions is enough to leave about 3" (7.5 cm) extra all around the design. If you like, you can purchase slightly less, but it is best to have a minimum of 2" (5 cm) of unworked canvas all around the edge to make blocking easier.

Although it may be possible to use substitute tapestry-weight yarns for the recommended yarns, it is best to use the brand and shade numbers I have specified if you want to duplicate my design exactly. The amounts listed for the yarns are on the generous side but are only approximate. It is not possible to be absolutely sure that they will be adequate for every single stitcher, as amounts needed can vary based on how loosely or tightly the stitches are worked.

EMBROIDERING THE DESIGN

Begin by marking the outline of the design on your canvas and, if desired, dividing it into tens just like the charted design, using a fabric marking pen. Note that each canvas intersection represents a stitch. Following the chart, work the embroidery in tent stitch, using one strand of wool tapestry yarn.

BLOCKING AND SIZING

You may find that your needlepoint looks slightly distorted as stitching progresses. Do not worry about this; the wool yarns can be blocked into shape after the stitching is completed.

To block the finished needlepoint, place it face down on a flat surface and dampen it thoroughly by spraying it with water or using a damp cloth or sponge. Then place the needlepoint face down on a large sheet of plywood. Begin nailing it to the plywood, stretching it out to approximately the finished measurements given in the instructions. Start with a tack in the center of each of the four sides of the needlepoint, nailing into the unworked canvas. Then add tacks from the centers outward toward the corners, using at least one tack per inch (2.5 cm).

Leave the needlepoint to dry completely, even if it takes several days. I then use wallpaper paste as a "size" to fix the shape. Mix the wallpaper paste to a fairly thick consistency. With the needlepoint still nailed in place, brush a light film of paste into the back. Remove only when completely dry.

MAKING PILLOW BACK

Each set of needlepoint instructions tells you how much fabric you will need to make a back for your pillow. Although you can insert a zipper in the pillow cover, it is easiest to create an "envelope" back. An envelope back consists of two panels of fabric that overlap at the center. The pillow form can be inserted or removed through the open overlap.

To make the back, after you have blocked your needlepoint, trim the empty needlepoint canvas around the embroidery to ¾" (2 cm). This is the seam allowance. Next, measure the size of the canvas in both directions. Each back panel should measure half the size of these measurements, plus an extension of 3" (7.5 cm) along the center (overlapping) edge.

After calculating the size of the back panels, cut out the two pieces. Fold and press ½" (12 mm) to the wrong side along the center (overlapping) edge of one piece, then press under ½" (12 mm) again to create a double hem. Machine-stitch the hem in place. Finish the center edge of the other panel in the same way. Next, lay the needlepoint face up on a flat surface. Lay the back panels face down on top of the needlepoint with the hemmed edges overlapping at the center and the raw edges aligned with the raw edges of the canvas. Pin and baste the back panels in place. With the needlepoint uppermost, machine-stitch close to the embroidery all around the edge. If you are sewing on a decorative cord, leave a ½" (12 mm) opening in the seam in the center of the bottom edge.

Trim the seam allowance to ⅝" (15 mm) and clip off the corners diagonally about ¼" (6 mm) from the seam. Turn the cover right side out. Lastly, sew on the decorative cord along the seam line, tucking the ends into the small opening in the seam.

BASKET

Enlarge these templates by 200% to achieve the correct size. Note that only half of template XX is given here; flop the template for the other half to create a full template. The solid lines on the templates represent the seam lines and the dotted lines the seam allowances. The arrows on the templates indicate the direction of the fabric grain. See pages 138–141 for the quilt instructions.

YY and YY rev

ZZ

center of the template

XX

align grainline along selvage

211

ATTIC WINDOW ON-POINT

The six templates needed for making this quilt are P rev (and P), Q (and Q rev and U) , N (and N rev), R, S, and T (and T rev). Enlarge these templates by 200% to achieve the correct size. Note that only half of templates R and T are given here; flop the templates for the other half to create full templates. The solid lines on the templates represent the seam lines and the dotted lines the seam allowances. The arrows on the templates indicate the direction of the fabric grain. Templates S and T (and T rev) can be found opposite. See pages 142–146 for the quilt instructions.

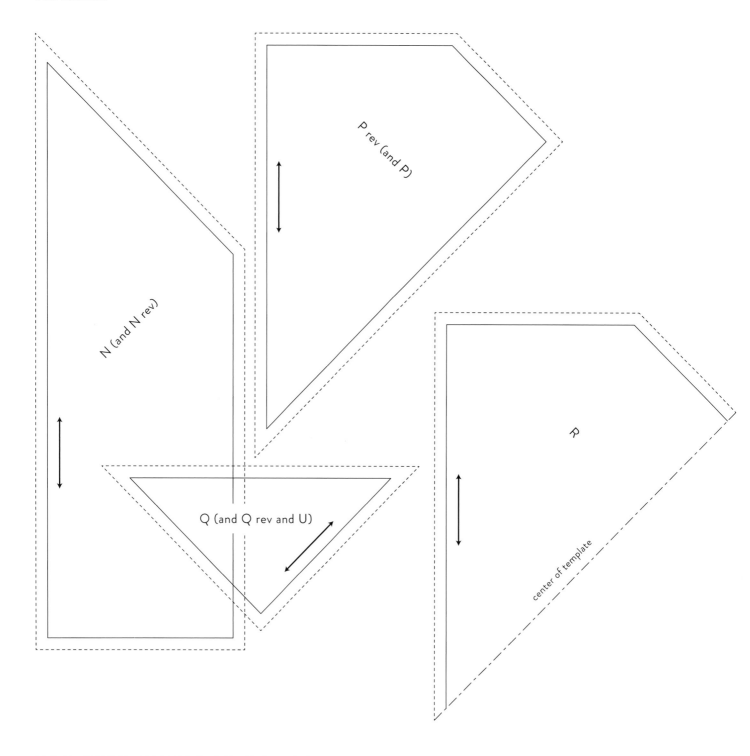

LEAFY APPLIQUÉ

Enlarge the eleven template squares (shown through page 218) by 200% twice (or 400%) to achieve the correct size (16" [40.6 cm] square). See pages 164–167 for the quilt instructions.

No. 1 (and No. 1 rev) Dahlia

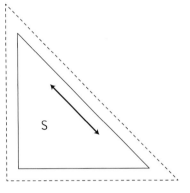

S

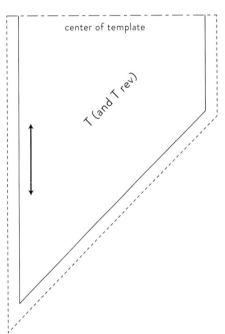

center of template

T (and T rev)

No. 2 (and No. 2 rev) Tulip

No. 3 (and No. 3 rev) Tomato

LATTICE WITH VASES

Enlarge the vase shape and Template F by 200% to achieve the correct size. The solid lines on the template represent the seam lines and the dotted lines the seam allowances. The arrows on the template indicate the direction of the fabric grain. See pages 173–176 for the quilt instructions.

No. 4 (and No. 4 rev) Daisy

No. 5 (and No. 5 rev) Sunflower

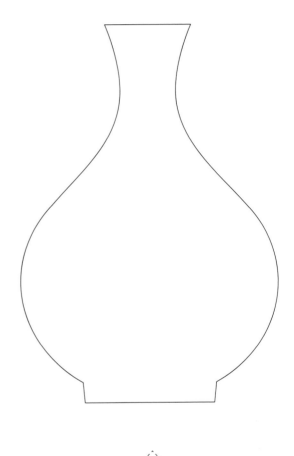

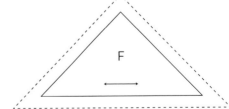

No. 6 (and No. 6 rev) Marigold

No. 7 (and No. 7 rev) Geranium

FLORAL OCTAGONS

Enlarge templates V, X, Y, and Z by 200% to achieve the correct size. The outer dotted outline of the octagon template (V) is for the fabric octagons, and the inner solid outline is for the paper octagons. The seam allowance on Template V is ⅜" (1 cm). For the other templates, the solid lines represent the seam lines and the dotted lines the seam allowances. The arrows on the templates indicate the direction of the fabric grain. Templates Y and Z can be found opposite. See pages 188–193 for the quilt instructions.

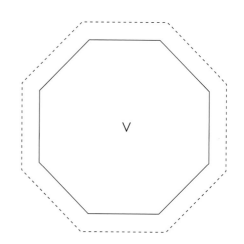

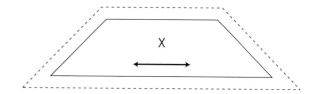

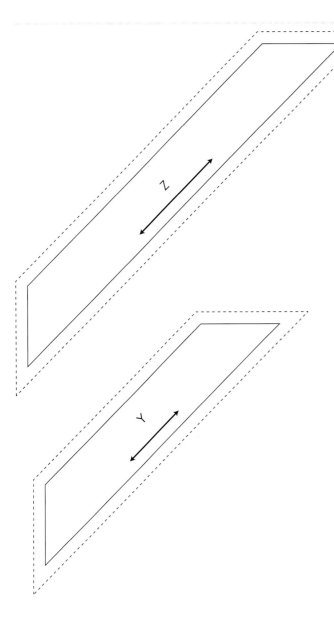

No. 8 (and No. 8 rev) Foxglove

No. 9 Radish

No. 10 Leaves & Buds in Pot

No. 11 Vase

TAWNY HATBOXES

The three templates needed for making this quilt are J, J rev, and K. The appliqué pieces (box lid, box lid rim, and box bottom) are incorporated within these templates. Enlarge the shapes by 200% to achieve the correct size. The solid lines on the templates represent the seam lines and the dotted lines the seam allowances. The arrows on the templates indicate the direction of the fabric grain. See pages 156–163 for the quilt instructions.

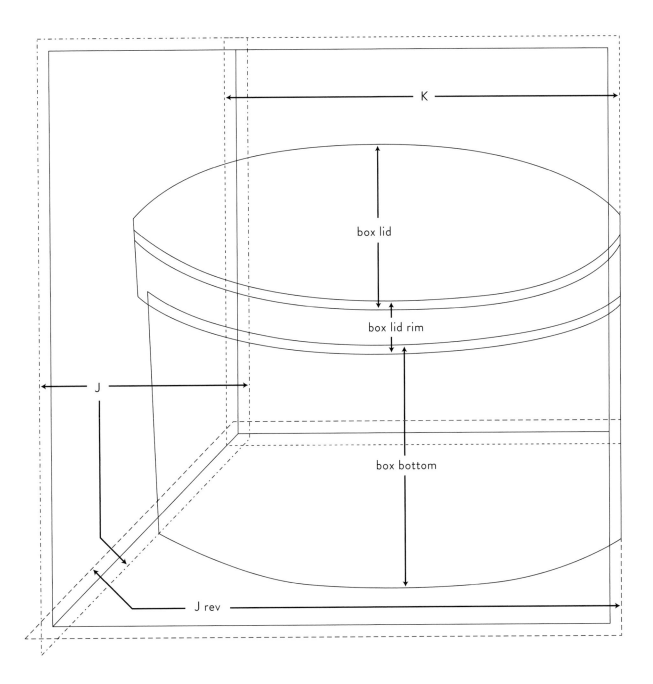

HEXAGON FLORETS

Template E appears at full size. The outer dotted outline of the hexagon is for the fabric hexagons, and the inner solid outline is for the paper hexagons. The seam allowance on this template is ⅜" (1 cm). See pages 154–158 for the quilt instructions.

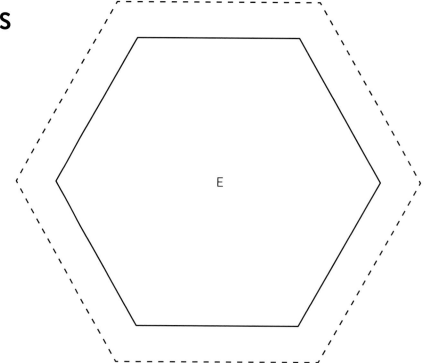

BLUE OHIO STAR

Enlarge Templates H and G by 200% to achieve the correct size. Note that only half of template G is given here; flop the template for the other half to create a full template. The solid lines on the templates represent the seam lines and the dotted lines the seam allowances. The arrows on the templates indicate the direction of the fabric grain. See pages 177–180 for the quilt instructions.

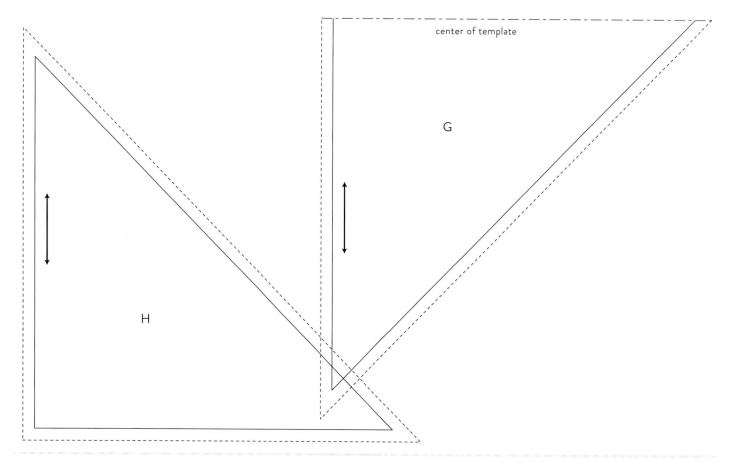

SOURCES

FABRIC

Many of the patchworks in this book contain Kaffe Fassett Collective fabrics. To use substitute fabric, see advice on page 204.

To find sources for Kaffe Fassett Collective fabrics and Kaffe's design-wall flannel, do a search on the Internet or contact one of the following:

U.S.A.
www.westminsterfibers.com

U.K.
www.coatscraft.co.uk or www.knitrowan.com

NEEDLEPOINT KITS

Kits for all of the needlepoints in this book are available from Ehrman. www.ehrmantapestry.com

ACKNOWLEDGMENTS

From Kaffe

My personal and heartfelt thanks go to Brandon Mably for his round-the-clock support and encouragement, and to Beth Sheard and Sally Harding, who gave so many hours of effort to this project.

From Liza

Thanks, first and foremost, to Drew, Alex, and Elizabeth Lucy, who endure living in fabric chaos when Kaffe and I are creating quilts for our books. I am grateful for your tolerance and encouragement.

To the talented sewers who generously lent a hand to help sew the quilt tops—Judy Baldwin, Corienne Kramer, Sally Davis, Julie Stockler, and Penny Jeffries—thank you.

It truly took a village to design and craft the Leafy Appliqué quilt. Many thanks for an intense and creative day of planning and designing this quilt to Julie Creus, Julie Parrish, Rose Lee Link, Beverly Sandvick, Stacey Whelan, Beverly Carter, Debbie Smith, Sara Barkley, Kay Garrett, Charmille Tamulinas, Delores Hernandez, and Marcia Shenk. The hand-appliqué was exquisitely stitched by Bekah Lynch, Sylvi Sealy, and Anita Brady. What talent— and patience!

The *glorious* quilting is an essential part of making these quilts. We are grateful to Judy Irish, Donna Laing, Bobbi Penniman, and Barbara Persing.

I am grateful to be an ambassador for BERNINA USA. All of the machine-pieced quilts in this book were made on my Quilter's Edition BERNINA.

Thanks to all of our helpful friends at Westminster Fibers who supplied us with glorious fabrics.

INDEX

QUILTS

Gray Random Strips
44, 120

Gray Blocks
46, 124

Radiating Bubbles
54, 128

Yellow Sunlight
56, 134

Basket
58, 138

Attic Window On-Point
66, 142

Seed Packet
68, 147

Round and Round
70, 150

Hexagon Florets
78, 154

Tawny Hatboxes
80, 159

Leafy Appliqué
88, 164

Leafy Medallion
90, 168

Lattice with Vases
92, 173

Blue Ohio Star
100, 177

Millefiore Snowball
102, 181

String Stripes
104, 185

Floral Octagons
112, 188

High-Contrast Squares
114, 194

NEEDLEPOINT PILLOWS

White Dahlia
48, 200

Bouquet
60, 200

Carlton Ware
72, 201

Pink Peonies
82, 201

Tulip Vase
94, 202

Dark Peony
106, 202

Carnations
116, 203

INSPIRATION COLLAGES

ANTIQUE TEXTILE INSPIRATIONS 16–17
It is always easier for me to create a new design based on an embroidered or printed flower rather than a more complex-looking live flower.

NEUTRALS & SOFT PASTELS 42–43
CLOCKWISE FROM TOP LEFT:
Detail of Gray Random Strips (page 44); my *Brassica* fabric; bouquet on vintage fabrics; close-up of rose from my front garden; needlepoint of magnolia blooms; hydrangeas; Chinese vase.

BRIGHT PASTELS 52–53
CLOCKWISE FROM TOP LEFT:
French wallpaper that inspired the needle-pointed Bouquet pillow (page 60); my *Big Blooms* fabric; a charity shop find; porcelain flowers on a shoe by Candace Bahouth; my painting of dahlias in a pink teapot; an amaryllis; Yellow Sunlight (page 56).

BRILLIANT HIGHS 64–65
CLOCKWISE FROM TOP LEFT:
My *Bekah* fabric; Russian Rose artwork; My *Lake Blossoms* fabric; a stunning flower-laden cake by Colette Peters; pages from my archive; detail of a Chinese fan; vintage flower jug.

SMOLDERING DEEP TONES 76–77
CLOCKWISE FROM TOP LEFT:
A Chinese porcelain box; my *Bekah* fabric; opium poppy; Chinese floral vase; me holding a poppy against Philip Jacobs's *Geranium* fabric; Chinese floral plate atop a wallpaper sample; Bekah Lynch's Bounce quilt.

LEAFY GREENS & FLOWERS 86–87
CLOCKWISE FROM TOP LEFT:
An antique carved vase that was the inspiration for the needlepoint on page 94; one of my knitwear designs; a formal English garden; a flea market find; wall painting in Fez, Morocco; one of sixteenth-century Italian artist Giuseppe Archibaldo's portraits made entirely of floral motifs; a Bird of Paradise quilt.

RICH, DARK TONES 98–99
CLOCKWISE FROM TOP LEFT:
Vintage velvet poppy print; embroidered shawl; photo by Steve Lovi of a dark brown iris; *Hollyhocks* by Philip Jacobs; arranging the dark flower bouquet on page 35; cloisonné vase; *Brocade*.

HIGH CONTRAST 110–111
CLOCKWISE FROM TOP LEFT:
My *Lotus Stripe* fabric; my *Brocade Peony* fabric; my collection of black-and-white rose vases; Marie-Christine Flocard's toile hexagon quilt; Victorian jug; opium poppy; morning glory.

Editor: Melanie Falick
Designer: Deb Wood
Production Manager: True Sims

Library of Congress Control Number: 2015955663

ISBN: 978-1-4197-2236-3

Printed and bound in China
10 9 8 7 6 5 4 3 2 1

Abrams books are available at special discounts when purchased in quantity for premiums and promotions as well as fundraising or educational
use. Special editions can also be created to specification. For details,
contact specialsales@abramsbooks.com or the address below.

ABRAMS The Art of Books
115 West 18th Street, New York, NY 10011
abramsbooks.com